Periodical Literature

in Eighteenth-Century America

Periodical Literature

in Eighteenth-Century America

Edited by Mark L. Kamrath
and Sharon M. Harris

The University of Tennessee Press / Knoxville

First Edition.

This book is printed on acid-free paper.

Library of Congress Cataloging-in-Publication Data

Periodical literature in eighteenth-century America / edited by Mark L.Kamrath and Sharon M. Harris.— 1st ed.
p. cm.
Includes bibliographical references and index.

ISBN 1-57233-319-7 (alk. paper)

1. American literature—Colonial period, ca. 1600-1775—History and criticism.
2. American literature—Revolutionary period, 1775–1783—History and criticism.
3. Periodicals—Publishing—United States—History—18th century.
4. Literature publishing—United States—History—18th century.
5. Books and reading—UnitedStates—History—18th century.
6. American literature—1783-1850—History and criticism.
7. United States—Intellectual life—18th century.
I. Kamrath, Mark. II. Harris, Sharon M.

PS193.P47 2005

070.5'72'097309033—dc22 2004014807

CONTENTS

Part III. The Early Republic and the 1790s 221

ILLUSTRATIONS

ACKNOWLEDGMENTS

This collection began as a conversation in Lincoln, Nebraska, and grew into a rich dialogue between the book's two co-editors and their contributors. As the collection took shape, we were fortunate to have the patience and persistence of fellow scholars from a wide range of disciplinary interests and institutions. Without such talent and dedication, this collection would not have been possible.

We are indebted to John C. Shields, Daniel E. Williams, and the anonymous reader at the University of Tennessee Press for their meticulous reading of the manuscript, and to Joyce Harrison, Stan Ivester, Bill Adams, Jennifer Siler, and the press staff for their encouragement and expertise throughout the editorial process. We believe that *Periodical Literature in Eighteenth-Century America* is a better book because of such support. Thanks also to Susan Belasco and Kenneth M. Price for their early encouragement with the collection, to Don Baumgartner at Computer Indexed Systems for help with access to the *Index to Early American Periodicals*, and to Roger Matuz for guiding us, early on, through the vast resource of the *American Periodical Series Online* database (ProQuest) and to Jo-Anne Hogan for assisting us in identifying particular texts. Our gratitude as well to Vincent Golden, Georgia B. Barnhill, and Terri Tremblay at the American Antiquarian Society for their generous help with background information and illustrations; and Ed Redmond, Kathryn L. Engstrom, and other reference specialists at the Library of Congress for their assistance.

Finally, Mark Kamrath wants to acknowledge the Department of English and the College of Arts and Sciences at the University of Central Florida for release time and research support for this project. He also wants to thank Cheryl Mahan and the University of Central Florida Library for their support in acquiring digital databases and related resources. Both editors thank fellow panelists and audiences for their comments and questions over the years in various conference panel discussions devoted to the subject of early American periodicals. We both also thank our families and friends who may have heard more than they ever cared to about periodical literature but whose support and interest has been invaluable.

Mark L. Kamrath and Sharon M. Harris

Introduction

> It may be necessary to appologize for the poor appearance of the work the last six months. The Magazine came into my hands when I was unprepared with a TYPE so good as I could wish for for the business, this evil would have been remedied but for the non-importation agreement, which it was MY DUTY to comply with: The ink also has been poor, but as it was of AMERICAN MANUFACTURE my customers were not only willing but desirous that I should use it. The first essay towards any new branch of business is always attended with difficulties, that was the case with the ink, experience alone must perfect it, the next I expect will be as much better than this, as this is better than the last.
>
> —Joseph Greenleaf, *Royal American Magazine*, 1774

Joseph Greenleaf's remarks to his subscribers in the December 1774 supplement to the *Royal American Magazine* about the "evil" of inadequate "TYPE" and, more important, the desire to use "INK" of "AMERICAN MANUFACTURE" even though it was "poor" earmarks a host of issues connected with the publication, circulation, and reception of eighteenth-century American periodical literature. As with numerous other prospectuses and prefaces, it references how political and financial situations—"non-importation" acts, postal regulations, inadequate numbers of contributors, and the delinquent payment of subscriptions—impeded the development of magazine production. It points, for instance, to the effort to improve upon the designs, engravings, and "ink" used in British or European periodicals as well as the need to run a successful business in an emerging market economy. It also recalls, especially before the Revolution, the emergent and often conflicted feelings of patriotism and the manner in which colonists increasingly imagined separation from British rule; expression of such thoughts was often at personal risk. Last, in addition to challenging colonial hierarchies, Greenleaf's commentary reflects a desire by Americans, despite an inadequate reading public, to be "independent" and to establish a national literature based on contributions from its citizens.

Although Greenleaf's remarks are geared toward the publishing circumstances of one particular magazine, most magazines, especially after the American Revolution, when magazine publication began to increase, were preoccupied with assessing American appetites and gradually including news, topics, or documents of domestic interest. The proliferation of magazine ventures in the mid- to late-1790s suggests that Americans were not only experimenting with the role of print in the public sphere but embracing it with an almost religious fervor and gusto. By the 1790s, in fact, American periodicals may be seen as drifting away from pre-Revolutionary or English influences—the idea, for instance, of the magazine as being primarily a repository for polite manners—and instead gravitating, often ambivalently, toward a kind of print capitalism that increasingly favored utility, native genius, intellectual eccentricity and other unique American interests. David D. Hall agrees, writing that the transformation of print culture that took place between the 1770s and 1850s was partly a result of "new printing and paper-making technologies," "a rapid increase in the rate of literacy, and a general speeding up of communication." With these changes, he writes, came "new literary genres" and a "new relationship between writers and their audience."[1]

Periodical literature, as early Americanists are rediscovering, provides a more extensive cultural record than previously recognized in regard to the material and literary processes that influenced authors, editors, publishers, and readers from approximately 1720 to the end of the century. Beginning, for instance, with Benjamin Franklin's *General Magazine, and Historical Chronicle, for all the British Plantations in America* (1741), periodical literature before the American Revolution records the negotiation of political and cultural identity in ways not usually documented in private letters or other manuscript materials. The wealth of religious hymns, European and domestic news, foreign-language translations, published debates, fragments, histories, slave advertisements, anecdotes, pseudonymous writing, biographies, circular letters, recipes for brewing beer, addresses, journal excerpts, fictitious dialogues, didactic tales, travel literature, prospectuses, literary reviews, editorials, and antislavery literature speaks to the heterogeneous ways periodical writing intersects with a range of cultural interests and rhetorical practices. This plethora of periodical genres offers a view of the manner in which certain discourses contested the status quo and others reinforced it, especially at the beginning of the American Revolution.

After the Revolution and especially during the 1790s, when periodical publication exploded, the magazine was still a relatively new cultural phenomenon, blending the reliability of annuals with the frequency of newspaper publications. As popular literature with increasingly commercial ties, periodicals reflected a rich diversity of cultural voices both from urban and rural areas. In fact, just as newspapers served as a medium for both dominant and counter-hegemonic discourses, so late-eighteenth-century American periodicals, as Steven Frye points out, also reflect the "enigmatic and complicated cultural demographics of the American postcolonial situation."[2] He remarks that, like the newspaper, "American periodicals manifested the 'dynamics of resistance,' reflecting both hegemonic and counter-discursive narrative elements."[3] What distinguished a newspaper from a magazine, in other words, was sometimes negligible in terms of content, format, and publication frequency. Of the 1790s, for example, Frank Luther Mott remarks in his now-classic study *A History of American Magazines 1741–1850*, "Just as the weekly paper invaded . . . the field of the general literary magazine and that of the religious journal in this period, so the daily threatened to usurp what had been from the first one of the leading phases of magazine interest—that of political record and discussion."[4] Despite the occasional blurring of the newspaper and the magazine in weekly publications such as the *American Apollo* (1792),[5] the magazine may be seen as playing an increasingly political and ideological role in the formation of national identity, mixing popular and elite forms of writing in an attempt to meet the moral, political, and educational needs of its citizenry. As such, post-Revolutionary periodicals, particularly as they distinguished themselves from their colonial predecessors and British or European counterparts, present an important and often neglected lens from which to view the emergence of early national culture and literature.

Periodical Literature in Eighteenth-Century America contributes to the rapidly changing, and intersecting, fields of early American studies and book history by revising the existing understanding of the cultural, ideological, and discursive contexts of early American literature. It examines how both early American newspapers and magazines provide fresh sites of critical inquiry for better understanding transatlantic and material contexts of print culture and production, especially the role of authors; relations between canonical and noncanonical writers as well as between popular and marginalized genres; representation of gendered and racial "Others"; the differences that emerged between pre- and post-Revolutionary periodicals; and the nature and function of "republicanism," including the rise of political parties and party politics, and similar ideological transformations as they were contested and negotiated in the public sphere.

Eighteenth-Century American Periodical Literature

In order to understand how the study of periodical literature has developed over the years and what promise it holds as an archive, it is useful to map some of the more significant studies or developments over the last several decades and to identify how each has attempted to clarify the importance of such material for literary and cultural studies. This is especially important as access to periodical literature in a digital medium increases and, in turn, provides alternative ways of accounting for, and constructing, relationships among magazines, readerships, and periodical content—especially material that was reprinted or appropriated and edited in various forms—and the manner in which a range of discourses circulated among and within various texts.

To begin, as Mott observes, "It was once the fashion, as it continues to be with a certain kind of critic, to assert that periodicals have in them little or nothing of reliable information or admirable literature."[6] While he acknowledges that periodicals are not "equally authoritative" and that alliances of editors and publishers and editorial bias sometimes color the contents of periodical material, he nevertheless accurately points to the inherent, cultural value of magazine material.[7] "Few fields of investigation," he argues, "are of more lively interest than that of the course of popular ideas. The thoughts and feelings of the people, the development of their taste in art and music and letters, their daily work and play, and even their fads, are inexhaustibly entertaining and instructive." "Where is there such a record," he continues, "of these things as we have in magazine files? Not in the newspapers, which tell of them with less skill and order; not in the books, which neglect some details of this web of life to overemphasize others."[8]

Although Mott may have overstated the differences among newspapers, magazines, and books, his points about the uniquely democratic appeal and format of magazines, their role in establishing a national literature, and their importance as part of a neglected historical archive ring true even today, some seventy-five years after the initial publication of his study.[9] Likewise, his assessment of periodical developments in the eighteenth century is also accurate. Specifically, in addition to identifying indifference by readers and writers, the absence of an effective means of distribution and collecting subscription payment, and "manufacturing embarrassments" as major reasons why (to quote Noah Webster) "The expectation of failure is connected with the very name of a Magazine," Mott points to the Postal Act of 1794 as a singularly important event in the development and publication of magazines.[10]

Because of the way the Postal Act of 1792 allowed for excessively high postage on magazines, thus retarding sales, the more liberal statute of 1794 reduced costs for magazine publishers, allowing, says Mott, for the "starting of a great many new magazines, and as a result more were begun in the final six years of the eighteenth century than in all the years from 1741 to 1794."[11] To be sure, he says, the Postal Act of 1794 did not bring about a millennium, but it did lead to unprecedented growth in the industry in terms of the numbers of magazines in circulation. Mott's study goes on to provide close and still invaluable analysis of specific magazines such as Benjamin Franklin's *General Magazine, and Historical Chronicle* (1741) and Matthew Carey's *American Museum, or, Universal Magazine* (1787–92), but Mott's primary scholarly contribution remains his close assessment of magazine print culture and the historical, political, and economic factors that affected magazine development, and his astute analysis of the early magazines' eclectic and "original" content despite an early reliance on material from English periodical publications.[12]

Also contributing to the heightened interest in periodicals at this time, but in other substantial ways, was Lyon N. Richardson's book *A History of American Magazines, 1741–1789* (1931). Almost forgotten now, his study nevertheless accurately documents the dearth of scholarship on periodicals up to 1927 and argues that while Mott provided the "first careful" reading of periodical material, he "accorded the eighteenth century limited and minor attention."[13] Richardson's full-length book, as its title suggests, focuses on the years 1741–89—from the publication of Franklin's and Bradford's magazines to the year George Washington was elected president—and covers the publishing circumstances and "literary and historical trends" of thirty-seven periodicals.[14] It is important to note that his study recognized that distinctions between a magazine and newspaper blur in specific cases, and his history relies, in part, on British periodicals to articulate his points. As he explains, "*The Penny Post*, a unique diminutive newspaper, but in some respects not unlike *The Instructor, The North-Carolina Magazine: or, Universal Intelligencer, The New Haven Gazette and the Connecticut Magazine, The Worcester Magazine*, and the *Courier de Boston*, periodicals which, though pamphlets or newspapers in the basic sense of the words, were printed on pages of less than folio size and were published as essay-journal-magazines or newspaper-magazines."[15]

Although Richardson's study rightly points to the relationship between political questions and their economic origins and how major political events such as King George's War, the French and Indian War, and the Revolutionary War affected magazine publication and content, he provided, unlike Mott, a more sustained analysis of magazine editors and editorial currents. He acknowledges the historical, political, and scientific controversies magazines hold, citing, for instance, how they record post-Revolutionary disillusionment concerning the absence of equality or how conservative and liberal forces in Protestant New England clashed over the question of universalism.[16] But the chief focus of his study are the "literary elements" of the magazines he has selected and the kinds of editorial decisions made by men such as Franklin, Thomas Prince, William Livingston, Judge Samuel Nevill, Benjamin Mecom, Christopher Saur, Isaiah Thomas, Hugh Brackenridge, James Freeman, Josiah Meigs, Mathew Carey, Noah Webster, and Nathaniel Coverly; this last named editor was among the first to solicit explicitly the support of women for his *Gentlemen and Ladies Town and Country Magazine*. In respect to detailing the specific print histories of particular magazines and editorial trends, Richardson's study still has no peer.

Although brief, James Playsted Wood's chapters in *Magazines in the United States* (1949) confirm, importantly, two points made by Mott and Richardson about the development of eighteenth-century periodicals: first, that many magazine subscribers considered themselves "patrons of an instrument that spread knowledge, advanced culture in the United States, and supported the literary and practical arts developing in the country"; and, second, that if books and magazines were valuable because so few were available, "Every page of every magazine was read carefully by a number of people," thereby making the influence of early periodicals both "intensive and extensive."[17] While later reception studies of individual magazines or periodicals produced in particular cities at particular times tend to confirm Wood's remarks, his study nevertheless identifies distinguishing elements of eighteenth-century periodical literature, and it is suggestive of the ways the discourses of sentiment, colonialism, self-liberation, and republicanism, to name but a few, could potentially intersect in the consciousness of American readers.

Almost seventy years would pass following Wood's observations before any other kind of synthetic statement would appear about the development and impact of periodical literature in early American history and culture. Michael T. Gilmore's remarks, for example, on magazines in *The Cambridge History of American Literature* (1994) are also useful but brief. He observes that periodicals in "both England and America evolved out of newspapers and were often indistinguishable from them," but that American periodicals "accommodated the popular reading habits of the nascent liberal order and opened their pages to voices that disputed established hierarchies."[18] Reflecting, he suggests, the "medium's newspaper origins," the contents of magazines "showed a diversity that could clash with the gentlemanly ethos."[19] This is evident not only in Judith Sargent Murray's essay serials, which Isaiah Thomas printed in the *Massachusetts Magazine* from 1792 to 1794, but also, writes Gilmore, in articles that affirmed "female accomplishments and argued for the importance of knowledgeable and patriotic mothers" or in periodical material that supported female education and occasionally advocated "sexual equality."[20] In short, Gilmore's observations highlight shifting attitudes toward periodical literature—importantly how new historicist, Marxist, feminist, and other critical approaches began to influence categories of interpretive analysis.

Subsequent studies such as William David Sloan and Julie Hedgepeth Williams's *The Early American Press, 1690–1783* (1994), David A. Copeland's *Colonial American Newspapers* (1997), Mary Ellen Zuckerman's *A History of Popular Women's Magazines in the United States, 1792–1995* (1998), and Ronald Lora and William Henry Longton's *Conservative Press in Eighteenth- and Nineteenth-Century America* (1999) have each, in their own way, called further attention to eighteenth-century periodicals. Copeland, for instance, updates our understanding of the content of colonial newspapers by providing data on the kinds of topics—from conditions or events at sea to news about Indian uprisings or religious revivals and sometimes sensational criminal reports—that were popular from one newspaper and one year to the next. And although it does not address women's periodical writing in the 1790s per se, Zuckerman's book calls attention to the *Lady's Magazine; and Repository of Entertaining Knowledge* (1792–93) and the need for a more comprehensive study of female readers, writers, and editors in eighteenth-century American periodical literature and the range of interests or subjects that contributed to a "female sphere."[21]

Additionally, formation of the Society for the History of Authorship, Reading, and Publishing, the Research Society of American Periodicals and its journal *American Periodicals*, as well as the Society of Early Americanists and publication of recent articles in *Early American Literature* have also refocused attention on the cultural contexts and importance of periodicals in American literature.[22] Likewise, in the last several years, interest in periodical literature has been spurred by publication of Kenneth M. Price and Susan Belasco Smith's *Periodical Literature in Nineteenth-Century America* (1995), a study that provides a major reference point for this present collection. Price and Smith further contribute to the history and study of American periodical literature by bringing together a collection of essays on a variety of texts and magazines that also addresses the "social history, publishing contexts, the literary marketplace, and the relationships between authors and editors" from the 1830s to the end of the century.[23] The patterns of development they identify with authors, publishers, and readers in nineteenth-century periodicals serve as a guidepost for our own inquiry into the literary marketplace of the eighteenth century.

However, a more directly useful resource for *Periodical Literature in Eighteenth-Century America* has been the comprehensive and detailed bibliographical work of Edward W. R. Pitcher. His *Fiction in American Magazines before 1800: An Annotated Catalogue* (1993) points to a range of issues with which essays in this volume, to one degree or another, concern themselves. In addition, for example, to confirming that there were "no universally accepted definitions for magazine and newspaper in the eighteenth century" and that magazines published news and newspapers published poems and prose tales, his study identifies several defining characteristics of eighteenth-century American periodical literature.[24] Chief among these are questions about what was considered factual or fiction during the period and what genres were dominant in American periodicals from one period to the next; the incidence, or rate, of "printing translated fiction in American magazines insomuch as that reflects the practices of editors or the taste of readers";[25] the role and identity of pseudonymous authors and the extent to which Americans authored original material, as opposed to reprinting it from British sources; and the degree to which certain texts were popular in American magazines and were republished in variant forms.

Pitcher's material suggests, in other words, several patterns of meaning, many of which essays herein illustrate and complicate. In terms of genre, for example, letters, tales or stories, anecdotes, and instances of public oratory seem to have been staples of magazine publication throughout the eighteenth century, with political and other speeches becoming both more popular and numerous shortly before as well as after the American Revolution. Also, while singular publications such as "Letter on Slavery. By a Negro," published in the *American Museum, or, Universal Magazine* (July 1789) and "On Sluttishness in Married Ladies," published in the *South-Carolina Weekly Museum, and Complete Magazine of Entertainment and Intelligence* (March 4, 1797), might be of interest to contemporary scholars for various cultural reasons, Pitcher's study reveals that certain texts were more popular than others, with some being reprinted no less than half a dozen times in various magazines.[26]

For example, "The Origin of Tobacco," also published by Franklin under titles such as "Remarks Concerning the Savages of North America," was first published in the December 31, 1784, issue of the *New Hampshire Mercury and General Advertiser* and then reprinted eight times in various magazines, including Philip Freneau's *Time Piece and Literary Companion* (1797). The anonymous "Journal of a Wiltshire Curate," first published in 1768 in the *Boston Chronicle*, was reprinted seven times, as was Richard Johnson's "Geographical Description of Bachelor's Island," first published in the *Boston Magazine* in 1783. The incidence of publication, in other words, in regard to Indian affairs, geography, or Arabian and Turkish tales is, as Pitcher suggests, richly revealing of the tastes and interests of readerships in eighteenth-century America and of the manner, historically, in which particular subjects gained more circulation than others.

Lastly, and more recently, searchable web versions of the American Periodical Series further testify to the growing interest in the content of American periodicals. Digital access to, or the ability to search among, the contents pages and indexes of almost ninety magazines has considerably broadened, and is even reshaping, the analytical categories scholars use with periodical texts for the study of early American literature and culture. As technological developments, such as the Index to American Periodicals of the 1700s and 1800s (CD-ROM and Internet) database and ProQuest's *American Periodical Series Online* (full-text digital facsimile), give us increased access to early periodicals, early Americanists are in a position to reassesses the thick structure of such terrain and to identify new categories of cultural and textual analysis. Indeed, scholars will not only be able to "more precisely and efficiently identify ideological inclinations of authors and patterns of verbal usage" but also "more comprehensively understand the historical, cultural, and literary contexts of an author's or era's works."[27]

For example, in addition to being able to identify numerous and perhaps even hundreds of other texts on a given topic—material, for instance, on the West Indies or female "taste"—scholars can also consider a range of alternative subjects, including children's reading, civil liberty, female slavery in South America, the history of "white negroes," methods of preventing suicide, the moral efficacy of dueling, delineating a female Republic, capital punishment, food consumption and economic statistics, hemp production, the treatment of Jews, prostitution, the success of paper money, the erotic content of Oriental tales, and so on.[28] Also, when one considers how publications such as Rev. Mr. Withers's "Thanksgiving Sermon, on Occasion of the Suppression of the Rebellion & c" were printed in the *American Magazine and Historical Chronicle* in April 1746 as an extract and reference political tensions at that time in the colonies, the number of ways periodical texts become culturally and rhetorically relevant is almost infinite.

To illustrate: the *Index to American Periodicals of the 1700s and 1800s* catalogues, for example, no fewer than 114 titles that contain the word *Indian*, as many as 367 entries or titles that include the word *speech*, 481 that reference *history*, and 1,397 that in one form or another are a letter. By contrast, however, an article title search of ProQuest's *American Periodical Series Online* yields 120 matches for *speech* and 202 matches for *Indian*. A keyword search, on the other hand, for *speech* records 890 matching articles for the same time period, 1740–99, while a similar search for *Indian* yields 3,010 articles. Likewise, the term *letter* lists some 1,327 matches by title, and some 7,777 by keyword search. By genre classification alone, in other words, digital access to the periodicals archive opens up a whole new world of texts for cultural and rhetorical study. Access by subject matter, title, or topic provides access to yet another layer of primary periodical source material.

Subjects such as these, then, as well as many others, appeared in a range of periodical venues, including relatively successful magazines such as the *New-York Magazine, or Literary Repository* (1790–97) and the *Massachusetts Magazine; or, Monthly Museum of Knowledge and Rational Entertainment* (1789–96), both of which lasted, for that time, an unprecedented seven years, and more eclectic ones such as the *Children's Magazine* (1789), the republic's only periodical aimed at youth; Thomas Coke and Francis Asbury's *Arminian Magazine: Consisting of Extracts and Original Treatises on General Redemption* (1789–90), the first American sectarian periodical; the *Humming Bird, or Herald of Taste* (1798), arguably the first magazine edited by a woman; the *Thespian Oracle, or Monthly Mirror* (1798); and the *Medical Repository* (1797–1800), the first American medical journal (see the appendix for a complete list of magazines contained in the APS series).

In short, as studies by Mott, Richardson, and others demonstrate, over the last several decades there has been an attempt to document more accurately both the archival and the historical, cultural, ideological, and rhetorical importance of eighteenth-century American periodical literature. Each successive generation of scholars has contributed to a clearer understanding of the contents periodical literature and how it, as part of a larger history of the book, can further illuminate

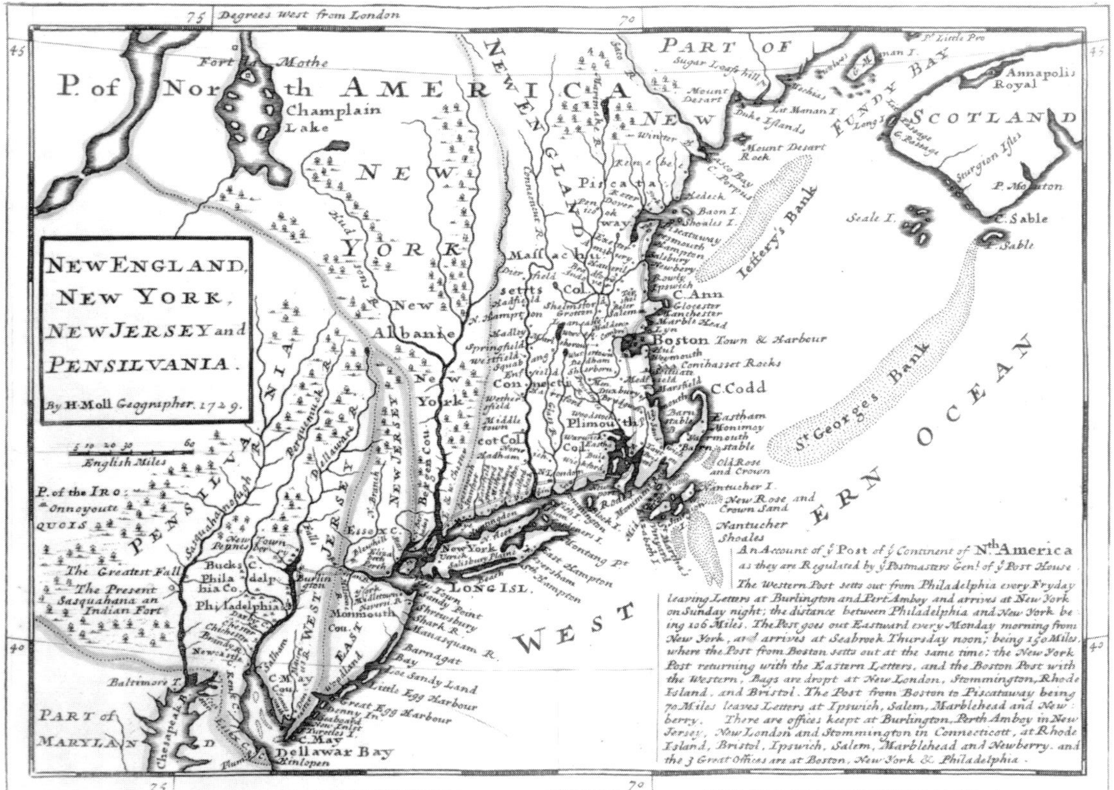

"New England, New York, New Jersey and Pennsylvania," from famous Dutch geographer and cartographer Herman Moll's *Atlas Minor* (1729), is the first postal map of the American colonies. It depicts the New England route for letters and other postal materials, including early newspapers such as John Campbell's weekly *Boston News-Letter* (1704-76). The map details roads, distances, the location of major urban postal offices, and where and when bags were "dropt." For a price, post riders completed other errands, including, as late as 1773, delivering a yoke of oxen in Connecticut. Postmasters such as Benjamin Franklin often used their postion to distribute their own publications. Later, as stage coaches became more common, delivery times became more regular, and subscriptions expanded, these routes became a means of distribution for other periodcal materials. Courtesy of Harvard College Library, Map Collection.

a range of issues and assumptions concerning the production and reception of such writing. Indeed, as access to periodical literature in a digital medium increases and, in turn, provides alternative ways of accounting for, and constructing, relationships between publishers, readerships, and periodical content, scholars will be able to appreciate more fully the range and importance of discourses and beliefs that circulated between—and within—both magazines and the deep structure of particular texts.

The Historical, Cultural, and Discursive Significance of Periodical Literature

Essays in *Periodical Literature in Eighteenth-Century America* investigate a range of texts and periodicals, some of which were widely read in the day and others that, for various historical, geographical, economic, and political reasons, were not. There are many and diverse periodicals which Americans in various regions of the country read and which our contributors examine specifically. In the Boston area relevant publications include James Franklin's *New-England Courant*, a newspaper that was published in Boston and the surrounding Massachusetts Bay colony in the 1720s and reflects the impact of pamphlets published in London; Thomas Prince's weekly the *Christian History* (1743–45); the *New-England Magazine of Knowledge and Pleasure* (1758–59); Isaiah Thomas's *Royal American Magazine, or Universal Repository of Instruction and Amusement* (1774–75); the *Boston Magazine* (1783–86); the *Massachusetts Magazine* (1789–96); and the *Gentlemen and Ladies Town and Country Magazine* (1789–90), which was contributed to by local women. Essays draw upon the *Worcester Magazine* (1786–88) of western Massachusetts, as well as the *New-Haven Gazette, and the Connecticut Magazine* (1786–88).

Looking to the New York and Philadelphia areas, essays examine the *New-York Mercury* (1752–63), the *New Jersey Magazine* (1786–87), and *Thomas Greenleaf's New York Journal* (1794–1800), as well as the century's longest-lived magazine, the *New-York Magazine, or Literary Repository* (1790–97). Philadelphia magazines include the *Pennsylvania Gazette* (1727–65); Benjamin Franklin's *General Magazine, and Historical Chronicle* (1741); German-language periodicals such as *Der Wöchentliche Philadelphische Staatsbote* (1762–79), *Ein Geistliches Magazin* (1764–72), and *Philadelphisches Magazin, oder Unterhaltender Gesellschafter für die Deutschen in America* (1798); *Columbian Magazine: or, Monthly Miscellany* (1786–90); Matthew Carey's *American Museum, or Universal Magazine* (1787–92); the *Universal Asylum, and Columbian Magazine* (1790–92); and the *Lady's Magazine; and Repository of Entertaining Knowledge*

(1792–93), a semiannual publication divided into monthly sections and aimed primarily at women.

And, last, from the middle and southern colonies and abroad, contributors use a range of periodicals, including the *General Magazine, and Impartial Review of Knowledge and Entertainment* (1798) and J. D. Cary's weekly *Key* (1798), both of Maryland; the *North-Carolina Magazine; or, Universal Intelligencer* (1764–65), a weekly newspaper that resembled a magazine in terms of format; and the *South-Carolina Weekly Museum* (1797–98), which was published in Charleston and is generally recognized as the most successful magazine south of Baltimore in the eighteenth century. In gauging various transatlantic shifts, essays in the collection also include various British periodicals such as the *London Magazine* (1747–83). These periodicals, like their domestic cousins, were also a means by which the early republic read and constructed itself.

In reassessing these materials, and their regional and national importance, some essays in this collection employ interdisciplinary methods of inquiry, with an emphasis, for instance, primarily on historical issues, materials, and methods of inquiry, or as a way of entering debates about the existence and effects of public spheres. Others employ narrative discourse and performance theories or use considerations of race, class difference, and ethnicity as a lens through which to more accurately gauge a text's meaning or cultural appropriation. Still others apply feminist interpretations of print culture and national identity as a way of identifying the role of gender and subjectivity in periodical production or they reexamine the reception of particular content in periodicals, relative to changing material and political relationships among publishers, printers, and readers and how they influenced constructions of republicanism or the status quo in the 1790s.

Using these methodologies, contributors explore alternative historical, cultural, and rhetorical assumptions and accurately identify the struggles of eighteenth-century publishers, such as that experienced by Greenleaf, and the issues they confronted. To provide focus on the collection's subject matter and how the essays reassess the eighteenth-century, the collection provides three categories of inquiry: "Atlantic Currents," "Revolutionary-Era Discourses," and "The Early Republic and the 1790s." Essays in each of these sections address issues that are unique to their relative categories but also to the larger print history of eighteenth-century periodicals.

In "Atlantic Currents," for example, essays by Carla Mulford, Timothy D. Hall, John Smolenski, and W. M. Verhoeven investigate issues from immigration and settlement to cultural representation in print in the public sphere to the ways that early colonists negotiated transatlantic change, foreign customs, cultural assimilation, and the impact of transculturation. From the ways, in other words, the Massachusetts Bay Colony used a print medium to deal with cultural predicaments to the manner in which German immigrant assimilation reflected anxiety about cultural difference and colonial identity, essays in this section probe a wide array of early newspaper and periodical print for a better understanding of how print culture mediated cultural instability and change in colonial New England. As such, essays in this section are concerned with issues of class expectations and realities as well as historical ethnic, racial, and religious differences and the multiple ways these cultural components intersected with a transatlantic print culture and early democratic modes of representation. Together, they provide insight into the diasporic conditions of colonial America and the manner in which a myriad of immigrant populations grappled with different cultural beliefs issues of identity and social stability.

Part II, on the other hand, "Revolutionary-Era Discourses," focuses more specifically on the manner in which periodical literature reflects a variety of colonial ideologies, absorbed Other discourses, and facilitated the development of national identity. From the circulation of classical materials and patriotic ideals to, for instance, the appropriation of American Indian oratory to respond to British colonial practices and the uses of sentiment in relation to the antislavery movements, essays by Chad Reid, Mark L. Kamrath, Robert D. Sturr, and Philip Gould show how newspaper and magazine publications increasingly practiced political dissent at the national, state, and local levels. This section pays particular attention not only to transatlantic influences but to the ways the provocative discourses of colonial resistance and dissent merged, often dialogically, with discourses of the ethnic or political Other and rehistoricize existing paradigms for understanding the formation of early national authorship and identity. As such, essays in this section raise important questions about the circulation of revolutionary or patriot rhetorics relative to racial and class markers and the manner in which such ideologies and political discourses were appropriated in a periodicals format and used to leverage both conservative and progressive political agendas.

In the last section, "The Early Republic and the 1790s," essays speak not only to the evolving changes in periodical print practices and distribution but the often innovative means taken by editors and readers alike to promote—or often contest—republican values in the public sphere. As such, essays by Beverly J. Reed, Frank Shuffelton, Lisa M. Logan, Seth Cotlar, and Sharon M. Harris recover an often neglected aspect of how Americans imagined themselves relative to Europe and a national body of literature in the face of unprecedented political, economic, theological, and moral changes in Anglo-American society. Specifically, essays in this section take into account the economic or commercial aspects of periodical production and consumption and the ways that emerging, and sometimes contradictory, representations of private and public "bodies" became a vehicle for understanding a range of debates concerning the formation of a democratic republic. As these essays demonstrate, for instance, the formation of political parties and platforms was intimately connected with periodical print matter.

Although in-depth study of American periodical literature has been relegated to a few efforts, most of which appeared before the advent of poststructuralism and the historical or cultural "turn," *Periodical Literature in Eighteenth-Century America* aims to reassess periodical literature in the eighteenth century and how it directly reflected and contributed to the formation of American national identity. As scholars continue to use interdisciplinary and emerging theoretical approaches with this body of literature, collaborations such as this collection deepen our understanding of both the material practices of American print culture and the historical, ideological, and literary significance of texts produced in that period.

If, as David S. Shields remarks, early Americanists need to navigate more effectively the unpredictable, discursive terrain of American literature and provide the kind of "thick description" that is necessary when dealing with a "mutable and expanding canon" and an archive rife with "undiscovered and unremarked works,"[29] the potential of recent cultural theories and digital access to periodical works holds great potential for redefining our current understanding of canonical and noncanonical American literature. Carla Mulford's recent remarks about the "renewed activity in archival recovery" and the risks of exclusionary research also speak to the kind of self-scrutiny that is necessary with American periodical literature in order to avoid "historical oversimplification" or the kind of "English and European overstory" that once dominated American studies.[30] Thus, just as scholarly inquiry into eighteenth-century American periodicals invites closer scrutiny of a host of other topics, including, for instance, the reception of Burke and *Clarissa* in America or how Oriental tales were appropriated by Americans, so such approaches promise to alter existing constructions of "republican virtue," the uses of sentiment, the role of print culture in the daily lives of American citizens, and so on, in imaginative and surprising ways.

Indeed, in the coming years, as early Americanists become familiar with and use full-text databases such as the *American Periodical Series Online*, we will be able to more thoroughly and accurately explore, word by word, the full range and contents of eighteenth-century American periodicals. Likewise, interpretive fields for understanding the colonial and early national periods will continue to evolve, thereby providing yet another platform or interpretive paradigm from which to understand the familiar discourses of colonialism, republican "virtue," sentimentalism, and dissent. Similar, in other words, to Greenleaf's understanding of periodical production and reception in his time—the idea that experience would enable his next publication to be "better than the last"—it seems that early Americanist scholars are finally in a position, theoretically and practically speaking, to access further and to understand more completely the multiple, and often embedded, ideological and discursive layers of eighteenth-century American periodical literature.

Notes

1. David D. Hall, *Cultures of Print: Essays in the History of the Book* (Amherst: U of Massachusetts P, 1996), 37, 11–12. Hall remarks that even as scholars of American literature are "reaching out to book history" so those interested in book history "must engage with questions arising out of literary and cultural theory—questions about authorship and intellectual property, representations of books and printing, the multivocality of texts, and the modes of 'domination,' as in forms of patriarchy, that infuse the definition of literature." Hall's observations call attention to the need for book historians to be aware of how literary theory can enhance scholarship, but, more important, his work points to the growing interdisciplinary interest in the historical contexts and cultural and literary significance of print culture, particularly American periodical literature.
2. Steven Frye, "Constructing Indigeneity: Postcolonial Dynamics and Charles Brockden Brown's *Monthly Magazine and American Review*," *American Studies* 39 (1998): 76.
3. Ibid.
4. Frank Luther Mott, *A History of American Magazines 1741–1850* (Cambridge: Harvard UP, 1930), 158.
5. According to the *Index for the Reel Guide to the American Periodical Series of the 1700s* (Indianapolis: Computer Indexed Systems, 1989), the *American Apollo* was published weekly in Boston from January 6, 1792, to December 25, 1794.
6. Mott 1.
7. Ibid., 4–5.
8. Ibid., 4.
9. Ibid., 2–4.
10. Ibid., 13.
11. Ibid., 18–19.

12. Ibid., 40.

13. Lyon N. Richardson, *A History of Early American Magazines, 1741–1789* (1931; rpt. New York: Octagon Books, 1966), ix.

14. Ibid., ix.

15. Ibid., x.

16. Ibid., 4–5.

17. James Playsted Wood, *Magazines in the United States,* 3d ed. (New York: Ronald Press, 1949), 25.

18. Michael T. Gilmore, "The Literature of the Revolutionary and Early National Periods," *Cambridge History of American Literature,* ed. Sacvan Bercovitch (Cambridge: Cambridge UP, 1994), 1:558.

19. Ibid., 562.

20. Ibid.

21. Mary Ellen Zuckerman, *A History of Popular Women's Magazines in the United States, 1792–1995* (Westport, Conn.: Greenwood P, 1998), 1. Zuckerman's earlier study with John Tebbel, *The Magazine in America 1741–1990* (New York: Oxford UP, 1991), also provides a brief sketch of early magazine history, noting, for example, that magazine growth between 1741 and the American Revolution was slow and that from 1741 "until 1794, there were never more than three magazines in the country at any one time, and half of those published in the period were issued during its last eight years." They also remark that "If there was one perennial subject in the journals, it was women, a topic explored from every conceivable angle, nearly always by men." See Zuckerman and Tebbel 5, 7. Also see Sloan and Hedgepeth Williams's *Early American Press, 1690–1783* (Westport, CT: Greenwood P, 1994); David A. Copeland's *Colonial American Newspapers: Character and Content* (Newark: U of Delaware P, 1997); and Ronald Lora's and William Henry Longston's *Conservative Press in Eighteenth- and Nineteenth-Century America* (Westport, CT: Greenwood P, 1999).

22. See, for example, Edward Larkin, "Inventing an American Public: Thomas Paine, the *Pennsylvania Magazine*, and American Revolutionary Discourse" in *Early American Literature* 33 (1998): 250–76; Jeffrey Pasley, "The Two National Gazettes: Newspapers and the Embodiment of American Political Parties" in *Early American Literature* 35 (2000), 51–86; and, more recently, Mark Kamrath, "*Eyes Wide Shut* and the Cultural Poetics of Eighteenth-Century American Periodical Literature," *Early American Literature* 37 (2002): 497–536.

23. Kenneth M. Price and Susan Belasco Smith, "Introduction: Periodical Literature in Social and Historical Context," *Periodical Literature in Nineteenth-Century America* (Charlottesville and London: UP of Virginia, 1995), 9.

24. Edward W. R. Pitcher, *Fiction in American Magazines before 1800: An Annotated Catalogue* (Schenectady, NY: Union College P in conjunction with: Antoca P, Lexington, KY, 1993), 1.

25. Ibid., 286.

26. The article in the July 1789 issue of the *South-Carolina Weekly Museum* on the moral etiquette or manners of married ladies also comments candidly on the "slobbishness of husbands."

27. Kamrath 522.

28. A publication laying out a "plan for admitting the female sex to an equal share in legislation" appeared in the April 6, 1786, issue of the *New-Haven Gazette, and the Connecticut Magazine*, while "The History of White Negroes" appeared in the April 13, 1786, issue of the magazine. For more on the roles of women in the Republic, see Lycurgus's letter in the *New-Haven Gazette, and the Connecticut Magazine*, April 6, 1786, 57.

29. David S. Shields, "Joy and Dread Among the Early Americanists," *William and Mary Quarterly* 57 (July 2000): 636.

30. Carla Mulford, "The Ineluctability of Peoples' Stories," *William and Mary Quarterly* 57 (July 2000): 632, 627–28.

PART ONE

ATLANTIC CURRENTS

In their provocative study *The Many-Headed Hydra: Sailors, Slaves, Commoners, and the Hidden History of the Revolutionary Atlantic*, Peter Linebaugh and Marcus Rediker remark that as the "hydra," or sailors, felons, laborers, and indentured servants, "dispersed in diaspora" so too the pressures to assimilate and to conform to authority were met with scrutiny and skepticism—a willingness to question the "authority of the minister and magistrate, the expansion of empire, the definition of private property, and the subordination of women."[1] Michael Durey concurs with their assessment of mass emigration and the presence of dissenting views insofar as he identifies the ways in which late-eighteenth-century Irish, English, and Scottish "political refugees" sought various types of religious, political, and economic reform.[2] Together, such scholarship calls attention to the manner in which a heterogeneous population, fresh on the docks of Boston and other port cities, attempted to navigate a multiracial, maritime economy whose magisterial authority was constantly threatened by internal political and social upheaval. It also points to the role that emerging public spheres and print culture played in establishing—and questioning—the boundaries of colonial authority and individual identity.

That is, if newspapers and magazines in the colonial period were more limited in number and distribution than they would be by the mid—eighteenth century, they were nonetheless important instruments for common people and the intellectual elites alike in recording and shaping the evolving nature of the colonial projects in the prenational era. While a few publishers and editors, such as Benjamin Franklin, had the status and ingenuity to advance their ideas to a wide audience, many of the periodicals from the 1740s onward were intended for small, more specialized audiences. Even so, because each colony had to negotiate its sense of some political autonomy with the realities of the power of the British Empire in mind, transatlantic themes prevailed in these early periodicals. Further, ethnically focused periodicals often looked to news and values from their readers' countries of origin. Thus, an often-conflicted dialogue of diasporic "self-hood" pervades the periodicals of the colonial period, often alongside broader, international themes such as new scientific and religious ideas. It was an era of constant negotiation for identity and assimilation, and the magazines and newspapers reflect the important bases on which colonial and ethnic selfhood was emerging.

In the colonial period, "political, religious, and social authority was remarkably local and decentralized in comparison with France, Britain, or Prussia";[3] therefore, unlike the later Revolutionary and Federal eras, discussions in periodicals—though often engaging transatlantic issues—largely remained centered in local, class-bound values. While international figures such as Benjamin Franklin and Thomas Jefferson are best known to students of early America, the localized debates were often rooted in political and cultural values specific to region and community. Not surprisingly, then, the boundaries of individual and community liberty form a major theme running through the periodicals of the colonial period.

Yet even in these decentralized discussions, the transatlantic influence of new scientific discoveries and philosophies and of ever-changing religious values and institutions affected the local, and periodicals' editors were particularly adept at negotiating these interrelated spaces. As many colonists were beginning to discover, religious and scientific questions often could not be separated. The influence of an Isaac Newton or a John Locke or of the significant body of scientists and philosophers examining the natural world was deeply felt within theological discussions. Add to these interconnecting if often conflicting new theories the impact of scientific discoveries relating to print culture, and the periodical emerges as one of the most important vehicles for expressing the conflation of the local, the international, and the philosophical.

The essays in this section expose the various ways in which communities—local and transatlantic—were negotiating these newly evolving ideas and technologies. Carla Mulford's "Pox and 'Hell-fire': Boston's Smallpox Controversy, the New Science, and Early Modern Liberalism," for instance, reveals the extent to which, for the first time in the Massachusetts Bay Colony, print media offered a vehicle for common people to discuss and debate their cultural predicaments, including issues of "polite" and "low" culture and the government versus the people. As the first case of freedom of the press in colonial British America, the James Franklin jailing controversy, she argues, called attention to scientific inquiry and emerging technologies that advanced the production and distribution of print culture. Both were simultaneously celebrated and condemned in the early eighteenth century, and those rivaling perspectives were important to the ways in which magazines and newspapers positioned themselves as part of the liberalizing movements or in opposition to them. Examining this debate through the lens of smallpox inoculation in Boston in the early 1720s, Mulford's analysis of Cotton Mather's perspectives on the crisis demonstrates that those adhering to older traditions could be surprising advocates of medical experimentation and that practices emerging from the new sciences could sometimes be seen as infringing on individual liberties. Mulford pushes the implications of the medical and civic debates surrounding smallpox inoculation to the complex ways in which such controversies signal the investment in cultural norms that are implied within the debates. As such, her essay not only probes how two modes of liberal inquiry—medicine and the public press—came into conflict, it also points to how the newspaper, like the pamphlet and other periodical formats, would become a public forum for navigating new, and often destabilizing, epistemological challenges of late Enlightenment "experimental knowledge."[4]

Timothy D. Hall, on the other hand, focuses in "Imagining a Transatlantic Awakening: the *Christian History* and the Hermeneutics of Revival" on questions of evangelicalism and empire, arguing that revivalists, and itinerant ministers in particular, perceived the Great Awakening not as a dispersed series of unconnected events but as a single, empirewide outpouring of the Spirit of God. Hall examines the multiple ways in which the *Christian History*'s emergence in the 1740s signaled a persuasive new vehicle that brought religious revivalism in dialogue with the considerable expansions in the transatlantic commercial empire. The weekly magazine also offered its revivalist readers an opportunity to participate in reconceptualizing an extended sense of their social world, and itinerant revivalism itself came under examination, focusing largely on the controversial James Davenport. Hall's investigation of one religious magazine's ideological and rhetorical content offers a model for examining a myriad of agendas and texts—sermons, letters, anecdotes, testimonials, foreign and domestic news, sketches, poetry, and more—in other religious periodicals as they relate to the history of modern evangelicalism, church formation, sectarian thought, and cultural change.[5]

John Smolenski and W. M. Verhoeven turn to the local and the ethnic shaping of community through periodical literature. In "'Incorporated . . . into a Body Politic': Clubs, Print, and the Gendering of the Civic Subject in Eighteenth-Century Pennsylvania," Smolenski examines Pennsylvania's most successful colonial newspaper, the *Pennsylvania Gazette* (1727–65), and its representation of various civic clubs and voluntary

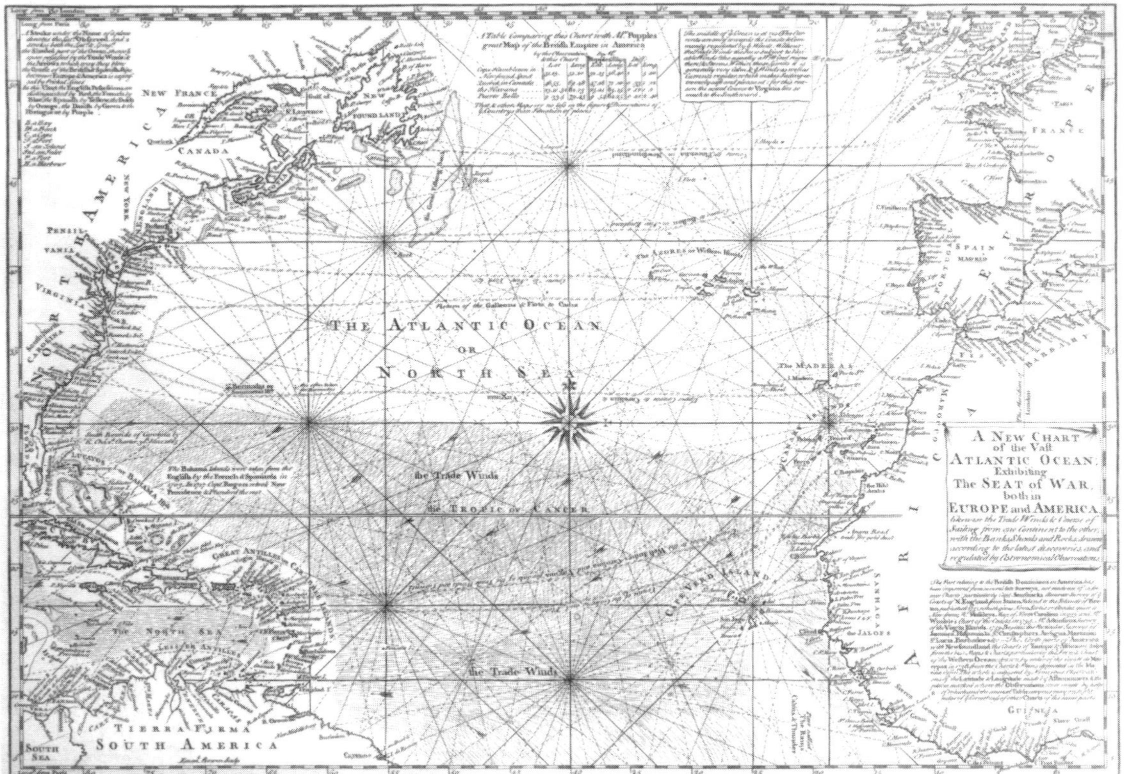

"A New Chart of the Vast Atlantic Ocean Exhibiting the Seat of War both in Europe and America" by F. Cooper. Printed in London in 1740, this map references the Jenkins Ear (war) and identifies how trade winds influenced currents near Europe, America, and Africa. Using the latest astronomical observations, it also charts the location of storms and the course of sailing from one continent to another, e.g., the "Usual course to the West Indies Carolina and Virginia." In identifying the course of British and Spanish ships between Europe and America as well as English, French, Spanish, Dutch, Danish, and Portuguese "possessions," the map represents colonial interests as well as commercial and ideological cross-currents within the Atlantic basin. Courtesy of the Geography and Maps Division, Library of Congress.

organizations such as the Masons and the St. Andrews Society. Smolenski marks the development of associational culture from the 1720s to the 1750s; important to such press coverage, he argues, is the ways in which newspapers used such events to influence their readers' interpretations of club and society activities as a means of defining what practices of public culture were valid for the public good. Far from cementing a common "republican" identity, he argues, printed representations of clubs produced a variety of different and notably masculine communal identities. Smolenski's essay illuminates how one particular periodical, at the local level, contributed to the construction of Pennsylvania's public sphere and how Pennsylvanians, as a region of readers, contributed to the development of a mass citizenship that was in turn influenced by various provincial interests along with issues of gender, class, religion, and ethnicity.

And last, in "'A Colony of *Aliens*': Germans and the German-Language Press in Colonial and Revolutionary Pennsylvania," Verhoeven draws attention to the significance of the German-language periodical press in eighteenth-century America—notably in Pennsylvania—before, during, and after the Revolution. Discussing the rivalry that erupted between the rural, sectarian German printers (such as the Saur family) and the urban printers, Verhoeven argues that the German immigrant assimilation into the socio-economic and political framework of eighteenth-century colonial and Revolutionary America was not, as is sometimes suggested, a matter of a "collective strategy" for the sake of ethnic survival, but a vociferous and at times painful process of transculturation marked by sharp ideological differences and divided loyalties. Being the largest non-British immigrant community and as such at the center of the national and transnational political and military tug-of-war, the Germans, more than any other non-British immigrant group, faced the daunting choice of whether to preserve and institutionalize their European ethnic and religious identity or to subscribe to the growing spirit of American patriotism and thus become Americanized at the expense of their German identity. The implications of his inquiry—to what extent this group's participation in the making of America affected their ethnic identity—is pertinent to all immigrant groups, from the colonial past to the present.

As these essays demonstrate, periodical literature in the colonial period deserves considerable attention for the ways it archives a diverse set of political, religious, social, and ethic interests, particularly at local and regional levels, amid rapid transatlantic cultural and social change. The diversity of opinion, particularly as it related to the needs and interests of working-class individuals and groups, becomes self-evident, especially in the manner in which weekly newspapers and magazines registered their concerns and conflicts. Among different types of cultural and ideological displacement, then, instances of provincial and international assimilation exist and act as a prelude to the debates that would lead to revolution and a desire for new political orders.

Notes

1. Peter Linebaugh and Marcus Rediker, *The Many-Headed Hydra: Sailors, Slaves, Commoners, and the Hidden History of the Revolutionary Atlantic* (Boston: Beacon P, 2000), 6.
2. Michael Durey, *Transatlantic Radicals and the Early American Republic* (Lawrence: UP of Kansas, 1997), 4.
3. Hugh Amory and David D. Hall, eds., *A History of the Book in America*, vol. 1, *The Colonial Book in the Atlantic World* (New York: Cambridge UP, 2000), 10.
4. See, for instance, "Of the late wonderful Discoveries, and Improvements of Arts and Sciences" in the *American Magazine and Historical Chronicle* of Boston, October 1743, and "Of the Sciences," April 24, 1755, in the *Instructor*, a weekly magazine printed and sold by J. Parker and W. Weyman in New York.
5. Other religious or ideological sites include magazines such as Thomas Coke and Francis Asbury's *Arminian Magazine* (1789–90); *Christian's, Scholar's, and Farmer's Magazine* (1789–91), *Theological Magazine* (1795–99), an irregular bimonthly magazine; *United States Christian Magazine* (1796); *Experienced Christian's Magazine* (1796–97), a monthly edited by Rev. W. Phoebus of New York; *Methodist Magazine* (1797–98); *Religious Monitor, or Theological Scales* (1798); *Christian's Monitor* (1799), a weekly published in Portland, Maine.

Carla Mulford

Pox and "Hell-Fire"

Boston's Smallpox Controversy, the New Science, and Early Modern Liberalism

> *This miserable Town, is a dismal Picture and Emblem of* Hell; Fire *with* Darkness *filling of it, and a* lying Spirit *reigning there; many members of our Churches, have had a fearful Share in the false Reports, and blasphemous Speeches, and murderous Wishes in which the Town is become very guilty before the Lord.*
>
> —Cotton Mather, diary, August 28, 1721, at the height of the smallpox controversy in Boston

Arguments over liberties of person and conscience and the freedom of the press are the fulcrum for the platform balancing the metaphysical and scientific revolutions of the seventeenth and eighteenth centuries. This becomes especially clear upon examination of the smallpox controversy in New England in the early eighteenth century. In particular, events in Boston in 1721 reveal the constellation of competing values inherent in a social formation moving, with liberalizing tendencies, from horologicals to chronometricals, from interpretations related to the presumed imperious order of an all-powerful Christian God (as dispensed through church and magistrate) to those relying upon scientific inquiry, the experimental method, and a conscious and rationalized pursuit and realignment of civic authority. For New Englanders, the smallpox crisis illustrated the crossroads between an occult interpretation of phenomena and total religious dependency, on the one hand, and the logical results from the new scientific experimental method on the other.

Taken in historical perspective, the smallpox crisis marks a crossroads in the formation of liberal subjectivity as fostered by new scientific technologies. Examination of the controversy's two sides, that of the Mathers and their interest in requiring smallpox inoculation and that of the Franklins and their interest in critiquing the decision-making of the ruling elite, illuminates the competition between two liberalizing scientific technologies, the technology of print and its implications for press freedom and (lacking a better term) the technology of the body in the form of determining a medical cure for smallpox.

Early Modern Liberalism and New Scientific Revolutions

In using the term *early modern liberalism* and focusing on the new scientific technologies of print and what one might call medicine, this essay takes up different strands on a thread of inquiry about liberalism that has been longstanding among scholars of early modern England.[1] Along with considering the extent to which Cotton Mather deployed occult interpretations during the smallpox epidemic, the linkages between Puritanism and the new scientific revolutions are also of interest. In 1938 Robert K. Merton argued in *Science, Technology, and Society in Seventeenth-Century England* what was then a provocative thesis that linked the development of Puritanism to the development of interest in science. Merton noted that in the latter half of the seventeenth century, a pronounced shift occurred in intellectual circles in England. He considered that "a well-defined social movement" toward what he called a "new fashionable" interest in the promotion of science brought about a complex of values one might call the *Puritan ethos* or a *Protestant ethic*.[2] More recently, Toby E. Huff has shown in *The Rise of Early Modern Science: Islam, China, and the West* that because of shifts in social, intellectual, and legal attitudes that began in the medieval era, institutions of higher learning in Britain and Europe assisted the process of the scientific revolution by offering an institutional framing through which intellectuals could be protected in their scientific endeavors. Despite what Huff rightly calls "the vested interests of the traditional religionists," multiple social and intellectual resources were called up to enable universities "to shape and instill a major commitment to the norms of disinterestedness and organized skepticism that are at the heart of modern science."[3] When sixteenth-century Europe underwent what Huff has called a "triple revolution"—a "revolution in cosmology," a "revolution in the disciplinary balance of the sciences" (creating a greater centrality for astronomy), and a "revolution in church authority"[4]—the result seems to have been that traditionalists in the Church, in attempting to restrict scientific discourse to the issuance of merely hypothetical statements, spurred the implementation of scientific procedures and protections in intellectual circles. Huff's point is that suddenly Europe and Britain had certain levels of protection offered by institutionalized structures. During the sixteenth and seventeenth centuries in England, these protections and encouragements were instituted in the founding of the Royal College of Physicians of London in 1518 and the Royal Society of London, officially chartered in 1662. It was not just in the career of Isaac Newton, in other words, that science was used to establish a greater sense of divine presence. The new science did not work against established institutions; instead, it was supported and enhanced by them.[5]

New Englanders did and did not take part in the institutional revolutions ongoing in England. Because of the special place of science in the Reformation Puritan practices later enhanced by Anglican writers after the Restoration of the British monarchy, New England theologians seem to have considered that they should hold particular status in scientific inquiry, for they could report back to England their findings about a natural world—North America—that was unknown to those in England. Yet this was not, in effect, the way that intellectuals in England conceived of New Englanders. While the findings of a Cotton Mather would be reported in the minutes of the Royal Society as pertinent to society inquiries and while individuals within the society might offer some British colonials a high degree of respect for their work, society members overall considered that colonials' primary information would be welcome but their analyses would need verification in England or Europe.

Cotton Mather perhaps more than any other American Puritan has come in for much criticism and negative psychoanalytical analysis because of what seems to have been close to a neurotic tendency to read in the natural world signs of the Puritan God's presence and judgment. Yet more than other American Puritans of his generation, Cotton Mather longed for international fame as a religionist *and* scientist. Mather presents a peculiarly interesting case for analyzing the tensions within the new scientific paradigms. As a younger man, Mather had recorded in his diary his high hopes about his father's and his own potential influence with churchmen back home, in England, even after the Restoration had clearly succeeded. Mather had remarkable capacities for work, especially for writing and seeking out the publication of numerous little treatises that would, he hoped, find their way back into England and even into the king's hands.[6] Mather busily sought prodigies to report as signs and wonders of their God and his God's bounty and beauty.[7]

Like his father, Cotton Mather became interested in the newer ways of looking at the world—ways that partook of Newtonian science and natural philosophy—and he considered that if changes were to occur in the interpretive framing of the Puritan God's universe, then those interpretive alterations ought rightly to occur in British North America, where people lived closer to the natural world and thus could be its best interpreters. Thus, for instance, Mather—knowing that his letters would reach the Royal Society—wrote to John Woodward, author of *An Essay toward the Natural History of the Earth: And Terrestrial Bodies, Especially Minerals . . .* (London, 1695; 2d ed., 1702), about what he called the giants of the Earth uncovered in America, at Claverack, New York.[8] In a letter dated November 17, 1712,

Mather thinly disguised his concern about Woodward's presumed superiority in science simply because he was English, making reference again and again to the importance of the discovery of the prodigy in North America.

Aware of metropolitan noninterest in publishing his writings on North American natural phenomena as signs of God's wonders, Mather ridiculed British and European ignorance about the New World by saying, "you must Look upon all the *American Curiosities* which are sent you, as being in some sort *Subterraneous,*" meaning less worthy. Mather's expressions indicate his frustration that British scientists and their publishers were being obstreperous in their refusal to take advantage of scientific knowledge Americans were offering. Indeed, Mather made much in his letter of the "subterranean" aspect of his speaking, given his sense that, despite his repeated efforts, London printers would not print his *Biblia Americana.* In the discussion about mastodon remains, Mather ranged through the writings of José de Acosta, Zoroaster, Egyptian traditions, the Christian Bible, Augustine, Virgil, Augustín de Zarate, scholastic writings, and Native peoples of the southern continent and those in the Albany area.[9] Regardless of his striving—or perhaps because of it—Mather was taken seriously only as a reporter of the natural phenomena, not as a scientific interpreter in his own right worthy of publication in England.

Throughout his life, Mather was interested in population numbers, population controls, and doing good in the world. This explains his fascination with finding a smallpox cure. The smallpox epidemic became Mather's opportunity to reveal his scientific knowledge to England and indeed all of Europe. It would provide him a means by which to bring acclaim to himself as a scientist and natural philosopher, and it might provide a means for gaining respect within an institutional structure that he acknowledged, for the most part, had been neglecting him. One has a sense, in reading through the materials related to the smallpox controversy, that Mather considered himself a man misunderstood and undervalued, not just by the local people but by Britons back in England.

Just as the new science effected changes in attitudes about the scientific inquiry into physiology and what today is called medicine, it brought about changes in information transmittal. The often-discussed printing revolution had its effects on James Franklin, who was in the process of articulating a posture of openness for his new newspaper, the *New-England Courant,* at precisely the time when smallpox was taking hold of the population in Boston. James Franklin, trained by printers working near the Inns of Court, came of age during the great era of increased vernacularization of the press in England. Well read in his uncle Benjamin's library, which included tracts associated with the Williamite Revolution of 1688, Franklin seems to have admired—as did his better-known brother, Benjamin—the alternative historians of England, the commonwealthmen who published and republished[10] the classic texts of John Milton, Algernon Sidney, James Harrington, Edmund Ludlow, Thomas Hollis, and Henry Neville.

When he finally felt pressed enough by the Mathers' and their followers' calumny against himself and his paper, James Franklin fought back, writing a brief in behalf of the toleration of all points of view fairly and publicly expressed. His apologia is an eloquent reflection of the commonwealth tradition he ad mired—"to anathematize a Printer for publishing the different Opinions of Men, is as injudicious as it is wicked. To use Curses without a Cause, is to throw them away as if they were *Nothing Worth*, and to rob them of their Force, when there is no Occasion for them," Franklin avowed. "The *Courant* was never design'd for a Party Paper," he continued,

> I have once and again given out, that both Inoculators and Anti-Inoculators are welcome to speak their Minds in it; and those that have read the Courants must know, that I have not only publish'd Pieces wrote among ourselves in favour of Inoculation, but have given as full an Account of the Success of it in England, as the other Papers have done. . . . What my own Sentiments of things are, is of no Consequence, nor any matter to any Body. I hereby invite all Men, who have Leisure, Inclination and Ability, to speak their Minds, with Freedom, Sense and Moderation, and their Pieces shall be welcome to a Place in my Paper.[11]

Here, as elsewhere, James Franklin framed his arguments along the lines of one of the central defenders of freedom of conscience and the press known to New Englanders, John Milton. Milton, whose influence over New England writers is well documented and whose books were in the libraries used by both the Mathers and the Franklins, is merely the best known of the writers on issues relevant to an inquiry into the cultural values related to freedom of conscience, freedom of person, and freedom of the press. As Milton had phrased it in 1660, the "whole freedom of man" consisted "either in spiritual or civil libertie." The primary concern in a free republic, according to Milton, is a "liberty of conscience which above all other things ought to be to all men dearest and most precious." For Milton, "the other part of our freedom consists in the civil rights and advancements of every person according to his merit."[12] Milton's *Readie and Easie Way to Establish a Free Commonwealth* was an argument against the return of the Stuarts to the throne. Milton proposed what Annabel Patterson has called a "massive decentralization of the law,"[13] and he pushed for fiscal clarity and a general leveling in terms of voting and office holding. In his famous *Areopagitica: A Speech for the Liberty of Unlicens'd Printing*, Milton proposed the best means toward the freedoms he was espousing as available in the practice of a free press. Milton, along with John Locke and Algernon Sidney, was highly regarded in New England particularly. Milton's writings on what he himself called the "good old cause" were part of a long line of arguments related to freedom of conscience, freedom of person, and freedom of the press in early modern England. They were as attractive to James Franklin as they were to his younger brother. When the ship *Sea-horse* reached the wharf in Boston Harbor, it set the stage for a most virulent debate not just about inoculation but about freedom of conscience and freedom of person. It was a debate wherein two complicated new scientific technologies—one, a technology of print bringing with it the liberalizing tendencies of the press, and the other, a technology of the body involving the liberalizing tendencies associated with the free practice of medicinal science—would collide.

The *Sea-horse*, Pox, and "Hell-Fire"

The *Boston Gazette* of April 24, 1721, reported as usual the arrivals and departures of ships, noting that the HMS *Sea-horse* had arrived at the port of Boston. Within a week, it became clear that the *Sea-horse* had carried a passenger who had contracted smallpox. The town of Boston first learned of the situation on May 8, when it was reported to the town commissioners,[14] and the *Boston News-Letter* for May 22 reported under the date Saturday, May 20, "This Day His Majesty's Justices, the Select Men, Overseers of the Poor and Constables of the Town of Boston, made a strict search and enquiry of the Inhabitants at their respective Houses, touching the Small-pox, and found none Sick of the Distemper, but a Negro Man at the House of Capt. *Paxton* near the South Battery, being the House that was first visited therewith: The Negro is almost Recovered, and will be in a Day or two removed to the Province Hospital at Spectacal Island."[15]

In removing the ailing man from proximity with others to an isolated place, the constables were following standard practice in Europe.[16] Quarantine and flight had been relatively successful when authorities sought to forestall an epidemic in Boston in late 1678. Of that earlier epidemic, Cotton Mather wrote to John Cotton in November:

> Never was it such a time in Boston. Boston burying-places never filled so fast. It is easy to tell the time wherein we did not use to have the bells tolling for burials on a Sabbath-day morning by sunrise, to have 7 buried on a Sabbath-day night after meeting, to have coffins crossing each other as they have been carried in the street, to have I know not how many corpses following each other close at the heels, to have 38 die in one week—6, 7, 8, or 9 in a day. . . . To attempt a bill of mortality, and the number the very spires of grass in a burying place, seem to have a parity of difficulty and in accomplishment.[17]

Mather was astonished at the losses in 1678, and although he was still a teenager, he vowed to attempt a cure the next time the smallpox reached Boston.

Such a mission provides evidence in Mather's thinking of an alliance between practices of new science and of divinity. An opportunity arose for him to attempt a cure in 1721, with the arrival of the *Sea-horse.*

On May 26, 1721, Mather wrote into his diary that "The grievous Calamity of the *Small-Pox* has now entered the Town. The Practice of conveying and suffering the *Small-Pox* by *Inoculation,* has never been used in *America,* nor indeed in our Nation. But how many Lives might be saved by it, if it were practised? I will procure a Consult of our Physicians, and lay the matter before them."[18] This 1721 diary entry summoned up a promise he had made to John Woodward of the Royal Society back in 1716: that if the smallpox ever came again to Boston, he would gather the physicians together and ask them to perform inoculations.[19] Mather had read in the 1714 Transactions of the Royal Society of London the work of inoculation carried on by a Greek physician and a fellow of the Royal Society, Dr. Emanuel Timonius, then living in Constantinople. In March 1717, Lady Mary Wortley Montagu, married to the British ambassador at Constantinople, brought attention to the inoculation process when she had her infant son inoculated. Eventually, the British royal family became interested in the procedures, and in the year 1721 inoculation against smallpox became a cause célèbre in Britain.[20]

Mather was evidently hoping to resolve the matter once and for all. He was well aware of the interest in inoculation in Britain at the time the *Sea-horse* arrived at Boston. But most Bostonians were uninvolved in the latest scientific news from abroad. As he insisted in his diary that he would, Mather consulted with the local doctors, who remained dubious about a cure by inoculation. Only one, Mather's friend Zabdiel Boylston, agreed to attempt the procedure. Boylston set to work on his own six-year-old son, along with two Africans kept as slaves. By September, Boylston had inoculated thirty-five people, with no deaths and indeed with scientific satisfaction as to the viability of inoculation as a means to ward off the smallpox.[21]

Despite his success and despite the numerous cases of smallpox that might have been saved by such experimentation,[22] the townspeople were immensely upset by Boylston's proceedings. They feared that inoculations were spreading the disease, and they were incensed that their personal liberties—liberties of conscience and liberties of civic action—were being sorely challenged. Both print and pulpit messages told citizens to accept smallpox inoculations. The *New-England Courant* was the central vehicle through which the controversy would be followed, and aired, before a confounded populace. The *Courant* provided the primary space where those who questioned the viability of inoculation and the seeming oppression of town leaders could air their opinions.

Three months after smallpox took over Boston, Cotton Mather was excruciatingly upset about the situation in which he found himself. He wrote in his diary on August 24, "The Town is become almost an Hell upon Earth, a City full of Lies, and Murders, and Blasphemies, as far as wishes and Speeches can render it so: Satan seems to take a strange Possession of it, in the epidemic Rage, against that notable and powerful and successful way of saving the Lives of People from the Dangers of the *Small-Pox.* What can I do on this Occasion, to gett the miserable Town dispossessed of the evil Spirit, which has taken such an horrible Possession of it? What besides Prayer with Fasting, for it?"[23] On August 28, he railed further that "This miserable Town, is a dismal Picture and Emblem of *Hell; Fire* with *Darkness* filling of it, and a *lying Spirit* reigning there; many members of our Churches, have had a fearful Share in the false Reports, and blasphemous Speeches, and murderous Wishes in which the Town is become very guilty before the Lord. Calling upon the Flock to prepare for the Table of the Lord, I warn them to repent of whatever may have been in them offensive unto GOD, and come with suitable Dispositions of Love to GOD and CHRIST and their Neighbour, lest they provoke Him to be terrible in His holy Places."[24]

Mather's clear alignment of some kind of divine wrath with the situation in which he found himself as someone attempting to attend to the physical well-being of godly people indicates his own conflicted assumptions about God's supposed divine plan and the uses to which science could be put by knowledge-able physicians in an effort to heal the sick (without any help from some other, mightier power). In his book *Popular Culture in Early Modern Europe*, Peter Burke writes about two stages of elite interaction with the general populace in seventeenth- and eighteenth-century Europe.[25] In the first stage, Burke argues, elites attempted to reform the general population while sharing many of its cultural presuppositions. In the second stage, Burke states, elites withdrew from the general culture. This withdrawal effected an installation of cultural differentiation that excluded, during and after the Restoration, any of the more general concerns of the population. As Michael P. Winship has pointed out,[26] Burke does not explore the tensions and struggles of moving between the stages, but his formulation provides a useful starting point for examining the ways in which Cotton Mather responded to the public outcry against him and for considering the ways in which that public outcry emerged.

A slightly broader picture of the historical context of the new science in New England emerges from a brief consideration of how elite groups in old England worked through issues in the new science in their founding of the Royal Society of London. Thomas Sprat, historian of the Royal Society, commented in 1665 on the general concern among the intellectual elite about the social and political tensions caused by what they characterized as religious extremism and religious disquietude in the earlier half of the century. In Sprat's words, "This wild amuzing mens minds, with *Prodigies*, and conceits of *Providences*," as he phrased it, "has been one of the most considerable causes of those spiritual distractions, of which our Country has long bin the *Theater*."[27] Indeed the concern in England about providences and prodigies, Sprat said, "affects men with fears, doubts, irresolutions, and terrors," to the extent that, in his view, there could be "nothing more injurious than this, to mens public, or privat peace."[28] By the end of the century, the British elite generally attempted to separate experiential and experimental science from the mere recording of what they continued to call "prodigies," or strange natural occurrences.

Yet in New England, well into the first quarter of the eighteenth century, indeed throughout the career of Cotton Mather—encouraged by Mather and men like him, and perhaps especially the Puritan theologians—people tended to look for signs of their God's wonder, and they interpreted events according to their perceptions of divine judgment. In this context, it is useful to reconsider the passage from Mather's diary. Mather, characterizing the town of Boston as an "emblem of Hell" filled with fire and darkness at once, reports his decision to exhort people to examine where in their lives they have been offensive to their God and to make amends accordingly. His resolution is not to secure their better understanding of inoculation procedures but instead—as he did repeatedly—to resort to an internal examination of conscience according to the lights of church and civil leaders such as Mather himself.

New Englanders were caught in a cultural lag in part foisted upon them by their church leaders. This is to say that members of the Royal Society had by the 1720s moved away from occult interpretations of natural phenomena to interpretations more readily based in what one would today call materialism. The Church of England and the Royal Society had, it would seem, provided sufficient neutral space for new scientific interpretation to become established. New Englanders by contrast, many of them following leaders such as Cotton Mather, adhered to an older tradition—indeed, a tradition fostered by none other than Isaac Newton of a generation before—of interpreting events according to divine intervention. Their interpretive environment differed from their counterparts in Britain, and the effects of new scientific experimentation were less available to them in their everyday lives. The New Englanders became exacerbated when church leaders such as Mather, well read in the new science, turned to occult interpretation rather than rational explanation. Mather had himself been keeping up with the new scientific findings of the Royal Society of London, and he had been reading and learning about the varieties of experiments used to take off the smallpox or even to prevent its attack on the body in the first place. But when Mather seemed, quite suddenly, to insist that there might be natural cures for smallpox, even as he, at the very same time, argued that an errant populace was to blame for their God's having given them the distemper in the first place, the argument confounded the townspeople. The churches in Boston were insufficient to provide Mather the space he would need to foist his scientific opinions on the people. Mather the churchman was experiencing a cultural lag that James Franklin readily understood.

The measure of the cultural lag regarding new science—both in Cotton Mather and in the population more generally—becomes clear on examination of the ways in which print media, especially the newspapers of Boston, were used for the first time in New England to carry on a public debate about matters that more typically fell under the sole purview of church and civil leaders. With the irony that only hindsight establishes, one recognizes a crossroads of early modern liberalism. In an interesting paradox, one of the outcomes of new scientific work (the technological advances of the printing and print's clearly vernacularizing tendencies) calls into question another outcome of new science (hypothetical scientific reasoning based on the experimental method put to use in behalf of medical cures).

Competing Technologies, Competing Sets of Men

Prior to the moment when print technology could foster general public scrutiny of leaders, church and civic leaders could operate within a closed system. Leaders such as Increase and Cotton Mather could, if they funded their efforts, make their own writings available to readers such as themselves—people from an intellectual and social elite already attuned to the questions and issues of central concern to the group. Until James Franklin came along, no space—because there was no medium for articulation of that space—had been available for the free and more general public enquiry. The *Boston Gazette*, like the earlier-established *Boston News-Letter*, was an organ largely of the governor and the political and economic elite. The editors of these newspapers carried on contentions against the Assembly, which they conceived to be more "popular," and they tended to support the clerical and intellectual leadership of the colony.[29] As Charles E. Clark has indicated, the *Gazette* and the *News-Letter* both "treated the lower orders of town and country with anonymity and occasional contempt."[30]

The debate about the smallpox came about in the way it did because James Franklin had collected around him a group of men who were willing to write for his new newspaper, the *New-England Courant*, with an expressed goal of entertaining any and all opinions on most matters. James Franklin hoped to entice to his newspaper a readership neglected by the *Boston News-Letter* and the *Gazette* by working largely in the belletristic tradition more commonly affiliated with genteel society in England.[31] It was a radical move on Franklin's part and an insightful one, for he was taking advantage of the shifting economic and political base that created a space for enterprising efforts. Franklin fostered an informal group of writers, probably not the club for which he has been credited,[32] and in so doing he sponsored, in effect, what Michael Warner has aptly phrased as "the Country posture without the Country"—that is, a culture of polite letters not for polite persons but for the everyday reader. Lacking a secure class position from which to speak of civic culture[33] and interested in the freedoms articulated by the commonwealth tradition, James Franklin worked to establish a sphere wherein authority would be challenged in open, public debate. The smallpox inoculations being foisted on the community by its leaders brought about just the right circumstances that Franklin believed essential as a forum for public information. He relied on the circumstantial necessity for open debate among members of the Boston community who had been, prior to this, kept largely outside of public discourse.

Franklin's efforts in the controversy illustrate the liberalizing tendencies of print media at a crucial time of emerging inquiry and emerging capital. In the *Courant*'s first number, James Franklin printed several notices written by a number of people, some of them affiliated with different churches (but especially the Anglican church), and one of them the Edinburgh-trained physician (the only person in the colony with such training), Dr. William Douglass. The opening article regarding the smallpox was written by John Checkley and published anonymously. Explaining the appearance of the newspaper, the article invited "conversation" to take place in the pages of the newspaper about a variety of matters. It was not long before the group of writers Franklin collected in his newspaper ended up being dubbed by the Mathers and their friends the "Hell-Fire club," after a club in London known for its scurrility.[34] Clearly the Mathers were distraught by the powerful effect of Franklin's newspaper in its garnering for itself a space for popular utterance that had been lacking in the other newspapers. The effort to denigrate Franklin's newspaper project by negatively labeling the writers a "club" indicates the strength of the distress among church and civic leaders caused by the *New-England Courant*'s criticisms of the reported progress of smallpox inoculations.

John Checkley's opening article concluded with a sly, negative glance at a letter written in behalf of Boylston's efforts in the smallpox inoculation and published in the *Boston Gazette* on July 21, 1721. Checkley called into question the rival newspaper's support of inoculation, even as it made slighting reference to the Mathers and their attempt to employ divinity on "their" side of the smallpox inoculation debates. Checkley's opener irked authorities interested in keeping the town as quiet as possible while the smallpox was being discovered and treated. Indeed the pretense of providing information and instruction seems to have been one of the goals behind the *Boston Gazette's* story about inoculation efforts. The *Courant*'s objectives seem to have been as much to inform local people about their rights as to inform them about the smallpox.

The *Gazette* for July 21 supported Boylston's efforts by citing his surgical successes. It aligned the inoculation project and its outcomes with divine sanction. In effect, the article indicated, whoever would question Boylston's work might be questioning "*All-wise Providence*," which had given over the inoculation method, as a generous gift, in the course of giving mankind the natural world. That letter, signed by Cotton and Increase Mather, along with four others, concluded with a series of rhetorical questions:

> Do we not in the use of all means depend on GOD's *blessing*? and *live* by that alone? And can't a devout heart depend on GOD in the use of *this* means, with much Gratitude, being in the full esteem of it? For, what hand or art of *Man* is there in this Operation more than in *bleeding, blistering* and a Score more things in *Medical use*? Which are all consistent with a *humble Trust in our Great Preserver, and a due subjection to His All-wise Providence?*[35]

Cotton Mather's hand is evident here, in the linking of subjection to God with subjection to the scientific "cure" under way.

The implication that the subjection of the people was necessary for the furtherance of God's ends, ends administered by church and town leaders, was the problem taken up for public scrutiny by Franklin and his writers, who constructed the situation as a challenge to freedom of person and of conscience. The *Gazette* article's conflation of science, the natural world, and medicinal practices with the notion of being duly subject to Providence—which in effect meant that the public should willingly submit to smallpox inoculation even though some of those inoculated were dying or dead—was not lost on the writers for the *Courant*, especially John Checkley. Checkley adopted typical early-eighteenth-century London club style, saying that he and his "set" were ready to take on the world. He concluded his remarks—in a direct address to his readers—by saying,

> And to engage the World to converse farther with us, they'll [readers will] find me in the good Company of a certain Set of Men, of whom I hope to give a very good Account,
>
> Who like faithful Shepherds take care of their Flocks,
> By teaching and practicing what's Orthodox,
> Pray hard against *Sickness*, yet preach up the POX![36]

Checkley's anonymous opening letter to the public was complemented by another anonymously printed letter by Dr. William Douglass. Douglass spoke to the town's disquietude about the inoculations. "Notwithstanding the general Aversion of the Town," Douglass wrote,

> *in Contradiction* to the declared Opinion of the Practitioners, *in Opposition* to the Selectmen, and *in Spite* of the discouraging

> Evidences relating to this Practice, *Six Gentlemen of Piety and Learning, profoundly ignorant of the Matter*, after serious Consideration of a Disease one of the most intricate practical Cases in Physick, do on the Merits of their Characters, and for no other reason, with a *Vox praeteriaq; nihil* assert, etc. If this Argument, *viz.* their Character, should prevail with the Populace (tho' here I think they have missed their Aim) who knows but it may oblige some prophane Person to canvas that sort of Argument. I think their Character ought to be sacred, and that they themselves ought not to give the least Occasion to have it called in question.[37]

Taking all of his rebukes of the inoculators into account, Douglass seems to have opposed the inoculation treatments supported by Cotton Mather and performed by Zabdiel Boylston, *not* on the grounds of their necessary faultiness but because the conditions under which Boylston's inoculations were performed and the unnecessary risks to others that the inoculations produced were, in his view, unacceptable and, worse yet, malicious.

Douglass expressed concern about the high-handed ways in which the inoculators were carrying on their treatments. In effect, the inoculators used the space created for them by the church and their leadership authority to detach themselves from the general population. They insisted, because of their character and station, that the authority for inoculation had been, in effect, given them by their God. As a trained physician, Douglass could challenge such authority and its impact as civic policy. He thus avowed his concern that public disruptions would occur if everybody chose to go out of his calling and have an opinion about scientific matters.

The *New-England Courant* was seeking, in front of public scrutiny and with an invitation that the people of the town contribute to the discussion, an accountability of its leaders. With Douglass, the other anti-inoculators opposed the treatments for differing reasons, with some of them disliking what might be called the "bully pulpit" method employed by both Mathers. For some time, the Mathers had been preaching pro-inoculation sermons that linked their authority with divine sanction. In effect, church leaders were presuming that their positions would secure them from question, much as might have happened in earlier days. Yet this was a different era, and the assumption that the church could provide security for scientific experimentation and speculation—that the church could, in effect, foster the new scientific technology of medical inquiry—proved incorrect. A new technology of print was emerging to challenge the authority that had formerly inhered in the established church. The space provided for public discourse in newsprint would promote a challenge to formerly authorized opinion.

The arguments against inoculation included observations that those in church and government ought not to interfere with the personal lives of the people over whom they were empowered. Still others questioned—with negative assumptions about "folk" remedies and the sources of Mather's information regarding the experiments—whether he had any greater authority than his own superstition.[38] Checkley's supposed "Set of Men" were not in any formal sense a club, but the group did include some of the better and more secularized (non-evangelical) writers of the community. It consisted of the printer James Franklin; Nathaniel Gardner, a poet and essayist; physicians William Douglass, George Stewart, John Gibbons (all Anglicans); Rev. Henry Harris (also Anglican); the soon-to-be-discovered Benjamin Franklin (whose Silence Dogood essays reached the pages of the *Courant* but who seems not to have entered the controversy);[39] and a few others. Under the pretense of the banter typical of the London club scene, they railed at the abuses of power that the Mather and pro-inoculation contingency were employing in the pulpit, in their publications in the *Boston Gazette* and the *Boston News-Letter*, and in separately published broadsides and pamphlets, such as Cotton Mather's *Sentiments upon the Small-pox Inoculated* (Boston, 1721), Increase Mather's *Several Reasons . . . proving that Inoculation is a Lawful Practice* (Boston, 1721) and *Some Further Accounts from London, of the Small-Pox Inoculated* (Boston, 1722), and Thomas Walter's *Little-Compton Scourge* (Boston, 1721).

Cotton Mather tended in private to demonize those who were arguing against the smallpox inoculation. In images of the town as full of hellfire and blasphemy, filled with a lying spirit, Mather captured his sense of failure before his God and his personal frustration with what he perceived at times to be the ignorance of his townspeople and at most other times the incursions of the Devil in a fallen people.[40] In worrying about whether he should inoculate his family, Mather had concern not just for his children but for the abuse it might raise against him should the inoculation not work. Mather worried about the extent to which members of his church were turning against him behind his back: "many members of our Churches, have had a fearful Share in the false Reports, and blasphemous Speeches, and murderous Wishes in which the Town is become very guilty before the Lord," he wrote on August 28, 1721.

After months of anguish, Cotton Mather, in severe personal sadness, announced at a meeting of ministers in January 1722 that he would retire from public life because he could not face the controversies and ire his writings and preachings were arousing. One response to Mather's personal anguish was that his relative Mather Byles used the term "Hell-Fire Club" in a letter published in the *Boston Gazette*, January 15, 1722, denouncing John Checkley (who had long before left off writing for the *Courant*) as "the Head of the Club" who had printed a pamphlet "to prove, That the God whom the Churches of New-England Pray to, is the Devil." "Be sure," Byles warned, "all the Supporters of this Paper"—referring to the *Courant*—"will be justly looked upon as the Supporters of a *Weekly Libel* written on purpose to destroy the Religion of the Country, and as Enemies of the faithful Ministers of it." Byles's attempt here was, like Mather's attempts in speaking of the men who wrote for the *Courant*, to link the Boston scribblers against inoculation with clubs reported to have been in London at the turn of the century, taking on and twisting names of biblical personages such as John the Baptist, offered blasphemous toasts to the devil and against those in authority in England.

For their parts, Mather and Boylston and those who supported inoculation believed they were following the latest news in treatments, and Mather seems honestly to have believed that by introducing the smallpox inoculation in the colonies, he was doing a service for the British nation. "The Notable Experience I now have of this New Method, for the Saving of many Lives, yea, and for the Abating and preventing of Miseries undergone by many who do live, and survive an horrible Distemper, enables me to recommend the matter so, that I hope it may be introduced into the English Nation, and a World of good may be done to the miserable Children of Men," he wrote in his diary on August 17, 1721. In the 1710s, Mather had published some of his findings in the *Transactions* of the Royal Society of London. In the early 1720s, he felt relatively secure about the procedures he was promoting, yet he received heavy resistance.

New Science, the Vernacularization of Culture, and Early Modern Liberalism

History has, of course, proved Cotton Mather, a minister, to have been right in this scientific matter. Yet it seems, on taking a sociological point of view for a moment, that the issues that the smallpox controversy raises are issues deeply rooted in cultural norms and the institutions that supported them. Here the question is not about whether Cotton Mather was correct or not, nor whether his findings were strongly or poorly supported by observational and experimental data and by series of testing circumstances in different environments. If the particular optimal circumstances for the smallpox experiments were sufficiently absent, then this situation attests to how courageous Cotton Mather was in setting forth his new medical findings.

The question really is whether a set of cultural institutions and a modicum of relatively value-neutral space for enquiry existed within which the merits of the Mathers' and others' new inoculation system could be debated without personal danger to those engaged in the enquiry. The question, in other words, is what kind of social and institutional supports existed for Mather and his physician friends that could provide them even a mere fair approximation of space for dispassionate evaluation of the clinical situation before them.

Had Mather been in old England, existing institutions could have assisted him. There was a solidified intellectual elite apart from the establishment theologians, and the Crown was supporting scientific inquiry, evidenced by its continued support of the Royal Society of London and of its members' ties to scientists on the Continent and in Asia. In addition, the religious establishment that had provided institutionalized protections for scientific inquiry had embraced the empirical method to such an extent that while concern about providence still informed the work of science, it did not drive empirical assumptions by any means. But Cotton Mather was in New England, not old England, and he was operating within a cultural system, which he himself supported, a system that in ideological terms dated a half-century earlier to a cultural framing that still linked godhead to natural phenomena, success in the natural world to spiritual agency with what was considered their next world. What is more, although Mather was himself well aware of the ongoing changes in the scientific establishment in England, the populace he addressed from his pulpit was not so informed. He seems to have been squarely rooted in the older system, too, which created affiliation between the phenomena of the natural world and what he perceived to be the divine providence of his God.

Mather and the Franklins were poised at a crucial cultural moment for the new science in New England, a moment that was, in religio-ideological terms, backward-looking, yet a moment that was remarkably forward looking in terms of practical scientific application (the smallpox inoculation) and practical technological innovation (the founding of several newspapers in Boston). With regard to print technology, the situation is a fine instance of what Benedict Anderson has called the vernacularizing thrust of print culture and print capitalism.[41] In the face of the newspaper debates, members of the elite tended to withdraw themselves from the increasingly displeased populace, a populace which for the very first time was not only invited but enabled to express its distrust of a ruling group that seemed autocratic and unconvincing in its articulations about the Puritan God and about new scientific measures. For those who participated in reading in and writing for newspapers and other periodicals, the culture of print created a signal opportunity whereby colonials could begin to imagine themselves as members of communities that would eventually become "nations" apart from Europe.[42] Print, then, provided an institutionalizing space for individuals to explore their beliefs about themselves, their God, and their ministers and physicians. In the context of print's liberalizing tendencies, James Franklin's insistence on providing a space for articulation of concerns and values ran counter to positions held by those in power. In effect, the situation indicates print's liberalizing tendencies—that is, print's ability to foster, indeed technologize, the invention of the citizen-subject.

The signal irony in this particular instance is that the *New-England Courant* did not seem to have had the totalized liberalizing tendency which Anderson has arguably credited to print culture at this time. To be sure, print enabled those in the general culture sufficient space to imagine a way of being in the world that would encourage independence of thought and action, apart from the directives of the cultural leaders in church and state. Yet the results of print use in this instance were conserving results: that is, print was used to fuel conservative cultural impulses antithetical to scientific inquiry and the experimental method.

In this single instance of the uses of the new science in New England, competing uses of new scientific experiences come to light, one a result of Cartesian studies productive of an exploratory-scientific paradigm in medicine and the other a result of technological innovations brought about by mechanization of language technologies. The competition seems to have resulted in politically liberalizing and culturally conserving tendencies at one and the same time, for the central issues of this debate were, on the one hand, theological questions about the nature of the world and, on the other, an institutional and disciplinary debate about who would have authority over the questions and the answers to the questions being raised. The new science provided, in light of this example from New England, a revolutionizing of the question of authority, but it provided, too (and ironically because of the vernacularizing tendencies of the press), a temporary restriction on the nature of the questions that would be asked. James Franklin would be jailed in June 1722 for a supposed "gross Affront" against the government—for making a facetious statement in an article about the town's fitting out a ship to go after pirates.[43]

Notes

1. See, for instance, Annabel Patterson, *Early Modern Liberalism* (Cambridge: Cambridge UP, 1997), and Joyce Appleby, *Liberalism and Republicanism in the Historical Imagination* (Cambridge, MA: Harvard UP, 1992).
2. Robert K. Merton, *Science, Technology, and Society in Seventeenth-Century England* (1938; rpt. New York: Harper and Row, 1970), 27–28, 43, 95–96.
3. Toby E. Huff, *The Rise of Early Modern Science: Islam, China, and the West* (Cambridge: Cambridge UP, 1993). See 321 ff.; quotations at 339.
4. Ibid., 356.
5. See Huff's chapter titled "The Rise of Early Modern Science," but see also the useful summary of these movements in Margaret C. Jacob, *The Radical Enlightenment: Pantheists, Freemasons, and Republicans* (London: Allen and Unwin, 1981), 20–64.

6. See, for example, *Diary of Cotton Mather*, vol. 1, 1681–1709 (New York: F. Ungar Publishing, [1957]), 168–69, 312, 314–15, 424.

7. In England at the time, such interest in or indeed obsession with anomalies of the natural world were taken as tokens of the strange absurdities of Puritan and later Dissenting thinking. The goal was to reduce the significations found in the natural world, to designify the natural world so that it could be studied carefully without any straining after peculiarities as if these were signs of the Dissenters' God's presence.

   Natural philosophy had been advancing under the auspices of royal authority in England. The work of John Spencer, an Anglican who had attacked prodigies as signs of Puritans' peculiarities during the Restoration era in the 1660s, was being taken up by most Nonconformists in England in the 1670s and 1680s and then in New England in the 1690s, marking what was perceived as an emancipation of natural philosophy from the taint of religious fanaticism.

8. This was the first of thirteen letters he wrote to Woodward and the Royal Society during twelve days in November 1712. He called the letters "Curiosa Americana" and hoped that they would be printed in England.

9. This situation is more fully discussed in Mulford, "Of Nature and of Nations: Anglicization, Creolization, and Finding an *American* Identity in Eighteenth-Century British America," in *Do the Americas Have a Common Literary History?*, ed. Barbara Buchenau and Annette Paatz (Frankfurt-am-Main and New York: Lang, 2002), 61–94, and Mulford, "New Science and the Question of Identity in Eighteenth-Century British America," in *Finding Colonial Americas: Essays Honoring J. A. Leo Lemay*, ed. Carla Mulford and David S. Shields (Newark: U of Delaware P, 2001), 79–103.

10. Annabel Patterson indicates that the publication history of these writers occurred first between 1697 and 1701 and in coordinated stages thereafter (13).

11. *New-England Courant*, no. 18 (November 27, 1721). The smallpox controversy is given able treatment by Arthur Bernon Tourtellot in *Benjamin Franklin: The Shaping of Genius. The Boston Years* (Garden City, NY: Doubleday, 1977).

12. Milton, *The Readie and Easie Way to Establish a Free Commonwealth* (London, 1660), in *Complete Prose Works*, ed. D. M. Wolfe et al., 8 vols. (New Haven: Yale UP, 1953–82), 7: 456–61. For general background on issues of press freedom in England, see Frederick S. Siebert, *Freedom of the Press in England, 1476–1776* (Urbana: U of Illinois P, 1952).

13. Patterson 5.

14. "A Report of the Record Commissioners of the City of Boston," *Boston Town Records* (Boston: Rockwell and Churchill, 1885), 13:81.

15. *Boston News-Letter,* May 22, 1721.

16. See Frederick F. Cartwright, *Disease and History* (New York: T. Crowell, 1972), 114–31.

17. Cotton Mather to John Cotton, c. November 1678, in *Selected Letters of Cotton Mather,* ed. Kenneth Silverman (Baton Rouge: Louisiana State UP, 1971), 7. See David Levin, *Cotton Mather: The Young Life of the Lord's Remembrancer, 1663–1703* (Cambridge: Harvard UP, 1978), 66–71.

18. *Diary of Cotton Mather,* 2:620–21.

19. This situation is discussed quite well by Ola Elizabeth Winslow in *A Destroying Angel: The Conquest of the Smallpox in Colonial Boston* (Boston: Houghton Mifflin, 1974), 33–37.

20. Cartwright 123–24.

21. Ibid., 124–25.

22. As a matter of medical ethics, some might argue that Boylston and Mather should not be exonerated for their activities because they behaved irresponsibly by engaging in these activities, especially in using slaves as part of their experiment. This argument is compelling, just as compelling as the one that suggests that any saved lives, even in experimental medicine, are lives well saved.

23. *Diary of Cotton Mather* 2:639.

24. Ibid., 2:641.

25. Peter Burke, *Popular Culture in Early Modern Europe* (New York: Harper and Row, 1978). See also Keith Thomas, *Religion and the Decline of Magic* (New York: Scribner, 1971).

26. This formulation follows the work of Michael P. Winship in his interesting essay on Cotton Mather, "Prodigies, Puritanism, and the Perils of Natural Philosophy: The Example of Cotton Mather," *William and Mary Quarterly,* 3d ser., 51 (1994): 93–94.

27. Thomas Sprat, *The History of the Royal-Society of London, For the Improving of Natural Knowledge* (London, 1667), 362. Qtd. in Winship, 96.

28. Sprat 362, 364, 360. Qtd. in Winship, 96.

29. See Charles E. Clark, *The Public Prints: The Newspaper in Anglo-American Culture, 1665–1740* (New York and Oxford: Oxford UP, 1994), 123–40.

30. Clark 123.

31. Ibid.

32. See Clark 124.

33. See Michael Warner, *The Letters of the Republic: Publication and the Public Sphere in Eighteenth-Century America* (Cambridge and London: Harvard UP, 1990), 66–67.

34. Clark argues that the "club" effect of Franklin's paper was a distinguishing characteristic of his forum. However, the group was too loosely knit to be considered a club of any kind. Franklin was gathering about him a cluster of potential writers for his fledgling newspaper.

35. *Boston Gazette,* July 21, 1721, 3.

36. *New-England Courant,* August 7, 1721, 1.

37. Ibid.

38. Mather had learned of the smallpox treatment methods used in Constantinople, then in England, through the *Transactions of the Royal Society.* Locally he learned of methods of inoculation from an African, his slave Onesimus. In the appendix to a chapter on smallpox in his manuscript *The Angel of Bethesda, An Essay Upon the Common Maladies of Mankind,* Mather clarifies the basis of his knowledge about smallpox:

> There has been a *Wonderful Practice* lately used in several Parts of the World, which indeed is not yet become common in our Nation.
>
> I was at first instructed in it, by a *Guramantee*-Servant of my own, long before I knew that any *Europeans* or *Asiaticks* had the least Acquaintance with it; and some years before I was Enriched with the Communications of the Learned Foreigners, whose Accounts I found agreeing with what I received of my own Servant, when he showed me the Scar of the Wound made for the Operation; and said, That no Person Ever died of the *Small-Pox,* in their Countrey that had the Courage to use it.
>
> I have since mett with a Considerable Number of these *Africans,* who all agree in one Story. . . . (Cotton Mather, *The Angel of Bethesda by Cotton Mather,* ed. Gordon W. Jones [Barre, MA: American Antiquarian Society and Barre Publishers, 1972], 107)

For further discussion of Mather's use of the African context of his findings, see Carla Mulford, "New Science and the Question of Identity in

Eighteenth-Century British America," in *Finding Colonial Americas: Essays Honoring J. A. Leo Lemay*, ed. Carla Mulford and David S. Shields (Newark: U of Delaware P, 2001), 79–103.

39. Kenneth Silverman has suggested that Franklin's Silence Dogood essays reflect—in the very name of the "author," Silence Dogood—a reference to Cotton Mather. See Silverman, 339.

40. For instance, he had written in his diary for July 18, "The cursed Clamour of a People strangely and fiercely possessed of the Devil, will probably prevent my saving the Lives of my two Children, from the Smallpox in the Way of Transplantation. So that I have no way left, but that of my continual and importunate Cries to Heaven for their Preservation. Accompanied with Admonitions unto them to make their own." *Diary of Cotton Mather* 2:632.

41. Benedict Anderson, *Imagined Communities: Reflections on the Origin and Spread of Nationalism*, rev. ed. (New York: Verso, 1991).

42. For Anderson, the "riddle" has to do with why creole communities, well before most of Europe, "developed so early conceptions of their nation-ness." Anderson maintains that the answer to the riddle lies primarily in the liberalizing tendencies of print technology. Useful discussions about issues in freedom of the press and the democratization of culture occur in Leonard W. Levy, *Freedom of Speech and Press in Early American History: Legacy of Suppression* (Cambridge: Harvard UP, 1960), and Jeffery A. Smith, *Printers and Press Freedom: The Ideology of Early American Journalism* (New York and Oxford: Oxford UP, 1988). But see Patterson and Caroline Robbins, *The Eighteenth-Century Commonwealthman: Studies in the Transmission, Development, and Circumstance of English Liberal Thought from the Restoration of Charles II until the War with the Thirteen Colonies* (Cambridge: Harvard UP, 1959) on the commonwealth tradition related to press freedom.

43. This essay was first presented to Columbia University's Seminar in the Atlantic World, May 2003. The author thanks the seminar participants and especially Herbert Sloan, Ned Landsman, Kathleen Wilson, seminar leaders, for a stimulating discussion of the matters this essay raises.

Tim D. Hall

Imagining a Transatlantic Awakening

THE *CHRISTIAN HISTORY* AND THE HERMENEUTICS OF REVIVAL

On March 5, 1743, Thomas Prince Jr. inaugurated a new era in American religious literature with the premier issue of the *Christian History*, the first exclusively religious periodical to appear on this side of the Atlantic. The magazine boasted an innovative format modeled in part on news weeklies of the day, printed on eight pages octavo to facilitate collecting and binding a year's issues into a single volume that could be indexed and sold in book form. A subscription fee of only two shillings per quarter made the *Christian History* much more affordable than newspapers typically costing more than three times as much, putting the magazine within the reach of a broad and highly motivated readership. The *Christian History* found inspiration in similar evangelical periodicals printed in England and Scotland, publications well adapted to the singular mission of reporting and interpreting the unprecedented revivals of religion then sweeping through the British Empire.[1] Like its transatlantic siblings, the *Christian History* provided its readers a key for imagining a new religious movement not only within a larger spacial dimension—the Atlantic world—but also within dramatic cultural changes that were altering how eighteenth-century men and women understood themselves and their place in the world.

The *Christian History* appeared in the midst of strident debate over the nature and legitimacy of the boisterous revivals then sweeping New England and parts of the middle colonies. Historians continue to debate those revivals' significance. Jon Butler has argued that contemporaries were witnessing a fresh outbreak of regional revivals similar to those that had characterized New England religious culture since the seventeenth century, one largely unconnected to revivals elsewhere in eighteenth-century British America.[2] More recently, others including myself and the historian Frank Lambert have responded that contemporaries both *perceived* the Awakening of the 1740s as "great and general," and revivalists consciously worked to "invent" what they believed was a unified transatlantic movement.[3] From this perspective, the Great Awakening of the 1740s constituted a system of meanings that became much more than the "happy instrument" through which thousands gained assurance of New Birth. It also provided participants with a powerful, persuasive account of the experience of rapid cultural change in an expanding commercial empire.[4]

Both supporters and critics of the revivals were responding to the religious dimensions of a much broader cultural crisis. Traditional assumptions of New Englanders, as of inhabitants throughout the British North Atlantic, were dissolving as colonists were drawn into a great commercial empire. By 1740 Boston had become the hub of a provincial market economy that was extending networks of credit and consumption into the New England countryside, enticing the children of the Puritans into greater dependence on England. Colonists rushed to purchase the latest English goods, acquiring a common set of tastes and experiences that bound them to other consumers throughout the Empire. Improvements in transportation and new tools of communication were shrinking the distance between the Old World and the New, drawing New Englanders closer to colonial neighbors and into greater participation in the Atlantic world. Public figures led effusive expressions of loyalty to the Crown, while Addisonian essayists filled Boston weeklies with celebrations of a provincial culture that was becoming more like London's.[5]

This growing preoccupation with commerce, the rush to acquire luxury goods, and the increasing links to a wider world all were accelerating the erosion of localism, an erosion that had begun in Europe during the seventeenth century and was now chipping away at New England localities as well. Religion played an important role in this local order by establishing moral boundaries for behavior and parish boundaries that differentiated the community's members from outsiders. Local histories of early modern England and America have shown that the conceptual horizons of individuals seldom extended beyond the boundaries of the parish, town, or county where they resided. Peculiarities of language, symbol, and ritual bounded people's experience and perceptions within specific locales, a phenomenon early-eighteenth-century English travelers still encountered in a bewildering array of local dialects, colloquialisms, and traditions.[6]

For its contributors and readers, the *Christian History* became an important instrument of the transatlantic breakdown of localism. As the published mouthpiece of one party in a vital public debate, the periodical played an important role in the emergence of the provincial public sphere of print discourse outlined by Michael Warner and others.[7] In the hands of Thomas Prince Jr. and his contributors, the periodical also became a powerful tool for the construction of what Benedict Anderson has termed an "imagined community," not of a nation, but of a transatlantic company of people transformed by empire-wide revival.[8] Collected accounts of correspondents from all parts of the British North Atlantic, supplemented by extracts from "famous old Writers," invited comparison with the revivals readers had experienced in their own communities. The similar structure and common language of the accounts encouraged readers to see conversions they themselves had witnessed or experienced as local manifestations of a vast and surprising outpouring of God's Spirit. Even so, the revivalists' use of print technology took a turn unexpected in the traditional narrative linking print, Protestantism, and the emergence of democratic nationalism, a narrative literary historian Sandra M. Gustafson has recently criticized for its neglect of eighteenth-century shifts in forms of oral communication. In New Light hands, revival narratives disseminated in correspondence, pamphlets, and evangelical periodicals often became a surrogate for the oral performance of a visiting itinerant minister, conveying a sense of immediacy and spiritual inwardness that complemented extemporaneous preaching and undercut the putative stability of print culture.[9]

The *Christian History* thus served as an interpretive tool through which revivalists articulated a new conceptual model of their social world. The revival community made it possible for individuals on the margins of a vast transatlantic empire to share a powerful, common experience of revival with people like them an ocean away. It relaxed spatial and social boundaries alike, freeing many converts to escape the bonds of traditional local constraints, to take on new roles and to assert themselves in unexpected and often disturbing ways. This new openness demanded of revivalists a critical examination, selective defense, and an effort to establish new boundaries where they seemed appropriate. Most readers of the day found the *Christian History*'s imagined world a persuasive interpretation of their own experience. Even opponents seldom attempted to deny the revivals' vast scope. The *Christian History's* narrative of eighteenth-century revival has enjoyed remarkable staying power, often in the face of formidable opposition.[10]

The impulse for publishing the *Christian History* arose in response to two important developments in the revivals after 1741. The first was the heightened awareness of the transatlantic scope of the movement as colonial newspapers published periodic accounts of George Whitefield's itineraries in England and his unprecedented revivals in Scotland. The newspaper reports were augmented by a growing transatlantic correspondence network among leaders of the revival movement who wrote concerning the progress of revival in various locales. Enterprising "friends of revival" in England and Scotland began publishing excerpts of these letters in weekly periodicals that followed a modified newspaper format.[11] Pastors throughout the British Empire, eager to spark revival in their own parishes or to inspire prayer for the spread of the "great and glorious work," spread the news to their congregations by reading accounts of distant revivals from their pulpits.[12]

The second development involved the disorders attending revival, especially the controversial proliferation of itinerants in the wake of George Whitefield's unprecedented tour of New England in 1740. The itinerancy of the Connecticut minister James Davenport quickly came to symbolize critics' worst fears concerning the revivals and helped to polarize New Englanders into prorevival New Light and antirevival Old Light camps. Opponents charged that Davenport's uninvited intrusion into others' parish bounds ran counter to the reverence for "religion and church-order" that in their view had prompted the fathers to establish New England's parish system. His "censoriousness" in declaring ministers unconverted violated eighteenth-century standards of decorum by challenging the figure who in most parishes anchored the deferential local order. Davenport urged parishioners to forsake "hireling" ministers, to cross parish bounds in search of converted pastors, to prefer converted lay itinerants' or even their own private readings of Scripture to the teaching of unconverted college graduates. Davenport's inflated claims to Divine guidance seemed to opponents nothing less than an "invasion of God's Prerogative."[13] His practices unleashed across New England a torrent of "Uneasiness, Jarring, Divisions, Discontent, uncharitable century and judging, and Separations."[14]

By the spring of 1743, the explosion of transatlantic revival and the threat of revivalistic excesses lent an urgency to Thomas Prince Jr.'s project of publishing an American evangelical magazine. The *Christian History*'s dual role in promoting a transatlantic awakening and defending it against critics are equally evident in the circular letter Prince published to solicit material for the periodical. Prince signaled his belief that the "Work" of Awakening was a single unified event by inviting ministers and other "*suitable Persons*" to submit "*particular Accounts* of the *Revival of Religion* in *every Town* in this remarkable Day of Grace." He also suggested an outline for the accounts that would attract the reader's attention while demonstrating the revivals' authenticity. They should describe "the *most Remarkable Instances* of the Power and Grace of GOD, both in *convincing* and *converting* Sinners, and in *edifying* Converts." Prince sought narrative examples of edified converts who could both authenticate the conversions and answer critics' charges of disorderliness: "Knowledge, Faith, Holiness, Love to GOD and their Neighbours, divine Joys, and an answerable Life and Conversation." Prince specified four "sorts of People" whose conversion accounts would be of special interest: the young, "*Immoral* Persons," persons who at first opposed the "Work," and "Those who have been before in Repute for *Morality* and *Religion.*" Finally, Prince solicited "*Attestations* . . . of some *creditable Persons*" to supplement the accounts. He also asked potential contributors to spread the word of his interest in collecting revival narratives.[15]

The historian Michael J. Crawford has observed that the structure of Jonathan Edwards's 1737 *Faithful Narrative of Surprizing Work of God* lay behind most revival accounts collected not only in the *Christian History* but in all the evangelical periodicals of the period.[16] This common narrative structure did not wholly suppress the peculiarities of distinct local revivals, which remain evident in many of the accounts. Nevertheless, it did contribute to the sense of shared experience among participants in hundreds of local revivals scattered throughout the British Atlantic world. In doing so it could function, as the philosopher Paul Ricoeur has argued concerning narrative, to provide a new model for religious experience in the world.[17] The revival accounts invited the converted self into a world with imagined horizons far beyond the parish bound while remaining in continuity with the older localist experience of Puritan conversion. While the local minister and congregation still exercised a significant role in testing a conversion's authenticity, few ministers, converts, or congregations imagined the event within a purely local context. An itinerant, an oral account of revivals elsewhere in the empire, a printed narrative, an audience swelled by participants from communities twenty or more miles away, all helped to situate individual conversions within a context of transatlantic revival.[18]

In the *Christian History*'s first issue, Prince explicitly set contents of the new periodical within their transatlantic context. He informed readers that his magazine would carry "authentic accounts" of revival not only from New England, but from England and Scotland and from other mainland colonies as well. At the same time, he expressed the hope that selections would help readers "guard against all extremes" and struck an irenic note by urging contributors to avoid "Personal reflections and angry Controversy."[19] Prince also set New England's awakening within a historical lineage that reached back through New England's founders to the Reformation. In the hands of the *Christian History*'s contributors, these themes formed the core of revival narratives that demonstrated the spiritual and historical authenticity of the revivals and shared useful methods for promoting them.

As narratives accumulated, the magazine became a manifesto for harnessing new techniques and new forms to the propagation of the age-old Gospel throughout the Atlantic world. The very act of publishing a revival account represented an effort to exploit a new means of communication made available by the market while contributing to the emergence of a discourse aimed at claiming the eighteenth-century world with the revivalists' Gospel. Its participants shaped their accounts into reasonable, progressive alternatives to the chaotic world of roving exhorters, the Old Lights' propensity to close the door on God's Spirit, and nascent Enlightenment attempts to assign God a distant role as the moral governor of an orderly Newtonian universe.

The centerpiece of the magazine's first volume was an interpretive history written by Prince for "the less knowing reader," using election sermons and revival accounts to demonstrate that the experience of New Birth, not the maintenance of ecclesiastical order, constituted the true legacy of New England's first settlers. Prince's interpretation depended heavily on a selection of quotations and use of language that permitted description of seventeenth-century piety in the vocabulary of the eighteenth-century revival. He shaped his narrative to show that decline and disorder set in, not as people began neglecting the external *forms* of godliness, but as they began denying its *power* by straying from the central message of the New Birth.

The "FATHERS of these Plantations," Prince asserted, were "bro't up by pious parents under the most *awakening Preachers*" of the English Reformation. The settlers established godly communities on New England shores, aided by the "lively, searching and awakening preaching of the *primitive Ministers*" whose proclamation of the "*absolute Necessity* of the NEW BIRTH" prompted tearful conversions in local meetinghouses. Only when conversion took place were "the *Colonies* united, and *Courts* united, and *Magistrates* united, and *Ministers* united, and *Churches* united, and *Plantations* united, &c." Subsequent generations neglected conversion to "increase Cent per Cent" through trade, forgetting that "Worldly gain was not the End and Design of the People of New England." Declension ensued as "Pride, Contention, Worldliness, Covetousness, Luxury, Drunkenness and Uncleanness broke in like a Flood," while those "outwardly conformed to good order *never Knew* what the New Birth means."[20]

In Prince's narrative history, seventeenth-century ministers affirmed the New Birth as the core of the New England identity by issuing unanimous calls for revival to reverse declension. Prince traced a succession of "transient Revivals of Religion" that had come in response to jeremiads, producing tears and cries of repentance while suppressing sinful disorders such as drunkenness and harlotry by reforming the hearts of sinners. The earthquake of 1727 ushered in a period of "more extensive revival" that broadened with the Northampton revivals of 1732–35 and surpassed all bounds during Whitefield's tour of 1740. Prince crowned his narrative with attestations of nearly 140 ministers to the authenticity of the "late revivals" under Whitefield and his successors.[21] In Prince's historiography, New Birth and revival were etched indelibly into New England's history and identity. Without them, Prince asserted, the fathers had unanimously declared its ecclesiastical order an empty husk.

Testimonies of contributors and extracts of "the best old authors" confirmed that the New Birth had always been central to the Protestant tradition itself.

Indeed their evangelizing zeal had often prompted ministers of the past to flout church order in pursuit of souls. During Elizabeth's reign, it spurred Richard Rothwell to undertake a traveling ministry that earned him the title "Apostle of the North." Godly English preachers ever since had been ready if necessary to ignore parish bounds to spread the message of New Birth. Excerpts from Richard Baxter's writings reminded readers that after the Restoration of Charles II in 1660, Baxter and other Nonconformists had defied church order to roam the English countryside preaching the Gospel. Baxter had also urged laypersons to cross parish bounds and "diligently attend" the preaching and counsel of a "judicious, faithful, serious, searching, powerful Minister" wherever one could be found. "Outcries attending the work of the Spirit" were "no new Thing;" Baxter and others often encountered and never condemned them. Excerpts from a tract by the seventeenth-century Boston divine John Wilson defended the "*Fervours* that appear in some in the exercise of Religion."[22]

Wherever Reformed Christianity had taken root, Prince's contributors asserted, the case was the same. James Robe of Kilsyth in Scotland cited the "Stewarton Sickness" of 1625 to 1630, a revival where Scots from scores of western Lowland parishes gathered in fields to hear the fiery preaching of Presbyterian ministers. The "field-preaching" of the ministers and the "groanings," "bodily distresses," and "sweet consolations" of the laity were the antithesis of order, but the New Birth that resulted formed the very core of Presbyterian faith. An excerpted address to Dutchmen by Hugh Kennedy, minister of the Scots church in Rotterdam, reminded readers that zeal for the New Birth stood at the center of the Dutch Reformed tradition. An account of the Pietist revivals narrated how German Christians had also battled "dead formalism" to return to the vital religion of the Scriptures and the Reformers.[23]

Prince's effort to find precedents for revivalism represented not a retreat to a mythical golden age, but a determination to demonstrate faithfulness to the unchanging Gospel of the Reformers while carrying it boldly into the eighteenth-century world. Just as the Reformers had laid aside tradition when the forms of godliness obstructed its power, so revivalists were prepared to exploit opportunities to spread the Gospel newly opened in this dynamic commercial empire. Mobility combined with participation in a long-distance network of communication; commerce and credit had begun to erode the localism that traditional forms of religious life had supported. The resulting openness to a world beyond local bounds had made colonists extraordinarily receptive to the "stranger ministers" who invaded their parish bounds with the message of the New Birth. In this new context, the forms of religious life that had well served the seventeenth-century fathers now constituted impediments to the movement of God's Spirit.

Prince and his contributors explicitly recognized the elements of historical change as well as continuity in this new outpouring of God's Spirit. Jonathan Edwards had already noted how increased mobility and more widespread communication had extended the reach of the Northampton revival of 1735—"*persons that came from abroad* on business," he had noted, were "savingly wrought upon" at Northampton and "went home rejoicing; 'till at length the *same Work* began evidently to appear in *several other Towns.*" American ministers noticed that newspaper reports of revival in Boston and Philadelphia sparked awakening in their own communities. Scottish ministers blessed God that printed accounts of the American revivals had sparked revival in parishes across the Atlantic. Indeed the publication of the *Christian History* and other revival magazines resulted from widespread recognition of print's facility for making people aware of events beyond their everyday frame of reference, coupled with a determination to exploit that potential to the fullest.[24]

George Whitefield and his colonial imitators had taken advantage of the era's mobility through itinerancy. The *Christian History*'s contributors recognized the new method would forever alter the dynamics of parochial ministry. Itinerancy challenged the parish minister's role as an anchor of New England's deferential, ordered communities. Critics saw it both as a potent symbol of a general loosening of eighteenth-century bonds and as an instrument by which they were further loosened. For converts it modeled an alternative way of situating the self in the open world envisioned in the *Christian History* and other prorevival publications.[25]

Itinerancy demanded that the parish minister accept a diminished role in the life of his community. Contributors to the *Christian History* expressed a willingness to do so because of itinerancy's remarkable facility for spreading revival. Jonathan Parsons of East Lyme, Connecticut, noted that strangers not entangled in the local network of deferential behavioral constraints could challenge the townspeople to examine their souls afresh: "*new* Faces, *new* Voices; a *new* Method, all tend to draw the Attention of *hearers;* and hence they were caught by the same Truths that had been offered them divers Times before." This effectiveness prompted many to follow John Porter of Bridgewater, Connecticut, in resolving like "St. John the *Baptist* to *decrease,*" relinquishing to itinerants the status his position had traditionally accorded him "so that CHRIST may *increase*" by the traveling preachers' message. John Willison of Dundee in Scotland, noting the suitability of Whitefield's gifts to his "new and singular Attempts for promoting true Christianity in the World," declared that a "standing Church office" of traveling evangelist would be to the world's advantage. Thomas Prince argued that itinerancy made perfect sense in a more pluralistic world where competing religious groups were rendering irrelevant the parish system. "Protestants preach in the Parishes of Papist Ministers in *Hungary* . . . Presbyterians, Congregationalists, Baptists and Quaker in the Parishes of Episcopalian Ministers in *England, Ireland, Virginia,* and *Carolina;* the Episcopalians, Baptists, and Quakers in the Parishes of Congregational Ministers in *New England.*" Much of the "Christian World" had in fact come to regard the invasion of parish bounds far preferable to the invasion of the "essential Rights of Conscience" that would result if itinerancy were forbidden.[26]

The experience of ministers such as Parsons, Bridgewater, and Willison suggests that pastors were often struggling to catch up with their parishioners in grasping the full implications of the new revivalism's model for action in the world. To be sure, many of the revival ministers consciously fostered a sense of wider regional and transatlantic connections, inviting itinerants to preach or preaching in neighboring parishes themselves. Joseph Park of Westerly, Rhode Island, welcomed the itinerant James Davenport into his parish to preach a "plain and awakening Sermon" that sparked revival among his British American parishioners as well as a congregation of praying Narragansetts. Park and neighboring ministers traveled throughout western Rhode Island and eastern Connecticut to fan the revival flames further.[27]

The *Christian History* and other revival accounts could provide powerful substitutes for an itinerant, approximating the oral immediacy of an evangelist's performance when read from the pulpit.[28] Henry Messinger and Elias Haven of Wrentham, Massachusetts, noted that "the *News of many Conversions in Northampton* . . . [and] some parts of *England* & *America*, were Means of sturring up *Thoughtfulness* in many."[29] Jonathan Parsons assiduously gathered revival accounts "from many places, attested by credible witnesses," and distilled them into a sermon that produced "greater visible Effects upon the Auditory than ever had I seen before in the Course of my Ministry."[30] Critics agreed that the *Christian History* and other revival accounts could "perpetuate the *evil Spirit*" of the revival as effectively as itinerancy. One complained that it was "publickly read on the Lord's Day in several Churches" and that its circulation had carried the "Spirit of Contention, Division, and Separation thro' all the American Provinces, and even beyond the *Atlantic.*"[31]

Such accounts make it clear that many laypeople acted on the relaxation of boundaries promoted by print and itinerancy, often pressing further than their ministers intended. They neither asked permission nor heeded a minister's prohibition to hear an itinerant in another parish. Those who sensed a prompting to exhort often spoke out boldly despite their lack of ordination. In such cases, Joseph Park judged that a minister's best course was to get out of the Spirit's way. He "countenanced" lay exhorters in Westerly despite the "rage" of opposing parishioners, concluding that "*the true Grace of* God must not be opposed, but encouraged where-ever God was bestowing it, and however he was sending it."[32] Other revivalists, though reluctant to go as far as Park, nevertheless recognized that laypeople often held the initiative in bringing the Awakening across local and regional bounds. They could either accommodate their parishioners' desire to participate in the "Work" or get trampled in a futile attempt to defend their parish line. A "Testimony and Advice" of ninety prorevival ministers therefore urged pastors to welcome ordained itinerants to their pulpits, "Being perswaded GOD has in this Day remarkably bless'd the Labors of *some* of his servants who have *travelled* in preaching the Gospel of Christ." They also warned "all sorts of people"—ministers and lay alike—"not to *despise* thes Out-pourings of the Spirit, lest a holy GOD be provoked to with-hold them."[33]

The *Christian History*'s spirited defense of itinerancy and its ready use of new forms of print commodities embroiled revivalists in a religious counterpart to the fierce debate that was engaging eighteenth-century political economists over the meaning of cultural change. Controversy over the Awakening aroused passions comparable to the fierce party rivalries of the 1790s, pitting prorevival papers such as the *Boston Gazette* against antirevival weeklies such as the *Boston Weekly Post-Boy*. The printed contest echoed contemporary debates over luxury, paper money, unregulated peddlers, and backcountry squatters as the two sides squared off over the nature of parish boundaries, the authenticity of conversions, and the propriety of accommodating popular choice.[34] By defending itinerancy's invasion of parish bounds and other revivalistic practices, Prince and his contributors opened themselves to charges of fomenting "Confusion in Towns; Contention in Churches; Alienations and Separations of People from one another and from their Ministers"—in short, the breakdown of community social order.[35]

Two themes emerged in the *Christian History*'s revival narratives as responses to the charge of fomenting disorder. First, narratives described techniques which contributors had found useful for controlling excesses. Second, they interpreted the apparent disorder as a genuine work of the Spirit of God on the souls of men. Publicity of the disorders had served as an unintended means of spreading revival across the Empire by drawing people's attention to the work of God taking place in regions far away. Both elements of the response helped to develop further the innovative model of eighteenth-century social reality that was emerging on the pages of the *Christian History*.

Prince established the advice-manual function of his magazine at the outset by devoting the first several issues to James Robe's narrative of the revival at the Scottish village of Kilsyth near Glasgow. The account described a revival thousands of miles away, yet remarkably similar to New England's in the number of conversions, attendant phenomena, and restoration of vital piety. Yet its writer went beyond a mere retelling of the main events to shape his narrative into a guidebook, recommending methods he had found useful for promoting revival while keeping it within acceptable bounds.[36] It provided a tool for interpreting the behavior both of converts and ministers, for judging which elements of their experience were legitimate and which were not. By following its example, others could join Robe in tailoring the revival to its proponents' expectations and its eighteenth-century context, articulating in the process a model of the world in which revival occurred.

Robe labored above all things to situate his revivals in a world that was radically open to the free activity of God's Spirit yet remained at the same time subject to the "God of order." He discovered early in the Kilsyth revival that the Spirit used his preaching of "the Terrors of the Law" to open parishioners to the Spirit's work, awakening them from their slumber before comforting them with the good news of Christ's forgiveness. He also found that the Spirit used the groaning and writhing of those "under conviction" to awaken others. Consequently, he recommended leaving the "distressed" in the assembly rather than risk quenching the Spirit by removing them. The effectiveness of evening meetings led by "stranger Ministers" prompted Robe to open both pulpit and private counseling sessions to fellow revivalists. He also opened the church doors to laymen from neighboring parishes, but he avoided undermining order by urging that lay strangers seek counsel from their own ministers concerning their souls.[37] The revival at Kilsyth took place in a world where the Spirit moved freely in people's hearts and where laypersons and ministers moved freely across parish lines to participate in the Spirit's work. Yet both took place without the revival devolving into chaos.

The "Testimony and Advice" of prorevival ministers complemented Robe's efforts to shape itinerancy with their own set of prescriptions for curbing excesses. Signers sought to separate "Antinomian disorders" from the "work of God" and warned readers against falling into this error. Laymen could avoid antinomianism by honoring their pastors, resisting the temptation to "invade the Ministerial Office" by preaching under pretense of exhorting. Ordained itinerants could avoid it by seeking permission from the resident minister to preach in any given parish "in ordinary cases," and pastors were urged to invite only itinerants qualified by ministerial training. Proper invitations could avoid much needless misunderstanding, while the clause "in ordinary cases" deliberately left it to "the serious *Conscience* both of *ministers* and *others* to judge when the Cases are *ordinary* or *not ordinary*."[38] Their world, like Robe's, remained open, mobile—a place of permeable boundaries where the Spirit remained free to work through the dictates of conscience.

Contributors to the *Christian History* frequently took their cues from the "Testimony and Advice" and Robe's account, using their narratives to shape the revivals into an open but orderly movement. Many recounted how itinerancy had been "wonderfully blessed of God" in bringing revival to their parishes. Many described in glowing terms their own itinerancy, their welcome by ministers and people, and the Spirit's blessing on their efforts. Several pled for tolerance among ministerial colleagues who encountered the disorders attending itinerancy. "Bodily agitations" might not necessarily signify the Spirit's presence, but none should judge too harshly when "illiterate Country men and others of small Experience are *ravished* with the Discoveries of *another World* and the *Knowledge of God in Christ*." If the convert's subsequent holiness and humility of conduct displayed the fruits of godliness then the revival must be regarded a work of God, despite temporary transgression of the "bounds of Decency."[39]

Prince crowned his interpretive effort by including James Davenport's *Confessions and Retractions* in the pages of the *Christian History*. The taming of the firebrand, who had become the symbol of enthusiasm for all parties, symbolized for revivalists the orderly adaptation of itinerancy to its eighteenth-century environment. They ensured that the document received as much publicity as had Davenport's antics. In addition to the *Christian History*, the *Confessions and Retractions* were published as a pamphlet and widely advertised in the newspapers.[40]

Davenport's retractions affirmed every guideline that revivalists had labored to formulate. He introduced his retractions with a reaffirmation of the "*glorious and wonderful Work of his Power and Grace* . . . in *New-England*, in the *neighbouring Governments* and *several other Parts*," reiterating his belief that "the Lord hath favour'd me, tho' most unworthy . . . in granting special Assistance and Success." Nevertheless, the repentant itinerant acknowledged that "misguided Zeal" and a "false Spirit" had spurred him to promote "Appendages" that had blemished the work of God. Davenport then listed five confessions and retractions, each of which supported some aspect of the effort to bring order to itinerancy and revivalism by restoring deference to certain shared behavioral norms. In the first two he repented the breaches he had opened in the social order by pronouncing so many settled ministers unconverted and encouraging parishioners to forsake them. The third repented his renunciation of the scripturally informed wisdom of community to order his conduct solely by private "Impulses and Impressions." The fourth retracted his encouragement of unqualified persons to "*a ministerial and authoritative Kind or Method of exhorting*" while the fifth repented his flouting of communal standards of decorum by frequent singing in the streets.[41]

Yet neither Davenport nor other contributors to the *Christian History* retreated to the parish-centered, deferential localism of pre-1740 practice. The periodical continued to endorse the new openness with descriptions of how God had "savingly used" ordained itinerants invited by local ministers to bring revival to the parishes of the North Atlantic world. The clause of the ministerial "Attestation" enjoining itinerants to seek permission "in ordinary cases" preserved the Spirit's liberty in extraordinary ones when an opposing minister's obstinacy might threaten his parishioners' eternal well-being. Revival narratives continued to endorse itinerancy by telling how the Almighty had used it to shock hearers out of their complacency, awaken them to their deplorable state, and open their hearts to the Spirit's conviction. Ministers refused to slight the Spirit by condemning instances of crying, "bodily distresses," or expressions of rapture. They attempted only to regain a measure of local control by suggesting that "hopeful conversions" be evaluated by a convert's ability to articulate his or her experience in reasonable, scriptural terms coupled with observation of the convert's subsequent conduct.

The *Christian History*'s interpretive effort to direct the spirit of revival was only partly successful. While many converts of the 1740s remained within the existing ecclesiastical order, many others burst weakened boundaries of place and station to form alternative expressions of evangelical faith. Separates formed New Light congregations within existing Congregational parish bounds. Separate Baptists fanned across New England and migrated south into the backcountry along the Great Wagon Road. They carried with them the strong inward strictures that they believed the Spirit instilled at conversion. They also retained the marks of the broader evangelical community—the distinct language of Awakening and conversion, itinerant preaching in the "old Whitefield style," and the use of correspondence, circular letters, and cheap printed literature to carry revival to an increasingly mobile British American population.[42]

Despite the limitations of the *Christian History's* hermeneutical project, its interpretation of eighteenth-century revival has exerted a powerful influence over subsequent historiography of the Awakening. Prince's account of New England history as a tale of early piety, subsequent declension, and revival formed the standard narrative outline for many subsequent histories of the Awakening. His appeal to the past has also informed more recent histories that treat the 1740s revivals as a retreat from incipient modernity into primitive Puritanism or revitalized ethnic traditions.[43] Contributors' millennial hopes that "the *Redeemer's* . . . spreading Empire" would soon "encompass the Earth" provide ample material for those exploring the revivalistic origin of British American millennialism.[44]

Yet as an interpretive artifact of what the revivalists themselves thought they were witnessing, the *Christian History* suggests that the Awakening's most important legacy lay neither in its putative primitivism nor in its millennial and prophetic fervor. Rather, it lay in adapting the old Puritan "heart religion" to the revivalists' own age, initiating the converted self into a transatlantic community mediated not by a learned clergy, but by a broadly shared language of print and itinerancy. Unlike most other eighteenth-century publications, which reshaped readers' perceptions through subtle, largely unconscious means, the *Christian History* explicitly promoted an expansive vision of its readers' world.[45] Under Prince's editorial hand, collected narratives from distant regions—Charleston, London, Aberdeen, Rotterdam, even Egypt—unfolded to readers a "SPECIMEN of that wondrous WORK of GOD," a Providential design of worldwide scope.

In its powerful interpretation of revival, the *Christian History* made a crucial contribution not only to "inventing" the Awakening, but to what the historian Harry S. Stout has termed the "rise of modern evangelicalism."[46] Its collected revival narratives worked hand-in-hand with itinerant preaching and mass meetings to produce revival on a scale hitherto undreamed of. Long after its self-appointed spokesmen pronounced the Great Awakening over in 1749, a continuous stream of itinerant evangelists drew on methods introduced in the 1740s to fan revival flames.

In so doing, the *Christian History* functioned as one of the American revivalists' most powerful interpretive tools in the construction of transatlantic evangelical revival, but other eighteenth-century journals and periodicals also contributed to this enterprise. Religion was a prominent theme in most print literature of the period. Indeed, the participation of clergy invoking religious perspectives on everything from transatlantic imperial tensions and warfare to Jacobitism suggests that religious figures and themes contributed as full members in the emergence of an eighteenth-century public sphere.[47] Revivalism in particular attracted attention in gentlemen's magazines, newspapers, and journals on both sides of the Atlantic during the 1740s and 1750s. Benjamin Franklin, for instance, sought to tap the market potential of controversy over Whitefield and his mid-colonial imitators by devoting a large proportion of space to the revival in his short-lived *General Magazine, and Historical Chronicle.* In 1741 Franklin opened the fledgling magazine's pages to a full-blown debate between pro- and antirevivalists in Pennsylvania over the propriety and authenticity of itinerancy and evangelical revival.[48] Even those opposed to the revivals contributed to the construction of the Awakening by addressing it as a category even as they denied its authenticity.[49]

Thomas Prince Jr.'s *Christian History* helped shatter an older religious world, radically reshaping it with a new model of religious experience that relied on print and itinerancy to carry the message of New Birth to the mobile, expansive population of eighteenth- and nineteenth-century America. Print played an important role in sustaining a succession of regional revivals that finally exploded into a second transatlantic outpouring of revival after 1800. Yet later revivalists merely acted on and enlarged a modern model of evangelism and conversion already sketched out in the pages of the *Christian History.* Nineteenth-century revivalism's itinerancy, its camp meetings, its massive output of cheap printed literature, and even its radical democratization were not so innovative as they are frequently portrayed.[50] Indeed, the preachers, missionaries, prophets, and hucksters of the Second Great Awakening only extended the story of modern revival that the *Christian History,* and the Awakening it helped to invent, had already begun.

Notes

1. Thomas Prince Jr., ed., *Christian History* (Boston, 1744–45). For subscription fees see Charles E. Clark, *The Public Prints: The Newspaper in Anglo-American Culture, 1665–1740* (New York: Oxford UP), 202–7. Earlier studies of the *Christian History* include L. N. Richardson, *A History of Early American Magazines* (New York: T. Nelson and Sons, 1931), 58–73, which provides a descriptive history of the magazine; Susan Durden, "A Study of the First Evangelical Magazines, 1740–1748," *Journal of Ecclesiastical History* 22, no. 3 (1986): 255–75, which treats the *Christian History* as one of several eighteenth-century revival periodicals; and John E. Van de Wetering, "The *Christian History* of the Great Awakening," *Journal of Presbyterian History* 44, no. 2 (1966): 122–29, which provides a brief analysis of the magazine's place within the New England revivals. Frank Luther Mott, in *A History of American Magazines*, 5 vols. (Cambridge: Harvard UP, 1938–68), is dismissive, sniffing that it can "scarcely be called a magazine" (1:25).
2. Jon Butler, "Enthusiasm Described and Decried: The Great Awakening as Interpretative Fiction," *Journal of American History* 64 (1982–83): 305–25.
3. Timothy D. Hall, *Contested Boundaries: Itinerancy and the Reshaping of the Colonial American Religious World* (Durham: Duke UP, 1994), 129–39; Frank Lambert, *Inventing the "Great Awakening"* (Princeton: Princeton UP, 1999), 222–50.
4. T. H. Breen and Timothy D. Hall, "Structuring Provincial Imagination: The Rhetoric and Experience of Social Change in Eighteenth-Century New England," *American Historical Review* 103 (1998): 1411–39.
5. T. H. Breen, "Empire of Goods: The Anglicization of Colonial America, 1690–1776," *Journal of British Studies* 25 (1986), 467–99; T. H. Breen, "'Baubles of Britain': The American and Consumer Revolutions of the Eighteenth Century," *Past and Present* 119 (May 1988), 73–104; Carole Shammas, *The Pre-Industrial Consumer in England and America* (Oxford: Clarendon P, 1990), 76–118; John Brewer and Roy Porter, eds., *Consumption and the World of Goods* (London: Routledge, 1993), 177–301.
6. Benedict Anderson, *Imagined Communities: Reflections on the Origin and Spread of Nationalism*, 2d ed. (London: Verso, 1991), 43–44; Barry Reay, "Popular Culture in Early Modern England," in *Popular Culture in Seventeenth-Century England, 1603–1660*, ed. Barry Reay (New York: St. Martin's P, 1985), 1–30; T. H. Breen, *Puritans and Adventurers* (New York: Oxford UP, 1980), 3–23.

7. Michael Warner, *Letters of the Republic: Publication and the Public Sphere in Eighteenth-Century America* (Cambridge: Harvard UP, 1990), 34–72; Jürgen Habermas, *The Structural Transformation of the Public Sphere: An Inquiry into a Category of Bourgeois Society*, trans. Thomas Burger with the assistance of Frederick Lawrence (Cambridge: MIT P, 1989), 27–56).

8. Anderson 37–46.

9. Sandra M. Gustafson, *Eloquence Is Power: Oratory and Performance in Early America* (Chapel Hill: U of North Carolina P, 2000), xvii, xxiii.

10. This study assumes a critical, dialectical relationship between language and social reality; that is, language shapes social reality within certain constraints imposed by human experience itself. People find accounts of social reality more or less persuasive as they help make sense of lived experience. For a fuller discussion see Paul Ricoeur, *Time and Narrative*, trans. Kathleen McLaughlin and David Pellauer, 3 vols. (Chicago: U of Chicago P, 1984–88), 1: 52–87; Gabriel M. Speigel, *The Past as Text: The Theory and Practice of Medieval Historiography* (Baltimore: Johns Hopkins UP, 1997), 44–56; Kevin J. Vanhoozer, *Is There a Meaning in This Text? The Bible, the Reader, and the Morality of Literary Knowledge* (Grand Rapids: Eerdmans, 1998), 201–80; Sara Maza, "Stories in History: Cultural Narratives in Recent Works in European History," *American Historical Review* 101 (1996): 1493–1515. For the role of print in the breakdown of local boundaries and creation of "imagined communities" of distant strangers, see Anderson 22–36.

11. Examples include John Lewis, *London Weekly History; Or, an Account of the Most Remarkable Particulars Relating to the Present Progress of the Gospel* (London, 1741); James Robe, *Christian Monthly History* (Edinburgh, 1743); and William M'Cullough, *Glasgow Weekly History Relating to the Progress of the Gospel at Home and Abroad; Being a Collection of Letters partly reprinted from the London-Weekly-History* (Glasgow, 1743). See Durden, "A Study of the First Evangelical Magazines," 255–75.

12. Susan O'Brien, "A Transatlantic Community of Saints: The Great Awakening and the First Evangelical Network, 1735–1755," *American Historical Review* 91, no. 4 (1986): 811–32; Lambert 156–71.

13. *Boston Gazette*, February 22, 1743.

14. *The Testimony and Advice of a Number of Laymen respecting Religion, and the Teachers of It* (Boston, 1743).

15. [Thomas Prince Jr.], *It being earnestly desired by many pious and judicious people, that particular Accounts of the Revival of Religion in every Town. . . .* (Boston, 1743).

16. Michael J. Crawford, *Seasons of Grace: Colonial New England's Revival Tradition in Its British Context* (New York: Oxford UP, 1991), 185.

17. Ricoeur 1:70–81.

18. For the social significance of seventeenth-century conversions, see Michael McGiffert, *God's Plot: Puritan Spirituality in Thomas Shepard's Cambridge* (Amherst: U of Massachusetts P, 1994), 147–48.

19. *Christian History,* 1:1.

20. Ibid., 1:58–100.

21. Ibid., 1:107–12; 93–124; 155–210.

22. Ibid.

23. Ibid., 1: 8, 287; 2: 267.

24. Ibid., 1: 122, 243, 7, 44–45, 358; compare Anderson 41–49.

25. Hall 71–100.

26. *Christian History,* 2: 144; 1: 404, 282, 198.

27. Ibid., 1: 205–10.

28. For the social significance of an itinerant's oral performance, see Gustafson 45–51.

29. *Christian History,* 1: 243.

30. Ibid., 2: 414–15.

31. *Boston Evening Post,* October 24, 1743.

32. *Christian History,* 1: 206.

33. Ibid., 1: 163.

34. Breen and Hall 1411–39.

35. *American Weekly Mercury,* December 28, 1744.

36. *Christian History,* 1:30.

37. Ibid., 1:40.

38. Ibid., 1:162–63.

39. Ibid., 2:131.

40. James Davenport, *The Reverend Mr. James Davenport's Confessions and Retractions* (Boston, 1744); *Boston Gazette,* August 14, 1744; *The Christian History,* 2:236–40.

41. *Christian History,* 2: 236.

42. Hall 129–39.

43. See, for example, Jon Butler, *Awash in a Sea of Faith: Christianizing the American People* (Cambridge: Harvard UP, 1990), 164–93.

44. *Christian History*, 2: 28; compare Ruth Bloch, *Visionary Republic: Millennial Themes in American Thought, 1756–1800* (Cambridge: Cambridge UP, 1985), 3–21; Susan Juster, "Demagogues or Mystagogues? Gender and the Language of Prophecy in the Age of Democratic Revolutions," *American Historical Review* 104, no. 5 (1999): 1560–81.

45. Compare Anderson 22–36.

46. Lambert 151–79; Harry S. Stout, *The Divine Dramatist: George Whitefield and the Rise of Modern Evangelicalism* (Grand Rapids: Eerdmans, 201–19.

47. For a few examples of a much more widespread phenomenon, see "Extracts from the Bishop of Salisbury's Sermon," *American Magazine and Historical Chronicle* (February 1746): 77–80; "Extracts from the Rev. Mr. Withers's Thanksgiving Sermon, on Occaision of the Suppression of the Rebellion," *American Magazine and Historical Chronicle* (April 1746): 166–69; "Extracts of a remarkable Sermon preached at Berlin by a Jew," *American Magazine and Monthly Chronicle for the British Colonies* (June 1758): 441–45.

48. See, for example, "Mr. Garden's Letters to Mr. Whitefield," *General Magazine, and Historical Chronicle* (April 1741), 263–68.

49. See Lambert's discussion of this, 185–221.

50. See, for example, Nathan O. Hatch, *The Democratization of American Christianity* (New Haven: Yale UP, 1989), 125–61; John H. Wigger, *Taking Heaven by Storm: Methodism and the Rise of Popular Christianity in America* (Urbana: U of Illinois P, 1998), 25–38.

John Smolenski

"Incorporated . . . into a Body Politic"

Clubs, Print, and the Gendering of the Civic Subject in Eighteenth-Century Pennsylvania

On March 1, 1729, the Society of Ancient Britons held their inaugural meeting in Philadelphia, at the Queen's Head, a tavern run by one Robert Davies. Then the Ancient Britons "walk'd in a regular Order with Leeks in their Hats, to the Church"—most likely Christ Church, the city's foremost Anglican church—"where was preach'd in the Old British Language . . . a excellent Sermon." The society's members then returned "in the like Order" to the Queen's Head for a sumptuous dinner. The evening concluded with several toasts, "drank under Discharge of Cannon" to the health of the King and Queen, the Anglican church, the proprietor, and the Ancient Britons in Pennsylvania. This festive procession and occasion was sufficiently important to merit two mentions in the *Pennsylvania Gazette*, one of the city's two newspapers; the first mention, published on February 25, advertised the coming event, while the March 4 issue offered a paragraph describing the affair in some detail.[1] The *Gazette*'s first discussion of any local clubs or similar organizations in Pennsylvania in the account of March 4 was also the first treatment of any public procession or parade.

In contrast to its relatively short account of the Britons' 1729 procession, the *Gazette*'s coverage of the 1755 ceremony marking the opening of the Masons' Philadelphia hall, the first such building erected in North America, was extensive. The newspaper described in great detail the Masons' processional march from their newly erected lodge to attend divine service at Christ Church, all the while "saluted by a Discharge of Nine Cannon from a Brother's Vessel, handsomely ornamented with Colours." The paper listed the order of all nineteen rows of Masons in the procession, from the "Sword Bearer, carrying a drawn Sword," to the "GRAND MASTER supported by two Brethren of Rank and Distinction," to the empty coaches and chariots (belonging to the Grand Master Mason, the provincial governor, and other Brethren) that brought up the rear. The *Gazette* then detailed the sermon preached by "fellow Brother" William Smith—itself published at the Masonic grand master's request—and described the Masons' celebratory dinner, including the fourteen toasts given "under repeated discharges of Cannon."[2] Both the proceedings themselves and the *Gazette's* coverage of them were more elaborate, in scale and in kind, than the Ancient Britons' inaugural meeting and its coverage in the press.

The contrast between these two accounts, separated by twenty-six years, reveals two interrelated changes that occurred during the middle of the eighteenth century in colonial Pennsylvania. First, it illustrates the evolution of an increasingly elaborate provincial associational culture, the nexus of clubs, societies, and organizations, which has been previously explored by David S. Shields. As he has illustrated, colonial clubs increased in size, number, and complexity; these institutions became an important site for public expression, ritual, display, and communication through processions (such as the Masons' or the Ancient Britons'), debate, and oratory.[3] The differences between the Masons' and the Britons' marches reflect this increasing ritual sophistication. But it also highlights another change: the shift in the *Gazette*'s practices of representing public or associational activities. The increase in the scope and complexity of public processions between 1729 and 1755 accompanied an even greater increase in the depth in which the *Gazette* covered them. This meant that not only did the *Gazette* publish the activities of organizations such as the Masons and the Britons in greater detail, the paper also offered more commentary on their actions, endorsing particular forms of associational activity. While the paper had in 1729 merely noted that the Britons had conducted themselves in "regular order," it elaborated in 1755 that at the Masons' celebration, "the greatest order and Regularity was observed" and that "Chearfulness, Harmony, and good Fellowship abounded." In other words, the increase in published description and information was accompanied by the paper's increasing willingness to offer cues intended to tell its reading public how to interpret the news it reported.

This essay explores these interrelated changes in associational activity and its public representations through an examination of the *Pennsylvania Gazette* from its establishment in 1728 through the outbreak of the imperial crisis in 1765. It analyzes the *Gazette* on two levels, exploring both the paper's coverage of clubs and associations and the language used to discuss public affairs within the paper itself. In this sense, it treats the *Gazette* as both a window onto provincial public activity and a discursive site in which public identities were debated and defined. By analyzing the relationship between these two aspects of the newspaper's relationship to colonial public life, this essay seeks to bridge a historiographic divide between print and ritual in the scholarship on provincial public culture.

For over a decade scholars of early America have explored the relationship between printed accounts of associational activity and the construction of public identities in early America. Influenced by Jürgen Habermas's conception of the public sphere, early American historians have analyzed the processes through which public culture was constructed, shaped, and negotiated.[4] These scholars have generally fallen into two camps. Many have emphasized the importance of the practices of public life "on the ground"—the rites of assembly of the Ancient Britons, for instance—in constructing public culture.[5] Others, such as Michael Warner and David Waldstreicher, have stressed the critical role played by print culture in constituting a conscious American public. While Warner sees print itself as the critical performative act embodying a public subjectivity, Waldstreicher argues that print and ritual public culture are so intertwined "that it becomes hard to tell where the ritual or reportage begins or ends."[6] In doing so, he treats ritual almost entirely in terms of discursive representation. Both Warner's and Waldstreicher's approach stress the "disembodied," or imagined, elements of early American public identity.

But those historians emphasizing the associational character of the public sphere and those highlighting its imagined character have operated under assumptions that have obscured the larger picture. On the one hand, those putting association at the center of public culture have, as Harold Mah has recently pointed out, conceived of the public sphere in "'spatialized' terms—that is, as a domain that one can enter, occupy, and leave."[7] While this approach has moved the study of the public sphere away from Habermas's bourgeois public and towards a more expansive, inclusive, and implicitly democratic public, it has also taken as a given that which Habermas sought to explain, namely the existence of a unitary public itself. Moreover, if different social groups are free to enter or leave the public sphere on their own terms, to what extent can "the" public—as opposed to multiple publics—be said to exist? On the other hand, those scholars tracing the role of print in the creation of an imagined public subjectivity have implicitly normalized particular forms of rational-critical discourse and specific types of individual subjectivity as general aspects of a colonial public sphere, as in the case of the "disembodied" bourgeois liberal subject at the heart of Warner's discussion.[8] Both approaches threaten to efface historical contingency within the history of the early American public sphere: while the first obscures the contingent emergence of the public itself, the second overlooks the instantiation of certain forms of publicity as normative. Frequent historiographic emphasis on one form of public expression over another at the expense of their interrelationship has exacerbated this problem.

As the opening vignettes of the Ancient Britons and the Masons suggest, the long-term story is not whether ritual or print is really constitutive of provincial public culture. Both are implicated. Rather, it is the history of particular forms of public expression claiming to voice, embody, or articulate a common public good. Provincials claimed that certain expressions of public culture were universally valid—thereby casting alternative or competing expressions of public culture as particularistic representations of special interests rather than the public's—and opponents accepted or rejected these claims. In provincial Pennsylvania, this process of defining public opinion involved not only the expressions of public sentiment themselves—the processions of the Britons and Masons—but also metacultural commentary about these cultural rituals, the cues interpreting the Masons' display as patriotic and public spirited. By examining both the practices of public culture noted in the *Gazette* and the paper's shifting metacultural cues for interpreting these practices, one can trace the emergence of an imagined public subjectivity firmly grounded in embodied ethnic, gendered, and religious practices.

An examination of the practice of print in the *Gazette* provides an ideal way of exploring these issues. Writing about early literary magazines, Mark Parker has argued that "scholars still tend to view magazines and periodicals merely as collections of discrete articles" without paying sufficient attention to the "dynamic relation among contributions [that] informs and creates meaning." He argues that only by looking at periodicals as composing a form in and of themselves—with their own conventions and practices—can one understand how the meaning of their content is shaped by silences, "appeals to what often goes without saying in a particular magazine or review innuendo familiar to its circle of readers, exaggeration discernable only by reference to the standard line of the periodical."[9] Parker's work also suggests possibilities for the study of early American newspapers, as well: if, as he has argued, early magazines seem promising subjects for exploration because they are collaborative texts, then newspapers would seem similarly promising. Although historians have done significant content analysis of colonial newspapers such as the *Gazette*—detailing such things as the proportion of space the paper devoted to news, advertising, announcements, or essays—they have yet to explore fully the ways in which newspaper conventions shaped the discursive work these texts accomplished.[10] By tracing the *Gazette*'s discussion of clubs and other forms of civic performance over nearly four decades, this essay demonstrates the necessity of understanding its reporting conventions—including "what often [went] without saying"—if we hope to understand how it shaped the meaning of civic discourse and action.

Although the Ancient Britons' inaugural march in 1729 was the first reported in the *Pennsylvania Gazette*, it was not the first significant procession in provincial history. Only three years earlier, Sir William Keith, the former lieutenant governor, had staged a disastrous political parade through the streets of Philadelphia following his election to the provincial legislative Assembly.[11] Appointed lieutenant governor in 1717 by Hannah Penn, proprietor of the colony and widow of provincial founder William Penn, Keith had proved himself a capable administrator during his nine-year tenure. He proved less successful, however, as a politician. Keith formed an alliance with David Lloyd, a populist Quaker politician who had clashed with both the proprietor and the Quaker faction that dominated the Assembly. He also established two organizations, the Gentleman's Club and the Leather Apron Club, to cultivate a following among elite and plebian Philadelphians, respectively. Keith's schemes led to repeated clashes with James Logan, secretary for the Penns' affairs in Pennsylvania; encouraged by Logan and unsure herself of Keith's motives, Hannah Penn discharged Keith as lieutenant governor in 1726. Keith responded to this slight by organizing a slate of candidates and running as a ticket for an Assembly seat, using meetings of the Gentleman's and Leather Apron Clubs to galvanize his followers.

Keith's election in the fall of 1726 was accompanied by "Mobs, Bonfires, Gunns, [and] Huzzahs." He planned a triumphal entrance to the state house for the opening of his first legislative session, which involved leading his followers—pointedly characterized by his political opponents not as "ye Wise, ye Rich, or the learned" but "mostly Rakes[,]Butchers[,] porters & Tagrags"[12]—in a parade through Philadelphia. The men marched two by two throughout the city streets, led by Keith himself on horseback; the procession ended finally at the statehouse. It was an amazing display of Keith's status and cultural authority, intended to impress Pennsylvania's citizens with his stature and sway legislators to elect him speaker of the Assembly. His gambit failed. Despite Keith's electoral skill, Lloyd had far more support among his fellow legislators than the former governor did. Sensing the inevitable outcome, even Keith's followers turned against him; most of the assemblymen who had run on the Keithian ticket failed to support his bid for speaker. Keith was humiliated after this fiasco, and his political career faltered; he soon left Pennsylvania. Without Keith, the Gentleman's and Leather Apron Clubs quietly faded away.

Within this context, certain elements of the Britons' procession become clearer. The "regular order" of the Britons' march went hand in hand with its apolitical character. While members of the club certainly dressed distinctively, the "Leeks in their Hats" did not obviously mark them as members or supporters of any particular political faction or social class. Their toasts to the queen, the proprietor, the provincial lieutenant governor, and Pennsylvania itself were nonpartisan and decidedly noncontroversial. The entire affair displayed the Britons' fellow feeling and public spirit for all to see but was not an attempt to influence public opinion. In all, the Britons' display and the *Gazette*'s reports of it suggest a disengagement from or innocence of public affairs. The Britons' procession was, in that respect, a typical public gesture among eighteenth-century clubs. Shields has argued that provincial clubs, fearful that their private meetings would arouse fear and suspicion among the general population, adopted two public personas: one "projected the innocence and charitability of private society," while the other exhibited a "frivolity that projected the impertinence, ridiculousness, and triviality of private society."[13] Not surprisingly, especially given the controversy that Keith's clubs and processions had earlier caused, the Britons chose the former strategy in planning and publicizing their inaugural event.

The *Gazette*'s coverage of other early provincial associations suggests that the Ancient Britons had reason to be concerned. Although the Britons were the first club covered by the paper, they were not the most oft-discussed; that honor belonged to the Philadelphia lodge of the Masons, founded around 1730.[14] The paper showed a fascination with Masons, printing more articles about the organization than any other provincial club in that period.[15] Many of these news items consisted of simple announcements giving brief information regarding the group's annual meetings, often including the results of elections for grand master and deputy master of the local lodge.[16] But the *Gazette* also carried more intriguing material, including a reprint of a London account that purported to reveal "The Mystery of Free-Masonry" through a series of queries and answers. The paper later published an article describing the Masons' great "Numbers and Character," noting that the group "consist[ed] principally of Persons of Merit and Consideration." Furthermore, it printed accounts of Masons elsewhere in North America and announced that a printed edition of the Constitution of the London Masons could now be purchased from Franklin.[17] As the *Gazette*'s editor and an enterprising bookseller, Franklin clearly thought his readers were interested not simply in accounts of Masonic behavior, but also in the rules that structured Masonic life.

One incident, however, raised public concern that the Masons' secrecy was not entirely innocent. In June 1737 and February 1738, the *Gazette* published multiple articles dealing with the death of the apprentice Daniel Rees, killed during a mock Masonic ceremony.[18] Apparently Rees had expressed an interest in Masonry to Dr. Evan Jones, his master. Jones—not a Mason—responded by staging, with several friends, an elaborate prank. Jones and his associates brought a blindfolded Rees into the doctor's garden to summon Satan, whose presence Jones claimed was required for initiation. After inducing Rees to offer hearty "Expressions of a true and faithful Allegiance to the Prince of Darkness," they gave the apprentice a cup filled with a strong emetic "in imitation of the Sacrament." The night's events concluded with another display of Rees' fealty to the "Masonic" cause: one of Jones' colleagues, identified only as "T," "indecently discovered his Posteriors, to which the Lad, under the same impediment of Sight was led to kiss, as a Book to swear upon."[19] Jones and his comrades greatly enjoyed their trick on the young apprentice, bragging about it publicly to Franklin—who as a Mason, was not amused—and inviting Rees to a second ceremony "on the pretense of raising him to a higher degree."[20] They arranged for a blindfolded Rees to meet them again in Jones's cellar, where they tried to scare him by dressing up as the devil's minions—one even dressing in a cowhide and horns to appear as Satan himself—holding pans of flaming brandy over their heads to give themselves a "ghastly and hideous" countenance. When Rees removed his blindfold and expressed no fear at their costumes, Jones threw his pan of burning alcohol on the apprentice, injuring him seriously. Rees died of his burns three days later.[21]

The *Gazette*'s extensive coverage of these events—its detailed account of Jones's trial and conviction for manslaughter was one of the longer pieces the paper published during this period—illustrates the extent to which this event played upon the public's fascination, and fear, of the Masons. The ceremonies staged by Jones and his friends were an inversion of contemporary cultural mores, mixing diabolism, homoeroticism, and Catholicism. Critically, it appears to have been the latter two elements that most disturbed many Philadelphians, including Franklin himself. He expressed great dismay about the emetic "Sacrament," the posterior kissing, and the diabolical oath involved in the ceremony, even telling Jones and a friend "that if they had done such things in England they would be prosecuted."[22] At the same time, he also borrowed a copy of the devilish oath from the tricksters and showed it to guests he entertained at his house, suggesting that he found the mock Satanism entertaining rather than objectionable. Likewise, the leaders of the city's Masonic lodge found themselves unable even to mention "T's" odious action by name, condemning the "Purging, Vomiting, [and] Burning" Rees endured as well as "the Terror of certain horrid and diabolical Rites" he was forced to undergo.[23]

In disavowing Jones's actions, the Masons sought to distance themselves not only from Rees's untimely death at his master's hands but also from the symbolism of these "horrid" rites. As Thomas A. Foster has pointed out, eighteenth-century anti-Masonic literature was especially posterior-centered, suggesting, among other things, that Masons "use[d] their shared preoccupation with their backsides to cement their fraternal bond."[24] In ritual terms, the Ancient Britons' procession had been described in the *Gazette* as the collective embodiment of a sober festiveness, a public-spirited private gathering. The parody of the Masons initiated by Jones, on the other hand, appears in the

Gazette as the literal embodiment of deviance, a performance violating appropriate standards of religion and masculine sexual practice. That Franklin, the publisher of the *Gazette*, and the local lodge leaders who submitted an advertisement "declaring the Abhorrence of all true Brethren to such Practices in general" would move so quickly and decisively to address the issue in print suggests the relationship between fear and fascination in the public's perception of Masonry. Paradoxically, their public denunciations helped news of the event circulate more widely than it might have otherwise, implicating Masonry into Jones's mock performance even as they ostensibly attempted to extricate it.[25]

The printed controversy over the Masons revealed the significant contestation over associational activity in eighteenth-century Pennsylvania. The debate over the Masons illustrated the role clubs played in the complex interactions between the development of a salon-style public sphere within private associations and the creation of an extended print public. In the aftermath of Keith's failed attempt to mobilize clubs for political ends and in an environment where private associations such as the Masons were awesome and awful at the same time, the *Gazette* circulated not only accounts of private organizations' public activities but commentary on them as well. Printed debate over associational behavior did not, however, take the form of abstract discussions of the public virtue. Rather, as in the case of the Masons, discussion focused on concrete practices and embodied figures. T's posterior, not the "disembodied" bourgeois liberal subject, occupied the center of this public sphere. Moreover the Masons' controversy did not simply illustrate the relationships among clubs, print, and the public sphere; it also foreshadowed problems other clubs would face in the coming decades

Although coverage of the Masons highlighted the cultural issues involved in discussions of clubs, it was not typical. More common was the *Gazette*'s coverage of organizations such as the Ancient Britons, the Library Company of Philadelphia (and other local library companies), the St. Andrew's Society, the Fort St. David's Fishing Club, and various local fire companies. While the *Gazette*'s treatment of these private associations was not uniform, an examination of their presence in the paper over time reveals some common themes. First, these clubs and associations were, in the main, frequently mentioned yet little discussed. Although they appear in the *Gazette* numerous times from 1728 to 1765, these brief mentions—many just a notice of the date, time, and place of the next meeting—often contain no record or description of the publicity or ritual in their activities. Missing from the bulk of this coverage is the ethnographic specificity present in the paper's discussion of the Masons' or even the Britons' inaugural processions. Of all the references to clubs and associations in the *Gazette*, fewer than one in six contained any extended discussion about the clubs or their activities; fewer still suggested what these clubs meant to their members or for the larger public.[26] Two types of organizations were the most consistently discussed in the *Gazette*: library companies and charitable or service associations.

Pennsylvania's library companies served multiple functions. The Library Company of Philadelphia, the first library company in the colony, was founded to achieve educational and civic ends. A member expressed the Company's goals in two addresses delivered before the Penn family in the library's early years. It aimed to promote "a publick generous Education . . . [and] to propagate knowledge, and improve the minds of Men, by rendering Science more cheap and easy of access." It was the next logical step in the province's maturation, as Pennsylvania moved beyond its "Infancy" when "the Refinements of Life . . . cannot be much attended to."[27] The company's desire to provide some measure of these refinements was connected with its expansive sense of how its actions might edify the public; in the eyes of its members, "the promoting of Knowledge and Virtue" were inextricably linked. Both the Library Company and the Penn family agreed that the group's activities would spread "Virtue, Learning, and True Religion" throughout Pennsylvania.[28] The message here was clear: if a library was a means of increasing civic virtue and wisdom in the colony, then the Library Company and its members must, through their association, be doing so as well. In republishing their addresses and the Penn's response, the company claimed to speak for society as a whole, defining its private activities as a public good.

Few of the other references to the Library Company in the *Gazette* offered such explicit commentary on the meaning of the group's behavior. Instead most provided oblique descriptions of the company's practices. One piece in the *Gazette*, for example, listed the Library Company's new bylaws; these regulations included "A Law for preserving a just Equality among the members . . . A Law for regulating the Election of Officers . . . [and] A Law preventing any Advantage by Survivorship among the Members of the Library Company."[29] These rules shed light on what kind of experience the Library Company collectively hoped its members might have. They represent the organization's attempt to be a participatory democracy of equal members, to level any advantages members would have by virtue of their birth or ancestry. And while the Library Company did not explicitly state whether it actually put these prescriptions into practice, the *Gazette* did show indirect evidence that it did. In advertising their annual meetings in the newspaper, the Library Company repeatedly publicized their practice of holding regular elections for officers and of supporting the organization through contributions from its members. Its competitors and imitators operated in a similar fashion. Perhaps because each saw itself as a miniature "Body politic" ruled by its own laws and regulations, as the Union Library Company of Philadelphia did, these groups regularly announced elections and contributions. The overwhelming majority of references to library companies during this period consisted solely of advertisements for forthcoming officer elections and calls for members to contribute their annual payment.[30]

Thus, while different from the Ancient Britons' and Masons more festive and ornate displays, these library companies did publicize a particular institutional culture. Their repetitive emphasis on a democratic process and equality among members provided these institutions and their members a powerful set of symbols and rituals; they suggest that members of the companies hoped—on the few occasions they made their views explicit—that participation within these institutions might be seen as publicly virtuous. This message was publicized, however, not through reasoned debate (in the Habermasian sense), but through representations of practice. Moreover these printed representations figured not only the character of appropriate civic behavior, but also the normative character of the civic actor, suggesting the possibilities and limits of such a role. If participation in the library companies was to be equalizing, it was not open to all, as the requirement of an annual payment illustrated.

Representations of fire companies in the *Gazette* were quite similar. Private associations performing a public good, these companies made implicit and explicit claims for their members' virtuous civic spirit. The *Gazette* first reported on the potential value of fire companies in early 1735, printing a letter (likely written by Benjamin Franklin under a pseudonym) praising "the Example of a City in a Neighboring Province." The letter told of a "Club or Society of active Men" jointly in charge of maintaining and operating fire-fighting equipment. For their services, the author suggested, these firefighters could be awarded "an Abatement or Exemption in the Taxes."[31] This call for virtuous men to assemble and fill a public need suggests the malleability of civic virtue; defined by activity and behavior rather than by birth and wealth, virtue was a choice. In linking private expressions of public virtue to taxpayer status, however, the piece demonstrated the gendered aspects of the performance of virtue. Philadelphia had the most egalitarian economic structure among eighteenth-century North American cities; nearly all men, whether unmarried or householders, were wealthy enough to pay some taxes. Nearly all independent women, whether unmarried or widowed, however, were poor enough to be exempt from taxes. Thus, the relatively greater degree of economic equality among men in Philadelphia was concomitant with the feminization of poverty.[32] The implied fire fighter, then, was decidedly active, virtuous, public spirited, and male.

References in the *Gazette* to the practices of fire companies and other fire-fighting organizations illustrated many of these themes. Subsequent discussions of the Union Fire Company, the city's first such club, displayed that group's attempts to institutionalize the civic and heroic qualities of fire fighting. In 1743, only a few years after its formation, the Union Fire Company published a handful of advertisements in the *Gazette* warning against arson and offering rewards for information regarding those who set fires or damaged fire pumps.[33] These warnings characterized arsonists and vandals as "evil minded, dissolute Persons," implicitly recognizing the fire fighters as public spirited and ethical. Even through the act of offering a reward—by symbolically and literally taking on a pseudo-governmental role—the Union Fire Company was claiming at least a limited authority over the public as a whole, not just its own members. Similarly, the Philadelphia Contributorship for Insuring Houses from Loss by Fire publicized its meetings in the paper regularly, generally issuing announcements twice a year regarding elections and changes in the group's policies. These announcements displayed the attempts to follow democratic procedures in running the association; one notice even discussed the group's attempts to make the policies more uniform, reducing the benefits wealthier homeowners could receive so that member contributions might stay lower.[34]

These references to library and fire companies thus left implicit a claim that these organizations provided legitimate forums to speak to and for the public. While this assertion was rarely challenged, it did not go entirely undisputed. An argument between "Tom Trueman" and "Obidiah Plainman" conducted in the pages of the *Gazette* in May 1740 demonstrated the controversial place voluntary associations still occupied in provincial political thought. What began as a debate over the closing of a "Dancing School Assembly and Concert Room" quickly turned into a debate on social distinction and public authority.[35] The exchange began in earnest with Tom Trueman's letter regarding revivalist George Whitefield's recent tour through Pennsylvania. Denying earlier reports in the *Gazette* that the trip had been a success, Trueman claimed that the tour had failed because "the better Sort of People in *Pennsylvania*" held the revivalist and his followers "in the utmost contempt."[36] The following week an author calling himself Obidiah Plainman took issue both with Trueman's assumption that he could speak for the province's "better Sort" and with his belief that the "better Sort" spoke for all Pennsylvanians. Trueman's implication that public rhetoric should be judged according to the social status of its speaker struck Plainman as pernicious; reason and virtue, he argued, not status, were better signs of authority. Urging Trueman to follow the examples of such legendary leaders as Demosthanes, Cicero, Sidney, or Trenchard, Plainman noted that "They never took upon them to make a Difference of Persons, but as they were distinguished by their Virtues or Vices." Plainman signed his letter "On Behalf of myself and the Rest of my Brethren of the Meaner Sort."[37]

It was the second exchange between Trueman and Plainman that highlighted the symbolic relationship between local clubs and the rhetoric of public authority. In responding to Plainman's letter, Trueman expressed doubts that the former actually represented public opinion in Pennsylvania; indeed, his criticism of Plainman focused on whether there was a "better Sort" and how those individuals might be identified. Rejecting Plainman's arguments, Trueman wrote that he had never argued that the virtue of a provincial elite was defined by birth. Instead their quality could be seen in what they did and how they acted; those individuals who participated in organizations such as the Library Company displayed and refined their superior public virtue. The participation "of Men of various Persuasions and Imployments" marked them, on the whole, as "the *better* sort of People." Referring to some people as the "better sort," he continued, did not mean that all those not specified as part of a virtuous elite were therefore the mob or rabble. Implying that Plainman's attempts to cast himself as part of a distinctive social class were a claim to political authority, Trueman wrote that Plainman must "imagine [him]self the Prince and Leader of a Set of People to me so little known, that till I had the Favour of yours, I never heard they made so great a Part of the Inhabitants of this Province."[38] Trueman argued for associational activity as both a sign of "better" character and an instrument for promoting civic character. He might not be able to specify all the differences between the rabble and its betters, but he knew the latter when he saw them.

Plainman's response dealt with the question of how an individual might speak on behalf of the public at large. Rejecting Trueman's claim to be merely representing the views of the "better Sort" impartially, Plainman wrote that "Tho' the Stile be in the third Person, yet, without any Prejudice to the Sense, it may be changed to the first[.]" Plainman thus argued that Trueman's letter was an attempt to speak *for* "the better Sort." In this respect, he continued, it differed from other social groups' public claims, such as "Boys at Bandy-Wicket, young Fellows at Foot-Ball, Magistrates on the Bench, Quakers with their Hats on, or the Library Company with their Hats off or on; for all those Persons are said to be OF the *Better Sort,* which does not exclude others from the same rank." Such an exclusive claim to represent civic virtue, Plainman argued, was tantamount to holding one's fellow citizens in contempt and subverting the public unity upon which the provincial government was grounded.[39] While both Trueman and Plainman agreed that participation in private associations had a public, civic dimension, they disagreed vehemently over how associational behavior should be interpreted. Was participation in a private association a legitimate means of self-improvement or an attempt to separate oneself from one's fellow citizens? Could members of private clubs speak for the public or merely speak publicly on behalf of their fellow club members? The vitriol of the commentary between Trueman and Plainman illustrates the important symbolic role that associational activity played in shaping notions of how citizens might legitimately embody public virtue.

Thus, representations of these organizations in the *Gazette* defined virtuous citizenship through examples of civic practices, expressed by private individuals on behalf of the public. While occasional pieces—such as the address to the Penns or the letter suggesting the formation of fire companies—offered more explicit interpretations of associational behavior, in general the meaning of these clubs' actions was left implicit. The articles in the *Gazette* rarely defined the rules governing civic behavior overtly. Instead these rules were most often expressed as latent aspects of social practices whose meanings were taken for granted; ambiguity was central to this process.[40] This practice of representing associational activities as virtuous naturalized the active, masculine subject who participated in fire and library companies as the imaginary civic subject at the center of provincial public life. In discussing the province's library and fire companies, the *Gazette* described the behaviors of these groups as both sign and process of civic identity. Virtue was not inherited, defined by birth or wealth; instead it could be cultivated and shaped in individuals and in society. For members participation in these clubs, publicized in the newspapers, signaled their public-spirited citizenship. At the same time, these activities were an ongoing process by which anyone might develop their civic virtue. Moreover, the *Gazette*'s reports of the library and fire companies emphasized the civic possibilities of associational activity, not the constraints (implicit or explicit) that limited participation or membership in these clubs.

This civic ideology embedded within the *Gazette*'s coverage was most clearly defined only when challenged. Trueman's explication of the ways in which associational participation produced a civic elite came in the face of Plainman's challenge. Each grounded his argument in assumptions regarding who constituted "the" people or "the" public. Neither doubted that associational practices were critical in shaping civic virtue, nor that individuals spoke to and for the public as members of different social groups. They differed merely on the limits of the "better sort," on who exactly might embody civic practice appropriately and on which bodily or embodied signs signified civic virtue. The powerful—and unspoken—role of associational practice in defining what a good citizen was and what a good citizen did was not at issue.

But while the *Gazette*'s coverage of fire companies, library companies, and social clubs such as the Masons, Ancient Britons, and St. Andrew's Society was important in shaping public conceptions of civic behavior, the most significant organization discussed in the *Gazette* was the provincial militia, called the "Association." Formed at a critical time when provincial public authority seemed weak and ineffective, the Association was a well-publicized attempt by private individuals to organize as virtuous citizens and act on behalf of the public as a whole. The group was formed as King George's War (1744–48) raged in the Atlantic world. By late 1747, Pennsylvanians had become increasingly worried that the war, which had heretofore avoided the Delaware Valley, would reach them. French privateers had choked off Pennsylvania's Atlantic trade almost entirely. Reports spread of French ships scouting the mouth of the Delaware River, raising the distinct possibility that a larger force might be on the way. The Quaker-led Assembly, adhering to its pacifist principles, refused to appropriate public monies or raise any troops for a military purpose—even for provincial defense. With the province left undefended, Pennsylvanians worried about the possibility of invasion.[41]

With the provincial government paralyzed, Franklin took matters into his own hands to convince private citizens to work collectively for the public good. In November 1747 he published, under the pseudonym "A TRADESMAN," a tract titled *Plain Truth*, which argued for the necessity of a citizen militia in Pennsylvania.[42] *Plain Truth* castigated Pennsylvanians for their attitudes regarding the British war with the French and Spanish, calling their collective inaction not only impractical but immoral as well. Mixing the civic, the historical, and the biblical, Franklin asserted that England was not the savior and deliverer of the American colonies; rather Pennsylvania and its neighbors would only be saved from destruction by raising their own armies and fighting for themselves. He buttressed his argument with a quotation from the Roman politician Cato in which the senator warned his countrymen that their government could be saved only by action, not by "timorous Prayers, and womanish Supplications." He further cited Cato's admonition that failure to take arms against enemies of the state was tantamount to "Effeminacy and Cowardice."[43] Franklin used biblical examples as well, citing from the Book of Judges the story of Laish, a defenseless city that was destroyed while it waited for outside deliverance. In making such a strong religious critique, Franklin had, without mentioning them by name, offered a stinging rebuke to those provincial Quakers who protested raising a militia. This implicit censure was even more striking given Franklin's praise for the collective valor of Pennsylvania's other citizens. He called upon the province's Britons to display "that *undaunted Spirit*, which has in every Age distinguished their Nation"; he also celebrated the thousands of members of "*that Warlike Nation*" who resided in Pennsylvania, the province's "*brave* and *steady* GERMANS."[44] *Plain Truth* framed participation in a citizen militia as the essence of good citizenship: it was an active embodiment of one's commitment to the body politic, a fervent display of a manly Christian civic virtue.

The publication of *Plain Truth* immediately generated public support for a citizen militia. Within a week of the tract's publication, Franklin had gathered together a group of individuals to settle on a plan for organizing a voluntary military association. Following meetings on November 21, 23, and 24, he drafted the rules and enlisted more than five hundred men for duty. The *Form of Association* was published immediately as a broadside and republished with added commentary in the *Gazette* on December 3.[45] This publication reiterated the impetus behind the Association and outlined the procedures by which it would operate. The Association, the tract announced, was a response by citizens concerned for their "mutual Defense and Security, and for the Security of our Wives, Children, and Estates" who were "unprotected by the Government under which we live"—an implicit but stern rebuke to Pennsylvania's provincial ruling fathers.[46]

The Association had an organization befitting its origins. Its charter called for members to arrange themselves into companies (by region or neighborhood) and meet on January 1, 1748, to elect officers for each company. The companies were intended to act like miniature democratic civil societies. The requirement that companies be organized by neighborhood was, as Franklin noted in the *Form of Association*,

> intended to prevent People's sorting themselves into Companies, according to their Ranks in Life, their Quality or Station. 'Tis designed to mix the Great and Small together, for the sake of Union and Encouragement. Where Danger and Duty are equal to All, there should be no Distinction from Circumstances, but All be on the Level.

Additionally, he continued, "frequent Elections secure[d] the Liberty of the People," one of the very things for which the Association was fighting. The charter called for the regular election of a general military council, intended to serve as "the Common-Band that unites all Parts of the whole Association into one Body."[47] Franklin and his fellow Associators hoped that their participation in the militia might not merely reflect a civic unity among male Pennsylvanians of all ranks and stations but effectively construct one through repeated civic practices.

While the Association's organizers made their intentions public through print, its rank-and-file members proceeded to express their civic solidarity as well. In mid-December, "a great Body of the Associators" gathered with their arms in the center of Philadelphia and marched down Market Street to the county courthouse. In a public meeting presided over by the governor and many members of the provincial council, the Associators divided Philadelphia's neighborhoods into companies for the upcoming election of officers. This gathering was followed the next day by "an excellent Sermon on the Lawfulness of Self Defence, and of Associating for that Purpose, to a very considerable Auditory" by Rev. Robert Jenny, rector of the city's Christ Church.[48] After electing officers on January 1, the Associators met again the very next day: "Nine Companies of the Associators . . . marched up and met at the State House" so that the officers might receive their commissions from the governor and Provincial Council and so that the general military council might be elected. After the selection of the military council, the Association "began its March through the Town, to the Court House, in Market Street." After dividing into three divisions, "three general Discharges from each Division" were fired. The *Gazette* deemed it a wonderful display of harmony among provincial citizens: "The whole was performed with the greatest Order and Regularity, and without occasioning the least Disturbance."[49]

The Association continued to receive coverage during the first months of 1748. On January 12, 1748, the *Gazette* printed a list of the "DEVICES AND MOTTOES painted on some of the Silk Colours of the Regiments of ASSOCIATORS." The regiments' displays were colorful, with each company's clothing decorated with icons such as lions, eagles, and even "the Figure of LIBERTY." The device and motto of one of the regiments listed in the *Gazette* suggested the impact that the threat of war had had on the Associators and, by implication, on Pennsylvania as a whole. The newspaper reported that this company's clothing contained "Three Arms, wearing different Linnen, ruffled, plain, and chequed; the hands joined by grasping each other's Wrist, denoting the Union of all Ranks. Motto, UNITA VURTUS [*sic*] VALET"—bravery united prevails.[50] The Associators' march was an assertion of martial solidarity in the face of a common military foe. Through their mottoes and their very existence, the Associators affirmed their solidarity with each other and with the colony, a common civic commitment that cut across lines of ethnicity and class.

Likewise, the *Gazette*'s second listing of the "devices and mottoes" of the Association regiments, three months later, described a similarly pluralist-minded militia company. Its symbol portrayed "Three of the Associators marching with their muskets shoulder'd and dressed in different Clothes, intimating the Unanimity of the different Sorts of People in the Association." The company's motto was "Vis Unit[i]s Fortior"—might made stronger through unity.[51] The "mottos and devices" of these and several other militia companies were on display several times in Philadelphia following their initial musters in December 1747 and January 1748. All in all, various companies in the Association met and marched more than a half dozen times from the Association's formation in December 1747 to September 1748.[52] The *Gazette* reported several of these militia musters, in addition to offering detailed accounts of the companies' insignia and lengthy lists of the company members' names. In so doing, the *Gazette* was not merely describing a nascent martial public identity but actively constructing it as well.

The Association constructed a distinct public culture in several ways. First, the Association fostered civic participation. Members met to elect officers; they marched in unison through Philadelphia's streets; and they wore insignia to mark their membership both in a specific militia and in the provincial militia as a whole. These rites of assembly were rituals of civic embodiment on two levels. On one level, individual Associators displayed and honed their patriotism by participating in these physical performances of civic identity, an outward embodiment of their inward allegiance to king and country. On the second level, these civic rituals joined the Associators into a single military "Body" that purported to represent all ranks, groups, and stations. Participation in the Association was said to level all distinctions and erased all differences, rendering those within the militia not merely united but equal, at least in the value and performance of their civic identities; the Association itself was the ritual embodiment of the body politic's civic spirit.[53] The Association, then, afforded another cultural site in which private individuals could influence the public good, similar to the private associations discussed above.

The Association that was represented was innovative for a second reason as well. The amount and kind of reportage the Association received in the colonial press cultivated a broader imagined public. Coverage of the Association in the *Gazette* was copious; twenty-seven separate issues of the paper (more than 87 percent of the total issues from November 19, 1747, to June 23, 1748) discussed the Association. This extensive coverage meant that the Association served a double public function, not only allowing the Associators to rehearse virtuous behaviors and ideals but also educating the *Gazette*'s public about civic responsibility. The *Gazette*'s metacultural commentary on the militia implicated the Association's practices into the print public sphere and allowed its message to reach an extralocal community of readers and citizens. If, as Benedict Anderson has argued, both print and collective ritual practices of liminality were implicated in the origins of "imagined community" in the eighteenth-century Americas, then the reportage of the Association seems to have combined the two in a particularly powerful way. Reading about the ritual performances through which the Associators displayed their allegiance to an imagined civic body was itself a ritual practice that allowed the *Gazette*'s readers to imagine themselves an integral part of the polity that the Associators had assembled to defend.[54]

As important as the frequency with which the *Gazette* wrote of the Association was the way in which its activities were described. The Associators described over and over again in the *Gazette*, however, were hardly the disembodied "negative" subjects at the center of Warner's description of the colonial public sphere.[55] Instead, the *Gazette* took pains to call attention to the masculine, ethnic, and class character of the Associators. The *Gazette*'s enumeration of the "Three Arms" wearing "ruffled, plain, and chequed" linen seems an obvious marker of social identity, particularly in a province where the Quaker plain style of clothing had assumed such a significant public meaning. As several other scholars have pointed out, both checks and ruffles on clothing and fabric were common and easily identified markers of working- and upper-class status, respectively.[56] Clothing also served in the reporting practices of the *Gazette* as a marker of ethnic identity.[57] It is too much to say that the *Gazette*'s readers necessarily interpreted this coverage as evidence of *actual* cross-class or interethnic unity. But these examples highlight the ways in which the Associators' participation in the print public sphere—as subjects in a metacultural commentary on their public civic practices—occurred not as "neutral" subjects but instead as actors whose identities were deeply inflected in ways that the reading public could easily imagine as ethnically loaded *and* ethnically open. Readers could find men of all classes and all social and ethnic groups embodied in these "mottos and devices" *except* Quakers, whose own plain style of speech and dress was a marker of their public identity and authority.[58] The Association had, through processional culture and print culture, fostered a public culture that delegitimated the privileged place in Pennsylvania's public imagination that provincial Friends had claimed. At the same time, it expanded both the number of citizens who could legitimately speak and act on the public's behalf and the variety of practices through which they might embody such public virtue.

The *Gazette*'s coverage of the Association marked a change in provincial public culture. The paper's discussion of associational ritual became more detailed, as the article on the Masons' 1755 march cited earlier illustrates. The *Gazette* also afforded private associations an opportunity to speak more directly to political concerns. In early 1765, for example, the paper reported the decisions of five local fire companies to forgo eating lamb that season, in order to bring the price of mutton down, to discourage its importation, and "to promote the Growth of Sheep in this Province." Later that year, members of the Heart and Hand Fire Company took an even stronger political stand. Declaring their opposition to "the late unconstitutional and oppressive Stamp Act," they threatened fellow company member John Hughes, the appointed provincial Stamp distributor, with expulsion from their ranks unless he heeded "the general Voice of his Country and Fellow Citizens" and resigned his office.[59] Yet this change likely reflected more than simply the paper's editorial policy; it also suggests that provincial clubs and associations had become more willing to go public in their activities and their assertions. The Association's activities, reported and subtly interpreted by Franklin in the *Gazette* and Franklin's other published writings, had legitimated club members' ability to speak—as members of private associations—to and for the public. Taken together with the broader evolution of clubs' place in the provincial public imaginary, both the Association's ritual culture and its printed representations in the *Gazette* had widened the scope of what constituted acceptable civic practice in colonial Pennsylvania. Following the Association, practices that had previously been deemed implicitly or explicitly suspect—such as secretive Masonic ritual—were now acceptable.

This local history of association and representation suggests that scholars' prevailing narratives about the emergence of public culture in early America need modification. As Mah has suggested, the "spatialized" conception of the public sphere employed by many historians does nothing to explain the emergence of a unitary public sphere, the nominal subject of Habermas's inquiry. Neither does it explain how the production of "the" public involved the development of new imagined citizenships. At the same time, this history of representation in the *Gazette* challenges the idea that the public emerged as a disembodied mass through the process that Mah has called "the imagined suppression of social particularity in the service of producing abstract individuals who then enter into discussion and debate in a spatialized public sphere."[60]

Far from suppressing social particularity, representations of public activity in the *Gazette* frequently emphasized particular social identities, including gender, religion, or class, even as those individuals highlighting these identities—such as Obidiah Plainman or members of several militia companies—emphasized their commonalities with the public as a whole. Thus, what Mah is describing is not the *actual* suppression of social particularity in public debate but instead the presumption that individuals "going public" have done so; his analysis—and, by extension, Habermas's and Warner's analyses—conflates claims to speak as an "abstract subject" with the messy realities of eighteenth-century public life. What this examination of public activity within the pages of the *Pennsylvania Gazette* suggests is that scholars of early American culture pay closer attention to the process by which specific identities or specific forms of embodying and articulating public virtue came to be accepted as general expressions of civic will. Here a deeper study of periodical literature—as sprawling, paradoxical, and internally contradictory as these texts are—might help illuminate the dynamics of this discursive process.[61]

Greg Urban's analysis of the dynamics of cultural conflict and the public sphere offers one way of understanding the representation of associational activity in the *Gazette*. Urban has pointed out that claims to speak for the public involve conflict between universalistic and particularistic cultural points of view. Those claiming to speak for "the" public, he argues, adopt what he calls an "omega" cultural perspective, implicitly or explicitly grounding their arguments in either a universal rationality or a general will.[62] Those claiming to voice the general will, he continues, often contrast the superiority of their "universalist" rhetorical position with the inferiority of other "particularistic" cultural perspectives, which he calls "alpha" culture. Urban notes that difference between omega and alpha culture is perspectival, not fixed; suggesting that the tension between alpha and omega cultural perspectives is a general feature of cultural conflict, he asserts that it is irresolvable.[63] There is nothing inherent in any culture, he argues, that allows it to claim superiority over any other culture. Culture, he writes, "is inert. It contains no force that would cause it to spread, to perpetuate itself, in the face or resistance or in the form of alternatives."[64] This motive force, the claim to authority over other cultures or peoples, he continues, can come only from arguing *about* culture. Claims to cultural authority are, in a word, metacultural.

And while all evaluative responses are, according to Urban, at some level metacultural, political and legal assertions are distinct from aesthetic ones. All three types of statements are self-conscious rankings of different cultural norms, meanings, and values. Political and legal statements, however, not only assert their own general validity over the peoples within that culture; they also cast competing metacultural expressions as subversive and dangerous, a threat to the unity and sovereignty of the political order. Urban describes the political dimensions of the tension between general "omega" cultures and particularistic "alpha" cultures as such:

> To talk about a contrast of this sort, that is, a contrast between a constituent subculture and the broader culture of which it is a part, would be in effect to assert the political autonomy of the subculture and to fracture the political union, at least under the present discursive construction of the nation-state.[65]

Thus, the fierce conflict over defining public opinion in provincial Pennsylvania took place not simply in the cultural domains of ritual association or print but also in the metacultural domain in which these cultural expressions were defined as legitimate expressions of public opinion. Articles in the *Gazette* condemning pseudo-Masonic ceremonies or celebrating the Association's musters were attempts to define the meaning of the very practices they represented. Moreover, as the debate between Trueman and Plainman made clear, attempts to define the relationship between specific groups and "the" public *were* viewed in political terms; Trueman's charge that Plainman had tried to declare himself king of a disgruntled mob is evidence of the potentially revolutionary dimensions of challenging perspectives that supposedly represented the general will. It would be a mistake, however, to overemphasize the importance of metacultural discourse in Pennsylvania during this period; as the foregoing analysis has shown, this was, in quantitative terms, a relatively insignificant feature of associational print discourse as a whole. Metacultural attempts to legitimate or delegitimate particular cultural practices of rhetorical strategies were occasional and situational. Nor were these debates ever definitively resolved. Just as Urban has argued that the tension between the omega and alpha elements of cultural systems is a general feature of culture itself, so too were attempts to define the parameters of provincial public expression themselves always open to challenge. An idealized, unitary public sphere was a practical impossibility.

Ironically, the two conditions that prevented the emergence of a unitary public sphere during this period—the relative paucity of metacultural discourse and the impossibility of ultimately settling those metacultural debates that did arise—were instrumental in the construction of a powerful, if only obliquely articulated, conception of the civic subject at the heart of Pennsylvania's public sphere. Because the *Gazette*'s discussion of private associations focused so heavily on describing their practices, the paper effectively naturalized some of the meanings latent in their activities. Print discourse in the *Gazette* rarely called the implicit assumptions behind these practices into question by debating them in the realm of public opinion. Nor did debates in the *Gazette* ever reach an ultimate conclusion fixing the meaning of associational practices or defining precisely what kinds of citizens participated in such activities. This ambiguity, however, effectively broadened the range of provincials who might imaginatively participate in the public identities constructed by private associations and print discourse. Participants' frequent refusals to enumerate those individuals excluded from civic action—accompanied by their occasional attempts to enumerate social and ethnic groups explicitly included in civil society—suggested that such activity was voluntary; civic identity was a product of volitional allegiance, not predetermined by birth. Men of all different ethnic, religious, and social backgrounds who were willing to embody the behaviors modeled in the *Gazette* could prove their civic worth. By thus implicitly and explicitly expanding the category of civic practice, participants in private associations and authors in the *Gazette* conflated civic embodiment with the embodiment of a martial masculinity. The "price of entry" for participation in Pennsylvania's public sphere was not the suppression all social identities, but the embodiment of an active martial, masculine citizenship.

This history of the *Pennsylvania Gazette* as both a window onto and an active site for the construction of Pennsylvania's public sphere does not address the normative concerns within the Habermasian public sphere project: one may still desire the creation of a twenty-first-century public sphere in which social differences between citizens may be suppressed in favor a purely rational-critical debate. However, it speaks to the emergence the eighteenth-century provincial North American public sphere, revealing elements of how and why the assumed subject at the center of that public emerged as it did. By figuring citizens as embodied, and not abstract, individuals, Pennsylvanians facilitated the development of a "mass" citizenship that was deeply, if subtly, inflected by gender, class, religion, and ethnicity.

Notes

An earlier version of this essay was presented at the 1999 annual meeting of The American Historical Association. I would like to thank Jon Butler, Eric Rauchway, David Waldstreicher, Karen Halttunen, Alan Karras, Richard Koufay, and the editors for their comments, suggestions, and assistance on this work in its various forms.

1. *Pennsylvania Gazette*, February 25, 1729; March 4, 1729. All dates given in this paper have been converted to "new style," with January 1 marking the start of each year.
2. Ibid., June 26, 1755.
3. David S. Shields, "Anglo American Clubs: Their Wit, Their Heterodoxy, Their Sedition," *William and Mary Quarterly*, 3d ser., 51 (1994): 293–304.

4. Jürgen Habermas, *The Structural Transformation of the Public Sphere: An Inquiry into a Category of Bourgeois Society*, trans. Thomas McCarthy (Cambridge: MIT P, 1989).

5. See, for example, Shields, "Anglo American Clubs" and *Civil Tongues and Polite Letters in British America* (Chapel Hill: U of North Carolina P, 1997); Steven C. Bullock, *Revolutionary Brotherhood : Freemasonry and the Transformation of the American Social Order, 1730–1840* (Chapel Hill: U of North Carolina P, 1996); Len Travers, *Celebrating the Fourth: Independence Day and the Rites of Nationalism in the Early Republic* (Amherst: U of Massachusetts P, 1997); Albrecht Koschnik, "Political Conflict and Public Contest: Rituals of National Celebration in Philadelphia, 1788–1815," *Pennsylvania Magazine of History and Biography* 118 (1994): 209–48; "Fashioning a Federalist Self: Young Men and Voluntary Association in Early Nineteenth-Century Philadelphia," *Explorations in Early American Culture* 4 (2000): 220–57; "The Democratic Societies of Philadelphia and the Limits of the American Public Sphere, circa 1793–1795," *William and Mary Quarterly*, 3d ser., 58 (2001): 615–36; Simon P. Newman, *Parades and the Politics of the Street: Festive Culture in the Early American Republic* (Philadelphia: U of Pennsylvania P, 1997); Peter Thompson, *Rum Punch and Revolution: Taverngoing and Public Life in Eighteenth-Century Philadelphia* (Philadelphia: U of Pennsylvania P, 1999).

6. David Waldstreicher, *In The Midst of Perpetual Fetes: The Making of American Nationalism, 1776–1820* (Chapel Hill: U of North Carolina P, 1997), 27.

7. Harold Mah, "Phantasies of the Public Sphere: Rethinking the Habermas of Historians." *Journal of Modern History* 72 (2000): 160.

8. Michael Warner, *The Letters of the Republic: Publication and the Public Sphere in Eighteenth-Century America* (Cambridge: Harvard UP, 1990), 38, 42.

9. Mark Parker, *Literary Magazines and British Romanticism* (New York: Cambridge UP, 2000), 3.

10. For an exceedingly thorough content analysis of the *Gazette*, see Charles E. Clark and Charles Wetherell, "The Measure of Maturity: The *Pennsylvania Gazette*, 1728–1765," *William and Mary Quarterly*, 3d ser., 46 (1989): 279–303.

11. The discussion of Keith's tenure in this and the following paragraph is drawn from John Smolenski, "Friends and Strangers: Religion, Diversity, and the Ordering of Public Life in Colonial Pennsylvania, 1681–1764" (Ph.D. diss., University of Pennsylvania, 2001), 264–66.

12. Isaac Norris to James Scarth, October 21, 1726, in Isaac Norris Letterbook, 1716–1730, Norris Family Papers, Historical Society of Pennsylvania.

13. Shields, *Civil Tongues and Polite Letters*, 176–77.

14. Bullock 46–47.

15. The *Gazette* published thirteen articles on the Masons from December 8, 1730, to March 30, 1738. By contrast, the Library Company of Philadelphia, the second most-mentioned provincial club, appeared in the *Gazette* only eight times during this same period.

16. See, for example, *Pennsylvania Gazette*, June 26, 1732; June 28, 1733; June 27, 1734; July 3, 1735; June 8, 1736; and June 30, 1737.

17. Ibid., December 8, 1730; May 13, 1731; April 18, 1734; May 16, 1734.

18. Ibid., June 16, 1737; February 7, 1738; February 15, 1738. See also Bullock 50–52.

19. *Pennsylvania Gazette*, February 7, 1738.

20. Ibid., February 15, 1738

21. Ibid., February 7, 1738.

22. Ibid., February 15, 1738.

23. Ibid., June 16, 1738.

24. Thomas A. Foster, "Antimasonic Satire, Sodomy, and Eighteenth-Century Masculinity in the *Boston Evening-Post*," *William and Mary Quarterly*, 3d ser., 60 (2003): 181.

25. On the paradox of such public denials of misdeed—statements that circulate spurious stories as much as they counter them—see Jane Kamensky, *Governing the Tongue: The Politics of Speech in Early New England* (New York: Oxford UP, 1997), 127–49; and Smolenski 132, 171.

26. There are 232 references to library companies, social clubs, service or charitable organizations, and other miscellaneous associations in the *Gazette* from January 1729 to December 1765; only 37 of these 232 mentions—15.9 percent of the total—contain any extended discussion of these clubs. The Association, Franklin's volunteer provincial militia, is not included in this count.

27. *Pennsylvania Gazette*, May 31, 1733.

28. Ibid., June 5, 1735

29. Ibid., April 8, 1742

30. Of the ninety-six references to library companies in the *Gazette* from 1728 to 1765, eighty-eight consisted entirely of such announcements, representing 91.7 percent of the total. The *Gazette* reported that the charter

granted the Union Library Company "hath incorporated them into a Body politic," *The Pennsylvania Gazette*, November 8, 1759.

31. *Pennsylvania Gazette*, February 4, 1735. For another discussion of the linkages between public spiritedness and fire fighting, see Benjamin L. Carp, "Fire of Liberty: Firefighters, Urban Voluntary Culture, and the Revolutionary Moment," *William and Mary Quarterly*, 3d ser., 58 (2001): 781–818.
32. On the absence of a poor, tax-exempt class of men in mid-eighteenth-century Philadelphia, see Gary B. Nash, *The Urban Crucible: Social Change, Political Consciousness, and the Origins of the American Revolution* (Cambridge: Harvard UP, 1979), 179. On the exemption of most independent women from taxes because of poverty, see Karin A. Wulf, *Not All Wives: Women of Colonial Philadelphia* (Ithaca: Cornell UP, 2000), 99.
33. *Pennsylvania Gazette*, November 29, 1744; February 5, 1745; March 26, 1745.
34. Members of the contributorship elected to limit claims to five hundred pounds per policy instead of five hundred pounds per house, which had been the previous limit; see the *Pennsylvania Gazette*, April 3, 1760.
35. Ibid., May 1, 1740.
36. Ibid., May 8, 1740.
37. Ibid., May 15, 1740.
38. Ibid., May 22, 1740.
39. Ibid., May 29, 1740.
40. This understanding of the power of latent social practices is based on Pierre Bourdieu's concept of the "doxa," which he defines as "the aggregate of 'choices' whose subject is everyone and no one because the questions they answer cannot explicitly be asked." Bourdieu argues that these "doxic," or aggregate, practices carry such defining force precisely because they are often unarticulated, uncontested, or unspoken: "The truth of the doxa is only ever fully revealed when negatively constituted by the constitution of a *field of opinion*, the locus of the confrontation of competing discourses" (*Outline of a Theory of Practice*, trans. Richard Nice [New York: Cambridge UP, 1977], 168).
41. Nash 231–32; Sally F. Griffith, "'Order, Discipline, and a Few Cannons': Benjamin Franklin, the Association, and the Rhetoric and Practice of Boosterism," *Pennsylvania Magazine of History and Biography* 116 (1992): 131–55; Barbara A. Gannon, "The Lord Is a Man of War, the God of Love

and Peace: The Association Debate, Philadelphia, 1747–48" *Pennsylvania History* 65 (1998): 46–61.

42. [Benjamin Franklin], *Plain Truth: or, Serious Considerations on the Present State of the City of Philadelphia, and Province of Pennsylvania*, in *The Papers of Benjamin Franklin*, ed. Leonard W. Labaree et al., 36 vols. (in progress) (New Haven: Yale UP, 1959–), 3:180–204.

43. The speech by Cato was cited in Latin on the title page of the first edition of *Plain Truth*, with an English translation printed in the *Gazette* two days later and on the second printing of the pamphlet. This citation of the English quotation of Cato is taken from the *Pennsylvania Gazette*, November 19, 1747.

44. [Franklin], *Plain Truth*, in *Papers of Benjamin Franklin*, 3:202–3.

45. *Form of Association*, in *Papers of Benjamin Franklin*, 3:205–12.

46. Ibid., 3:206.

47. Ibid., 3:206, 209–11.

48. *Pennsylvania Gazette*, December 12, 1747).

49. Ibid., January 5, 1748.

50. Ibid., January 12, 1748.

51. Ibid., April 16, 1748.

52. The *Gazette* describes eight different musters either reported after the fact or scheduled to occur in the near future (dates listed in *Gazette* in parenthesis): December 5, 1747 (December 12, 1747); January 2, 1748 (January 5, 1748); February 17, 1748 (January 26, 1748); April 12, 1748 (March 29, 1748); May 24, 1748 (March 29, 1748); June 3, 1748 (June 9, 1748); June 15, 1748 (June 23, 1748); August 29, 1748 (September 1, 1748).

53. This understanding of the equalizing possibilities ritual affords is drawn from Victor Turner's analysis of "liminality" within the ritual process. See his *Ritual Process: Structure and Anti-Structure* (New York: Aldine DeGruyer, 1969).

54. See Benedict Anderson, *Imagined Communities: Reflections on the Origins and Spread of Nationalism*, 2d ed. (New York: Verso, 1991), esp. 53–54 (on Turner's ritual process); 37–46 (on print's role in constructing a public imaginary); and 47–66 (on the operation of this process in the Americas). Interestingly, Anderson singles out Franklin as the archetypal creole nationalist, arguing that his profession was central to his nationalism (61). Franklin's role as both the organizer and chief reporter of the Association would seem to confirm Anderson's hypothesis.

55. Warner 38, 42.

56. Richard L. Bushman, *The Refinement of America: Persons, Houses, Cities* (New York: Vintage, 1992), 71; Claudia B. Kidwell and Margaret C, Christman, *Suiting Everyone: The Domestication of Clothing in America* (Washington, D.C.: Smithsonian, 1974), 33; Edward Warwick, Henry C. Pitz, and Alexander Wycoff, *Early American Dress: The Colonial and Revolutionary Period* (New York: Amaryllis P, 1965).
57. The majority of times an individual's ethnic identity was mentioned or discussed in the *Gazette* from 1727 to 1765, clothing was used to describe his/her appearance.
58. On the distinctiveness of Quaker dress, see Smolenski, "Friends and Strangers"; and Joan C. Kendall, "The Development of a Distinctive Form of Quaker Dress," *Costume* 19 (1985): 58–74.
59. *Pennsylvania Gazette*, February 28, 1765; March 7, 1765; March 14, 1765; April 11, 1765; May 16, 1765; December 19, 1765.
60. Mah 170.
61. For a more general assessment of the possibilities of the study of periodical literature, see Mark Kamrath, "*Eyes Wide Shut* and the Cultural Poetics of Eighteenth-Century American Periodical Literature," *Early American Literature* 37 (2002): 497–536. While this particular essay examines one specific newspaper, this approach toward analyzing magazines and other forms of eighteenth-century periodical literature can yield insight into the struggle to define legitimate public expression. In the early republic, for example, magazine authors frequently engaged in debates over associational practices, and often these discussions went beyond simple descriptions of a club's actions and became metacultural commentaries on the meaning of associational activity itself. An investigation of the competing metacultural cues intended to shape how readers interpreted associational activity might reveal something about the process by which particular expressions of the public good came to be legitimated as expressions of "the" public good. See, for example, the debate over the "character" of a proper club in "Description of a Club," *Massachusetts Magazine: or, Monthly Museum of Knowledge and Rational Entertainment* (April 1789): 219–21, and Ruricola, "Description of a Rural Club," *Massachusetts Magazine* (May 1789): 260–61; the discussion of the character of club members in Z, "The Club—No. II," *New-York Magazine, or Literary Repository* (July 1790): 379–81; and Acasto M, "The Club—No. IV," *New-York Magazine* (September 1790): 498–500.
62. Greg Urban, "Culture's Public Face," *Public Culture* 5 (1993): 216–18.

63. For example, while U.S. culture might claim "omega" cultural status in reference to "alpha" ethnic subcultures within the country, it would appear as merely one "alpha" culture among many in reference to other national cultures.

64. Urban 228.

65. Ibid., 216.

W. M. Verhoeven

"A Colony of *Aliens*"

Germans and the German-Language Press in Colonial and Revolutionary Pennsylvania

> This will in a few Years become a German Colony: Instead of their Learning our Language, we must learn their's, or live as in a foreign Country. Already the English begin to quit particular Neighbourhoods surrounded by Dutch, being made uneasy by the Disagreeableness of disonant Manners; and in Time, Numbers will probably quit the Province for the same Reason.
>
> —*The Papers of Benjamin Franklin*

Benjamin Franklin is not known for being a close friend of the immigrant Germans in Pennsylvania. Seeing them initially, in the 1730s, as a mere nuisance, or at best as an unwieldy tool in his own political schemes, Franklin came to regard the Germans as a serious threat to British American identity, even to the very future of Pennsylvania, as German immigration rapidly increased in the 1740s and 1750s. The fact that as early as 1732 it was Franklin who published the first German-language newspaper in America should therefore be treated with considerable suspicion: rather than a gesture of cross-cultural goodwill or—as has been suggested—a shrewd business initiative in a growing market for German-language printing,[1] *Die Philadelphische Zeitung* was in fact a calculated attempt to break the German-Quaker alliance that dominated the Pennsylvania Assembly and held sway over local politics in the colony.[2]

Franklin's pioneering venture into German-language printing was the beginning of a long and complex history of the German press in colonial and Revolutionary America—a history that reflects perhaps most signally, as some have argued, how the Germans turned the balance in favor of the drive for independence and thus decided the outcome of the War against Britain.[3] Being the largest of the non-British European immigrant groups that shaped eighteenth-century American culture and demographics, the German-language immigrants were a cultural and political force to be reckoned with—a position that was rendered even more significant because the large majority of German immigrants settled in segregated, tightly organized ethnic enclaves in a relatively confined geographical area. Nearly 80 percent of the German-speaking immigrants went to Pennsylvania, at least initially, and Pennsylvania accounted for a similar share in the number of German-language newspapers and periodical publications in British North America and the United States prior to 1830.[4] Also, in terms of circulation, German-language periodicals and newspapers far outnumbered those in any other foreign language. Although in absolute numbers they represented only a small percentage of the total number of periodicals and newspapers published in British North America as a whole, German-language publications clearly constituted a significant presence in the public sphere in eighteenth-century America, especially given their concentration in Pennsylvania and surroundings states.

When considering German-language publications in the eighteenth century, it is important to be aware that there were no clear generic markers distinguishing one periodical publication from another. Though this may to some extent be true for English-language publications as well, the situation appears to be particularly murky for the German-language periodicals. Thus, several of the "newspapers" discussed here offered themselves to the public as "Zeitung" but would not qualify as such today; conversely, some of the "periodicals"—often called "Magazin" or "Wochenschrift" (weekly)—might qualify today as newspapers, be it that in most cases they appeared less frequently than newspapers. Frequency of publication is in fact almost never a clear distinguishing feature, nor is content or subject matter. What is probably the first German-language periodical, Christoph Saur's *Ein Geistliches Magazien* (1764–72) was in fact a free supplement to a newspaper—or rather a personal gift from a benevolent publisher, who was concerned about the spiritual well-being of his subscribers. If that does not disqualify it as a periodical, its highly erratic appearance rate might, for the magazine appeared whenever the publisher had time and copy to print. The first German-language magazine that explicitly affiliated itself as such was *Das Philadelphisches Magazin* (1798), published by H. and J. R. Kämmerer Jr. Unlike *Ein Geistliches Magazien, Das Philadelphisches Magazin* was launched to be published on a periodical basis (once every three months—though it did not survive beyond the first issue); however, its contents—a blend of domestic and foreign news, remarkable events, "curious histories," "heroic adventures," advertisements, anecdotes, and an occasional piece of verse—barely distinguished it from periodicals appearing at the same time under the banner of "Zeitung" or "Geschichts-Schreiber" (chronicler).[5] Topicality directing the choice of the events and the issues covered is an obvious feature of a newspaper; yet few German-language newspapers in eighteenth-century America had anything of the temporal immediacy one would expect from a newspaper. Of course, news in general, and foreign news in particular, traveled slowly in the eighteenth century and was often old news by the time it was printed, but this was especially so in the case of German and other foreign-language newspapers simply because most news items had to be translated before they could be printed. Not surprisingly, with some regularity German printers complained that their subscribers failed to appreciate the additional cost and effort involved in producing a German-language periodical or newspaper in America. Add to the translation issue the delay with which news from Germany (often not published elsewhere) reached the German printers in America, and it becomes obvious why an eighteenth-century German-language newspaper would often read like a weekly or a monthly—even though it might appear three times a week.

All this is not to say that there were not any German-language newspapers that could face the competition with their English-language counterparts: on the contrary. Thus, despite the proliferation of German-language printing in the eighteenth century, it is still little known that the very first announcement of the adoption of the Declaration of Independence was printed not in English but in German, in Henrich Miller's *Pennsylvanischer Staatsbote* of July 5, 1776; it was the same Miller who on July 9 printed the first translation of the complete text of the Declaration—being only the third printing of the text in American newspapers. Also, during the Revolutionary War, the German press was courted and sponsored at various points by both the loyalists and the patriots as part of their strategic propaganda campaigns. If, as Christopher Looby has argued in *Voicing America*, "Nations are not born, but made. And they are made, ineluctably, in language," then the German printers and pamphleteers were prominent among the makers of the Republic.[6]

One should not underestimate either the significance or the complexity of the German-language press in eighteenth-century America, before, during, and after the Revolution.[7] The German immigrant assimilation into the socio-economic and political framework of eighteenth-century colonial and Revolutionary America was *not*, as Aaron Fogleman has recently suggested, a matter of a "collective strategy" for the sake of ethnic survival, but a vociferous and at times painful process of transculturation marked by sharp ideological differences and divided loyalties—both before and after July 1776.[8] Being the largest European immigrant community and as such at the center of the national and transnational political and military tug-of-war, the Germans, more than any other non-British immigrant group, faced the daunting choice of whether to preserve and institutionalize their European ethnic and religious identity and—as Franklin put it—"by herding together establish their language and Manners to the Exclusion of [the English]"[9] or to subscribe to the growing spirit of American patriotism and thus become Americanized at the expense of their

German ethnic identity. In the predominantly retrospective historiographical accounts of Revolutionary and early-national America, the dynamic of this crucial choice of cultural (trans-)formation has so far been underexposed.[10] The question, in other words, that still needs to be addressed today is to what extent did the Germans "unmake" themselves while "making" America?

Roughly speaking, the German-language printers in Pennsylvania in the pre-Revolutionary period consisted of two distinct groups: there was the Saur dynasty of Germantown (Christoph Saur I, his son, Christoph Saur II, and his grandsons, Christoph Saur III and Peter), and a number of their satellites and associates;[11] and there were Saur's competitors, mainly located in Philadelphia, where Anton Armbrüster and, notably, Henrich Miller were the leading figures.[12] The basis for this division is to be found in the two main religious denominations among the German settlers in Pennsylvania: on the one hand, there were the so-called sectarians, or "mystics" or "radical pietists," which included the Mennonites, the Amish, the Dunkards, the Schenkfelders, and the Waldensians; and on the other hand, there were the more liberal, nonsectarian "Church people," notably the Lutherans and the German Reformed; the Moravians were positioned somewhere in between, now siding with this group, now with the other, depending on the issue.[13] The former were opposed to legal procedure, higher education, an educated clergy, all worldly rituals and forms, and war and military service; the latter believed in higher education, in simple ritual, an educated clergy, in formal legal procedure, and in military service when necessary.[14] Both groups, however, had a strong love for the German language, which went far beyond the linguistic and the folkloristic: both the sectarians and the moderates believed—at least until the 1790s—that in the preservation and protection of the German language lay the preservation and protection of their faith, their freedom, indeed, their very survival, both in cultural and in ethnic terms. Characteristically, Christoph Saur I took great pride in the fact that the Bible that he printed in 1743 was the first to appear in America in a European language; writing in 1763 in the preface to the second edition, his son, Christoph Saur II no less proudly observes: "Es erscheint nun zum zweytenmal in diesem Americanischen Welttheil die Heilige Schrifft, die Bibel genannt, in hochteutscher Sprache in öffentlichem Druck; zum Ruhm der Teutschen Nation, indem keine andere Nation wird aufzeugen können, dass die Bibel in diesem Welttheil in ihrer Sprache sen gedruckt worden."[15] This triumphalist claim may sound slightly immodest for a pious sectarian, but the record of the Saur printing house fully justifies this momentary lapse: together the elder Saur and his son printed more than 150 books, an annual almanac, a newspaper, and countless pamphlets and broadsides. During the first half of the eighteenth century, the center of the German-language press and book distribution was in rural Pennsylvania and was dominated by the pacifist German sectarians. It was more than anything else their *pacifism* that would ultimately undermine the position of the sectarian printers: first the French and Indian War and then the build-up to the Revolutionary War increasingly compromised the sectarian Germans and their press, while the nonsectarian, Philadelphia-based printers, who were more sympathetic toward the national cause, gradually began to get the upper hand in the course of the 1760s and 1770s.

Among those who played a crucial part in trying to obfuscate the significance of the sectarian Germans and their press in the colonial and early-Revolutionary period was one of the very shapers, and printers, of American identity, that is, Franklin himself. Thus, one of the earliest and most influential of German printers, Christoph Saur I (1694–1758), is conspicuously absent from Franklin's *Autobiography*, even though Saur repeatedly frustrated Franklin's political schemes, which included setting up English-language schools among Germans, invalidating public documents written in German, banning from public office those who did not speak English, and closing Pennsylvania to further German-speaking immigrants. It must have taunted Franklin that while his own *Philadelphische Zeitung* folded after the second issue, mainly because of a boycott by German readers, Christoph Saur, a pious but tough Anabaptist in Germantown, was running the widely read and much-trusted *Der Hoch-Deutsch Pennsylvanischer Geschicht-Schreiber*, as well as a German-language almanac, *Der Hoch-Deutsch Americanische Calender*, that was a direct competitor of Franklin's own *Poor Richard* (the German calendars were selling at 120,000 copies a year). It was Saur's paper—now renamed *Pensylvanische Berichte*—that in 1747–48 dared to launch an attack on Franklin's plan for an association for the defense of Pennsylvania and thereby, to Franklin's deep disgust, managed to persuade the Germans to avoid the Association. Significantly, there is no mention of Saur's media victory over Franklin in the *Autobiography*. Indeed, while Franklin briefly refers to the German translation of his "Fast proclamation," which was intended to drum up support among the Germans for the Association, he misleadingly observes that such support "would probably have been general among all but Quakers if the Peace [of Aix-la-Chapelle, October 1748] had not soon interven'd."[16] The influence of Saur's paper among the German immigrants was so great that in 1755 Franklin was driven to finance a rival German press in an attempt to force Saur out of business—a scheme that sadly failed: Franklin's *Die Philadelphische Zeitung*, printed by Anton Armbrüster, folded in 1757, Saur's paper continued to thrive.[17]

An extraordinary letter to Peter Collison of May 1753 confirms in the most revealing way that it was above all the independent German-language press, and especially its capacity to render the German settlers inaccessible to his ideological mission of "whiting" America, that madc Franklin dread the German predominance in Pennsylvania so much:

> Not being used to Liberty, they know not how to make a modest use of it. . . . They behave, however, submissively enough at present to the Civil Government which I wish they may continue to do: For I remember when they modestly declined intermingling in our Elections, but now they come in droves, and carry all before them, except in one or two Countries; Few of their children in the Country learn English; they import many books from Germany; and of the six printing houses in the Province, two are entirely German, two half German half English, and but two entirely English; They have one German News-paper, and one half-German. Advertisements intended to be general are now printed in Dutch [i.e. German] and English; the Signs in our Streets have inscriptions in both languages, and in some places only German: They begin of late to make all their Bonds and other legal Writings in their own Language, which (though I think it ought not to) are allowed good in our Courts, where the German Business so encreases that there is continual need of Interpreters; and I suppose in a few years they will be also necessary in the Assembly, to tell one half of our Legislators what the other half say. . . .[18]

Saur may have been a devout and god-fearing Christian, but when it came to defending the freedom of his religion, his language, and his cultural heritage, he could wield a pen as sharp as any. Thus, in a 1755 broadside titled "Eine zu dieser Zeit höchstnöthige Warnung und Erinnerung an die freye Einwohner der Provinz Pensylvanien von Einem, dem die Wohlfahrt des Landes angelegen und darauf bedacht ist,"[19] Saur in glowing language reminds his readers that their freedom is their "natürliches Recht" (their natural right) and that they should therefore no longer feel like second-rate citizens. In what seems like a direct challenge to what Franklin described as the Germans' "intermingling in our Elections," Saur strongly urges his countrymen to go out and vote during the upcoming elections for the Assembly, so that the candidates who are most likely to defend their rights and freedom will be elected, rather than "die Feinde euer Freyheiten" (the enemies of your liberties):

> Ihr habt das Recht zu allen Freyheiten eines Englisch-Gebohrnen, und habt das Antheil an den Grund Gesetzen des Landes. Ihr sind Menschen, die Verstand haben; lasset mich euch nochmalen ermahnen, das ihr euren guten Verstand auch gebrauchet, euch ermuntert, und eure Freyheit behauptet.[20]

And he reminds his fellow countrymen what would happen if they did not vote in the right members: "Die unglückliche Deutschen würden viel ein schwerreres Joch tragen müssen, als diejenige Tyrannen war, warum sie aus ihrem Lande entflohen sind" (the unfortunate Germans would have a much heavier cross to bear than was the tyrant because of whom they fled their country). The reference here is almost certainly to the act being prepared in the Assembly providing for a militia, of which the governor was to act as commander in chief—a militia which, Saur comments sarcastically, was not meant to provide protection against "den Einfällen der fremden Feinden" (the attacks from foreign enemies), but "nur eure Rechte and Privilegien sollen aufgegeben und überliffert werden in die Hände eurer Einheimischen Feinden" (only to curtail your rights and privileges, and deliver them into the hands of your domestic enemies).

Saur does not mention Franklin by name as one of the Assemblymen who were antagonistic to German freedom and rights, but it may be more than a coincidence that Saur's broadside appeared in the same year—1755—in which Franklin, in his essay "Observations Concerning the Increase of Mankind," notoriously referred to the Germans as "Palatine Boors" who were allegedly about to take over Pennsylvania from the British.[21] Whether Franklin actually meant "hogs" ("boars")—and not "peasants"—when he used the word "boors" was and still is a moot point,[22] but what *is* clear is that there was an element of racial prejudice in the way he worded his resentment against the German settlers. Referring to German immigrants (along with the Spaniards, Italians, French, Russians, and Swedes—though not the Saxons) as being "of what we call a swarthy Complexion," Franklin ponders,

> "Why should Pennsylvania, founded by the English, become a Colony of *Aliens*, who will shortly be so numerous as to Germanize us instead of our Anglifying them, and will never adopt our Language or Customs, any more than they can acquire our Complexion. . . . I could wish their Numbers [of "purely white People"] were increased. And while we are, as I may call it, *Scouring* our Planet, by clearing America of Woods, and so making this Side of our Globe reflect a brighter Light to the Eyes of Inhabitants in Mars and Venus, why should we in the Sight of Superior Beings, darken its People?"[23]

If Franklin—be it only from the early 1770s onward—increasingly began to manifest himself as an active campaigner in the Abolitionist movement, both inside and outside of politics, this only adds further weight to the suspicion that for Franklin (and for the British Americans in Pennsylvania in general) the rural Germans were a potentially bigger threat than black people—in cultural, economical and political terms.[24] Unlike the black population, the German immigrants, many of them well-trained craftsmen or land-owning farmers, were for the most part literate; moreover, thanks to printers such as the Saurs, they were well informed about events outside their communities, in the Pennsylvania Assembly as well as further afield, in other parts of America and in Europe. Seeing that the German immigration from the Palatinate and other regions in the southwest of Germany peaked in 1753 and that these particular immigrants tended to travel and settle in close family units, it is not surprising that it was precisely in the early 1750s that Franklin began to develop pre-Malthusian concerns about the increase of population in general and about the increase of the German population in Pennsylvania in particular.

In terms of numbers, the Germans would easily have been able to dominate the Pennsylvania Assembly in the 1740s and 1750s, had they wished to do so. Of those Germans that bothered to exercise their right to vote, most—notably the peace-loving sectarians—had traditionally used their vote in support of the Quaker party, effectively handing the Quakers political control over the colony even though they were a minority. However, in the wake of the buildup to the military conflict between the English and the French and the resulting militarization of the political agenda (with calls for the introduction of a militia, taxation, conscription), pressure increased on the Germans to show where their true allegiance lay—and Franklin's efforts both to woo and to shame the Germans into jumping on his military bandwagon are to be seen as part of this process. It was clearly Saur's "Urgent Warning" and similar pamphlets, though, that won the day in the pamphlet wars occasioned by the 1754 and 1755 Assembly elections; Saur not only succeeded in persuading the peaceable German settlers to come to vote, but also to vote out the "Governor's Party" led by Franklin.[25] Measured by its immediate political impact, the mid-1750s marked the high point of the Saur press. However, two developments were soon to break the hegemony of Saur's press and his control of the German vote: the defeat of General Braddock's army in July 1755 and the effects on the electorate of a crucial shift in German immigration patterns. The former event left the Germans settlers in the western Pennsylvania hinterland defenseless against increasingly brutal Indian raids upon their settlements—which not only triggered a mass exodus to towns in the east of the province but, more important, had an immediate impact on the German vote as a whole from the 1756 Assembly elections onward.[26] At the same time, with the immigration of the peace denominations having virtually ceased by 1725 and the immigration of the more liberal "Church people" having peaked in the early 1750s, the Saur empire began to run into opposition from within the German immigrant community itself. Significantly, at the 1756 Assembly elections, the liberal Germans, throwing their weight in with the Scotch-Irish Presbyterians (whose religious beliefs were close to their own) voted against the Quakers—thereby effectively ending Quaker control of the province.

Not only was he a formidable defender of the sovereignty of his ethnicity and his language, the elder Saur was also a key player in the fierce battle over the introduction of the so-called charity schools among the German-speaking immigrants in Pennsylvania—a battle with a complex, transatlantic twist. In order to combat the growing power of the German language, Proprietor Thomas Penn founded the "London Society for the Support of Schools among the German Protestants in Pennsylvania" in 1753. A scheme that was well backed financially by the highest British authorities, including George II, Penn's "charity schools" were actually an attempt to anglicize the German immigrants and thereby to curb the influence of the various German religious enclaves. For a while Penn's ambitions coincided with similar attempts undertaken by the church authorities in Germany and Holland (notably the German Reformed synods in Amsterdam), who, as a result of the sharp increase of emigration in the 1740s and 1750s, were beginning to dread the loss of souls as well as of bodies in the migration. However, the members of the Dutch Synod soon began to realize that Penn's charity schools were not intended to educate poor German immigrants but to teach the Germans English, possibly even English religion. While the Dutch Synod began to redirect its educational initiatives in Pennsylvania by setting up its own schools, it was Christoph Saur with his paper *Der Hoch-Deutsch Pennsylvanische Geschicht-Schreiber* who led the attack against the hated charity schools from within Pennsylvania itself.[27]

Saur's *Pennsylvanische Geschicht-Schreiber*, which ran (under different names) for an unprecedented thirty-eight years (from 1739 to 1777), has been described as "the most influential German journal of the early Colonial period."[28] Its purpose was not merely to provide news, but primarily to offer stories which might promote Christian devotion, meditation, and "Furcht Gottes" (fear of God). For in the final analysis, Saur regarded his activities as a printer—from his more worldly newspaper, to his calendar, to his editions of the Bible—as part of God's divine plan: even though, as in the case of the charity schools, the moral purpose of his paper would sometimes acquire less pious overtones, he would use his publications as downright political tools only when the freedom of his faith, or his political interest, came under attack. His most spiritual (noncommercial, nonpolitical) publication was a periodical in the narrow definition of the term, which he published out of a sense of religious duty and for the mere pleasure of printing itself: he once referred to the production of his magazine as "Liebes-Arbeit" (labor of love).[29]

Generally regarded as the first religious periodical in America, *Ein Geistliches Magazin* appeared at irregular intervals between 1764 and the 1770s. The eight-page issues were numbered but not dated. Since they were distributed free of charge as a supplement to his son's newspaper, the issues appeared whenever Saur had sufficient copy and time and paper to print it. In his preface to the first issue, he explained the genesis of his magazine. It had saddened him that there were so many families he knew in Germantown who had no religious books other than the Bible, often because they were too poor to buy any; hence, he suggested that if they simply stitched the issues together after a while, they would thus acquire "ein schönes Haus-Magazien" (a nice family magazine) free of charge.[30]

The issues of *Ein Geistliches Magazien* would typically be filled with religious observations; extracts from German religious books and translations from similar works in English; narratives designed for moral instruction ("Warnung an die Jugend vor Verführung zum Bösen" [A Warning to the Young against Temptation to Evil]); and articles on the religious education of children ("Hundert nöthige Sitten-Regeln für Kinder" [One Hundred Necessary Moral Rules for Children]). Whenever he was low on copy from contributors, which seems to have been the case frequently, Saur would choose extracts from his own favorite religious publications, and thus in one sense *Ein Geistliches Magazien* became the spiritual autobiography of its printer. In his choice of texts Saur revealed a clear predilection for unworldly, pious, and devout men of faith, in particular mystics. In the second issue, for instance, Saur reprints sections from *A Serious Call to a Devout and Holy Life* (1728), the most influential book by the English nonjuror and mystic William Law (1686–1761). He continues printing extracts from Law's *Ernstlichen Ruff* in issues 3 and 4. In the eighth issue Saur begins extracting a biography of the German mystic and itinerant preacher Hans Schwärmer Engelbrecht (1599–1642), whose popular following among the poor incited the wrath of the church authorities. *Das Leben Hans Engelbrechts* would fill another five issues of *Ein Geistliches Magazien*. In what is probably his own translation, Saur devotes two issues (31 and 32) to the remarkable lectures and sermons of another devout man of God, the French Huguenot theologian and "sehr Gottesfürtichtigen Prediger" (very God-fearing preacher), Andrew Rivet (1573–1651). Occasionally, when no copy had been submitted for some time, Saur offers his readers a reflection on his own faith and on his life with and for God, as in issue 21. But even then he remains a meek and God-fearing man whose only certainty in life is that without God, man is doomed to a life of evil and sin, since evil and sin are firmly lodged in man's "eigenen Alt-Adamisch-verdorbenen Herzen."[31] In the last four issues of the first series, Saur reprints *Das Geheimniss der geistlichen Geburt Christi in uns* (The Mystery of the Spiritual Birth of Christ in Us), a little-known spiritual treatise by Adam Gottlieb Weigen (1677–1727).

Despite the magazine's intensely spiritual mission, with Saur deliberately having steered clear of any denominational or doctrinarian issues, some of his readership had apparently taken offence at his private initiative to instill the fear of God in his fellow countrymen. In the afterword to the fiftieth issue, Saur resolutely brushes aside all criticism of his magazine and shows himself determined to continue it. But at the same time he announces that he will temporarily have to suspend the publication of *Ein Geistliches Magazien* because the new

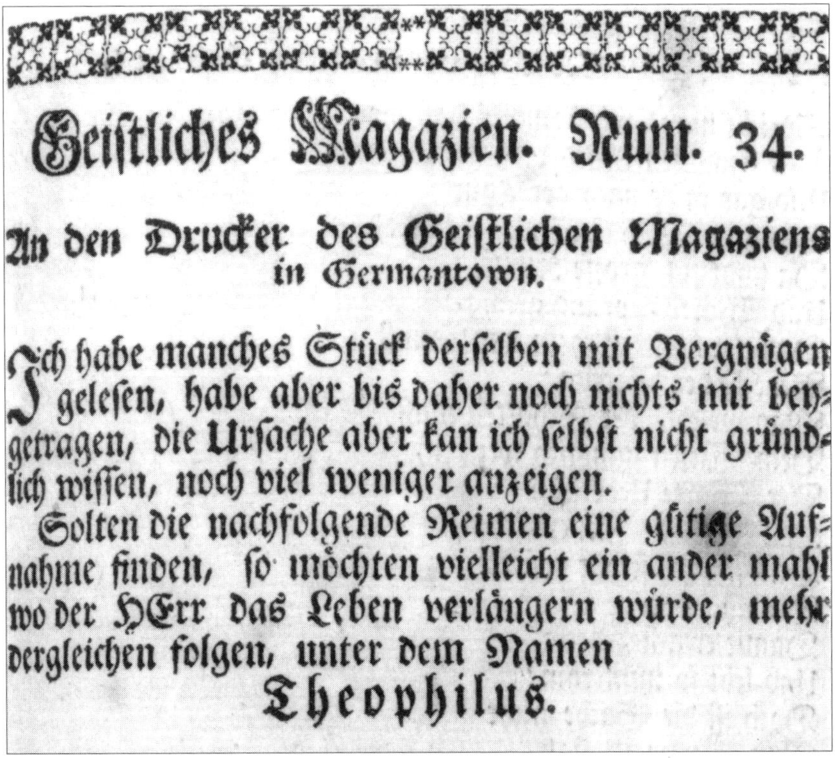

Geistliches Magazien. Num. 34.

An den Drucker des Geistlichen Magaziens
in Germantown.

Ich habe manches Stück derselben mit Vergnügen gelesen, habe aber bis daher noch nichts mit beygetragen, die Ursache aber kan ich selbst nicht gründlich wissen, noch viel weniger anzeigen.

Solten die nachfolgende Reimen eine gütige Aufnahme finden, so möchten vielleicht ein ander mahl wo der HErr das Leben verlängern würde, mehr dergleichen folgen, unter dem Namen

Theophilus.

Title page from *Ein Geistliches Magazien, oder: aus den Schatzen der Schrifftgelehrten zum Himmelreich gelehrt, dargereichtes Altes and Neues,* "An den Drucker des Geistlichen Magaziens in Germantown," no. 34 (1764). A reader of Christoph Saur's *Ein Geistliches Magazien* writes that he has enjoyed earlier issues of the journal but that he regrets not having contributed himself. Under the pen-name "Theophilus," he offers a German translation of an English poetic dialogue between a scholar and a woman, which a friend of his had read in the *Pennsylvania Chronicle* the week before. His remarks illustrate how German and English texts circulated as part of one print economy in eighteenth-century Pennsylvania, with the German press sometimes following, at other times leading, the English-language press. Courtesy of the Historical Society of Pennsylvania.

edition of the Bible that was being printed in the Saur print shop at the time was absorbing all the type, paper, labor, and resources that were available.

Saur was true to his word, for in 1770 he started the second series of *Ein Geistliches Magazien*, which would ultimately comprise another fifteen issues. In the preface to the first issue of the new series, Saur lifts the veil a little on the nature of the controversy that the first series of the supplement had caused among some of the newspaper's subscribers. Apparently some people had complained that he had launched his magazine merely to promote certain schools of faith and to denigrate others; some of the newspaper's more secular subscribers had resented Saur's interfering with what he calls their "Fleisches-Ruhe und sündlichem Leben."[32] Indeed, there had been those, Saur goes on to report, who had burned issues of his magazine in rage, while others had expressed their resentment by folding the magazines and using them as paper bags.[33] Though perhaps only anecdotal evidence, the episode certainly suggests that by the early 1770s Germantown was by no means the uniform, homogenous ethnic enclave that many have assumed it was. Despite opposition from some corners, however, Saur remained true to his spiritual mission. Only for a brief moment did the proud printer in him outweigh the devout Christian when Saur notified his readers at the end of the twelfth issue that it had been printed using "the first type ever cast in America."[34] The last issue of *Ein Geistliches Magazin* appeared in 1772.

The elder Saur was an Anabaptist and a conscientious objector to all war (hence his stand against Franklin's militia); his son, Christoph II (1721–1784), was an orthodox Dunkard, and as such also opposed to war; however, soon after he took over his father's newspaper in 1758 (renamed to *Germantowner Zeitung*), Christoph II was to find that the rising tensions between the loyalists and the patriots no longer allowed a sectarian printer to remain quite so unworldly and politically circumspect as the newspaper's founder had been. There is no definite evidence to suggest that Christoph II either favored or opposed the War of Independence (for one thing, only five issues of his paper from the war period survive), but it is likely that, like most of the peace-loving sectarians, he would have sided with the British in the conflict.[35] He was detained by the patriots for a few days after having spent some time with his sons in Philadelphia in October 1777. Squashed between the conflicting political forces of the patriots and the British and distrusted by both sides, Christoph II soon found himself without any space for maneuvering. Thus, rather abruptly and inauspiciously, the sectarian German-language press and propaganda in Germantown had ended.[36]

During the British occupation of Philadelphia (1777–1778), Christoph III and Peter continued their father's *Germantowner Zeitung* as *Der Pennsylvanische Staats-Courier*, but they turned it into a radically different newspaper. A coarse and rabid Tory paper, *Der Pennsylvanische Staats-Courier* catered in part for the thousands of German mercenaries in Philadelphia—something that earned the brothers the dubious sobriquet of "General Howe's German Printers." In the issue of February 18, 1778, the Saur brothers published a bitter attack on the patriots, denouncing ministers of the Gospel such as Peter Muhlenberg as political market criers and depicting Benjamin Franklin as a dismissed postmaster now appointed ambassador to a royal court.[37] When the British evacuated Philadelphia (June 16, 1778), the brothers hastily fled to St. Johns, New Brunswick, where they published another Tory paper, the *Royal Gazette*. Their press and their possessions in Philadelphia were confiscated by the patriots and subsequently sold. By then Christoph II had already returned to Germantown, where he was arrested by the patriots for refusing to take an oath of loyalty to the new government—after which his property, too, was confiscated and sold at an auction.[38]

While the services of the German sectarian printers were enlisted in the war by the loyalist side, those of the more liberal German printers were sought after by the patriots—illustrating the crucial role played by German-language printing in the critical years during which the future of British North America was decided. When it first appeared on January 18, 1762, John Henrich Miller's *Der Wöchentliche Philadelphische Staatsbote* became the first serious competitor to the hegemony of the Saur press.[39] Through its subtitle the paper immediately distinguished itself from the Saur press: whereas Saur's *Pennsylvanische Geschicht-Schrieber* was subtitled "Sammlung Wichtiger Nachrichten aus dem Natur- und Kirchen-Reich" (A Collection of Important News from the Realms of Nature and the Church), Miller's *Staatsbote* announced in its subtitle that it would be concerned with "den neuesten Fremd- und Einheimisch-Politischen Berichten" (the latest foreign and domestic political news), adding in smaller print that it would also report on "den von Zeit zur Zeit in der Kirche und Gelehrten Welt sich ereignenden Merkwürdigkeiten" (interesting developments taking occasionally place in the church and the scholarly world). The four-page paper appeared twice a week, on Tuesdays and Fridays. Apart from a handful of advertisements (not infrequently offering rewards for information concerning runaway servants), the newspaper printed a wide array of news items, mostly translations from stories and notices carried in the English-language press. Since Miller had to do the translating as well as the printing, news items appeared in the *Staatsbote* a few days after they had appeared in the English newspapers.

Johann Henrich Müller (1702–1782), or Henry Miller, as he was known among English-speaking Americans, was a man with a wide experience in the printing business. Having served his apprenticeship in Basel, he was a journeyman printer in various European countries before coming over to America for the first time in 1741 with the Moravian leader Count Zinzendorf (whom he joined on his first missionary campaign to the Indians a year later). During a second stay in America (1751–1754), Miller worked for a while in Franklin's shop as the supervisor of his German-language printing; it is likely he also saw Franklin when both men stayed in London between 1757 and 1761, during which time Miller printed a newspaper for the fourteen thousand Hessians then quartered there.[40] Given that they knew each other and had worked together and given that Franklin continually backed other German papers, it is quite possible that Franklin was the spiritual, if not the financial backer of Miller's *Staatsbote*.

With tensions beginning to rise between the colonies and the mother country in the early 1760s, Miller chose a propitious time to launch his newspaper. Thus, the first announcement that the British government was contemplating the introduction of the Stamp Act appeared in the *Staatsbote* on April 2, 1765—which marked the beginning of Miller's long and bitter campaign against the hateful act. Miller was doubly aggrieved by the Stamp Act, seeing that it was very much an anti-German act, levying higher taxes on the German-language printers.[41] He compared the introduction of the act on November 1, 1765, to the Lisbon earthquake, which also occurred on All Saints' Day, and he suspended publication of the *Staatsbote* between the October 31 issue and the November 18 issue, when the paper reappeared—on unstamped paper. Without actually calling for a revolt against the British authorities, Miller never left off hammering on about what he called "colonial rights," which he insisted the British had to respect, lest things should get out of control.

Being the main medium of German-American patriotism, Miller's *Staatsbote* is a fascinating account of the events that crowded the period between the repeal of the Stamp Act (March 1766) and the first rumblings of the war as experienced by the tens of thousands of nonsectarian Germans in Philadelphia and increasingly beyond (hence the change of name to *Pennsylvanischer Staatsbote* in January 1768). Initially merely distrustful of British intentions yet conciliatory, Miller gradually grew more militant; from 1775 onward there is a distinct trend toward armed resistance. Thus, the May 2 issue of the *Staatsbote* in that year is packed with extracts from letters that had arrived in various towns in the country and from other sources reporting that Gage's troops had marched on Lexington and Concord on April 19 and had clashed with the "Minutmänner" (Minutemen). Accounts of the number of casualties on both sides vary greatly from report to report, but all correspondents agree that it was a treacherous and unprovoked attack. While Miller abstains from any sort of comment, it is clear from his selections where his sympathies lie and what kind of response he is trying to evoke in his readers. Several of Miller's correspondents express their utter dismay at how the British regulars opened fire "ohne den geringsten erhaltenen anlaß, und ohne daß unsere leute einen einzigen schuß thaten" (for no apparent reason, and without a single shot being fired by our people) on a small group of Lexington Minutemen at their morning drill—who in one report were unarmed and in another armed with unloaded rifles. The same issue of the paper reports that five days after the skirmishes at Lexington and Concord eight thousand patriots met in Philadelphia "um maaßregeln zur erwägen, die bey dem gegenwärtigen verwirrten zustande Americanischer sachen befolgt werden sollen" (to consider measures that have to be taken in the present confusing state of American affairs); it also prints a call from "Die Committee für die Graffschaft Philadelphia" (the Committee for the County of Philadelphia) to meet on May 8 to discuss "sachen von der allergrößten wichtigkeit" (matters of the utmost importance).

In the weeks and months following Lexington and Concord, Miller's *Staatsbote* develops into what can be called the German-language branch of the propaganda network of the Continental Congress and the Pennsylvania Assembly, forming the logistical link between the American patriots and the German community. In the July 2, 1776, issue, for instance, Miller printed an appeal from Congress for the recruiting of four companies of German soldiers in both Pennsylvania and Maryland, which together were to form "das Deutsche Battallion." As the armed conflict deepened and the situation in Philadelphia became more and more hectic each day, Miller stepped up the frequency of the paper's appearance to several issues a week, especially during the months leading up to the adoption of the Declaration of Independence, which the *Staatsbote*, as previously noted, was the first newspaper in America to announce—and to state proudly—on July 5: "Gestern hat der Achtbare Congress dieses Vesten Landes die Vereinigten Colonien Freye und Unabhängige Staaten erkläret. Die Declaration in Englisch ist jetzt in der Presse; sie ist datiert, den 4ten July, 1776, und wird heut oder morgen im druck erscheinen."[42] This announcement of the Declaration was followed on July 9 by the full-text German translation.

Described by one commentator as an "unintentional autobiography,"[43] Miller's paper offers a vivid insight into daily life in Revolutionary Philadelphia during the first months of America's bid for freedom. Apart from the many detailed and unusually long reports and proceedings from the Continental Congress and the Pennsylvania Assembly, one may come across an advertisement for someone who could cast cannons (August 8, 1776); a notice that copies of "The American Crisis" 1 and 2 were now available at two pence and four pence, respectively (January 29, 1777); reports about the Revolutionary troops being quartered in schools and churches; and, as the weather got colder, calls to provide firewood at a patriotic price (December 19, 1776). There are also recurring reports on the recruitment of German mercenaries by the British authorities (April 2, 1777), Franklin's diplomatic mission to France (April 2, 1777; "Alle Augen von Europa sind auf den Doctor gerichtet" [All eyes of Europe are focused on the doctor]), and an announcement that Congress has chosen the flag of the United States (August 27, 1777). It is a sign of Miller's dedication to the patriotic cause that despite the sharp increase in the price of paper and the fact that more and more of his readers stopped paying their subscriptions, he continued to print—even though in December 1776 he was forced to reduce his paper to a weekly, single-sheet issue. While the English-language papers had already increased their subscription rates in the course of 1776, Miller held out until August 1777, when "Mit dem größten Verdruß" (to his deep regret) he had to announce that he, too, was forced to increase the subscription fee to the *Staatsbote*.

Then, on September 25, 1777, in one of the most dramatic moments in the paper's history, Miller had to flee from Philadelphia in a panic as General Howe's troops occupied the city. He did not have time to take his press with him, and the publication of the *Staatsbote* was suspended between issue 877 (September 9, 1777) and issue 878 (August 5, 1778). The British must have been well aware of the importance of Miller's press for the patriotic side, for when they evacuated Philadelphia in June 1778, General Howe's English printer, James Robertson, came with the king's wagons and men to haul away the Miller press to the ships (Franklin, we recall, had lost his own printing press to the looting Hessians shortly before). On July 22, 1778, Miller published a broadside ("Henrich Millers des Buchdruckers in Philadelphia, nöthige Vorstellung an die Deutschen in Pennsylvanien" [A Necessary Expostulation from Henry Miller, Printer in Philadelphia, to the Germans in Pennsylvania]), printed on a borrowed press, in which he accused the younger Saur of having appropriated from his press what Robertson had left behind, and of having destroyed the rest—presumably, Miller speculates, because Saur was convinced that Franklin had had a great stake in his press. Miller neither denies, nor confirms Saur's (alleged) conjecture, but he does end his broadside with an appeal to the authorities that they compensate him for his loss, being "ein nützlicher Mann dieser Stadt, ein ehrlicher Mann und wohlbekannter und bewährter Freund von America" (a useful man of this town, an honest man and a well-known and respected friend of America).

On a borrowed press and with the remainder of the German type that the robbers had left behind, Miller was back in business on August 5, be it only once a week (on Wednesdays), in a half-sheet size, but with his patriotic zeal unabated. However, Miller was approaching the age of eighty by now and was finding it harder and harder to do all the legwork and to generate enough interest in his paper to enable him to stay in business. In the September 30, 1778, issue, he complains that "Wenig Leute verstehen was für Mühe der drucker einer Deutschen zeitung hat: Fast jede Zeile muß übersetzt werden. Viele sind auch schon dazu gewöhnt, daß man ihre Anzeigen nicht nur umsonst übersetzt, sondern auch sogar aufsetzt. Wer alles dieses, und noch mehr, vernünftig überlegt, hat wol keine Ursach sich über den Preis dieser Zeitung zu beschweren."[44] The December 9 issue opens with his own advertisement announcing a vacancy for "ein ehrlicher frischer und starker Mensch von etwa 20 Jahren, der kein ordentlich Handwerk hat und die Preß-Arbeit in der Buchdruckeren lernen möchte,"[45] no doubt because Miller was at this time planning his retirement. Dwindling readership, competition from the English newspapers, rising prices, and the effects of old age finally forced Miller to end the *Staatsbote* on May 26, 1779. He spent his last days in the Moravian settlement in Bethlehem, where he died in 1782. His apprentices Steiner and Cist continued the patriotic mission of Miller's paper until the turn of the century.

The end of the Saur dynasty and the demise of Miller's empire by no means signaled the waning of the German-language in Pennsylvania. Even though for the urban German immigrants in particular English more and more became the language used in the public realm, reducing German increasingly to the language of the home and a ceremonial language of cultural memory, German printers continued to launch new newspapers and other periodicals well into the post-Revolutionary period. In the 1780s and 1790s several new German-language newspapers appeared, notably in urban centers, and in direct response to the growing tensions generated by the widening political divide in the country. And again, as during the Revolution, the German-American section of the population was split right down the middle, even while trying to hang on to their common German language and heritage. Thus, in 1790 a new German-language weekly, *Die Chestnuthiller Wochenschrift*, appeared in Philadelphia, printed by Samuel Saur (the youngest son of Christoph Saur II). It was a staunchly republican paper, which documented not only the political developments in the young Republic (including proceedings from "Der neuen, Deutschen, republicanischen Gesellschaft" [the New German Republican Society] in Philadelphia), but also covered at length the evolving Revolution in France during the early 1790s. Its Jacobin leanings were most apparent in its detailed and sympathetic accounts of discussions in the National Assembly and the Paris Jacobin Club. However, such an explicitly pro-French stance was increasingly hard to maintain in the political climate of the day, and the paper folded after less than three years in 1794.

Die Chestnuthiller Wochenschrift was the kind of "un-American" newspaper that came under heavy fire from one of the most curious German-language periodical publications, *Der Deutsche Porcupein, und Lancäster Anzeigs-Nachrichten* (The German Porcupine and Lancaster Advertiser). This weekly federalist newspaper was originally launched in Lancaster on August 8, 1787, as the *Neue Unpartheyische Lancäster Zeitung, und Anzeigs-Nachrichten* (New Independent Lancaster Newspaper and Advertiser) by the printer-publishers Anton Steimer, Johann Albrecht, and Jacob Lahn. Steimer is believed to have been apprenticed to Christoph Saur III; Albrecht was an apprentice to Christoph Saur II, and had come to Lancaster in 1788.[46] The paper's beginnings were innocent enough, for in the first issue the publishers stated that their only mission was to provide those German readers in Lancaster County that were "not too familiar with the English language" *unpartheyische* (nonpartisan) accounts of "alle verhandlungen der regierung, wichtige vorfälle und nachrichten" (all proceedings of the government, important events and news). And indeed, initially, the weekly adopted a rather pedestrian mode, providing a mixture of brief local, domestic, and foreign news items; pieces on the blessings of an agricultural existence;

announcements and advertisements; and "Freundschafliche Correspondenz" (polite correspondence). Steiner died in April 1788, and from the August 16, 1788, issue on the paper was published by Albrecht and Lahn, carrying on in much the same vein.

Then, out of the blue, the December 24 issue (73) opens with an extraordinary "Address to the Germans in America." Directed to the "Deutsche Männer" in particular, the author of the article starts off by reminding them they "are descended from a people that has no equal on earth, and no civilized nation exists at this time that is as old as the German nation; no nation was as courageous as the German, and none can claim that they are more enlightened" (my translation). The author subsequently launches into an excessive panegyric of the German people, claiming that the Germans made the Roman Empire tremble; conquered and occupied Italy, Spain, France, and Britain (among others), and repeating again and again that no nation on earth is as old, brave, and enlightened as the German nation. Shifting focus, the article then goes on to criticize the German Americans for having betrayed their proud heritage by not having acquainted themselves sufficiently with matters of state and government and for having allowed the English to run America by themselves. To amend this situation, the author proposes to write a ten- to twelve-volume history of all known peoples in human history, including an analysis of their customs, laws, religions, and forms of government. Since he estimates it will take him five to six years to complete it, the author ends by inviting the paper's readers to underwrite the publication.

The author of this article remains anonymous, but since it is the issue's opening piece and since it covers almost two entire pages out of a total of four, it can have appeared only with the moral support of the publishers. At any rate, the change of tone signaled in the address is symptomatic of the political course the paper took in subsequent months. After Lahn retired, the paper continued from March 1790 on under the responsibility of "Johanna Albrecht & Company"; it also began increasingly to reflect a Federalist bias. As the "Federalist reign of Terror" began to gain momentum in the second half of the 1790s, so did Albrecht's zealous support for the Federalist cause. On November 1, 1797, he discontinued the *Neue Unpartheyische Lancäster Zeitung* to relaunch it on January 3, 1798, now showing its true colors under its new title *Der Deutsche Porcupein, und Lancäster Anzeigs-Nachrichter.* Albrecht, too, had now thrown off all pretense. Immediately engaging in patriotic diatribe against the alleged enemies of the United States, Albrecht proudly announces his ambition to become the German-language equivalent of the "English Porcupine," launched by William Cobbett on September 6 the year before; he even sets himself the goal to surpass the three thousand subscriptions *Porcupine's Gazette* had attracted. Addressing the rhetorical questions, "Why a German Porcupine?" and "Aren't there enough newspapers as it is?" (my translation). Albrecht retorts that indeed there are too many newspapers, "aber diese haben unserm Lande mehr geschadet, als alle dessen offenbare Feinde je gethan haben oder thun können: Sie haben die franzosen darzu gebracht, das sie von einem Grad der Unverschämtheit zum anderen gegen uns gegangen sind, bis endlich ihre Gesandten unserm Washington Troz geboten."[47] And if that were not bad enough, Albrecht writes, the French had started pirating their defenseless merchant vessels, causing damage of more than twenty-five million dollars, as well as the nation's monetary crisis. Albrecht is clear about how to turn the tables on the Jacobins:

> "Das einzige Mittel ihnen [the French newspapers] entgegen zu arbeiten, isst eine dergleichen Zeitung, und die Feinde unsrer Regierung, fremde oder einheimliche zu entlarven—Der best Weg isst denen Democraten, Jacobinern und Unruhstiftern, sie auf ihrem eigenen Boden anzugreifen, ihnen Fus gegen Fus zu setzen, ihnen nicht ein Haarbreit nachzugeben, sie mit ihrem eigenen Waffen zu bekämpfen, und ihnen zwey Streiche für einen zo geben. . . . Denn eine Unwahrheit oder Falschheit der Jacobiner, welcher nicht widersprochen wird, wird für wahr gehalten."[48]

The year 1798, Albrecht threatens, will not be a happy one for the Democrats.

His subscribers and readers were less convinced of his new editorial course than Albrecht himself, for in the second issue of *Der Deutsche Porcupein* Albrecht reports of the dismay the newspaper's new title had caused and of the many poisoned letters he had received. He defends his decision by saying that with a title such as *Der Deutsche Porcupein,* unlike those other "unpartheyische" (nonpartisan) German newspapers, his newspaper at least could never be suspected of pocketing British and French gold. Proudly calling himself "ein alter 1776ger Americaner," Albrecht flatly refuses to budge and vows to continue to fight the "französisirten Americaner" (Frenchified Americans). So obsessed was Albrecht with "exterminating . . . the new French philosophy, and . . . Jacobin principles," that in the issues of February 14 and 21, 1798, he printed a proposal in English to publish a new newspaper, to be titled *The Times; or, Weekly Porcupine.* No such newspaper ever appeared, which suggests that Albrecht's zeal was a little too much for the Lancaster community to absorb. In December 1799 Albrecht quietly drew the curtain on his *Deutsche Porcupein;* tucked away on the bottom of page 3 of issue 104 appeared a three-line statement saying that the newspaper would reappear in the new year under a new title.

In retrospect, Johann Albrecht's German-dubbed Federalist zeal comes across as almost endearingly naïve, yet as his January 1798 manifesto makes clear, that same passion to be "ein wharer Americaner," or "a true American," only barely covers a crippling existential dilemma: whether to be a true American or a true German. The transculturation of the German immigrant population in America *was* such a torturous process because, being the largest non-English ethnic group, they had real choices—as Franklin realized only too well. But for the sharp divisions between the rural and the urban communities, and between the Federalists and the Democratic-Republicans, the Germans in America could have remained a distinct ethnic and cultural group for much longer, and German might have been the second official language of Pennsylvania after all. How unrealistic this turned out to be in hindsight is aptly illustrated by the "Address to the Germans in America": somehow the author of that document fails to see the discrepancy between talking about an undivided, world-encompassing German nation and the fact that most of them had come to America fleeing religious or political persecution or starvation back home. The sectarians never came to America to be Americans: they were ethnical purists, who wanted to be left alone, to their faith, their traditions, and their language. But the American Revolution did not leave them alone, and, like the loyalists, they discovered that neutrality was not an option; nor was cultural neutrality, after the war was over and the nation began to reinvent itself. As for the nonsectarian, urban German immigrants, they often all too eagerly chose to become Americans in the decades before the Revolution, in the expectation that they would be able to cling to their ethnic roots at the same time. Henrich Miller's story reveals that this was not the case. Those same nonsectarian Germans were subsequently drawn into America's postwar soul-searching, as the nation tried to figure out what the Revolution had really been about; as an ethnic group they emerged from this process as divided as was the nation as a whole.

The role of the German-language press in the 1790s rapidly changed as the consolidation of the American Revolution began to put more pressure on ethnic minorities to assimilate—on the urban settlers more so than on the rural sectarians. Although the Germans in America continued to speak German, marry Germans, and live among Germans, many of them (notably those in Philadelphia and communities in the east of the state) profiled themselves proudly and self-consciously as *Americans*—albeit Americans who happened to speak both English and German. Whereas for the sectarians clinging to the German language was a matter of safeguarding the position of the German religious denominations and hence of maintaining their European heritage (as with the dogmatic use of Dutch by the Dutch Reformed in Michigan until well into the twentieth century), for republicans such as Henrich Miller and Samuel Saur it was something different: their use of the German language was part of their heritage, not of their future; it was part of what they had been, not of what they wanted to be. This explains why among the urban Germans who subscribed to Miller's and Saur's newspapers the inclination to think American, to behave

American, and to speak English was stronger than among the rural Germans. It was the same process of voluntary assimilation among urban Germans that put a stake through the Kämmerers' ambition to create in America the first periodical aimed at a genteel, German-speaking readership. Ironically, precisely the patriotic, hyphenated German readers to whom *Das Philadelphisches Magazin* was catering would be the first Germans in America to abandon their German language and ethnicity and happily blend into mainstream, British American culture. Thus, in ethnic terms, the urban, nonsectarian Germans in Pennsylvania became the victims of their own successful assimilation: the price they paid for being loyal supporters of the American Revolution and for helping to consolidate it was the loss of their own ethnic identity. They printed "America" but effaced themselves. But what is perhaps even more ironic, if not tragic, is that it had been the same highly successful liberal German-language press that in the 1760s and 1770s had significantly contributed to silencing the once formidable propaganda machine of the independent sectarian Germans. For even though they still stubbornly refused to become a part of the mainstream of American life, at the end of the Revolutionary War the sect people no longer stood in the way of Americanization of Pennsylvania and of its general population. Where Franklin had failed, Henrich Miller and his fellow printers had triumphed. But at what price? The full history of the Germans and the German-language press in colonial and Revolutionary America is a tale that still needs to be told.

Notes

1. Karl J. R. Arndt, "German as the Official Language of the United States of America?" *Monatshefte* 68, no. 2 (1976): 129.
2. See Francis Jennings, *Benjamin Franklin, Politician* (New York and London: Norton, 1996), 72–80. The first issue of *Die Philadelphische Zeitung*, the first German-American newspaper, appeared on Saturday, May 6, 1732, under the imprint "B. Francklin." It was badly edited, was in very poor German, and soon folded. See "The First German Newspaper Published in America," *Pennsylvania Magazine of History and Biography*, 24, no. 4 (1900): 306–7 (includes a facsimile reproduction of the text of the second issue of *Die Philadelphische Zeitung*).
3. Arthur D. Graeff, "The Relations between the Pennsylvania Germans and the British Authorities (1750–1776)" (Ph.D. diss., Temple University, 1939), 239–52.
4. Aaron Spencer Fogleman, *Hopeful Journeys: German Immigration, Settlement, and Political Culture in Colonial America, 1717–1775* (Philadelphia: U of Pennsylvania P, 1996), 12; Christopher L. Dolmetsch,

"Locations of German Language Newspapers and Periodical Printing in the United States: 1732–1976," *Monatshefte* 68, no. 2 (1976): map 2.

5. The main difference perhaps is that *Das Philadelphisches Magazin* was more generally geared toward entertaining its urban, middle-class readers, rather than merely informing them or pastoring their souls (hence the subtitle, *Unterhaltender Gesellschafter* [Entertaining Companion]. *Das Philadelphisches Magazin,* had it survived beyond its first issue, in May 1798, would have been the closest German-language equivalent to the English-language magazines that it was trying to emulate—such as, say, the *Weekly Magazine of Original Essays* (Philadelphia, 1798–99) or the *Monthly Magazine and American Review* (New York, 1799–1800). Aiming to cater for German bourgeois readers in America, the publishers self-confidently pledge their subscribers in their preface, "Wir werden weder Mühe noch Kosten sparen, dieses Magazin so unterhaltend als möglich zu machen, under wir schmeicheln uns, dass die Deutschen, die doch sonsten so sehr für Cultur sind, uns ihren Schutz nicht enthalten werden" (We will spare no trouble or expense to make this magazine as entertaining as possible, and we flatter ourselves that the Germans, who have always been so supportive of the arts, will not withhold their patronage from us) (2). All translations from the German are the author's, unless indicated otherwise.

   Those cultured Germans were treated in the first issue to brief pieces on subjects such as a medicinal spring in Pennsylvania, Indian self-sacrifice, Colley Cibber's travels through France, and Turkish bathing rituals, as well as "true" narratives about a case of female heroism, an inhuman landowner, a fortunate escape, and an unfortunate girl. The issue ended with some "poetical attempts" and a "political journal." That the publishers were explicitly targeting a patriotic, *hyphenated* German audience (as opposed to an ethnically purist, sectarian one) is clear from the commemorative portrait of Washington that they printed as their frontispiece, as well as from their opening essay, a rousing biography of the recently deceased president (which is followed by a vignette about Mount Vernon).

6. Christopher Looby, *Voicing America: Language, Literary Form, and the Origins of the United States* (Chicago and London: U of Chicago P, 1996), 1.

7. The present essay deals only with the German-language press in Pennsylvania, in the late-colonial and Revolutionary period. It has been estimated that a total of around eighty-five thousand German-speaking immigrants arrived in the thirteen colonies between 1700 and 1775, the bumper years being between 1730 and 1770, with the period 1750–1760 showing the highest decennial immigration (Fogleman 2, table 1.1). The

great majority of these landed in Philadelphia, and although many of them quickly moved on to join their countrymen dispersed throughout western Pennsylvania, German settlers could be found in states all along the Atlantic coast, notably in Maine, New York, Maryland, Virginia, the Carolinas, and Georgia.

8. Fogleman 11.

9. Benjamin Franklin, *The Papers of Benjamin Franklin*, ed. Leonard W. Labaree et al., 36 vols. to date (New Haven: Yale UP, 1959–), 4: 234.

10. It is symptomatic of scholars' neglect of the role German immigration played in the making of America that the massive German settlement in Pennsylvania is missing from Bernard Bailyn's classic studies, *The Peopling of British North America: An Introduction* (New York: Knopf, 1988), and *Voyagers to the West: A Passage in the Peopling of America on the Eve of the Revolution* (New York: Knopf, 1986).

11. One of the most intriguing printing communities in rural Pennsylvania was founded by Conrad Beissel (1691–1768) in Ephrata. Having had an "awakening" when he was twenty-five and still living in Germany, Beissel decided to immigrate to America to escape religious persecution. Beissel arrived in Germantown in 1720, but after about a year withdrew to an isolated spot at what is now Ephrata, Lancaster County, where he founded a mysticist sect that in its heyday had around three hundred members. Among the sect's main principles of faith were adult baptism, celibacy, what amounted to self-flagellation, and extreme piety. The Ephrata community became one of the most active centers of printing and book production in rural Pennsylvania outside of Germantown. The "Ephrata Cloister," as it is now called, had its own paper mill, print shop, bindery, and even a scriptorium, where some of the most beautiful calligraphy of the colonial period was produced. Obviously, the Ephrata community produced religious texts only—hundreds of original hymns, as well as sheets of music. After Beissel's death, the community was led by the Indian negotiator Conrad Weiser. However, by that time, the community was already in decline. The long-term effects of the Ephrata's celibacy principle led to its ultimate demise. See Guy T. Holliday and Christoph E. Schweitzer, "The Present Status of Conrad Beissel/Ephrata Research," *Monatshefte* 68, no. 2 (1976): 171–78.

12. For a more-detailed picture of the remarkable spread and diversity of the German-language press in America in the eighteenth and nineteenth centuries, see the excellent bibliography by Karl J. R. Arndt and Reimer C. Eck, eds., *The First Century of German Language Printing in the United States of America*, 2 vols. (Göttingen: Niedersächsische Staats- und

Universitätsbibliothek, 1989). A good narrative survey is provided in the opening chapter ("The Newspapers and Their Publishers") of James Owen Knauss, *Social Conditions among the Pennsylvania Germans in the Eighteenth Century, as Revealed in German Newspapers Published in America*, Proceedings of the Pennsylvania-German Society, vol. 29 (Lancaster, PA: New Era Printing, 1922), 1–36.

13. This broad division in religious orientation of the German settlers is reflected in the shift in immigration patterns. Until the end of the Thirty Years' War in 1648, predominantly Germans from the north-German towns of the Hanseatic League and surroundings areas immigrated to America; after 1648, large numbers of Germans from the southwest of the country (the "Palatine") left for the New World. The latter were predominantly Lutheran and German Reformed.

14. John Joseph Stoudt, "The German Press in Pennsylvania and the American Revolution," *Pennsylvania Magazine of History and Biography* 59 (1935): 75.

15. "This is now the second time that the Holy Writ, called the Bible, appears in print on the American continent in the German language to the renown of the German nation, no other nation being able to claim that the Bible has been printed in their language on this continent" (from the "Verrede" [preface]). Twelve hundred copies of the 1743 edition of the German Bible were printed; two thousand copies were printed of the second edition.

16. Benjamin Franklin, *Autobiography*, eds. J. A. Leo Lemay and P. M. Zall (1868; New York and London: Norton, 1986), 93. Even today's scholars still sometimes take Franklin's version of the history of the Association simply at face value. Thus Robert Middlekauff observes in his recent book *Benjamin Franklin and His Enemies* (Berkeley, Los Angeles, and London: U of California P, 1996) that Franklin's campaign "to lead to war a province whose leaders had long espoused pacificism" was "an extraordinary achievement," especially because it was done "without alienating any save a few members of the Society of Friends" (38). An analysis of the long-neglected relation between Franklin and the German-language press would have revealed that the support for Franklin's plans for a militia was far less widespread than he himself suggested and that he actually alienated more than a mere handful of Quakers—notably the sectarian German immigrant population of Pennsylvania.

17. See Jennings 72. Between 1749 and 1762 Franklin may have been involved—as financial backer or publisher—in up to five other attempts to establish German-language newspapers, sometimes in cooperation with the *Deutsche Gesellschaft*. None of these newspapers had much impact,

and they quickly collapsed. Although it is surmised that he was behind *Das Hoch-deutsche Pennsylvanische Journal* (1743) and Gotthart Armbrüster's weekly of 1748, Franklin is likely to have had a hand in Johann Böhm's *Philadelphier Teutsche Fama*, while his name appears as publisher of the Philadelphia bilingual paper of 1751 and of the *Philadelphische Zeiting* (1755–57). He certainly controlled H. Müller and S. Holland's *Die Lancastersche Zeitung* of 1752–53. See Knauss, *Social Conditions among the Pennsylvania Germans*, 8, and also Stoudt, "German Press in Pennsylvania," 80.

18. Franklin, *Papers*, 4: 484.
19. "An Urgent Warning and Reminder for the Free Inhabitants of the Province of Pennsylvania, by One Who Is Greatly Concerned about the Well-Being of the Country."
20. "You have the same rights and liberties as any English-born have, and share the Constitution of the country. You are people of reason and common sense; so let me summon you once again to use your common sense, to assert yourselves, and to uphold your liberties. . . ."
21. Franklin wrote his essay *Observations Concerning the Increase of Mankind* in 1751, but it was not published until November 1755 in Boston with S. Kneeland. It is reprinted in Franklin, *Papers*, 4: 225–34. The citation is on page 234.
22. Franklin was attacked over the use of the phrase in the *Pennsylvania Journal* (September 27, 1764, supplement), but he received support from *The Plot* (Philadelphia, 1764). See also Middlekauff, *Benjamin Franklin and His Enemies*, 98–99.
23. Franklin, *Papers*, 4: 234.
24. A slave owner in the 1750s and 1760s, Franklin first publicly denounced the slave trade in 1772; in 1787 the Quakers made him president of the "Pennsylvania Society for Promoting the Abolition of Slavery" and the "Relief of Free Negroes Unlawfully Held in Bondage." In the late 1780s he drew up a "Plan for Improving the Condition of the Free Blacks," raised funds for the abolitionist cause in a public address, and signed a petition to the U.S. House of Representatives. For a brief survey of Franklin's changing attitude toward slavery and the slave trade, see Paul W. Conner, *Poor Richard's Politicks: Benjamin Franklin and His New American Order* (London, Oxford, and New York: Oxford UP, 1965), 77–84.
25. See Glenn Weaver, "Benjamin Franklin and the Pennsylvania Germans," *William and Mary Quarterly* 14 (January 1957): 542.
26. Ibid., 542–47.

27. See Jennings 73–80. For a detailed account of Franklin's role in the charity schools affair, see Whitfield J. Bell Jr., "Benjamin Franklin and the German Charity Schools," *Proceedings of the American Philosophical Society* 99 (December 1955): 381–87. For a short history of the charity schools, see S. E. Weber, "The Germans and the Charity School Movement," *Pennsylvania German* 8 (July 1907): 305–12.

28. Stoudt 76. *Der Hoch-Deutsch Pennsylvanische Geschichts-Schreiber* was published quarterly from August 20, 1739, to 1741; monthly from 1741 to July 1756; biweekly from August 21, 1756, to December 1774; and weekly from January 1775 to October 1777. It was published in quarto (7 x 9.5"), later in large quarto (8 x 13"); each issue was usually four pages, two columns each. At its peak, it had about four thousand subscribers; it was circulated also in Virginia, Georgia, and the Carolinas. It was edited and published by Christoph Saur from August 1739 to September 1758, by Christoph Saur II from September 1758 to 1776, by Christopher Saur II and his son Peter in 1776, and by Christoph Saur III and Peter Saur from September 11, 1776, to October 1777. It was continued in Philadelphia as *Der Pennsylvanische Staats-Courier*. See Karl J. R. Arndt and May E. Olsen, *German-American Newspapers and Periodicals, 1732–1955: History and Bibliography*, vol. 1 of *Die deutschsprachige Presse der Amerikas, 1732–1968: Geschichte und Bibliographie*, 2d rev. ed. (1962; New York: Johnson Reprint Corporation, 1965), 523–24.

29. Christoph Saur, *Ein Geistliches Magazien*, 1st ser., 50 (Germantown, n.d.): [410].

30. Saur, *Ein Geistliches Magazien*, 1st ser., 1 (Germantown, n.d.): [vi].

31. Saur, *Ein Geistliches Magazien*, 1st ser., 42: 335; (own, old-Adamic depraved heart).

32. Saur, *Ein Geistliches Magazien*, 2d ser., 1: 2; (fleshly peace and sinful life).

33. Ibid.

34. Saur, *Ein Geistliches Magazien*, 2d ser., 12: 136.

35. See Stoudt 76–77.

36. It is ironic in this context that in 1772 Christoph II printed and published a 264–page language manual and grammar intended for newly arrived German immigrants and those who had no access to English-language teachers to learn to read and speak English. It has to be said, though, that in an appendix he adds an abbreviated German grammar, "Whereby an Englishman may easily attain to the knowledge of the German language" (see *Eine nützliche Anweisung oder Beyhülffe vor Deutsche um English zu lernen*, Germantown, 1772).

37. Stoudt 77.

38. Arndt 133.

39. *Der Wöchentliche Pennsylvanische Staatsbote*, as Miller's newspaper came to be called in 1768, was published weekly from January 18, 1762 to May 16, 1775 (no. 1–695); semi-weekly from May 23, 1775 to July 23, 1776 (no. 696–818); weekly from July 30, 1776 to May 26, 1779 (no. 819–920). The size varied: usually large quarto (9 x 14"), each issue 4 pages, but during the War frequently 2 pages; after December 19, 1776, the paper was printed on a half sheet. Various special supplements were issued, such as a special farewell number which appeared on October 31, 1765, on the eve of the implementation of the Stamp Act, and at the occasion of the Repeal of the Stamp Act. Circulation of the *Staatsbote* has been estimated at 6500; it also had readers in Georgia, the Carolinas, Virginia, New Jersey, and New York (see Arndt and Olson 567–68.)

40. Stoudt 80–81.

41. According to Arthur D. Graeff, "The duty, if imposed under its original terms, would have fallen more heavily upon the German rather than upon any other group of colonists. The Act provided that a double duty be laid where the instrument, proceedings, etc. shall be engrossed, written, or printed within the said colonies and plantations, in any other than the English language." Arthur D. Graeff, "The Relations between the Pennsylvania Germans and the British Authorities(1750–1776)," *Pennsylvania German Society Proceedings* 47 [1939]: 20).

42. "Yesterday the honorable Congress of this continent declared the united colonies free and independent states. The Declaration, in English, is in press at this moment; it is dated July 4th, 1776, and will appear in print today or tomorrow."

43. Charles Frederick Dapp, *The Evolution of an American Patriot, Being an Intimate Study of the Patriotic Activities of John Henry Miller, German Printer, Publisher and Editor of the American Revolution* (Ph.D. diss., University of Pennsylvania, 1924), 6.

44. "Few people understand how much it takes to print a German newspaper: almost every line has to be translated. Many also find it normal that their advertisements are not only translated, but also set up in type free of charge. Whoever seriously considers all this, and more, will surely have no cause to complain about the price of this paper."

45. "An honest, energetic and strong young man of approximately twenty years of age, who has no regular employment and who is eager to learn the skills of operating the printing press."

46. Karl J. R. Arndt and May E. Olson, *Die deutschsprachige Presse der Amerikas, 1732–1968: Geschichte und Bibliographie*, vol. 2 of *Die deutschsprachige Presse der Amerikas, 1732–1968: Geschichte und Bibliographie* (Pullach bei München: Verlag Dokumentation, 1973), 523.

47. "but these have caused more damage to our country than all those public enemies have or could have done. They have sympathized with the French to the point where they inflicted one deed of aggression after another against us, until at last their envoys were stopped by our Washington."

48. "The only counter-measure against them is a similar newspaper, and to exterminate the enemies of our government, both foreign and domestic— The best way is to attack the Democrats, Jacobins and agitators on their own turf, to confront them head-on, not to yield an inch to them, to fight them with their own weapons, and to answer every strike with two of our own. . . . For any untruth or lie from the Jacobins that is not rectified, will be held to be true."

PART TWO

REVOLUTIONARY ERA DISCOURSES

As recent studies of the American Revolution and the performative use of language have shown, there is ample reason to examine more closely how an emerging print culture, and periodicals in particular, provided a stage or venue for constructing a liberal-democratic republic. The "prehistory of American liberal democracy" and its "confrontation with liberal ideology," observes Nancy Ruttenburg, need to be reassessed along with the crises and compulsive public responses that contributed to colonial America's "distinctive mode of political (and later, literary) subjectivity."[1] She further states that the performative circumstances of such crises or struggles and the emergence of a democratic ethos represent a process of "individuation" and political utterance—a "democratic personality"—that precedes the rational and structured debates of the public sphere during the Revolutionary era.[2] The "theaters" of such struggle, sometimes "nonliberal," collectively represent the earliest articulations of consensual politics and efforts in developing a democratic form of government.[3]

Along with seeing the founding of the early republic as being tied to a series of speech acts and print responses, it is also necessary to read colonial and Revolutionary texts against each other and against "Other" language or discourse systems of the day.[4] Intercultural exchange, in other words, also afforded the opportunity for rhetorical and ideological integration between, and even within, British American traditions of writing and speech and disenfranchised classes, including Native American and African American populations. "The forms of state power," remarks Sandra M. Gustafson, "that white men designed in the early republic were shaped in crucial ways by their proximity and resistance to the speech of white women, native Americans, and African Americans."[5] While Gustafson's study focuses primarily on an "oratorical public culture" during the Revolutionary era, there exists a largely untapped reservoir of print texts and debates in periodical literature of this time that further illuminates the impact of the spoken word and the dynamics of cultural contact and difference in Revolutionary-era print culture.

Essays in this section, then, cohere chronologically but also focus specifically on the manner in which newspaper and magazine publications archive a variety of colonial and Other discourses that eventually contributed to the development of national identity. Beginning with, for instance, the circulation of classical materials and patriotic ideals in newspaper formats and the appropriation of American Indian oratory to respond to British colonial practices, arguments here demonstrate how periodical publications intervened in political debate at the national and more local levels. Similarly, essays on the conflicting views of Shays's Rebellion and the hybrid format of some magazines and the uses of sentiment and satire in relation to the antislavery movements also bring into relief the multiple ways a periodical format boldly facilitated the construction of democratic ideals and the realization of a new republic founded on equality and liberty. As such, the essays focus not only on transatlantic influences and how the periodical format evolved but also on how the multiple discourses of colonial resistance and dissent emerged and intersected, often dialogically, with discourses of an ethnic or political Other. As a consequence, recovery of the polyphony of voices and ideologies revises existing paradigms for understanding the formation of early national identity and print culture.

Specifically, "'Widely read by American Patriots': The *New-York Weekly Journal* and the Influence of *Cato's Letters* on Colonial America," by Chad Reid, reevaluates the impact of Cato's ideas and ethics in the American colonies, showing how John Peter Zenger's aggressive print practices spilled over from the printing press into political thought and became a deeply embedded vehicle for disrupting British royalist control. He argues that the increasing dissemination of news and information, the intensive reading practices of American colonists, and the explosion of political battles in newspapers enabled *Cato's Letters* to dominate the average colonist's awareness of politics and social freedoms. Almost forgotten now, the Roman ideals embedded in *Cato's Letters* were influential in helping the laboring class and the elite alike in becoming acutely aware of their political rights and liberties. The print history of *Cato's Letters* in the media and its focus on civil liberties strengthens the argument, he says, that the public sphere is one of a widespread, popular readership, not the fractional representation of the populace that Habermas's theory puts forward.

Mark L. Kamrath's "American Indian Oration and Discourses of the Republic in Eighteenth-Century American Periodicals" returns to the longstanding debate about the role and impact of the American Indian on the eve of the American Revolution; he argues that the appropriation of native oratory or "speeches," real or imagined, in periodicals such as the *Royal American Magazine* (1774–75) inscribe the native Other and, at the same time, also enabled colonists to articulate a radical, patriotic response to British colonial practices. Specifically, he identifies how Indian speeches such as "Specimen of Indian Eloquence" ("Mingo") and "An Indian ORATION" (Creek) enact an ethos of resistance to English colonization and oppression and circulated in early American periodicals. Such appropriation or imitation of Indian oration by American colonists, he suggests, deepens our knowledge of events between the Stamp Act of 1765 and the eve of the American Revolution as well as how the rhetoric of native resistance commingled dialogically with the rhetoric of sympathy and dissent and, ultimately, the patriot discourses of freedom, liberty, and independence. As such, it also forces a reassessment of early representation of the Other, the way in which the melding of classical, late Enlightenment, and American Indian ideologies enabled American colonists to forge a uniquely American Revolutionary rhetoric and to write and speak back to imperial authority, and the historicization of the processes of American "decolonization."

"Civil Unrest and the Rhetoric of the American Revolution: Depiction of Shays's Rebellion in New England Magazines of the 1780s," by Robert D. Sturr, examines reactions to Shays's Rebellion in the *New-Haven Gazette, and the Connecticut Magazine* (1786–89) and the *Worcester Magazine* (1786–88). Both had previously been newspapers and were founded during a period of constitutional and political crisis. These magazines, he argues, offered dramatically different reactions to a crisis that threatened the viability of the early republic. The attempt by conservative intellectuals in New Haven to blunt the impact of Shays's Rebellion with satire and scorn is contrasted with the effort of Isaiah Thomas in the mercantile center of Worcester to present a more-balanced range of responses to backcountry agitation. The differences between these two magazines, particularly in their respective views on the War of Independence, explain and elucidate both the growth of conservative political trends in the late 1780s and the potential of periodical publications from diverse regions to intervene in national political debate. Although different in rhetorical mode and political orientation, each of these magazines sought to offer remedies for republican government that spoke to then-emerging principles of sovereignty and representation, making such periodicals "intermediary institutions" between the people and their representatives and dispelling the myth that American periodicals were primarily a repository for upper-class morals, polite manners, or exclusively academic perspectives.

Finally, Philip Gould's "The African Slave Trade and Abolitionism: Rereading Antislavery Literature, 1776–1800" rereads antislavery literature in post-Revolutionary magazines such as Matthew Carey's *American Museum, or, Universal Magazine* (1787–92) as a shaping force in the continual articulations of republican politics and culture, arguing that discourse that was often sentimental or satirical dominated antislavery literature during this era and functioned as a way of articulating the proper and moral terms of free labor, commercial exchange, and international trade. Periodical antislavery literature, he argues, that was published between the 1770s and 1810s provides an important but neglected link between Revolutionary American antislavery and antebellum abolitionism. One sees in such literature, often reprinted, not only a range of genres including poetry, sketches, and anecdotes but also an appeal to the sensibilities of readers that includes use of emancipation rhetoric and the voice of "piccaninny" black dialect. As such, this literature simultaneously highlights two kinds of enslavement—the brutal treatment of African captives and the "cultural depravity" of recently liberated, supposedly civilized British Americans. It also calls attention to how readerships at this time navigated, often ambivalently, the "middle passage," or moral ambiguities, between slave commerce and late Enlightenment Protestant Christianity.

In short, essays in this section seek to account more carefully for the full range of cultural and ideological discourses that permeate colonial America up to, and shortly after, the American Revolution. To the extent that the dynamics of contact and racial and class difference inform how this era constructed itself relative to a European past, essays in this section collectively examine the rhetorical impact of such differences and how the weekly and monthly periodicals often became a medium for cultural self-examination and ideological change. In this way, the essays here offer perspective not only on lingering colonial loyalties and cultural diasporas but also on the dramatic shift in the early 1790s from a virtuous republic to a liberal market economy of individualism and political self-interest.[6]

Scholars looking, then, to reassess the periodicals archive relative to the Revolutionary era will find a range of discourses tied to the subjectivities of multiple, and sometimes overlapping, groups and individuals. The manner in which various cultural, ethnic, and political discourses were appropriated, in other words, and became embedded in periodical print calls attention to how this material embeds or encodes the discourses of dissent and offers an "alternative platform" from which to assess questions of "empire, authority, slavery, and oppression."[7] The full range and multiple forms of such discourses and their various modes of resistancc and dissent remain to be examined as does their influence on the ideology and language of the American Revolution.

Notes

1. Nancy Ruttenburg, *Democratic Personality: Popular Voice and the Trial of American Authorship* (Stanford: Stanford UP, 1998), 3.
2. Ibid.
3. Ibid., 2–3.
4. For groundbreaking work on the revolutionary founding of the Republic, acts of voice, and the role of print, see Christopher Looby's classic study *Voicing America: Language, Literary Form, and the Origins of the United States* (Chicago: U of Chicago P, 1996). For a more recent and localized study on Revolutionary-era discourses and change, see Christopher Grasso's *A Speaking Aristocracy: Transforming Public Discourse in Eighteenth-Century Connecticut* (Chapel Hill: U of North Carolina P, 1999).
5. Sandra M. Gustafson, *Eloquence Is Power: Oratory and Performance in Early America* (Chapel Hill: U of North Carolina P, 2000), xix.
6. See Steven Watts's *Republic Reborn: War and the Making of Liberal America, 1790–1820* (Baltimore: Johns Hopkins UP, 1987), xvii, 9–13.
7. Mark L. Kamrath, "*Eyes Wide Shut* and the Cultural Poetic of Eighteenth-Century American Periodical Literature," *Early American Literature* 37 (2002): 523.

Chad Reid

"Widely Read by American Patriots"

The *New-York Weekly Journal* and the Influence of *Cato's Letters* on Colonial America

> He rose, dread Foe to Priests and Fetters,
> Deep skill'd in Church and civil Matters;
> For he had read all Cato's Letters
>
> —*The New York Mercury*, July 23, 1753

In 1778 Samuel Johnson proclaimed that "society is held together by communication and information."[1] The result of this dialectic is increased knowledge. But knowledge does not germinate in an isolated environment; it grows through the continual interaction of people. Simply by walking down the street and overhearing a conversation, attending a funeral, sitting in a tavern and listening to someone read aloud the latest news from across the ocean, or borrowing a neighbor's book, the wealth of an individual's knowledge accumulates.[2] From the literature that people acquire and the news that they hear, a new world of understanding unfolds. For colonists, acquiring knowledge through reading was a cherished activity and resource. "As if in compensation for the limits on supply," David D. Hall writes, "people read with care the texts that came to hand."[3] Samuel Goodrich of Ridgefield, Connecticut, describes the essence of his pastime. While reflecting on early childhood experiences from the 1790s, he declares, "Books and newspapers—which are now diffused even among the country towns, so as to be in the hands of all, young and old—were then scarce, and were read respectfully, and as if they were grave matters, demanding thought and attention."[4]

More than any other literature of the Enlightenment, *Cato's Letters* traversed the colonies through traditional methods of idea diffusion and communication. After arriving in 1721, *Cato's Letters* would repeatedly emerge from the colonies' early printing presses to receive the focus and concentration that

Samuel Goodrich outlines.[5] The dissemination of knowledge and colonial attention are foundational to Cato's impact.[6] The majority of contemporary scholarship writes that *Cato's Letters* was the colonists' own "British-penned bible," "widely read by American Patriots," and "popular enough in the colonies to be quoted in every colonial newspaper from Boston to Savannah," with its authors, John Trenchard and Thomas Gordon, becoming "the most important disseminators of ideas to Americans in the prerevolutionary generations."[7] All of the above phrases are now axiomatic. But how were these ideas transferred and embedded into the populace? To what extent and circumstance did Cato become so often read? Unfortunately few historical examinations actually supply details rather than broad generalizations in regards to Cato's popularity and presence within the colonial mind. Works from Elizabeth Cook, Clinton Rossiter, Bernard Bailyn, and Gary Huxford provide examples of reprintings in newspapers and political pamphlets, scraps and ideas regarding Cato's repetition and popularity within colonial print culture and politics.[8] One author who focuses exclusively on *Cato's Letters* is Marie P. McMahon. Her book, *The Radical Whigs, John Trenchard and Thomas Gordon: Libertarian Loyalists to the New House of Hanover*, describes Trenchard and Gordon's writings within the British political environment of the early eighteenth century.[9] Although McMahon's research investigates the categorization of *Cato's Letters* within the writings for that era, she does not concern herself with the colonial American landscape.[10]

In volume 1 of the *History of the Book in America, The Colonial Book in the Atlantic World*, James N. Green announces that the *New-York Weekly Journal*'s "politician editors wrote every word of it [the newspaper] except the advertisements and the news notices, and they conducted a lively, witty newspaper that was exceedingly popular."[11] The *New-York Weekly Journal* was indeed popular. With the early appearance of *Cato's Letters* in what seems to be one issue after another, it is hard to exaggerate its role not only in early colonial newspapers, but also its importance within the scope of the colonial political mind.[12] As a result of the intensive reading practices of American colonists and the widespread, repeated dissemination of information from political battles, newspaper feuds, and reader interaction within the pages of the *New-York Weekly Journal, Cato's Letters* dominated the formation of the colonial everyman's politics and awareness of social freedoms in the early eighteenth century.[13] In addition, despite his initial English appearance over a decade ago in Michael Warner's *Letters of the Republic*, Jürgen Habermas's writings on the public sphere remain hotly debated. The usage of *Cato's Letters* in the media—in conjunction with Richard Brown's and Robert Darnton's examples on how knowledge disperses—strengthens the argument that the public sphere is one of a widespread, popular readership and not the fractional representation of population that Habermas's theory enunciates.[14]

Cato's Letters is a series of 138 essays written in Britain as a reaction to the South Sea Bubble.[15] Because of their tremendous popularity in the *London Journal* and the *British Journal,* Trenchard and Gordon's writings soon expanded from malevolent political incidents to religion, the liberties of individuals, and the conduct of government, while advertising their anti–High Church/Lockean biases. With Algernon Sidney as one influence, Trenchard generally "wrote what he thought, and wrote it for no other reason than because he thought it and that it would be of service for his country to know it."[16]

The "Cato" moniker is named after Marcus Porcius Cato, or Cato the Younger (95–46 B.C.E.), a virtuous Roman general who, after reading Plato's *On the Soul* (a treatise on the immortality of the soul), committed suicide rather than falling captive to the armies of the tyrannous Julius Caesar. A handful of quotations and a letter to Cicero are the only original, surviving items left in his name. The main sources for which Trenchard and Gordon understood his motivations and beliefs come from Plutarch's *Parallel Lives of Illustrious Greeks and Romans* and Joseph Addison's popular 1713 theatrical play, *Cato.*[17]

Marcus Porcius Cato was a courageous leader, both militarily and politically, who held the laws of the state in high regard—so much so in fact that "everything he said was for the interest of the state."[18] He was a republican who advocated the public possession of the Roman government. This leader of the people often took up political positions in order to act as a watchdog against the machinations of Caesar and his quest for autonomous government power.[19] Despite these autocratic tendencies, Cato hoped that the current political environment would adhere to the constitution of pre-Gracchan days. In that era, men strongly believed in the importance of attaining virtue within their lives and everyday activities. This goal of a virtuous lifestyle complemented Cato's Stoicist education.[20] Before his death in Utica, people closest to Cato believed that "he was incapable of a dishonest or deceitful action."[21] They loved him for his courage and virtue, and he strove to protect the people from corruption in government.

Trenchard and Gordon—themselves creating a modern, British Cato through *Cato's Letters*—also believed in the social contract of the government and the people. Consistent with the ideological convictions of Marcus Cato, the two men observed that the people are as knowledgeable in governmental procedures as the Crown who ruled over them. Monarchs should be valued for their political and social achievements, not for their appearance or empty words. The English Constitution upholds the basic and necessary rights of Englishmen, protecting them from government and individuals in power. If the government were to break this contract with the people, every movement for redressing the people's grievances was just. Any individual whose liberties were infringed upon has the right to protect and regain them. Obedience to these English common laws parallels Marcus Cato's esteem for ancient Roman laws. The British authors also believed that the nature of man slides towards corruption whenever a sparkle of power appears before him. Upon its first taste, man will stop at nothing to satiate a desire for expanded powers. He will cast aside every moral fiber in his body to gain more.

In addition, the authors of *Cato's Letters* were extremely suspicious and "frankly against all authority in matters spiritual but that of the individual conscience."[22] Their original essays favor Deist attitudes in regards to the creation of the universe and provide a keen distaste for the clergy. Man possesses his own individuality from which the innumerable strains of religion derived. Religion molds to his preferences, a concept that Marcus Cato did not subscribe to within his polytheistic world. Thus, there were obviously many parallel ideas and conflicting beliefs between classical Cato and the British Cato of Trenchard and Gordon.[23] Most important, the aspects of virtue, liberty, and adherence to a government of the people (aspects which both Catos supported), were the tenets that synthesized early political thinking within the colonies.[24]

One example of the prestige of *Cato's Letters* in colonial America lies within the pages of the *New-York Weekly Journal.* New York's second newspaper, the *Journal* appeared on November 5, 1733. It was originally designed as a political adversary for William Bradford's *New-York Gazette.* Previous to the *Journal*'s founding, Governor William Cosby had allowed the *Gazette* to enjoy a media monopoly over the city in order to maintain a strong British influence. As a reaction to the *Gazette*, Cosby, and traditional royalist power, the *Journal* "was the first newspaper in America to be established as a political party newspaper."[25] Subsequently the *Journal*'s printer, John Peter Zenger, and Bradford "carried on a paper war against each other."[26] The community quickly noticed a discrepancy in the politics of the two newspapers. The "*Journal* soon assumed political features which excited general attention in the colony; several writers in the newspaper attacked the measures of government with a boldness which was unusual in those days."[27] Governor Cosby was never depicted favorably.[28]

The Zenger camp utilized the rhetoric of *Cato's Letters* to represent their alternative political position in New York.[29] Evidence of the magnitude and popularity of Cato within Zenger's paper is abundant. In respect to this celebrity, the prose of Trenchard and Gordon appeared prominently in eight out of seventeen *Journal* issues from November 1733 to February 1734.

Many newspaper editors inserted Cato's prose to fill space, provide the public with knowledge on political and social theories, and instigate local political criticism. In most instances, *Cato's Letters* were introduced with only a few words addressing the relevance of the essay's subject to the current political occasion. In other times, the prose from an "Admired Writer" gushed through the pages.[30]

Newspaper symbols never represented *Cato's Letters.* Either a small hint in the introductory preface or the simple mark of "CATO" was all it took.

Cato's words often mirrored the beliefs of the newspaper editors who printed them but were then masked only as an opinion or partisan position in print.[31] Occasionally newspaper editors devised their own letters to the editor. "The editors of the *Journal* resorted to a device commonly used among colonial editors," Huxford notes, "i.e., writing letters to themselves." He argues that *Journal* editors wrote the preface to the December 10, 1733, issue.[32] The preface announces, "Mr. Zenger, If You'll give a Place in your Paper to the following Sentiments of (I had almost said, the Divine) English CATO; I have Reason to believe they will not be disagreeable to your Subservers." On the one hand, Huxford does not furnish sufficient evidence to prove his case since the text does not support his argument. On the other hand, Benjamin Franklin, his brother James (the editor), and a group of writer-friends nicknamed the "Hell-Fire Club" often contributed their own articles to the *New-England Courant* during the 1720s. Editors of the *American Weekly Mercury* did the same. So Huxford's analysis is plausible if one follows this trend into the 1730s for the *Journal.* Determining whether letters to the editor were the work of a newspaper's readers or its editors is extremely difficult. Nonetheless, Cato's thirty-eighth essay, "The Right and Capacity of the People to judge of Government," accompanies the preface of this December issue.[33]

The printed treatise comes after the *Journal*'s attack of the previous week against Cosby "for permitting French warships to enter the harbor and spy out on the fortifications of New York."[34] Cato's polemic concerns the role of the people in directing their own government. Trenchard and Gordon declare that the majority of those who are in positions of power are corrupt. A large amount of editorial emphasis is placed on certain words and ideas to supplement Cato's prose. Zenger capitalized these words in order to promote his own beliefs. His version begins, "Some have said, IT IS NOT THE BUSINESS OF PRIVATE MEN TO MEDDLE WITH GOVERNMENT." Other Cato phrases the printer accentuates are, "GOOD GOVERNMENT," "LIBERTY," "*Publick Truths ought never to be kept secret,*" and, "*it is the Duty of every Individual to be concerned for the Whole, in which himself is included.*" The essay itself took up half the newspaper—two full pages! Cato's assertions enunciate Zenger's current political grievances. Arguments for the people's control of government reprinted in the *Journal* were an effective political weapon against Governor Cosby.[35]

The purpose of Zenger's accentuation is evident. He used his newspaper not only as a tool to disseminate local and foreign news to the public, but also to educate his audience on certain liberties he believed colonists should be more fully aware and take advantage of, such as freedom of speech. But these conventions of emphasis sometimes led to reader confusion rather than comprehension.

The next week's December 17 issue possesses an unsigned letter to Zenger questioning the printer's highlights. "What is the Meaning of the big and different Letters for some Words and Sentences in Cato's Sentiments in that Paper?" the author writes,

> For Example, in describing the Causes of the Happiness and Misery of Government, the Character of Order is little, and that of MISMANAGEMENT great. Is there not (said he) something like Punn in this? Pray (sais he) where it there little Order and great Mismanagement?. . . I hope in some of your Papers to know the Success of his Inquiry.

Zenger does not answer the author's query, but the solution is obvious. The highlighted expressions were to support Cato's and his own arguments.

While communication networks and the rest of the city froze from the cold of these wintry months, Zenger writes a warm note to his readership thanking them for the newspaper material they had sent.[36] He announces, "Now when Foreign News is not to be had, and all other News Writers in these Countries are at a Loss how to continue their Papers, and what to fill them with; I must acknowledge my Obligations . . . that you do so plentifully supply me . . . I have now Supplies sufficient to fill above seven weekly Papers more." Thus, despite the frequent application of mutual copying of essays and articles between regional newspapers, readers were still able to influence their local newspaper's content. Whether Cato was the material Zenger's readers provided, it is difficult to tell. But after his statement, the *Journal*'s next issue begins a long series of reprinted Cato sermons.

The January 28, 1734, edition opens with paragraphs concerning the "SCHEMES OF GENERAL OPPRESSION AND PILLAGE, SCHEMES TO DEPRECIATE OR EVADE THE LAWS, RESTRAINTS UPON LIBERTY AND PROJECTS FOR ARBITRARY WILL." Cato's myriad of opinions lends a word or two to this sinister topic. Embedded within the text of Zenger's front page essay is Cato's treatise on men and self-love. The work comes from *Cato's Letters*, no. 112, "Fondness for Posterity nothing else but Self-love. Such as are Friends to publick Liberty, are the only true Lovers of Posterity."[37] Although the words of the two authors are connected, the mood and style of Zenger's diatribe varies with Cato's sections. Zenger is adamant and tense in comparison to Cato. With yet another jab at Governor Cosby and Bradford, this essay argues that man's ambition is for posterity and fame. All obstacles are only momentary for those who do "wicked things."[38] Among various other phrases, the editor intensified "INSTRUMENTS OF PUBLICK RUIN" and "A LAWLESS DAGGER" for readers to discern. A judicial assault by Chief Justice DeLancey (a Cosby appointee) in this month of January is the motivation underlying Zenger's latest venomous print. But despite charges of usurping Cosby's power and slandering his administration, a grand jury refused to prosecute Zenger and company, men who seemed to have "gain'd some credit among the common People."[39]

Zenger's use of Cato contrasts with his rival. With a heavy reliance on Joseph Addison and Richard Steele's *Spectator* (usually selections on scandal and lying), Bradford's *Gazette* "took the conservative, aristocratic point of view in governmental affairs."[40] Zenger sorely dismissed Bradford's royalist actions, for he describes the *Gazette* as "a Paper known to be under the Direction of the Government, in which the Printer of it is not suffered to insert any Thing but what his Superiors approve of, under the Penalty of losing 50 L. per annum Salary, and the Title of The King's Printer for the Province of New-York."[41]

As the drama between the two newspapers continues, a February *Journal* issue contains a letter to Bradford.[42] Here Zenger writes a lengthy reply concerning the contents of the latest *Gazette*. He declares, "ADDISON STEEL and the ENGLISH CATO have been Men ALMOST DIVINE, we can hardly Err if we agree with them in Political Sentiments; And yet we ought not to give up our Reason to them Absolutely, because they were Men, and as such Lyable [to] Errors tho I know not on one Error in either of them." Thus, no matter what the moral mortal arguments were, *Cato's Letters* and the *Spectator* were the authorities for both sides. The Divine Cato was always correct. Zenger found it inconceivable for the two sides to be arguing when using the same sources. The proper usage of Cato in newspapers is then the subject for Zenger's upcoming edition.

In the *Journal*'s next issue, the citation of *Cato's Letters* in a recent newspaper discussion again draws the attention of Zenger.[43] In a letter addressed to his adversary, Zenger quibbles with Bradford's acknowledgments to Trenchard and Gordon. Zenger then extends the disagreement in another section of the same newspaper, denigrating the *Gazette* author for his woeful argumentative usage of Cato. Zenger admonishes, "CATO (by which I always have meant and shall mean *Gordon* and *Trenchard;* or one of them, by their public Works, if not otherwise expressed) says, *That Envy always praises those it rails at.*"[44] Further on in his tirade against Bradford, Zenger applauds "the most masterly Hand of CATO." These laudatory comments expose remarkable significance hidden in the shadows of the text. First, Zenger's designation of Cato as an eminent literary authority in recent *Journal* issues directs an impact upon his readers. Anyone who reads the words of *Cato's Letters* in the future will take notice because they have been previously regarded as important. Second, because Zenger uses text from the "masterly Hand" of Cato to corroborate and emphasize his arguments there is less effort to convince his reading audience that his side is just, since an eminent literary authority supports his own words.

A week later, Zenger prints Cato's fifteenth treatise, "Of Freedom of Speech: That the same is inseparable from publick Liberty."[45] In addition to the Cato work, a letter to the editor discusses the usage of literary sources in recent newspaper essays. The writer complains of Zenger's own words surrounding those of Cato. "One of the Writers of Bradford's Paper," he announces,

> makes *Zenger's* Types to swell *Gordon's* Letters to Gyganitck size, for omitting some Parts of them. I, on the other side, should have thought, that by omitting any thing he had made it less than it was before, and made them Pigmies instead of Giants, thus Parties differ. However, he grants the Materials are rich, tho' tacked together with course Stuff; let it be so if he pleases, make use of the rich Materials and throw away the tacking, and make the best of them.

Thus, the sharp attention of New York readers developed into more sophisticated preferences for the reprinting of libertarian material. An evolution of procedure has occurred. Through repeated reprintings, intense colonial reading practices, and reader feedback, editors must now adhere to a positive usage of Cato for Cato quotes to be adequately cited and for Cato's words to stand alone and apart from any other editorials.[46]

Zenger's next *Journal* issue on February 25 reprints Cato's thirty-second essay, "Reflections upon Libelling."[47] It is prefaced, "As Libeling seems at Present the Topick that is canvassed both at Court and among the People, I must beg you will insert in your weekly Journal; the following Sentiments of CATO." The monograph, as titled, concerns the subject of libel. At the bottom of the newspaper's front page, the author then switches Cato essays. A passage from Cato no. 13, "The Arts of misleading the People by Sounds," begins.[48] Only a few paragraphs emerge from this work, which contains such notable phrases as, "In short the People often Judge better [than] their Superiors." The author's contributing prose then switches back to Cato no. 32. A week later, the March 4 *Journal* issue continues to reprint the last portions of no. 32.[49] This presentation of *Cato's Letters* is confined to the front page as Zenger omits every other paragraph from the original essay because of space restrictions. Not to abandon the political connection between himself and Cato versus Bradford, Zenger then makes room for an additional letter about the ongoing newspaper war. These recent reprints and letters were reactionary attacks against the Cosby-Bradford alliance, for only a month before Chief Justice DeLancey had attempted to have both the *Journal* and the Morrisite faction indicted for libel.[50]

"Johannis Eboracus" submitted an article for the *Journal*'s May 27 issue. The work is in fact two Cato essays molded together. The first section of *Cato's Letters* no. 75, "Of the Restraints which ought to be laid upon publick Rulers," covers most of the front page.[51] The article then shifts to Cato no. 115, "The encroaching Nature of Power, ever to be watched and checked."[52] Only a few paragraphs from this tract are used. Hence, not unlike the *Journal* issues of two months previous, the article is a mishmash representation of Cato. A few paragraphs are deleted from the original version of no. 115, presumably to fit in only the more significant passages. This publication is another example of writers using Cato essays to present their ideas. With the frequent reprintings of Cato, the public readership became increasingly familiar with Trenchard and Gordon's theories and beliefs.

Chief Justice DeLancey's third attempt to imprison Zenger and company for libel occurred in October of 1734. Again, jurors were unwilling to contest Zenger's innocence. Governor Cosby then moved to have the assembly order the destruction of the *Journal* issues he deemed libelous. Legislators refused. On November 2, the governor and council declared the *Journal* seditious and urged the attorney general to undertake legal action.[53] Discussions concerning the liberties of the press, the English Constitution, and the politics of governors began to reemerge within the *Gazette* and the *Journal.* In response to these proceedings, Cato stepped onto the stage and into the limelight. A November contributor humbly exclaims, "I am not sure that any Thing I can offer of my own will not be deemed a Libel, I chose to send you Part of one of Cato's Letters, the Publication of which I hope will be acceptable to your Readers." Cato's fifteenth, "Of Freedom of Speech: That the same is inseparable from publick Liberty" follows, covering almost three full pages of the newspaper.[54] Representative of the printer's high esteem for this particular essay, there are only minor editorial intrusions to the reprinting. Zenger was keenly aware of the legal troubles developing around him as he quickly reprinted this popular work on individual rights and freedoms. Authorities arrested him soon after the edition was published.

On November 17, 1734, John Peter Zenger was brought to court under the instructions of Governor Cosby for "publishing several seditious libels" that provoked "Seditions and Tumults among the People of this Province."[55] On the twenty-third, *Journal* issues were burned in New York's streets.[56] Appropriate for the occasion, the December 9 *Journal* features Cato's hundredth letter, "Discourse upon Libels."[57] "As Naration seems at present what you Aim at," the introduction exclaims, "I send you one of Cato's Letters, which was read in the House by Lewis Morris, junr." Taking three out of the edition's four pages, the Cato essay is reprinted in its entirety. It is not a coincidence that Morris read Cato "in the House" for he was one of the main conspirators against Cosby. He helped establish the *Journal* in the first place.

After a nine-month imprisonment, Zenger was finally brought to City Hall for trial on August 4, 1735. His lawyer, Andrew Hamilton, developed his main arguments on libel from *Cato's Letters* no. 100. Hamilton's premise contended that Zenger's libel is legal when proven true.[58] When the court rejected this reasoning, Hamilton took issue with Zenger's right as a printer to publish material critical not only of Governor Cosby, but also of the rulers and governments of the colonies.

A jury of his peers acquitted Zenger of all charges. Sidney Kobre asserts, "the jury, like the newspaper, was reflecting the rising tide of commercial and political independence and the general resentment against the royal governor and crown."[59] A combination of tension against representatives of the Crown and a belief in individual liberties must have affected the jury's decision.[60]

Despite the trial's end, Cato continually reappeared in the *Journal.* As if to reiterate his previous actions as just and not illegal, Zenger immediately printed Cato's sixtieth essay, "All Government proved to be instituted by Men, and only to intend the general Good of Men." Without any significant emendations, the work is published in both the August 25 and September 1, 1735, issues.[61] It contains several phrases arguably construed as snipes at Cosby's royal position. "Nor can any government be in fact framed but by consent," Cato declares, "since no man, or council of men, can have personal strength enough to govern multitudes by force."[62] On August 28, Governor Cosby attempted to remove Van Dam, Alexander, and Morris from their respective political positions, but the Privy Council refused to act.

The paper war between the *Gazette* and the *Journal* resulted with the latter transplanting several important ideas of liberty and individual freedom onto the reading public. Richard Bernstein declares that "the Zenger case had no direct doctrinal impact in America or in Britain."[63] But the influence of Cato is evident. With a jury of his peers validating not only Zenger's actions, but also Cato's arguments for his defense, the ideas of *Cato's Letters* reached new heights in colonial influence. Since there were readers of the newspaper battles, buyers of the newspapers, and audiences of the court, Cato's repetition and presence led to a higher level of political awareness—a presence that dominated colonists' political thinking during the pre-Revolutionary decades.[64]

In *The Structural Transformation of the Public Sphere,* Jürgen Habermas also writes of the reading habits of people and their politics. These activities evolved into critical public debate through a republic of letters and newspapers.[65] One viewpoint may claim that Habermas's ideas about the public sphere correspond with several examples in this article. As detailed above, colonists possessing an intensive style of reading often petitioned Zenger to print a Cato treatise or demanded that Cato be accurately and respectfully represented within the *Journal*'s pages. This parallels Habermas's writings as his public sphere rationally debated literary works like Trenchard and Gordon's. Perhaps colonial newspapers are not the appropriate venue for this discussion since the *Journal* was not always an instrument of rational, critical thinking with people who intellectually reasoned about the prose at hand and in print. The *Journal* was a political instrument of polemics used by a cadre of selfish men preoccupied with power in colonial New York.[66] *Cato's Letters* was reprinted to represent the people, or any non-elite readers that would follow Morris, Van Dam, and Alexander. Over time, this ploy soon developed into the real thing as readers formulated their own political sensibilities through a continuous presence of Trenchard and Gordon. The *Journal* was not the only media outlet to project Cato, but it was the most overtly political during this clamorous period.

The Structural Transformation of the Public Sphere pertains to the decorum of reading and the activities of the higher male orders of society.[67] Through various information circles and the proliferation of newspapers in the colonies, *Cato's Letters* reached readers of both sexes, of varying age and status. The next step, perhaps, would be to acknowledge the possibilities of embedded motivations in American culture towards a popular political system, one not solely consisting of elite colonial males. With this broad readership of political ideas and knowledge, could these readings in colonial American culture hint at the early formations of a more sustained, democratic movement in the Western world?

One work that tries to account for the origins of American culture and society is John C. Shields's book, *The American Aeneas: Classical Origins of the American Self.* Shields argues that American identity consists of two elements, one of the Judeo-Christian influence and the other based on Roman classical literature. From the writings of Cotton Mather, William Livingston, Phillis Wheatley, Herman Melville, and others, Shields demonstrates that the classical works of Virgil and Ovid and Joseph Addison's play, *Cato,* were colossal influences reciprocating religion's dominance in colonial society and the American self of today. Since *Cato's Letters* contains numerous examples of classicism within its text and was named after the Roman general, the impact of Trenchard and Gordon's 138 essays substantiate the popularity of this classicism. *Cato's Letters* in New York helped to construct not only political identity but also Shields's colonial American identity.[68] Since *Cato's Letters* represents a product of Roman classicism and since these essays influenced the colonial public (from the higher elite of Thomas Jefferson and John Adams to the lower ranks of the populace) in its politics, then these findings strengthen Shields's classical DNA strand and that which acknowledges the political ideology of American identity.[69]

Within his study on the Declaration of Independence, Carl L. Becker proclaims, "Generally speaking, men are influenced by books which clarify their own thought, which express their own notions well, or which suggest to them ideas which their minds are already predisposed to accept."[70] This line of thinking applies to Cato's popularity within the colonies. Several letters to the editor believed that Cato's arguments were politically and morally enticing to readers. In addition, *Cato's Letters* possessed a lighter, more attractive argumentative style of writing compared to other writers of the period.[71] *Cato's Letters* eclipsed colonial America's politics as a result of its repetition in political battles and reader interaction with newspapers. As their political polestar, the letters became a ready conduit of expression for both editor and reader. Early editorial propaganda excoriated royal institutions and figures through the italicization, capitalization, and persistence of Cato's tracts. For readers, *Cato's Letters* became a set of words to which editors must also apply a standard of reverent depiction. In an era when the newspaper industry was still in its nascence and when acquiring information from around the colonies and empire was of everyday importance, the colonial reading public also submitted *Cato's Letters* to newspapers for publication during breaks in the news. If there was not any news to read, why not broadcast another Cato treatise? From these situations, it is evident why newspaper editors reprinted Cato so often, whether or not a political tussle was present. In 1735 New York newspapers "seemed to embody public opinion as never before."[72] With the media's reliance on the words of Cato, the public's political opinion was *Cato's Letters.*

By the 1760s and 1770s, an abundant supply of local news, foreign news, colonial essays, and political pamphlets such as Thomas Paine's *Common Sense* began crowding Cato's space.[73] Cato was indeed subject to references and reprintings in newspapers and various political pamphlets during the Revolutionary period (such as John Dickinson's *Late Regulations respecting the British Colonies . . .* of 1765 and John Chalmers's *Plain Truth* of 1776), but his overt prominence in the 1720s, 30s, and 40s declined in the public eye.[74] In the latter decades, *Cato's Letters* was more likely quoted, footnoted, or paraphrased than presented as essays in their entirety.[75]

The Revolutionary generation was imbued with Trenchard and Gordon's ideals and argumentation. By comparison, the music of the Beatles is not as overtly apparent in today's popular culture as in the 1960s. Yet today's music still draws tremendous influence and inspiration from their work. The Beatles are ingrained within society and noted as a classic. The same situation parallels Cato's in the later decades of the eighteenth century.[76] Stepping back into the colonial period, several questions may be asked. What about the reading knowledge of the lower orders in the 1750s and beyond? Do the essays play a direct ideological role for people during the Seven Years' War? Were colonists reluctant to fight for the British because of such readings? In these years leading up to the Revolution, how did the nonelite use these ideas of Cato in the world around them? In addition, weekly and monthly magazines were another type of print that excelled within colonial politics. This highly influential format of political discourse may foreshadow several fruitful conclusions on further study of Cato and the colonial reading public.[77]

Colonial newspapers reprinted Cato during times of political and newspaper scandal, or during times without any incident at all. In periods of war or political dispute, the importance of maintaining the people's freedoms often reemerges. This enunciation of liberties also appears again and again in today's society wherever an enemy is perceived—domestically or internationally. In most instances, people can recite the exact section or article of the Constitution documenting their infringed-upon freedoms. This alert, carefully articulated knowledge evolved from Cato's outlines of liberties before the Revolutionary period and ratification of the Constitution. Because of their celebratory status in such a large and important era of American history, *Cato's Letters* supplied a foundation in early eighteenth century political thought that still lingers in the speeches of today's political watchdogs and civil rights organizations.

For many years, historians have labeled *Cato's Letters* as "a classic for many Americans."[78] Unfortunately they have failed to prove exactly how this reputation developed. With the intense concentration of a reading public as described by Samuel Goodrich, the innumerable strands of proliferating news, and the great frequency and recognition of *Cato's Letters* within colonial society, Cato was successful in making individuals (elite and nonelite) acutely aware of their rights and liberties in colonial print and their surrounding political environment. This tradition foreshadowed the cries for liberty and justice in the eighteenth century through to modern America.

Notes

I would like to thank Jamie Bronstein, James Matray, William Eamon, Robert Buckingham, James Tagg, Ronald Hamowy, Adrian Johns, Charles E. Clark, Tracy Wong, John C. Shields, the anonymous reader of this volume, and the editors—Mark L. Kamrath and Sharon M. Harris—for their helpful advice, patience, and encouragement on earlier drafts of this essay.

1. Richard D. Brown, *Knowledge Is Power: The Diffusion of Information in Early America, 1700–1865* (New York: Oxford UP, 1989), 269.
2. Ibid., 30, 39. A visual companion to Brown's communication networks and the circulation of information is found in Robert Darnton, *The Forbidden Best-Sellers of Pre-Revolutionary France* (New York: Norton, 1995), 189. For enlightenment and news transferring in taverns and coffeehouses, see David W. Conroy, *In Public Houses: Drink and the Revolution of Authority in Colonial Massachusetts* (Chapel Hill: U of North Carolina P, 1995), and David S. Shields, *Civil Tongues and Polite Letters in British America* (Chapel Hill: U of North Carolina P, 1997), 55–65.
3. David D. Hall, "Introduction: The Uses of Literacy in New England, 1600–1850," in *Printing and Society in Early America*, eds. William L. Joyce et al. (Worcester, MA: American Antiquarian Society, 1983), 21.
4. Goodrich is the affluent author of numerous children's books in the nineteenth century under the pseudonym "Peter Parley." See Samuel G. Goodrich, *Recollections of a Lifetime, or Men and Things I have Seen*

(New York: Miller, Orton, and Mulligan, 1857; rpt. Detroit: Gale Research, 1967), 1: 86, and Hall, "Introduction," 21, for the quotation. For a further glimpse of Goodrich and his popularity in America, see John C. Shields, *The American Aeneas: Classical Origins of the American Self* (Knoxville: U of Tennessee P, 2001), 196–97.

5. Other examples of intensive eighteenth-century reading practices are found in William J. Gilmore, *Reading Becomes a Necessity of Life: Material and Cultural Life in Rural New England, 1780–1835* (Knoxville: U of Tennessee P, 1989), 266, and with the proprieties of Lord Chesterfield in Richard L. Bushman, *The Refinement of America: Persons, Houses, Cities* (New York: Knopf, 1992), 86. For discussions on intensive and extensive reading, see Hall, "Introduction"; Darnton, "Forbidden Best-Sellers," 218–19; Cathy N. Davidson, *Revolution and the Word: The Rise of the Novel in America* (New York: Oxford UP, 1986), 72–73; and Roger Chartier, *The Cultural Origins of the French Revolution*, trans. Lydia G. Cochrane (Durham: Duke UP, 1991), 67–91. A short bibliography of the important groundbreaking works by Rolf Engelsing, Rudolf Schenda, and Erich Schon is found in Darnton 422.

6. This essay highlights the proliferation of information, cultural influence, and reading among all orders of society (especially for the nonelite) in the early decades of the eighteenth century. For discussions on bottom-up and top-down influences, see Brown, *Knowledge Is Power*, and Peter Burke, *Popular Culture in Early Modern Europe* (New York: Harper and Row, 1978). With literacy rates estimated at 80 percent for men and 40–45 percent for women within New England, upper-class travelers such as Dr. Alexander Hamilton should not have been surprised in 1744 upon meeting the inarticulate, "a rabble of clowns" as Alexander puts it, who were just as knowledgeable as they on certain subjects; see Kenneth A. Lockridge, *Literacy in Colonial New England: An Enquiry into the Social Context of Literacy in the Early Modern West* (New York: Norton, 1974), 13–42, and Carl Bridenbaugh, ed., *Gentleman's Progress: The Itinerarium of Dr. Alexander Hamilton, 1744* (Chapel Hill: U of North Carolina P, 1948), 162–63. Responding to literacy and the transfer of information amongst the common people, Gary B. Nash writes that "the literacy rate was high in colonial America and especially widespread in the cities. Population density made it easy to pass broadsides and pamphlets from hand to hand or to read them aloud in the taverns." See Gary B. Nash, *The Urban Crucible: Social Change, Political Consciousness, and the Origins of the American Revolution* (Cambridge: Harvard UP, 1979), 200.

7. Arthur M. Schlesinger, *Prelude to Independence: The Newspaper War on Britain, 1764–1776* (New York: Knopf, 1957), 137; Forrest McDonald,

Novus Ordo Seclorum: The Intellectual Origins of the Constitution (Lawrence: UP of Kansas, 1985), 47; Elizabeth C. Cook, *Literary Influences in Colonial Newspapers: 1704–1750* (New York: Columbia UP, 1912; rpt. Port Washington, NY: Kennikat P, 1966), 81; Nash, *Urban Crucible*, 348.

8. Cook 81–90, 125–30; Clinton Rossiter, *Seedtime of the Republic: The Origin of the American Tradition of Political Liberty* (New York: Harcourt, Brace, 1953), 141–45, 492; Bernard Bailyn, *The Ideological Origins of the American Revolution* (Cambridge: Belknap P of Harvard UP, 1967; rpt. 1992), 35–45, 49–53; Gary Huxford, "English Libertarian Tradition in the Colonial Newspaper," *Journalism Quarterly* 45 (Winter 1968): 677–86. Huxford, most notably, has outlined the prominence of *Cato's Letters* amid various political disputes.

9. Marie P. McMahon, *The Radical Whigs, John Trenchard and Thomas Gordon: Libertarian Loyalists to the New House of Hanover* (Lanham, MD: UP of America, 1990).

10. Both David L. Jacobson and Ronald Hamowy have compiled and edited *Cato's Letters* (the former, a select few; the latter, the entire series). The two collections furnish readers with excellent surveys of Trenchard and Gordon's authorial histories, their beliefs, and the impact of their prose in Britain and the American colonies. In his introductory essay, Jacobson also cites several examples of *Cato's Letters* reprintings in colonial newspapers. See John Trenchard and Thomas Gordon, *The English Libertarian Heritage: From the Writings of John Trenchard and Thomas Gordon in "The Independent Whig" and "Cato's Letters,"* ed. David L. Jacobson (Indianapolis: Bobbs-Merrill, 1965), and Trenchard and Gordon, *Cato's Letters or Essays on Liberty, Civil and Religious, and Other Important Subjects*, ed. Ronald Hamowy (Indianapolis: Liberty Fund, 1995).

11. James N. Green, "English Books and Printing in the Age of Franklin," in *A History of the Book in America*, vol. 1, *The Colonial Book in the Atlantic World*, eds. Hugh Amory and David D. Hall (Cambridge: Cambridge UP, 2000), 254.

12. Circulation statistics underestimate the capacity of information recycling from one reader to the next. But they nonetheless provide initial clues to measuring the influence and dissemination of political works such as *Cato's Letters*. See Isaiah Thomas, *The History of Printing in America, with a Biography of Printers & an Account of Newspapers*, ed. Marcus A. McCorison, 2d ed. (New York: Weathervane, 1970), 14; Charles S. Brigham, *Journals and Journeymen: A Contribution to the History of Early American Newspapers* (Philadelphia: U of Pennsylvania P, 1950), 19–22; Charles E. Clark, *The Public Prints: The Newspaper in Anglo-American*

Culture, 1665–1740 (New York: Oxford UP, 1994), 206, 258–59; and Amory and Hall, ed., *A History of the Book in America*, 234, 293, 340, 361. For newspaper recycling see Harry B. Weiss, *A Graphic Summary of the Growth of Newspapers in New York and Other States, 1704–1820* (New York: New York Public Library, 1948), 6.

13. In order to address the increased politicization and awareness of liberties by the public through the exposure of *Cato's Letters*, one must quickly assess the status of politics within the public sphere. What is the positioning of this politicization before *Cato's Letters*? Colonists were well aware of their general rights as humans from sources of natural law, the moral economy of society, and the Magna Carta. Although here the argument is for the establishment of a more-individualized political awareness, Richard Merritt provides a useful look at the development of a group-orientated "political community" within the colonies; see *Symbols of American Community, 1735–1775* (New Haven: Yale UP, 1966).

14. Jürgen Habermas, *Structural Transformation of the Public Sphere: An Inquiry into a Category of Bourgeois Society*, trans. Thomas Burger (Cambridge: MIT P, 1989), and Michael Warner, *The Letters of the Republic: Publication and the Public Sphere in Eighteenth-Century America* (Cambridge: Harvard UP, 1990). A small sample of works that discuss and challenge Habermas's thesis includes the collected essays in Craig Calhoun, ed., *Habermas and the Public Sphere* (Cambridge: MIT P, 1992), and Robert A. Gross, "Print and the Public Sphere in Early America," an unpublished paper presented to the Omohundro Institute of Early American History and Culture, October 31, 2000. While this chapter argues for the dissemination and prominence of *Cato's Letters* in the minds of the pre-Revolutionary reading public, one should not discount the relevance of other realms of influence for an increasingly politicized public. For example, economics, religion, and political parties also contribute to an individual's awareness of political situations and the environment around him or her. For more on these factors and the growth of colonial politics within Boston, New York, and Philadelphia, see Gary B. Nash, "The Transformation of Urban Politics, 1700–1765," *Journal of American History* 60 (December 1973): 605–32, and Nash, *Urban Crucible*, 124, 141–47.

15. Discussions on the South Sea scandal are found in John Carswell, *The South Sea Bubble* (London: A. Sutton, 1960); Charles B. Realey, "The *London Journal* and Its Authors, 1720–1723," *Bulletin of the University of Kansas* 36, no. 23 (1935): 1–34; and Ronald Hamowy, "*Cato's Letters*, John Locke, and the Republican Paradigm," *History of Political Thought* 11 (Summer 1990): 273–94.

16. Realey, "The *London Journal* and Its Authors," 3.
17. For scholarship pertaining to Addison's play, see Henry C. Montgomery, "Addison's *Cato* and George Washington," *Classical Journal* 55 (February 1960): 210–12; Fredric M. Litto, "Addison's *Cato* in the Colonies," *William and Mary Quarterly*, 3d ser., 23 (July 1966): 431–49; Albert Furtwangler, "Cato at Valley Forge," *Modern Language Quarterly* 41 (March 1980): 38–53; and Randall Fuller, "Theaters of the American Revolution: The Valley Forge *Cato* and the Meschianza in Their Transcultural Contexts," *Early American Literature* 34 (1999): 126–46.
18. Plutarch, *Cato the Younger* no. 14 (London: London Association of Classical Teachers, 1984), 33. The following works have informed this discussion on the beliefs and attitudes of Marcus Porcius Cato: Lily Ross Taylor, *Party Politics in the Age of Caesar* (Berkeley: U of California P, 1949; rpt. 1971), and Erich S. Gruen, *The Last Generation of the Roman Republic* (Berkeley: U of California P, 1974).
19. Julius Caesar was not his only adversary. In 53 B.C.E. Marcus Porcius Cato successfully thwarted Pompey's initiatives to form a dictatorship.
20. Taylor 167–68.
21. Plutarch 43.
22. Caroline Robbins, *The Eighteenth-Century Commonwealthman: Studies in the Transmission, Development and Circumstance of English Liberal Thought from the Restoration of Charles II until the War with the Thirteen Colonies* (Cambridge: Harvard UP, 1959), 117.
23. For more discussion on the beliefs and writings of *Cato's Letters*, see Realey; McMahon; Hamowy, "*Cato's Letters*, John Locke, and the Republican Paradigm"; Jacobson xxxiii–xlvii; Robbins 115–25; Isaac Kramnick, *Bolingbroke and His Circle: The Politics of Nostalgia in the Age of Walpole* (Cambridge: Harvard UP, 1968), 243–52; and J. G. A. Pocock, *The Machiavellian Moment: Florentine Political Thought and the Atlantic Republican Tradition* (Princeton: Princeton UP, 1975), 467–77.
24. Later references to "Cato" in this essay pertain strictly to *Cato's Letters*, and should not be confused with Marcus Porcius Cato or Addison's play.
25. Sidney Kobre, *The Development of the Colonial Newspaper* (Gloucester, MA: Peter Smith, 1944; rpt. 1960), 64; see also Cook 121–49.
26. Thomas 463.
27. Ibid., 462.
28. It should be noted that James Alexander was the *New-York Weekly Journal*'s editor, with Francis Harison holding the *New-York Gazette*'s

respective position. Stanley Katz proclaims that Alexander was the "guiding genius" behind the *Journal*, transforming "virtually every department of the *Journal* into a vehicle for criticism of the Governor." See James Alexander, *A Brief Narrative of the Case and Trial of John Peter Zenger, Printer of the New-York Weekly Journal*, ed. Stanley N. Katz (Cambridge: Belknap P of the Harvard UP, 1963), 8–9, and Vincent Buranelli, "Peter Zenger's Editor," *American Quarterly* 7 (1955): 174–81. Although one could debate Alexander's status within the workings of the *Journal*, this essay presents Zenger as the newspaper's main figurehead because of the fact that numerous newspaper essays, letters, and correspondence are solely addressed to and from him.

29. In his description of New York's political environment, Richard Bernstein writes, "Cosby had few qualifications to be governor . . . he saw his governorship as a means to rebuild his shattered finances" and "to wring as much money out of his post as he could. Cosby made matters worse for himself with his contempt for those whom he was sent to govern, and his clumsy and arrogant interventions in the politics of colonial New York." Richard B. Bernstein, "Review of Paul Finkelman, ed., *A Brief Narrative of the Case and Tryal of John Peter Zenger, Printer of the New-York Weekly Journal*," H-Law, H-Net Reviews, January 2000. URL: http://www.h-net.msu.edu/reviews/showrev.cgi?path=132509487544459. These political intrusions hindered the plans of Lewis Morris, James Alexander, and Rip Van Dam, men who had a vendetta against Cosby for usurping their political power in New York (and thus hiring Zenger for the antagonist position). Scholarship on this group's political and literary activities is found in Stanley N. Katz, *Newcastle's New York: Anglo-American Politics, 1732–1753* (Cambridge: Belknap P of the Harvard UP, 1968), 61–90, and Alison Olson, "The Zenger Case Revisited: Satire, Sedition, and Political Debate in Eighteenth-Century America," *Early American Literature* 35 (2000): 223–45.

30. Important indications as to the range of readership demographics for the *Journal* and the scope of the impact of *Cato's Letters* on the New York populace (other than wealthy gentlemen of prominent social standing) during this period are found in letters to the editor from sailors (December 17 and 24, 1733), carpenters (January 7, 1734), housekeepers and maids (January 21 and 28, 1734), other tradesmen (July 8, 1734), women (February 18, August 19, September 9 and 23, December 23, 1734; May 12, 1735; February 23, 1736), and the poor (January 14, September 2 and 16, 1734; April 21, December 1, 1735).

31. See Cook 82 and Clark 207–14.

32. Gary Huxford, "The Old Whig Comes to America: A Study in the Transit of Ideas" (Ph.D. diss., University of Washington, 1963), 151–52.

33. *Cato's Letters*, vol. 2, ed. Hamowy, no. 38, "The Right and Capacity of the People to judge of Government." All subsequent page citations of *Cato's Letters* refer to the modern Hamowy edition.

34. Kobre 65. These attacks concerning French observations continued to fester among the pages of the *Journal*, becoming an easy, early target for dispute against Cosby's gubernatorial abilities.

35. In his discussion on propaganda and the effectiveness of newspapers during the American Revolution, Schlesinger points out that newspapers of the 1760s and 1770s contained similar editorial employments of italicization and capitalization; see *Prelude to Independence*, 59.

36. *Journal*, January 21, 1734.

37. *Cato's Letters* 3, no. 112, "Fondness for Posterity nothing else but Self-Love. Such as are Friends to publick Liberty, are the only true Lovers of Posterity."

38. Ibid., 787.

39. Frank Luther Mott, *American Journalism, A History: 1690–1960*, 3d ed. (New York: Macmillan, 1962), 33.

40. Cook 126. She also writes, "Zenger was reprinting not only *Cato's Letters* but any other essays or verse that would strengthen or illustrate his point of view"; see also 129–30 and Mott, *American Journalism*, 33. The others failed to reach Cato's frequency or impact.

41. *Journal*, December 17, 1733.

42. Ibid., February 4, 1734.

43. Ibid., February 11, 1734.

44. This quote comes from *Cato's Letters* 4, no. 113, "Letter to Cato, concerning his many Adversaries and Answerers," 792.

45. *Cato's Letters* 1, no. 15, "Of Freedom of Speech: That the same is inseparable from publick Liberty," *Journal*, February 18, 1734.

46. The *New-York Gazette*'s perspective is found in its January 28, February 25, and March 4, 1734, editions. Similar developments emerged in other cities as well. The priorities of Cato's Philadelphia readers were seen three and a half years earlier in the *American Weekly Mercury*. There a reader had written to the newspaper complaining of the improper usage of *Cato's Letters* within the essays of "Brutus or Cassius"; see *American Weekly Mercury* (Philadelphia), August 4, 1729. Hints at the refinement of Cato and *New-England Courant* readers are also found. In 1722, *Courant* editors

had to correct a misprinted Cato essay from their May 14 edition. The next week, a blurb inserted near the advertisements confirmed, "*In our last Paper (in the Extract from the* London Journal*) at the End of a Sentense quoted from* Seneca, *was omitted the two Words,* multis negas*: The whole runs thus,* Vitam tibi ipsi si negas, multis negas." *New-England Courant* (Boston), May 21, 1722. The mended sentence belongs within *Cato's Letters* 2, no. 42, "Considerations on the Nature of Laws," 292. Hence, readers in New York, Philadelphia, and Boston grew to recognize and insist on perfect replications of *Cato's Letters* in the newspapers they read.

47. *Cato's Letters* 1, no. 32, "Reflections upon Libelling."
48. *Cato's Letters* 1, no. 13, "The Arts of misleading the People by Sounds."
49. *Cato's Letters* 1, no. 32, "Reflections upon Libelling."
50. Cosby and DeLancey were unsuccessful in incarcerating Zenger and company, as jurors were "reluctant to act against Zenger"; see Katz, *Newcastle's New York,* 76.
51. *Cato's Letters* 3, no. 75, "Of the Restraints which ought to be laid upon publick Rulers."
52. *Cato's Letters* 3, no. 115, "The encroaching Nature of Power, ever to be watched and checked."
53. Katz, *Newcastle's New York,* 76.
54. *Cato's Letters* 1, no. 15, "Of Freedom of Speech: That the same is inseparable from publick Liberty," *Journal,* November 11, 1734.
55. Thomas, *History of Printing in America,* 487, and *Journal,* November 25, 1734. Foreshadowing this colonial American drama, British Parliament charged the *London Journal* for libel against the government soon after it started publishing *Cato's Letters* in May 1721; see Realey, "The *London Journal,* 1720–1723," 19–26.
56. Katz, *Newcastle's New York,* 76. Governor Cosby designated four specific issues for burning; December 17, 1733; September 23 and 30, 1734; and October 7, 1734; see Alexander 117–32. Interestingly, none of the above "libelous" *Journal* issues features a *Cato's Letters* reprinting. This again reflects the esteem held for the Cato literature by both sides of the Cosby-Morrisite struggle.
57. *Cato's Letters* 3, no. 100, "Discourse upon Libels," *Journal,* December 9, 1734.
58. Leonard W. Levy, *Freedom of Speech and Press in Early American History: Legacy of Suppression* (New York: Harper Torchbooks, 1963), 36.
59. Kobre 67.

60. It is difficult to accurately pinpoint their motives, but current trends seen within past newspapers provide relevance to the above factors. In September 1729 Philadelphia's Crown authorities were dissuaded from charging *Mcrcury* cditor Andrcw Bradford for libcl duc to thcir lack of confidence in a conviction. This example and Bernstein's previous description of New York politics demonstrates that a general atmosphere of colonial tension predominated with its governors.

61. *Cato's Letters* 2, no. 60, "All Government proved to be instituted by Men, and only to intend the general Good of Men."

62. *Cato's Letters* 2, no. 60, 414.

63. Bernstein, Review of "A Brief Narrative," H-Law, January 2000; see also Leonard W. Levy, "Did the Zenger Case Really Matter? Freedom of the Press in Colonial New York," *William and Mary Quarterly*, 3d ser., 27 (January 1960): 35–50.

64. As a consequence to the Morris-Cosby feud, factious pamphlets multiplied during this tumultuous political era. Nash points out that "the Morris-Cosby struggle for power brought twenty-seven pamphlets from the presses between 1732 and 1734, when only an occasional piece had appeared before"; see "Transformation of Urban Politics," 616. These findings discount the political works within the *Journal* and the *Gazette.*

65. Most notably, see Habermas 43–51.

66. Habermas claims that newspapers were "the hobbyhorses of the money-aristocracy" in Great Britain, which was similar to the situation in New York; see 182.

67. The original arguments that inform and support this discussion are from Nancy Fraser, "Rethinking the Public Sphere: A Contribution to the Critique of Actually Existing Democracy," in Calhoun 115–117. Bruce I. Weiner's unpublished paper, "Republican Culture and Early American Magazines, 1750–1800," presented at the Second Biennial Meeting of the Society of Early Americanists in Norfolk, Virginia, on March 8, 2001, pointed the way to these pages.

68. Shields's meticulous examinations of Virgil within the works of Mather, Wheatley, Melville, and others should lead to a new perspective on colonial newspapers, manuscripts, and diaries and provoke further examinations on the depth of Roman classicism in popular American culture. Scholars will now be forced to question the origins behind the text. This work elicits extended questioning in regards to the range and depth of classicism within the nonelite readers of colonial America. From *American Aeneas*, scholars may discern the intellectual elite's immersion

into the realms of Virgil and Ovid, but did regular people embrace this classicism? Did the reading public ever draw a connection between Virgil and Mather? And, finally, to what extent does Virgil, as an example, appear in colonial newspapers and magazines?

69. See John C. Shields xlv. As part of Shields's theory on the foundations of American culture, he describes how the Judaeo-Christian heritage and classical heritage are actually "two strands coming together, intertwining and interconnecting so as to accommodate virtually infinite possibilities . . . of Americanness" (xlv). To explain this phenomenon further, Shields equates his two templates with the analogy of a double helix of human DNA.

70. Carl L. Becker, *The Declaration of Independence: A Study in the History of Political Ideas.* (New York: Knopf, 1922; rpt. Vintage Books, 1958), 28.

71. Huxford, "English Libertarian Tradition," 686.

72. Green, "English Books and Printing in the Age of Franklin," in Amory and Hall 255.

73. Articles by Donald Lutz and the team of David Lundberg and Henry May confirm the expanse of literature coming into the colonies. The latter authors illustrate that Cato's prevalence rested in the early decades of the eighteenth century. By looking at collections and library catalogues, Lundberg and May found that *Cato's Letters* was present in 37 percent of the holdings between 1700 and 1776. This percentage falls down to 21 and then 13, and then increases to 18 for the periods of 1777–1790, 1791–1800, and 1801–1813, respectively. See David Lundberg and Henry F. May, "The Enlightened Reader in America," *American Quarterly* 28 (Summer 1976): 279. Cato's presence within colonial newspapers supports a similar declining trend. According to Donald Lutz's statistics, Cato was only seventh among the most cited authors within colonial literature. Montesquieu topped the list between 1760 and 1805; see Donald S. Lutz, "Late Eighteenth-Century American Political Thought," *American Political Science Review* 78 (March 1984): 194. Because Lutz's study begins in the latter half of the eighteenth century, its scope truncates Cato's more formidable periods. As illustrated in the list below, *Cato's Letters* was already widely reprinted.

74. In contrast, Charles E. Clark argues for a "full-scale rediscovery and adaptation" of *Cato's Letters;* see Clark, "Early American Journalism: News and Opinion in the Popular Press," in Amory and Hall 350. Another theory for the decline of popularity in *Cato's Letters* is found in Jacobson lix.

75. To add to this implicitness, scholars have often commented on the similarities of phraseology between *Cato's Letters* and Revolutionary

documents. For example, Richard Buel points to Cato as an influence in the "Address to the Inhabitants of Quebec" in 1774, Pauline Maier denotes George Mason's 1776 draft of Virginia's Declaration of Rights, and Elizabeth C. Cook acknowledges some parallels with the Declaration of Independence. See Richard Buel Jr. "Freedom of the Press in Revolutionary America: The Evolution of Libertarianism, 1760–1820," in *The Press and the American Revolution*, eds. Bernard Bailyn and John B. Hench (Worcester, MA: American Antiquarian Society, 1980), 69; Pauline Maier, *American Scripture: Making the Declaration of Independence* (New York: Knopf, 1997), 127–28; and Cook, *Literary Influences in Colonial Newspapers*, 82.

76. Most recently, the controversy concerning authorship of several Beatles songs has reemerged. Paul McCartney and his recording company have tampered with the writing credits to many songs from the "Lennon/McCartney" duo. McCartney has attempted to correct history by switching the "Lennon/McCartney" tag to "McCartney/Lennon" for songs that he had predominantly written. People are outraged, lawsuits suggested. Thus, as expressed within colonial newspapers and important cultural influences like *Cato's Letters*, the issue of accuracy remains timeless. See Jenny Eliscu, "McCartney Reignites Beatles Feud," *Rolling Stone* 26 (December 2002): 19–20.

77. Cursory investigations concerning *Cato's Letters* have shown approval and usage from several magazines; see *American Museum* (Philadelphia, December 1791); *Massachusetts Magazine* (Boston, September 1792); *Cato's Letters* 2, no. 49, "Of the Power of Prejudice," *New Hampshire Magazine or the Monthly Repository of Useful Information* (Concord, October 1793); *Cato's Letters* 2, no. 40, "Considerations on the restless and selfish Spirit of Man," *New Hampshire Magazine* (November 1793); and a small quotation from Cato in "An Eulogy on Ugliness," *Weekly Magazine of Original Essays, Fugitive Pieces, and Interesting Intelligence* (Philadelphia, February 9, 1799).

78. Pauline Maier, *Resistance to Revolution: Colonial Radicals and the Development of American Opposition to Britain, 1765–1776* (New York: Knopf, 1972; rpt. New York: Norton, 1991), 27.

Cato's Letters in Colonial American Newspapers

Below is a list of early American newspapers and the corresponding published dates that contain references to *Cato's Letters*. The contents of the newspapers range from issues holding an entire Cato essay to a small quotation to a Trenchard or Gordon reference to someone who pretended to write a Cato letter (through form or end signature). The essays and debates by the Catos of the Revolutionary era as written by George Clinton, Abraham Yates Jr., and George Mason are not included. Since every newspaper printed in colonial America has not been examined and the chart is incomplete, further amendments and additions are still to come. But as a complement to the above article, this list provides an important perspective of Cato's presence within eighteenth-century America.

Date	Newspaper	Cato's Letters Content
Sept. 11, 1721	*New-England Courant (Boston)*	*No. 32: "Reflections upon Libelling"*
Oct. 9, 1721	*New-England Courant*	*No. 34: "Of Flattery"*
Oct. 16, 1721	*New-England Courant*	*No. 34: "Of Flattery"*
Oct. 23, 1721	*New-England Courant*	*No. 33: "Cautions against the natural Encroachments of Power"*
Oct. 30, 1721	*New-England Courant*	*No. 33: "Cautions against the natural Encroachments of Power"*
Dec. 4, 1721	*New-England Courant*	*Editor quotes Cato within a letter to religious community*
Feb. 20, 1722	*American Weekly Mercury (Philadelphia)*	*No. 38: "The Right and Capacity of the People to judge of Government"*
Mar. 15, 1722	*American Weekly Mercury*	*No. 40: "Considerations on the restless and selfish Spirit of Man"*
Mar. 29, 1722	*American Weekly Mercury*	*No. 34: "Of Flattery"*
Apr. 2, 1722	*New-England Courant*	*Letter by "Philanthropos," rephrasing Cato No. 57: "Of false Honour, publick and private"*
Apr. 19, 1722	*American Weekly Mercury*	*No. 35: "Of publick Spirit"*
May 7, 1722	*New-England Courant*	*No. 27: "General Corruption, how ominous to the Publick, and how discouraging to every virtuous Man. With its fatal Progress whenever encouraged"*
May 14, 1722	*New-England Courant*	*No. 42: "Considerations on the Nature of Laws"*

Date	Newspaper	Cato's Letters Content
May 21, 1722	*New-England Courant*	*Announcement regarding a misprinted quote from Cato No. 42: "Considerations on the Nature of Laws."*
May 28, 1722	*New-England Courant*	*Letter to the editor possessing a quote from Cato No. 27: "General Corruption, how ominous to the Publick, and how discouraging to every virtuous Man. With its fatal Progress whenever encouraged"*
May 31, 1722	*American Weekly Mercury*	*Cato mentioned by "Americo-Britannus"*
June 7, 1722	*American Weekly Mercury*	*No. 36: "Of Loyalty"*
June 21, 1722	*American Weekly Mercury*	*"Americo Britannus" again refers to Cato's Letters No. 33: "Cautions against the natural Encroachments of Power"*
July 9, 1722	*New-England Courant*	*"Silence Dogood" [Benjamin Franklin] reprints No. 15: "Of Freedom of Speech: That the same is inseparable from Liberty"*
July 16, 1722	*New-England Courant*	*A passage from No. 15: "Of Freedom of Speech: That the same is inseparable from Liberty" is reprinted in a letter to the editor*
July 23, 1722	*New-England Courant*	*"Silence Dogood" includes a passage from No. 31: "Considerations on the Weakness and Inconsistencies of human Nature"*
Jan. 7, 1724	*American Weekly Mercury*	*No. 131: "Of Reverence true and false"*
Jan. 14, 1724	*American Weekly Mercury*	*No. 131: "Of Reverence true and false"*
Feb. 11, 1724	*American Weekly Mercury*	*No. 128: "Address to such of the Laity as are Followers of the disaffected Clergy, and of their Accomplices"*
Feb. 18, 1724	*American Weekly Mercury*	*No. 128: "Address to such of the Laity as are Followers of the disaffected Clergy, and of their Accomplices"* *No. 130: "same address continued"*
Feb. 25, 1724	*American Weekly Mercury*	*No. 130: "same address continued"*

Date	Newspaper	Cato's Letters Content
Mar. 3, 1724	*American Weekly Mercury*	*No. 130: "same address continued"*
Mar. 20, 1729	*American Weekly Mercury*	*"The Busy-Body" [Joseph Breintnall] reprints No. 100: "Discourse upon Libels"*
Apr. 17, 1729	*American Weekly Mercury*	*"The Busy-Body" reprints No. 102: "The Contemptibleness of Granduer without Virtue"*
May 1, 1729	*American Weekly Mercury*	*"The Busy-Body" reprints No. 106: "Of Plantations and Colonies"*
May 22, 1729	*American Weekly Mercury*	*Female reader: "palming your Cato's"*
Aug. 14, 1729	*American Weekly Mercury*	*Reader complaining of Cato being plagiarized*
Sept. 18, 1729	*American Weekly Mercury*	*"The Busy-Body reprints passages from: No. 39: "Of the Passions; that they all alike good or all alike evil according as they are applied," No. 40: "Considerations on the rest less and selfish Spirit of Man" No. 115: "The encroaching Nature of Power, ever to be watched and checked" No. 96: "Of Parties in England; how they vary, and interchange Characters, just as they are in Power, or out of it, yet still keep their former Names"*
Apr. 9, 1730	*American Weekly Mercury*	*Reprints No. 45: "Of the Equality and Inequality of Men"*
Apr. 16, 1730	*American Weekly Mercury*	*Reprints No. 111: "The same Subject continued" [from No. 110, Of Liberty and Necessity]*
Apr. 30, 1730	*American Weekly Mercury*	*No. 111: "The same Subject continued"*
May 14, 1730	*American Weekly Mercury*	*No. 123: "Inquiry concerning Madness, especially religious Madness, called Enthusiasm"*
May 21, 1730	*American Weekly Mercury*	*No. 123: "Inquiry concerning Madness, especially religious Madness, called Enthusiasm"*
May 28, 1730	*American Weekly Mercury*	*No. 124: "Further Reasonings upon Enthusiasm"*
June 4, 1730	*American Weekly Mercury*	*No. 124: "Further Reasonings upon Enthusiasm"*

Date	Newspaper	Cato's Letters Content
Dec. 10, 1733	*New-York Weekly Journal (New York)*	*No. 38: "The Right and Capacity of the People to judge of Government"*
Dec. 17, 1733	*New-York Weekly Journal*	*Letter to the editor questioning his representation of Cato*
Dec. 31, 1733	*New-York Weekly Journal*	*No. 131: "Of Reverence true and false."*
Jan. 28, 1734	*New-York Weekly Journal*	*No. 112: "Fondness for Posterity nothing else but Self-love. Such as are Friends to publick Liberty, are the only true Lovers of Posterity"*
Jan. 28, 1734	*New-York Gazette (New York)*	*Proper usage of Cato's Letters acknowledged*
Feb. 4, 1734	*New-York Weekly Journal*	*"English Cato have been Almost Divine"*
Feb. 11, 1734	*New-York Weekly Journal*	*Rebuttal letter to the New-York Gazette on their ill usage of Cato in a previous newspaper* *Quote from No. 113: "Letter to Cato, concerning his many Adversaries and Answerers"* *No. 14: "The unhappy State of despotick Princes, compared with the happy Lot of such as rule by settled Laws. How the latter, by abusing their Trust, may forfeit their Crown"*
Feb. 18, 1734	*New-York Weekly Journal*	*No. 15: "Of Freedom of Speech: that the same is inseparable from Liberty"* *Zenger swells "Gordon's Letters to a Gygantick size"*
Feb. 25, 1734	*New-York Gazette*	*Letter to the editor regarding Gordon's and Zenger's swelling fonts*
Feb. 25, 1734	*New-York Weekly Journal*	*No. 32: "Reflections upon Libelling"* *No. 13: "The Arts of misleading the People by Sounds"*
Mar. 4, 1734	*New-York Gazette*	*Letter to the editor: "with all possible deference to the profound Admirer of Cato"*
Mar. 4, 1734	*New-York Weekly Journal*	*No. 32: "Reflections upon Libelling"*

Date	Newspaper	Cato's Letters Content
Mar. 11, 1734	*New-York Weekly Journal*	*No. 33: "Cautions against the natural Encroachments of Power"*
Mar. 21, 1734	*Pennsylvania Gazette (Philadelphia)*	*Cato's Letters volume advertised for sale*
Mar. 25, 1734	*New-York Gazette*	*Mentioning of "American Catos"*
May 27, 1734	*New-York Weekly Journal*	*No. 75: "Of the Restraints which ought to be laid upon publick Rulers"* *No. 115: "The encroaching Nature of Power, ever to be watched and checked"*
Nov. 11, 1734	*New-York Weekly Journal*	*No. 15: "Of Freedom of Speech: that the same is inseparable from Liberty"*
Dec. 9, 1734	*New-York Weekly Journal*	*No. 100: "Discourse upon Libels"*
Dec. 30, 1734	*New-York Weekly Journal*	*Quotes from No. 113: "Letter to Cato, concerning his many Adversaries and Answerers"*
July 7, 1735	*New-York Weekly Journal*	*No. 42: "Considerations on the Nature of Laws"*
July 14, 1735	*New-York Weekly Journal*	*No. 42: "Considerations on the Nature of Laws"*
July 21, 1735	*New-York Weekly Journal*	*No. 37: "Character of a good and of an evil Magistrate, quoted from Algernon Sidney, Esq."*
Aug. 25, 1735	*New-York Weekly Journal*	*No. 60: "All Government proved to be instituted by Men, and only to intend the general Good of Men"*
Sept. 1, 1735	*New-York Weekly Journal*	*No. 60: "All Government proved to be instituted by Men, and only to intend the general Good of Men"*
Sept. 8, 1735	*New-York Weekly Journal*	*No. 62: "An Enquiry into the Nature and Extent of Liberty; with its Loveliness and Advantages, and the vile Effects of Slavery"*
Sept. 15, 1735	*New-York Weekly Journal*	*No. 62: "An Enquiry into the Nature and Extent of Liberty; with its Loveliness and Advantages, and the vile Effects of Slavery"*

Date	Newspaper	Cato's Letters Content
Sept. 23, 1735	*New-York Weekly Journal*	*No. 62: "An Enquiry into the Nature and Extent of Liberty; with its Loveliness and Advantages, and the vile Effects of Slavery"*
June 10, 1736	*Pennsylvania Gazette*	*No. 128: "Address to such of the Laity as are Followers of the disaffected Clergy, and of their Accomplices"*
June 12, 1736	*South-Carolina Gazette (Charles-Town)*	*No. 15: "Of Freedom of Speech: That the same is inseparable from publick Liberty"*
May 4, 1738	*American Weekly Mercury*	*"Cato, Jr." paraphrases No. 38: "The Right and Capacity of the People to judge of Government"*
Mar. 26, 1739	*New-York Weekly Journal*	*No. 56: "A Vindication of Brutus, for having killed Caesar."*
Apr. 2, 1739	*New-York Weekly Journal*	*No. 56: "A Vindication of Brutus, for having killed Caesar."*
Apr. 9, 1739	*New-York Weekly Journal*	*No. 56: "A Vindication of Brutus, for having killed Caesar."*
Jan. 11, 1748	*Independent Advertiser (Boston)*	*Paraphrase from No. 45: "Of the Equality and Inequality of Men"* *Paraphrase from No. 62: "An Enquiry into the Nature and Extent of Liberty; with its Loveliness and Advantages, and the vile Effects of Slavery"*
Jan. 21, 1748	*Boston Weekly News-Letter (Boston)*	*Cato's Letters volume advertised for sale*
Jan. 25, 1748	*Independent Advertiser*	*No. 35: "Of Publick Spirit"*
Feb. 29, 1748	*Independent Advertiser*	*No. 38: "The Right and Capacity of the People to judge of Government"*
Mar. 14, 1748	*Independent Advertiser*	*"No Mob's" letter to the editor complaining of Cato plagiarism*
May 16, 1748	*Independent Advertiser*	*No. 37: "Character of a good and of an evil Magistrate, quoted from Algernon Sidney, Esq."*
June 13, 1748	*Independent Advertiser*	*No. 26: "The sad Effects of general Corruption, quoted from Algernon Sidney, Esq."*

Date	Newspaper	Cato's Letters Content
July 7, 1748	*Boston Weekly News-Letter*	*Cato's Letters quote prefaces front page*
July 16, 1748	*South-Carolina Gazette*	*No. 15: "Of Freedom of Speech: That the same is inseparable from publick Liberty"*
July 25, 1748	*Independent Advertiser*	*Cato's Letters volume advertised for sale*
July 29, 1748	*South-Carolina Gazette*	*No. 37: "Character of a good and of an evil Magistrate, quoted from Algernon Sidney, Esq."*
Aug. 8, 1748	*Independent Advertiser*	*Cato's Letters volume advertised for sale*
Aug. 8, 1748	*South-Carolina Gazette*	*No. 38: "The Right and Capacity of the People to judge of Government"*
Aug. 22, 1748	*Independent Advertiser*	*No. 43: "The natural Passion of men with Superiority"*
Oct. 24, 1748	*Independent Advertiser*	*No. 40: "Considerations on the restless and selfish Spirit of Man"*
Dec. 19, 1748	*Independent Advertiser*	*No. 73: "A display of Tyranny, its destructive Nature, and its Tendency to dispeople the Earth"*
Dec. 26, 1748	*Independent Advertiser*	*Phrase from No. 34: "Of Flattery" in front page essay*
Feb. 13, 1749	*Independent Advertiser*	*No. 87: "Gold and Silver in a Country, to be considered only as Commodities"*
Mar. 13, 1749	*Independent Advertiser*	*Paraphrase from No. 31: "Considerations on the Weakness and Inconsistencies of human Nature"*
Mar. 20, 1749	*South-Carolina Gazette*	*No. 99: "The Important Duty of Attendance in Parliament recommended to the Members"*
June 26, 1749	*Independent Advertiser*	*No. 67: "Arts and Sciences the Effects of Civil Liberty only, and ever destroyed or oppressed by Tyranny"*
May 28, 1753	*New-York Gazette*	*Cato's Letters volume advertised for sale*
June 11, 1753	*New-York Mercury (New York)*	*Cato's Letters volume advertised for sale*

Date	Newspaper	Cato's Letters Content
July 23, 1753	*New-York Mercury*	*Cato's Letters reference on front page*
Sept. 20, 1753	*Independent Reflector (New York)*	*No. 131: "Of Reverence true and false"*
Mar. 3, 1755	*New-York Mercury*	*Thomas Gordon is mentioned, Cato's Letters quote used in preface*
Apr. 21, 1755	*Boston Gazette (Boston)*	*No. 15: "Of Freedom of Speech: That the same is inseparable from publick Liberty"*
May 12, 1755	*Boston Gazette*	*No. 38: "The Right and Capacity of the People to judge of Government"*
May 19, 1755	*Boston Gazette*	*No. 38: "The Right and Capacity of the People to judge of Government"*
June 23, 1755	*Boston Gazette*	*No. 24: "Of the natural Honesty of the People, and their reasonable Demands. How important it is to every Government to consult their Affections and Interests"*
Apr. 26, 1756	*Boston Gazette*	*Phrases from No. 15: "Of Freedom of Speech: That the same is insepa rable from publick Liberty"* *Passage from No. 70: "Second Address to the Freeholders, &c. upon the same Subject" used in a letter to the editor*
Feb. 23, 1758	*Pennsylvania Journal and Weekly Advertiser (Philadelphia)*	*"The Watchman" quotes a section of No. 15: "Of Freedom of Speech: That the same is inseparable from publick Liberty"*
Mar. 2, 1758	*Pennsylvania Journal and Weekly Advertiser*	*Letter to the editor applauds the usage of Cato's Letters*
Mar. 9, 1758	*Pennsylvania Journal and Weekly Advertiser*	*Passage quoted from No. 17: "What Measures are actually taken by wicked and desperate Ministers to ruin and enslave their Country"*
Mar. 16, 1758	*Pennsylvania Journal and Weekly Advertiser*	*Letter to the editor requesting an portion of No. 32: "Reflections upon Libelling" for print*
Apr. 6, 1758	*Pennsylvania Journal and Weekly Advertiser*	*Cato's Letters mentioned in a letter to the editor*
Aug. 26, 1765	*Boston Evening-Post (Boston)*	*No. 106: "Of Plantations and Colonies"*
Aug. 26, 1765	*Connecticut Courant (Hartford)*	*Essay signed by a "Cato"*

Date	Newspaper	Cato's Letters Content
Sept. 26, 1765	*New-York Gazette*	*No. 106: "Of Plantations and Colonies"*
July 13, 1767	*Connecticut Courant*	*Cato's Letters advertised for sale*
July 27, 1767	*Connecticut Courant*	*Cato's Letters advertised for sale*
Nov. 9, 1767	*Boston Gazette*	*No. 15: "Of Freedom of Speech: That the same is inseparable from publick Liberty"*
Jan. 21, 1768	*Maryland Gazette (Annapolis)*	*Portion of No. 106: "Of Plantations and Colonies" quoted in "Letters from a Farmer in Pennsylvania" [John Dickinson]*
Sept. 14, 1769	*South-Carolina Gazette*	*Phrases from No. 87: "Gold and Silver in a Country to be considered only as Commodities."*
Apr. 19, 1770	*Maryland Gazette*	*No. 32: "Reflections upon Libelling" from the Bristol Gazette*
Mar. 28, 1771	*Massachusetts Spy (Boston)*	*No. 15: "Of Freedom of Speech: That the same is inseparable from publick Liberty"* *No. 100: "Discourse upon Libels"*
Apr. 19, 1771	*Massachusetts Spy*	*No. 15: "Of Freedom of Speech: That the same is inseparable from publick Liberty"* *No. 100: "Discourse upon Libels"*
Apr. 25, 1771	*Massachusetts Spy*	*No. 15: "Of Freedom of Speech: That the same is inseparable from publick Liberty"* *No. 100: "Discourse upon Libels"*
May 2, 1771	*Massachusetts Spy*	*Cato's Letters cited*
May 6, 1771	*Boston Gazette*	*No. 15: "Of Freedom of Speech: That the same is inseparable from publick Liberty"*
June 24, 1773	*Maryland Gazette*	*"A Planter" uses quotes from No. 36: "Of Loyalty" and another Letter*
Sept. 23, 1773	*Maryland Gazette*	*"A Very Great Patriot" includes Cato's Letters within his educational reading list*
Oct. 21, 1773	*Maryland Gazette*	*"A Clergyman of the Established Church" references Cato's Letters with a letter to the editor*

Date	Newspaper	Cato's Letters Content
Mar. 30, 1775	*Pennsylvania Evening Post (Philadelphia)*	*Cato's Letters cited*
Apr. 4, 1775	*Pennsylvania Evening Post*	*Cato's Letters cited*
May 10, 1775	*Massachusetts Spy*	*False "Cato" essay, neither authored by Trenchard or Gordon*
Mar. 7, 1776	*Maryland Gazette*	*"Rationalis" quotes a passage from No. 60: "All Government proved to be instituted by Men, and only to intend the general good of Men"* *A series of false "Cato" essays begin, debates with "Cassandra" and "The Forrester" ensue*
Dec. 11, 1777	*Massachusetts Spy*	*False "Cato" essay appears*
Dec. 19, 1777	*Massachusetts Spy*	*Another false "Cato" essay*
Jan. 22, 1778	*Massachusetts Spy*	*False "Cato" essay*
Aug. 14, 1780	*Boston Gazette*	*No. 15: "Of Freedom of Speech: That the same is inseparable from publick Liberty"*
Aug. 16, 1787	*Maryland Gazette*	*"Pubicola" quotes from No. 75: "Of the Restraints which ought to be laid upon publick Rulers"*

Secondary Sources

Numerous secondary sources have mentioned *Cato's Letters*, often supplying token newspaper dates within their notes. The following works provided a skeletal assemblage for the above table. Other tidbits and trivia are found in sources previously cited.

Bailyn, Bernard. *The Ideological Origins of the American Revolution.* Cambridge: Belknap P of Harvard UP, 1967. Rpt. 1992.

——. *The Origins of American Politics.* New York: Vintage Books, 1967.

Colbourn, Trevor. *The Lamp of Experience: Whig History and the Intellectual Origins of the American Revolution.* Chapel Hill: U of North Carolina P, 1965. Rpt. Indianapolis: Liberty Fund, 1998.

Cook, Elizabeth C. *Literary Influences in Colonial Newspapers: 1704–1750.* New York: Columbia UP, 1912. Rpt. Port Washington, NY: Kennikat P, 1966.

Huxford, Gary. "English Libertarian Tradition in the Colonial Newspaper." *Journalism Quarterly* 45, no. 4 (Winter 1968): 677–86.

Maier, Pauline. *Resistance to Revolution: Colonial Radicals and the Development of American Opposition to Britain, 1765–1776.* New York: Knopf, 1972. Rpt. New York: Norton, 1991.

Nash, Gary B. *The Urban Crucible: Social Change, Political Consciousness, and the Origins of the American Revolution.* Cambridge, MA: Harvard UP, 1979.

Rossiter, Clinton. *Seedtime of the Republic: The Origin of the American Tradition of Political Liberty.* New York: Harcourt, Brace and Co., 1953.

Trenchard, John and Thomas Gordon. *The English Libertarian Heritage: From the Writings of John Trenchard and Thomas Gordon in "The Independent Whig" and "Cato's Letters."* Ed. David L. Jacobson. Indianapolis: Bobbs-Merrill, 1965.

Mark L. Kamrath

American Indian Oration and Discourses of the Republic in Eighteenth-Century American Periodicals

> Whether they were or not, to a transient observer they appear'd as *such*, being cloath'd in Blankets with the heads muffled, and copper color'd countenances, being each arm'd with a hatchet or axe, and pair of pistols, not was their *dialect* different from which I conceive these geniuses to *speak*, as their jargon was unintelligible to all but themselves.
>
> —John Andrews, from a letter to a friend two days after the Boston Tea Party, December 18, 1773

Reasons why colonists chose to dress as American Indians when protesting the East India Company and British policy concerning the importation of tea have traditionally focused on the use of simple disguise and convenience or the symbolism of resistance. As various documents attest, the men who dumped the tea referred to themselves as "THE MOHAWKS." But the reason, observes Benjamin Woods Labaree, "they dressed this way and called themselves Mohawks is unknown."[1] Philip J. Deloria in his recent study *Playing Indian* concurs in part, arguing that as an "attempt to deflect blame, dressing like an Indian had, at best, limited use."[2] Even though the participants "took pains to offer up Indian identities, grunting and speaking stage Indian words that had to be 'translated' into English," Boston, he writes, "knew its popular street-gang leaders." "Dressing as an Indian allowed these pretend Mohawks to translate texts, images, and ideologies into physical reality . . . [to live] out the cultural ideas that surrounded Noble Savagery as concrete gestures that possessed physical and emotional meaning."[3]

Although it is difficult to pinpoint the precise reasons why Boston patriots dressed up as Mohawk Indians and imitated them in dress, dialogue, and deed, Deloria's observations about American willingness to "translate texts, images, and ideologies into physical reality" invites inquiry into the ways these various representations of the American Indian entered the public consciousness, local or otherwise.[4] In fact, if discourse about the native dates back to Columbus's inquiry into the origins, character, and treatment of indigenous tribes, European publications—French and British representations in particular—have shaped the earliest terms of reference by which colonial Americans constructed native peoples. However, just as American periodicals represent the native in ways that resemble their European counterparts, so they seem to distinguish themselves by recording representations of American Indians that reference native speech or "oration," either in translation or as part of an increasing appropriation of native discourse and values.

Using postcolonial and narrative discourse theories to identify the dialogical contexts or "thick" dimensions of native oration is key in examining how native speech in American periodicals increasingly informs the ways colonial Americans constructed the native Other and themselves, especially before the American Revolution. That is, many magazine publications that contain this type of dialogue, such as Franklin's *General Magazine, and Historical Chronicle, for all the British Plantations in America* (1741) and the *South-Carolina Weekly Museum and Complete Magazine of Entertainment and Intelligence* (1797–98), illustrate a range of ways "oration" or native speech is evident and in dialogue with other more dominant discourses. However, when the content of such magazines is compared with the *New England-Magazine of Knowledge and Pleasure* (Boston, 1758–59) and, for instance, revolutionary rhetoric in the *Royal American Magazine* (Boston, 1774–75), a distinct discursive and ideological continuity between American Indian oratory and American Revolutionary rhetoric emerges.

In other words, beyond identifying "the existence of a resistance literature arising from indigenous, colonized inhabitants of the Americas" or how Native American Indians "write back" as colonial subjects,[5] analysis of the intersection between Native American oratory and periodical publications elucidates the ways print culture appropriated native oratory and used it as a means of inscribing the native and, at the same time, articulating a radical, patriotic response to British colonial practices. Such appropriation not only deepens our understanding of the ideological circumstances and discursive structures that informed events between the Stamp Act of 1765 and the eve of American Revolution, but also poses questions about the origins and meaning of American "decolonization"—the way in which "speech acts" or the blending of American Indian and late Enlightenment rhetorics, particularly in periodical literature, shaped both Revolutionary discourses and national identity.[6]

Europe and the American Indian

To begin, interest in the American Indian is, of course, part of a long transatlantic tradition in which extracts from letters or travel literature and various fictional accounts attempt to render the image and identity of the American

Indian or some aspect of native ideology and language. Aside, for example, from the way French writing such as Jean-Jacque Rousseau's popularized or romanticized the native or, as in the case of François Marie Arouet de Voltaire's *Sincere Huron* (1753), provided the Indian with a fictional voice, English publications such as Thomas More's *Utopia* (1516) and, later, the contents of English periodicals such as Ralph Grifftbs's *Monthly Review* (1749) also represented the native in positive albeit sometimes idealized ways—reprinting, for example, excerpts from Mailett's *Discourses between an Indian Philosopher, and a French Missionary.* (See Albert V. Carozzi's edition of *Telliamed; or, Conversations between an Indian Philosopher and a French Missionary on the Diminuation of the Sea.*) As Michelle Burnham has demonstrated, Unca Eliza Winkfield's *Female American* (1767) also mimics Indian language and provides a "fascinating, complex, and important text that adds a great deal to our understanding of the cross-articulation of gender, empire, and race in the early Anglo-American novel."[7] Of course, many other texts represented the native as "savage" or "Other," the subject of scientific and philosophical inquiry.[8]

In fact, alongside accounts of native atrocities in *Mercurious Civicus* (1645), a London newspaper, one can locate in English periodicals several emerging and ongoing debates concerning the origin of native peoples and similarity to people of ancient India and various Jewish tribes. Scientific or "objective" inquiry, in other words, into native habits and "genius" based on speech or language patterns was common. In fact, so persuasive was the transatlantic influence of such literature that William Penn, one of the descendants of the famous founder of Pennsylvania, would declare in a letter to English friends, printed in 1775 in the *Pennsylvania Magazine: or, American Monthly Museum*, that he was "ready to believe" that American Indians were "of the Jewish race."[9]

This interest in understanding the American Indian occasionally gave rise to explicit transatlantic dialogue, as in 1755 when the *London Magazine* published a Maryland man's letter on proper English "methods to civilize the Indians" and when American periodicals such as the *Monthly Miscellany or Vermont Magazine* (July 1794) published articles titled "The Savage and the Civilized Man. An European Picture" and "The Civilized Man and the Savage. An American Picture."[10] Such publications suggest the deeply self-conscious manner in which Americans considered the increasingly divergent and sometimes political ways Europeans and they themselves had come to characterize the native. Indeed descriptions of England, *not* colonial America, in these magazines as "haughty" or "proud" suggest the extent, especially on the eve of the American Revolution, to which colonists felt comfortable in appropriating characteristics ascribed to natives and using such stereotypes as a means of resisting an economic and political oppressor.

But even as transatlantic dialogue about the Indian in periodical literature presents interesting and unique patterns of ideological and discursive appropriation, one is prompted to ask how the appropriation of Indian characteristics, particularly that of speech or voice, came about at the Boston Tea Party. What cultural, political, or rhetorical circumstances prompted colonists to identify themselves as "MOHAWKS," to imitate Indian speech, and to rebel against the English? Was it merely an impromptu disguise meant to mock the English? Or was it symbolic? Returning to Deloria's observations about the "performance of Indian Americanness" and the pursuit of national identity, what amid these periodical or discursive contexts clarifies colonial willingness to "translate texts, images, and ideologies into physical reality?"[11] How and where, in other words, did native "speech acts" come to be synonymous with an act of political or economic resistance? To what extent, if any, does such discourse compete with negative representations of the Indian? If, in other words, nineteenth-century native speeches revealed native virtues such as "directness, courage, and spiritual grandeur,"[12] does such discourse have a history or deep structure, print or otherwise, in eighteenth-century periodicals? The answers to these questions vary, but there also appears, with some exceptions, to be identifiable patterns in how colonists appropriated Indian images or represented them as part of their pursuit of independence and national identity.

For instance, early colonial newspapers, as David A. Copeland points out in *American Newspapers: Character and Content*, largely reported frontier encounters, often portraying the native negatively in print. Such representations appear in a variety of genres, including frontier news and congressional reports, anecdotes, poems, serial fiction, and essays, and in a range of magazine publications from Benjamin Franklin's *General Magazine, and Historical Chronicle* (1741) and the *New American Magazine* (1758–59) to the *Lady's Magazine; and Repository of Entertaining Knowledge* (1792–93) and the *New-York Weekly Magazine; or, Miscellaneous Repository* (New York, 1795–97). Copeland observes that "From Boston to Savannah newspapers reported atrocities inflicted upon white settlers by 'the Sculking Indian Enemy,' a phrase John Campbell repeatedly used in the *Boston News-Letter* [1704–25] to describe Native Americans."[13]

Thus, even as American magazines such as the *North-Carolina Magazine; or, Universal Intelligencer* (June 14, 1764) published similar articles reporting "Indians killing and captivating daily"[14] and focused on debates about race, the genius of, and relations with the native, they distinguished themselves from *both* colonial newspapers and British periodicals by actively printing a variety of texts that contain American Indian oratory or speech—that is, discourse about native resistance to white encroachment. Of the many magazine publications that contain such dialogue, Franklin's *General Magazine, and Historical Chronicle* illustrates early on the particular ways oration or native speech was presented in the context of early American periodical literature. It provides an alternative vantage point for understanding how the image and ideologies of "the Indian" found their way into colonial American consciousness.

Franklin's *General Magazine, and Historical Chronicle*

Benjamin Franklin's *General Magazine, and Historical Chronicle*, the earliest publication of its kind, despite troubles with John Webbe and Andrew Bradford, appeared on February 16, 1741, and ran through June of that year, when the last issue was published. As Frank Luther Mott remarks, "In the six numbers published, proceedings of parliament and of the state assemblies and state papers in general occupy about one-third of the pages, discussions of the currency question are prominent, and religion is by no means neglected."[15] Although the currency issue and Rev. George Whitefield's "activities and opinions" dominate the pages of Franklin's magazine,[16] the magazine also contains "some sketches of history; a few dialogues, characters, and essays; a manual of arms; a monthly department of current events, called 'Historical Chronicle'; and rates of exchange and prices current in Philadelphia."[17] James Playsted Wood observes that the magazine contained about seventy-five pages and because there were no subscribers and Franklin relied on single sales it "sold for sixpence sterling the single copy."[18] The magazine, he says, was not edited for Philadelphia or Pennsylvania but "for the colonies as a whole."[19]

Among the many proceedings Franklin printed was the New York Indian Treaty of 1740, which included the "answer made by the Six Nations" over a period of several days in August of that year to George Clarke, the lieutenant governor, and other commissioners for "managing Indian affairs."[20] The appearance of translated and transcribed native voices within reprinted treaties, especially in eighteenth-century periodical literature, has received minimal scholarly attention, but as Daniel K. Richter points out they are important sources of information on "issues of intercultural diplomacy."[21] Of the specific importance of treaty minutes and Indian speeches, he writes:

> Such records are fraught with problems: interpreters' linguistic skills are suspect; clerks frequently tired of long Indian 'harangues' and noted only what they considered to be the high points; and deliberate falsification sometimes occurred. Nevertheless, in no other source did ethnocentric Euro-Americans preserve with less

distortion a memoir of Indian thoughts, concerns, and interpretations of events.[22]

In short, Richter points to the treaties and the speeches themselves as a potentially valuable site for gaining perspective on colonial-Indian relations. Because texts such as these are in translation, they are, without doubt, subject to interpreter bias and various kinds of misinterpretation. The same is true for any instance of Indian oratory that is represented as authentic or as an instance of native speech. Nevertheless, they draw attention to the ways colonists interacted with native peoples, both ideologically and discursively.

To illustrate: the text Franklin reprints begins by relaying Clarke's understanding of why the Mohawks, Oneidas, and others are interested in strengthening or brightening the "*Covenant-Chain,*"[23] a reference to treaties drawn up in 1677 between the Mohawks and Mahicans and the colonies of Massachusetts and Connecticut.[24] It rapidly moves, however, to Clarke's concern with younger warriors "joining the *French* parties" and destabilizing relations with the English, and his request for unilateral agreement on behalf of the Six Nations. "In this Difference of our Conduct," he remarks, "and that of the *French,* may be seen the Difference between *Freedom* and *Slavery,* between *Englishmen* and *Frenchmen.*"[25]

Clarke goes on to alert the tribes to the political and moral dangers of consorting with the French, reminding them, for instance, of what constitutes "true Notions of Liberty, Virtue and Honor" and that if they neglect his advice, they will "sooner or later have Cause to repent it."[26] After giving the tribal leaders a belt of wampum, Clarke continues his paternalistic remarks by expressing his dissatisfaction over the news that "some of the *Onondage Sachims* went to *Canada*" to speak with its governor and by addressing other developments that he sees as contributing to trade relations, preventing the French from building a fort near Tierondequat, or preserving the "Peace and Happiness of all his [the King of England's] Children and Subjects."[27] He concludes by giving the tribe's leaders yet another "Belt of *Wampum.*"[28]

Where native oratory or speech becomes readily apparent is the "*Answer made by* the Six Nations *of Indians,*" which Franklin prints in italics. Addressing "Brother Corlaer" and acknowledging that the Six Nations also wish to "*renew that ancient* Covenant-Chain," the Indian speaker responds to concerns about breaking treaties with the English and going to Canada, saying that they had hoped such an initiative would be "*for the advantage of us all.*"[29] However, it is in reference to a trading post on Indian lands and the kind of advantage white traders seem to have that the speaker responds directly and forcefully to Clarke's complaints. Acknowledging that the trading post is an advantage to the Six Nations because of the availability of material goods, the native speaker also remarks, "But we think, Brother, that your People, who trade there, have the most Advantage by it, and that it is as good for them as a Silver Mine."[30] While he clarifies their position on other points, he also requests that powder and lead be sold more cheaply and that "*none of the Traders at* Oswego *may give any Reason, or to be the Occasion of any Quarrel or Disturbance between us.*"[31] "*We desire also,*" he says, "*that Brother* Corlaer *will take care that we may be better paid for building Houses at Oswego.*"[32] The chief's remarks are then accompanied by the giving of strings of wampum, a performative element of the oration.

Although Clarke responds by restating his request that travel along roads and trade not be interrupted and by explaining how he has no control over market forces or "how the Traders shall sell their Goods," he appears willing to promote fair trade and to recommend to traders that they "give no Occasion of any Quarrel or Disturbance. . . ."[33] However, the Indian speaker continues to assert the interests of the Six Nations, especially its political ones, when he says of Tierondequat that "*We perceive, that both you and the* French *intend to settle that Place; but we are fully resolved, that neither you nor they shall settle there. There is a Jealousy between you and the Governor of Canada about that Place.*"[34] Between the exchange of political desires and wampum, in other words, is resistance to French and English settlement—a request for political and cultural sovereignty.

The treaty ends with a difference of opinion as to the appropriateness of having sachems from southern tribes physically participate in strengthening the Covenant-Chain: Clarke claiming he represents the views of Indians living toward the south, and the Six Nations desiring the presence of sachems from the south in order to "strengthen and confirm" the treaty.[35] Just as one might infer that Clarke was motivated to exclude sachems from southern tribes because they might compromise treaty negotiations, so the treaty Franklin reprints also records the Six Nation's reluctant willingness to "agree to the Terms required by . . . [the English]."[36] It ends, in other words, on a note of compromise, though the agreement is weighted in favor of English interests.

Significantly, then, the treaty records native remarks or speech that indicate acute awareness of colonial or hegemonic discourses. Such marginalized discourses or texts begin to illustrate the ways periodical literature such as Franklin's *General Magazine, and Historical Chronicle* helps "translate texts, images, and ideologies into physical reality" (Deloria 6). That is, reprinted texts such as the New York Indian Treaty of 1740 record representations of Indians that reference native American speech or oration and more fully document the manner, besides news of the "Skulking Indian," in which colonists came in contact with native values and perceptions. Of course, after the French and Indian War (1754–63) and the American Revolution, native tribes were defeated in battle and increasingly displaced. And the Indian once again became a focal point of cultural tensions, symbolically or otherwise, as Americans sought to settle the Ohio Valley and other areas and construct, says Eric Hinderaker, a "dynamic national empire."[37]

However, even as such historical and cultural events took place, periodical literature continued to record ongoing cultural contact between British Americans and native peoples. As the next section demonstrates, regional differences, as can be seen in the *South-Carolina Weekly Museum*, also led to distinct representations or use of American Indian oratory, especially after the American Revolution. At the same time, the particular print and cultural contexts of publications in one area of the country can offer perspective on how Indian images, ideologies, and texts are represented in the print culture of another.

The *South-Carolina Weekly Museum*

In contrast to Franklin's magazine, periodical publications at the beginning of the nineteenth century present a sharply different picture of the Indian. As Philip Gould remarks, early-nineteenth-century representations of Native Americans such as Metacom—or "King Philip"—embody the "tenuous relations between republicanism and sentimentalism."[38] If, as Gould argues, the benevolent heart and sad death of Mctacom become "the site of both cultural and literary transformations"[39] in the 1820s and after, so in the 1790s, after the American Revolution, tales or oratory concerning Indian resistance, especially in periodical literature such as the *South-Carolina Weekly Museum*, also provide a platform for defining republican virtue. Such material offers insight into how Americans in the post–Revolutionary era valued or appropriated Native American culture and ideologies. In particular, the manner in which various narratives embed Indian oratory—sometimes authentic, sometimes not—provides a stark contrast of how Americans negotiated national identity in light of ethnic difference and a colonial past.

Publication, in other words, of texts such as "Yonora; An American Indian Tale" and specifically "Specimen of Indian Eloquence" (a speech by Tachnedorus, or John Logan), which fascinated Thomas Jefferson, in the *South-Carolina Weekly Museum* and their rhetoric of virtue and colonial resistance document some of the broader cultural shifts or changes in British America toward the native American body and its importance as a site for cultural change. These pieces map how American Indian resistance in reprinted treaties in periodical publications such as Franklin's moved toward a more affective or sentimental construction of American Indian identity and, at the same time, national self-consciousness. Whether or not this larger shift in sentiment over a period of almost sixty years is tied to how the American Indian was represented in print culture in 1773, shortly before the American Revolution, remains to be seen. Nevertheless, magazines such as the *South-Carolina Weekly Museum* record important cultural perceptions of Native Americans, especially as they pertain to the ways the content and effect of Indian speech or oratory—its political rhetoric—intersected with various changes and emerging practices in periodical publishing.

The *South-Carolina Weekly Museum*, a thirty-two page weekly published on Saturdays from January 1797 to July 1798, was first printed by William Primrose Harrison at 32 Church Street near the city theater in Charleston. Its pages were full of a rich variety of genres and documents, including, for example, a speech by George Washington to Congress on December 7, 1796, concerning domestic relations with the Creek nation in Georgia and tensions with Great Britain, and a "List of Acts passed by the [State] Legislature [of South Carolina]"

In addition to various literary fragments, essays, and, on occasion, patriotic letters to the editor that called for America's sons to exhibit the "independence and manliness of sentiment" of their fathers,[40] stories about the Orient, news about West India, and anecdotes reprinted, for instance, from Leland's *History of Ireland* all point to the increasing interest in other cultural norms and people's roles as political subjects. However, even as European reprints, travel literature, and missionary reports became popular and made their way into the *South-Carolina Weekly Museum* and contributed to specific attitudes toward the Orient, so interest in the American Indian—sentimental stories or tales in particular—also increasingly manifested itself.

To be sure, images of the "Skulking Indian Enemy" remained, but sometime after the American Revolution sentimentalized accounts of American Indians became prevalent. Indeed texts such as "The Humane Indian," which was reprinted widely in the 1790s,[41] Rev. J. Wharton's "The Dying Indian," and "The Victim, An Indian History" document not only the popularity of "noble savage" or how a culture of sentiment or sympathy contributed to the "cult of the vanishing Indian" but how, as in the *South-Carolina Weekly Museum*, such discourse reflects a republican "ambivalence"—what Edward Watts calls the "nation's constant anxiety over the issue of its colonial origins."[42]

Although several texts appear in the *South-Carolina Weekly Museum* that speak to the status of the American Indian and the "Second World" or conflicted condition of the early republic, "Yonora; An American Indian Tale" (published on January 28, 1797) is typical of how the discourses of sentiment and colonial resistance *intersect* and use a suffering female or male figure to map appropriate moral behavior in the new republic. "Yonora," for instance, concerns the lovely daughter of Chief Logan, whose nation, the Ichitimachas, live on the banks of the Mississippi bordering Louisiana. Her separation from her father, Logan, and her lover, Piomingo, as a result of war with neighboring tribes leads to her capture by French troops and a twelve-year captivity. Her servitude, or oppression, under the French comes to a halt after her tribe agrees to identify and return the Indian responsible for killing a French missionary.[43] And on the occasion of her redemption, her lover delivers an impassioned speech recalling Logan's attempts to be just and their efforts to live peaceably with the whites. Yonora's bliss, however, is short-lived when her lover and father, both of whom desire a "Treaty of amity with the whites," are ambushed by an enemy tribe intent on disrupting peace negotiations. The story ends with the reader's learning that "She wished to follow them to those regions of bliss, where the winds of nature blow not, nor bring on their pinions the vicissitudes of human life" and thus committed suicide—a path that "philosophers have vindicated" and "Christians condemn" but that "delivered Yonora, at least, from all sublunary pains."[44]

Whether, as the editors of the *South-Carolina Weekly Museum* note, the "speech is genuine," is difficult to determine. Yet it appears to have been taken "with some of the circumstances of [the] story, from a now obscure, yet revealing, 1758 history of Louisiana" by M. Le Page du Pratz.[45] The tale is important then because of the ways it records both a desire for peace with the French and, in the context of sentimental language and suffering, a discourse of colonial resistance and dissent. One needs only to note what precipitates the murder of the missionary—that is how Indian-white relations are described by the narrator. Commenting, for instance, on how the French had settled Louisiana and how their missionaries were "zealous for the extension of their religion" and interested in making "proselytes of them to their religion," the narrator remarks, "The Indians in many instances did not like this description of people, although they silently submitted to their dictates—the nature of their religion being too morose and severe for the genius of a barbarous people."[46] While the narration here embodies ethnocentric attitudes about savage peoples, it nevertheless records the rhetoric of resistance—and feeling.[47] It articulates Logan's desire to "protect his country from the ravages of its enemies" but, at the same time, depicts the natives in subordinate and sympathetic ways. It uses emotion, in other words, to identify ethnocentric or colonial attitudes, thereby contextualizing the tale's "Indian speech" in ways that appeal to one's sense of injustice and, as the case may be, native virtue in light of ideological and cultural oppression.[48]

If, as Michelle Burnham notes in *Captivity and Sentiment: Cultural Exchange in American Literature, 1682–1861*, "sites of colonial contest" provide "terrain for elaborating strategies of selfhood . . . that initiate new signs of identity, and innovative sites of collaboration, and contestation, . . ."[49] material such as "Logan's Lament," as it was usually called, is telling. Jefferson appears to have received "the 'translation' of it [that] he had been given in 'my pocket-book of 1774,'" and it was then published in the January 20, 1775, issue of the *Pennsylvania Gazette* and later in Jefferson's *Notes on the State of Virginia* in 1787. Often reprinted along with Jefferson's remarks, the speech by the Cayuga chief John Logan—a text which appears in slightly variant form in the March 4, 1797, issue of the *South-Carolina Weekly Museum*—explicitly embodies the discourses of sentiment, "virtue," and colonial resistance.[50] As Jay Fliegelman points out, addressed to Lord Dunmore, "Logan's speech, with its mixture of conciliation and anger, offered a displaced articulation of colonial grievances" and suggests that it had been "heard through the filter of both Ossian and the Gospel of John." However, despite its "unintended political resonance," Jefferson clearly was deeply impressed by American Indian oratory and, says Fliegelman, his "insistence on the interchangeability of himself and Logan as 'Americans'" (Jefferson was wrongly accused of having fabricated Logan's speech) may be understood as both his testimony to the "native genius of oratory" and a reflection of how that discourse contributed to the construction of an "American" people.[51] The speech, in other words, dramatizes the "nation's ambivalence" over its status as the colonized and the colonizer: the manner in which "colonized peoples seek to take their place, forcibly or otherwise, as historical subjects" and male sentiment, not late Enlightenment reason, contributes to the "stirrings of literary and cultural decolonization."[52]

To illustrate in another way: just as the tale of Yonora combines efforts to live peaceably with whites and Logan's defiant posture with the suffering image or oppression of a female Other, so "Specimen of Indian Eloquence" embodies a masculine suffering figure to prompt sentiment or national self-consciousness about appropriate moral behavior in the new republic. It begins with editorial comments about Jefferson's assessment of the "genius and mental powers of the Indians" and the fact that "American Indians are formed, in mind as well as in body, on the same model with the *homo sapiens Europeans.*"[53] But it quickly turns to the subject of native bravery and underscores Jefferson's remarks that "we," meaning America, have examples of Indian oratory of a "superior luster," some of which may "challenge the whole orations of Demosthenes and Cicero."[54]

After noting, for instance how the authenticity of Logan's speech to Lord Dunmore, then governor of Virginia, is unquestionable, the editor relates how in the spring of 1774 two Indians of the Shawanese tribe robbed and killed an inhabitant on the Virginia frontier, an event that in turn prompted the formation of a posse, led by Michael Cresap, that was designed to carry out revenge against the natives. The white retribution that takes place wipes out the family of Logan, a reputed "friend of the whites," and causes him to retaliate against the colonists for several months, killing many frontier families.[55] Logan's tribe, however, is eventually defeated and his speech to Lord Dunmore widely printed. Although, as Anthony F. C. Wallace points out, Jefferson censored information concerning Cresap's innocence,[56] the speech epitomized events—namely, Indian extinction—that were part of a larger historical process.[57] Moreover, in a way that is similar to the resistance articulated in Franklin's reprinted treaties and the speech and actions in "Yonora," Chief Logan's oratory disrupts or challenges the narrative of English colonization; it enables Americans to practice "sympathetic identification" with a racial Other—a male figure of suffering.

Echoing the rhetoric of resistance in "Yonora," Logan's speech is as follows:

> I appeal to any white man to say if he entered Logan's cabin hungry, and he gave him no meat; if ever he came cold and naked, and he clothed him not. during the course of the last long and bloody war, Logan remained idle in his cabin, an advocate for peace. Such was my love for the whites, that my countrymen pointed as they passed, and said, *Logan is the friend of the white men.* I had even thought to have lived with you, but for the injuries of one man. Colonel Cresap, the last spring, in cold blood, and unprovoked, murdered all the relations of Logan, not sparing even my women and children. There runs not a drop of my blood in the veins of any living creature. This called on me for revenge. I have fought it: I have killed many: I have fully glutted my vengeance—for my country, I rejoice at the beams of peace; but do not harbour a thought that mine is the joy of fear; Logan never felt fear. He will not turn on his heel to save his life. Who is there to mourn for Logan?—Not one.[58]

Beyond the manner in which Logan's speech references historical fact and his efforts to accommodate British settlement and, later, American imperialism, it clearly records his resistance on the eve of the American Revolution to the totalizing narrative of colonization. The revenge he exacts against white settlers who murdered his relations speaks, in other words, to a colonial ethos and the continued subordination and extermination of native peoples. It operates as a counter-narrative to—or critiques—the act and rhetoric of English colonization.

However, the speech also serves as a kind of cultural or moral barometer for the nation. The "sad lament," writes Wallace, and its "lugubrious last words, 'Who is there to mourn for Logan?'"—became famous as a "kind of epitaph for a doomed race."[59] As Jefferson himself observes in *Notes on the State of Virginia,* it was reprinted countless times both at home and abroad and regularly rehearsed as "an exercise" in schools.[60] The question, though, is in what ways or, more importantly, *why* might the suffering figure of Logan—or the act, as Elizabeth Barnes puts it, of "sympathetic identification"[61] have appealed to the imagination of the republican reader? To what extent does the speech demonstrate or enact a "correspondence or unity between subjects" that also speaks to the formation of American national identity?[62] How does it serve as a platform for navigating or negotiating republican virtue?

On comparing the discourse of resistance in Franklin's reprinted treaties with Logan's speech some fifty years later, is there a plain and neat trajectory from political sympathy, in Franklin's case, to cultural or national sentiment about the "vanishing Indian"? Or is it possible that yet another ideological or discursive dynamic is present, especially in the years before the American Revolution, that provides insight into, or raises further questions about, still other ways American Indian oratory, real or imagined, was appropriated for the purpose of nation building?

Both Franklin's publication and the *South-Carolina Weekly Museum* provide perspective on why, for instance, Boston patriots dressed up as Mohawk Indians and imitated them in dress, dialogue, and deed. The use of Indian oratory in these publications enables a clearer understanding, as Deloria observes, of why Americans were willing to "translate texts, images, and ideologies into physical reality," particularly on the eve of the American Revolution. By juxtaposing instances of Indian oratory as they appeared in periodicals at different times during the eighteenth century, one can more accurately gauge how, or how significantly, a pattern of American Indian oratory and resistance to the colonial status quo—from Franklin's treaty to Logan's speech—informs colonial America's understanding of its relationship to England and the kinds of political rhetoric that were generated around the time of the American Revolution.

That is, if a postcolonial consciousness is by definition disruptive of imperial power or hegemony, instances of American Indian oratory that resist the status may be seen as illuminating the political discourse of colonial America before the American Revolution. Beyond historicizing the role of male sentiment in constructing a narrative of nationalism and virtue, publication of oratory such as Logan's further historicizes America's ambivalence about its role as the colonized and colonizer. It offers a useful model for interrogating the discourses of empire and points, arguably, to the ideological and rhetorical conditions, especially before 1776, under which Americans appropriated various texts, images, and ideologies from the American Indian in an effort to resist British tyranny. Events such as the Boston Tea Party in 1773, including why colonists chose to imitate Indians in speech and appearance, gain additional clarity when they are juxtaposed discursively with Indian oratory in magazines such as the *New-England Magazine of Knowledge and Pleasure* or with representations of "native genius" in other periodicals.

Boston's *New-England Magazine of Knowledge and Pleasure* and "An Indian ORATION"

Along with the question of why participants in the Boston Tea Party dressed up as Mohawks,[63] a long-standing debate concerning the influence of the Six Nations Iroquois Confederacy on the framers of the Constitution has been raging ever since Donald A. Grinde Jr.'s publication of *The Iroquois and the Founding of the American Nation* (1977) and Bruce E. Johansen's publication of *Forgotten Founders: Benjamin Franklin, the Iroquois and the Rationale for the American Revolution* (1982). Like those studies, Johansen's *Debating Democracy: Native American Legacy of Freedom* (1998) argues that "Native American confederacies (especially the Haudenosaunee Confederacy) helped shape the intellectual development of democracy in the United States. . . ."[64] John Adams, he asserts, requested "a more accurate investigation of the form of governments of . . . modern Indians" (qtd. in Grinde 52), and papers of the fifty-five delegates to the Constitution Convention clearly document interest in adapting Indian principles of democracy and government.[65] If what Johansen and others suggest about Indian ideologies and influence is true, the publication of Indian speeches, especially on the eve of the American Revolution, also argues for the existence of political, ideological, and rhetorical continuity between cultures.

So, even as periodicals record political interactions between natives and colonial leaders—treaties, for instance, agreed to after 1741 and until the eve of the American Revolution—magazine publications increasingly began to associate a native discourse of resistance with American desire to free itself from British domination. Nowhere is this more evident than in the rhetorical and ideological similarities between the March 1759 publication of "An Indian ORATION" (ostensibly from the Creek Indians in regard to the French and Indian War and their conflicts) in the *New-England Magazine of Knowledge and Pleasure* and the political discourse associated with the Boston Tea Party printed in publications such as the *Royal American Magazine*, also published in Boston. The contrapuntal relationship between these texts is especially provocative and suggests explicit ways, to recall Deloria, in which the language and images of native protest translates into a colonial American rhetoric that challenged political tyranny.

First, as with many of these types of texts, there is controversy about the history and authenticity of "An Indian ORATION." In his study *Deadly Medicine: Indians and Alcohol in Early America* (1995), Peter Mancall, for instance, remarks that the British version of the speech—*The Speech of a Creek-Indian, against the Immoderate Use of Spirituous Liquors*—published in London in 1754 was purportedly based on an edition (now apparently lost) printed earlier in New York and provided sensational evidence about the destructive impact of alcohol on Indian communities. . . ."[66] "Its rhetoric," he says, "suggests that it was probably the work of a Briton or colonist engaged in the battle against distilled spirits then raging in England," and it illustrates the "public nature of the assault on the liquor trade carried out by the Indians."[67] To be sure, Mancall is accurate in recalling how the speech echoes Indian "appeals for temperance" and even a "total ban on the alcohol trade"[68] as well as in suggesting how it intersects with the temperance movement in England. However, a more historically and textually accurate reading emerges when one compares the London publication of the speech with its counterparts in American magazines and the manner in which they present or contextualize the text.

The *Universal Asylum, and Columbian Magazine*'s June 1790 introduction to the speech, which has been neglected until now, provides a provocative, and potentially accurate, history of the text's apparent origins and transmission. The introduction states that the speech "exposes the abominable vice of drunkenness" and that it compares favorably in terms of form with the "best rhetorical compositions of the ancients."[69] Additionally, we are told:

> The first draft of this celebrated speech is said to have been taken, in short hand, in a council of the Creek-Indians, about the year 1748. It came into the hands of a deputy of Sir William Johnson, a gentleman of the name of WRAXAL, in the year 1752, who communicated his notes of it to a gentleman, (then living at *New-York*) who has long been honourably distinguished in the *republic of letters*, in Pennsylvania, who is particularly eminent in *rhetorical compositions*, and whose writings, even now, not withstanding his advanced age, discover all the fire and energy of the most lively youthful imagination. After having been first published in a New-York Gazette, it was, by the same gentleman, republished with some other Indian compositions, in London, about the beginning of the year 1753, and a very high character is given of the work in the *Monthly Review* for April, in that year.[70]

It is important to note that this introduction provides several pieces of information Mancall did not have at his disposal. In addition, for example, to documenting within a year William Smith's London publication of the speech, it also identifies historically accurate relations between Peter Wraxal, secretary of Iroquois Indian affairs in New York from 1750 to 1759, and Sir William Johnson, who was also distrustful of the Albany Indian Commissionaires and who later had "sole Management and Direction of the Affairs of the Six Nations and their Allies."[71] Wraxal, for instance, lived in New York in May 1752 and could have passed along some version of the speech to Smith, who lived in New York from 1751 to 1753. Even more significant, however, it identifies the *New-York Gazette, or Weekly Post-Boy* as the initial source of publication, which is historically accurate.

What is more difficult to verify, of course, is the extent to which the speech is in fact that of a Creek named "Onughkallydawwy Garangula Copac," whether its translation is reliable, and to what degree the content of the speech has been altered, at different times, by American and British editors.[72] That is, if the content of the speech, especially on familial relations, does not seem to resemble Creek rhetoric in the late 1740s, one might argue that the speech, if it came through Wraxal, might more properly be identified as Iroquois. One question

From an old American News-Paper.

Mr. *Parker*,

THE CREEK Indians *are ſettled between the Rivers* Halbama *and* Loucuſhatche, *about five or ſix Hundred Miles weſtward of* Charles-Town, *in* South Carolina : *They are eſteemed a brave, poliſhed, and wiſe People. Upon the breaking out of the late War, the* Engliſh, French, *and* Spaniards *made Application to them for their Alliance ; they were at the ſame Time at War with ſome other* Indian *Nations. As they found themſelves in a very critical Situation, a National Council was aſſembled, in which the following Speech, or Harangue was delivered.*

Though your Paper circulates amongſt a People whoſe Laws, whoſe Religion, and Civil Accompliſhments, elevate them above the Enormities which gave Riſe to this Oration, yet ſuch is the Mutability of human Affairs, and ſo frail is the Texture both of publick and private Virtue, that we hope the Publication of this Patriot Remonſtrance, will be deemed no unneceſſary Beacon : We flatter ourſelves that it cannot diſpleaſe the Wiſe and the Good ; and though it may produce no Advantage, yet it may perhaps entertain your Readers. When, therefore, you have nothing more worthy to fill up your Paper, we deſire you will inſert it.

We will only add, that a literal Tranſlation of the Indian Phraſeology, *is ſcarce poſſible into our Language : Their Orators have a certain Loftineſs of Expreſſion, and a Pomp of Imagery, which we have not Abilities to naturalize ; tho' we have endeavoured to ſupport the Spirit of the Original ; yet we hope the* Matter, *rather than the* Form, *will employ the Attention of your Readers. As to the Critics, we are not a Subject worthy their Sovereignty.* We are, &c.

AN INDIAN ORATION.

Fathers, Brethren, and Countrymen,

IN this ſolemn and important *Council*, before the Wiſdom and Experience of ſo many venerable *Sachems*, and having the Eyes of ſo many Heroic Chieftains upon me, I feel myſelf ſtruck with that awful Diffidence, which I believe would be felt by any one of my Years, who had not reſigned all the Modeſty of his Nature.

Nothing

"An Indian ORATION," title page and adjoining page of text from the *New-England Magazine of Knowledge and Pleasure*, March, 1759. Addressed to "Mr. *Parker*," the prefatory material claims the "Patriot Remonstrance" occurred at a national council near the Halbama and Loucushatche rivers. Whether factual or not, the "Indian Oration" addresses the Creeks about the evils of alcohol but also, importantly, embeds italicized print type that references revolutionary era political language and ideas—a practice familiar to colonial printers and readers. Courtesy of the American Antiquarian Society.

Nothing, *O ye Creeks!* could enable me to bear the fix'd Attention of this *Assembly*, and give to my Youth the Power of an unembarrassed Utterance, but the animating Conviction, that there is not one Heart amongst us, but glows for the Dignity, the Glory, the Happiness of his Country. In *those Principles*, how inferior soever my Abilities may otherwise be, I cannot, without violating my own Consciousness, yield to any One the Superiority.

Fathers, Friends, and Countrymen,

We are met together to deliberate upon no less a Subject, than *Whether we shall, or shall not, be a People.* — On the one Hand we are at War with a Nation of our own Colour —brave, active, and sagacious. They bear us an inextinguishable Hatred, threaten us with all that *Prudence* ought to fear, and that *Valour* should be excited to repel; on the other, we are surrounded and courted by three powerful Nations, of Colour, Laws, and Manners different from our own. I say *courted.* And though each is Rival to the other; yet we have Reason to apprehend they mean not our Prosperity.

I do not stand up, *O Countrymen!* to propose the Plans of War, or to direct the Wisdom of this *Assembly* in the Regulation of our Alliances. My Intention is to open to your View, a Subject not less worthy your deliberate Notice; and though equally glaring, though equally consequential to your Existence and Happiness, yet from the bewitching Tyranny of Custom and the Delusions of Self-Love, if it has not escaped a general Observation, has eluded public Censure, and been screened from the Animadversions of our National Councils.

I perceive the Eye of this *August Assembly* dwells upon me. Oh! may every Heart be unvailed from its Prejudices, and receive with Patriot-Candour, the disinterested the Pious, the filial Obedience I owe to my Country, when I step forth to be the Accuser of my Brethren! —— not of Treachery, not of Cowardice, not of a Deficiency of the noblest of all Passions, the *Love of the Public*: These I glory in boasting are incompatible with the Character of a *Creek.* The Traytor, or rather the *Tyrant*, I arraign before ye, *O Creeks!* is no Native of our Soil, but a *lurking Miscreant*, an *Emissary* of the evil Principle of Darkness. 'Tis that PERNICIOUS LIQUID, which our pretending that emerges then is the following: if this was an Iroquois speech delivered by an Iroquois headman and transmitted through an Englishman with connections to the Iroquois, then why did someone bother ascribing it to the Creek?[73] While it is difficult to answer that question, primarily because it assumes Iroquoian features are exclusive to the text and that Wraxal had no contact with Indian commissioners south of New York (for instance, William Pinckney of South Carolina), one might reasonably speculate that the British version of the speech reflects British interests and the American versions reflect American concerns, such as an interest in "independence and bravery not available in one's own society"[74] at particular times. It is also useful to consider how the speech, in some sort of Creek form, might have found its way to Wraxal and then to Smith sometime in 1751.

First, evidence for suggesting that the speech was in fact authored by a Creek named Copac exists in the address to "Mr. Parker" that precedes the speech.[75] Both in the December 30, 1751, *New-York Gazette, or Weekly Post-Boy* publication and the March 1759 *New-England Magazine of Knowledge and Pleasure* publication of the speech, there is, as in the 1754 London pamphlet, specific and generally historically accurate information about the place and time of the speech. The *New-England Magazine of Knowledge and Pleasure* prints the following:

> The Creek Indians are settled between the Rivers Halbama and Loucushatche, About five or six Hundred Miles westward of Charles-Town, in South Carolina: They are esteemed a brave, polished, and wise People. Upon the breaking out of the late War, the English, French, and Spaniards made Application to them for their Alliance; they were at the same Time at War with some other Indian Nations. As they found themselves in a very critical Situation, a National Council was assembled, in which the following Speech, or Harangue was Delivered.[76]

Just as the Popple map of 1733 identifies the "Halbama" River and the "Locushatche" River, so the Mitchell map of 1755 locates a western route from "Charlestown" to the Mississippi River that passes over the "Locushatchee" River and through territory occupied by the "Upper Creeks." Also, the British, French, and Spanish were in a contest concerning territory near the Alabama River, near modern-day Montgomery. In fact, as Daniel H. Thomas points out, English traders regularly traveled between Charleston and Fort Toulouse at the head of the Alabama River, where the Coosa and Tallapoosa rivers converge.[77] The distance, he says, between the two points was about "425 miles."[78] While nearby tribes fought over land and trade rights, the "first formal war" involving the post, remarks Thomas, was "King George's War between Britain and France, 1744–48."[79] David H. Corkran concurs, adding that though there were disparate tribes, they were held together by ancestral languages, "intermarriage of clans, and the annual national meetings and frequent regional meetings of village headmen."[80] In addition, he notes that "During the late winter of 1747–48, Creek intercourse with the Spaniards continued" and that "By mid-1748 the Creeks were asking Governor Glen of South Carolina to intervene to bring a peace in the Cherokee war."[81]

Although it is difficult to verify all the relevant facts, there are enough to suggest that the speech probably had some sort of historical basis and that, whether real, fictitious, or just edited by the "fire and energy of the most lively youthful imagination" of William Smith or some other intermediary, it *seemed real* and was of importance to the British in England in 1754 for social reasons that seem to be tied to the temperance movement and the preservation of "Family-Virtues."[82] Clearly, by attributing the speech to "Onughkallyawwy Garangula Copac," the son of "the great *Garangula,*" the British version of the speech, like the 1790 American version but unlike the 1751 and 1759 versions, attempts to authenticate native virtue in regard to "Children" and the preservation of a people. Additionally it places more emphasis on the benefits of sobriety and the "Pleasures," sentimental and carnal, of women if one embraces the "Cup of Moderation," not drunkenness.[83] As Shirley Samuels has adeptly demonstrated, the desire, especially in the early republic after 1776, was to use "the family" as "model for government and the socializing unit that will make government tenable."[84] This aspect of republican virtue became increasingly more pervasive in the print culture and public sphere of the 1780s and 1790s.

The perception, in other words, that the speech was of American Indian origin (specifically Creek) was sufficient. Whether the speech was historically accurate in an autobiographical or ethnographical sense (and blended Iroquoian names with Creek facts, or vice-versa) made little difference in this case. As Gordon M. Sayre remarks about an Onodagan or Iroquoian orator who was also named "Garangula," in his speech to the French on September 5, 1684, "The voice of Grangula is at once Other and a projection of the self through the Other, for as a celebrated instance of Indian oratory, it fulfills Euroamerican ideals of a defiant chief, a cherished image that is in part a projection of desires for an independence and bravery not available in one's own society."[85] The manner, suggests Sayre, in which Lahontan's version of the "harangue" differs widely from the "official text of the negotiations preserved in the French colonial archives"[86] points not only to problems of translation and authenticity with these speeches but highlights the manner in which Indian oratory was regularly used at particular times by particular people for particular rhetorical purposes.

This kind of discursive appropriation is also readily apparent in the manner in which the 1751 and 1759 American publication of "An Indian ORATION" differs from its 1754 English counterpart and even the 1790 American version and their emphasis on the didactic or moral significance of the speech's content, not its political or patriotic references. For example, the "Introduction; By the Translator" in the London edition begins by saying "Of all the Vices which prevail in the World, none more degrades human Nature, and dishonours the glorious Image of the Deity, than immoderate *Drinking*; and there is none against which more has been said, both from the Press and Pulpit: Yet still this Vice rears its shameless Front, and reels from Street to Street in Broad Day."[87] The translator of the text, in other words, emphasizes the didactic value of the speech, particularly as it pertains to temperance issues in England. This is reinforced not only by repeated reference to the word *vice* but also by the assertion that the "Sentiments of a Heathen"—or oratory from a people the British "esteem *Barbarians*"—is uncommonly exceptional and therefore, in this case, somewhat useful.[88]

By contrast, while the introduction in the *Universal Asylum, and Columbian Magazine* (1790) version of the speech is in full agreement with its English counterpart on the point of its didactic value, stating that the author "justly observes" that no vice in the world is worse than "'immoderate drinking,'"[89] "An Indian ORATION" is pitched quite differently in the *New-England Magazine of Knowledge and Pleasure* (1759). Like the earlier version of the speech that appeared in the *New-York Gazette, or Weekly Post-Boy* (1751), the introductory material omits reference to the word *vice* altogether, saying only that the texture of both "publick and private virtue . . . [is] frail."[90] Also, while the New York version of the speech italicizes or draws attention to words such as "*Indian Phraseology*" and the "Rivers *Halbama* and *Loucushatche*," which the London version does as well, the *New-England Magazine of Knowledge and Pleasure* does not italicize those words or phrases.

Instead it emphasizes language referring to the historical nature and circumstances of the Creek, specifically the state of relations with "*other* Indian *Nations*" and what "*a brave, polished, and wise people*" they are relative to other peoples and cultures.[91] In addition to acknowledging the difficulty of a "*literal* Translation" and seeking "*the Attention*" of the magazine's "*Readers*," it also states the desire that "*the Publication of this Patriot Remonstrance, will be deemed no unnecessary Beacon*" for readers.[92] To be sure, the London edition of the speech uses such language as well—but it is overshadowed by a heavy dose of moral didacticism and ethnocentrism. In the 1759 version of the speech, the word *barbarians*, for example, does not appear, nor does it appear in the 1751 New York version. Thus, unlike other magazine contexts for the speech, the content and typography of the introductory material for the Boston version establishes a unique tone or subtext and prepares the reader to be receptive to discourse in the speech which underscores both moral righteousness *and* political—or "*Patriot*"—principles.

To illustrate: on one level, the speech clearly addresses the threat of an outside enemy—alcohol—and its effect on the Creek nation. The native speaker begins by addressing those in "*Assembly*" as "*Fathers, Brethren, and Countrymen*" and "*Fathers, Friends, and Countrymen*" and then saying:

> We are met together to deliberate upon no less a Subject, than *Whether we shall, or shall not, be a People*—On the one Hand we are at War with a Nation of our own Colour—brave, active, sagacious. . . . I do not stand up, *O Countrymen!* to propose the Plans of War, or to direct the Wisdom of the *Assembly* in the Regulation of our Aliances. My Intention is to open to your View, a Subject not less worthy of your deliberate Notice. . . .Oh! may every Heart be unveiled from its Prejudices, and receive with Patriot-Candour, the disinterested[,] the Pious, the filial. . . . The Traytor, or rather the *Tyrant*, I arraign before ye, *O Creeks!* is no Native or our Soil. . . . Tis that PERNICIOUS LIQUID, which our pretending white Friends artfully introduced and so plentifully pour in amonst us. O that a Man should let a Thief within his Mouth to steal away his Brains! . . .[93]

Similar to the voices of Indian resistance in Franklin's *General Magazine, and Historical Chronicle*, this oration records a confrontation between the colonial subject and the colonizer, particularly in the way it associates deception and the use of alcohol as a means of stealing native identity and lands. Surely, the impassioned rhetoric, as the anonymous editors suggest, is augmented by appeals later in the speech to native pride and ultimately to the "Love of Women" in order to practice moderation and preserve the country.[94] The discourses of sentiment and virtue, in other words, blend with the language of indignation to produce a speech that records resistance to the political status quo by a subject people. Also missing from the speech are specific markers to "family-virtues" and "children."

However, when language such as "Patriot-Candour" and "People," which alludes to aspirations for political sovereignty at that time, is read as part of a larger discursive reference to the political and economic tyranny of England, the speech becomes dialogically significant. Rather than being rhetorically consistent with the didactic context and emphasis of the London version of the speech or even that of the *Universal Asylum, and Columbian Magazine* of 1790, both of which highlight the speech's moral or domestic pull concerning drunkenness and temperance, the typographical interventions and patriotic overtones of the 1759 speech are overtly political and much more closely resemble the 1751 printing. Like the 1751 publication, editorial emphasis is clearly on how the speech operates as a "Patriot Remonstance" or protest—that is, on the kind of political appeal or model the Creek speech has. This is especially evident when words such as *tyrant* are italicized in the 1751 and 1759 versions of the speech but not in the post-Revolutionary version or the earlier London edition. Just as the Indian speech, in other words, can be seen as highlighting temperance issues and "family virtue" on the one hand, so it can also be seen, on the othcr, as a vehicle for patriotic dissent or an ethos of political resistance and autonomy. That is, whether real, fictitious, or hybrid, the discursive and political genealogy of "An Indian ORATION" in periodical publications provides a means of identifying a range of ideologies and cultural attitudes—some of which may seem contradictory—concerning the American Indian and national identity in the early republic.

Nowhere is this rhetorical and political dialogism or ambivalence more clear than in some of the revolutionary discourse in circulation at the time, particularly in Boston around the time of the French and Indian War (1758–60). During this period, British officials in the colonies began to favor a tax on the colonies and actively recommended such measures to Parliament. In 1759, for example, several Virginia and South Carolina laws were nullified and royal control over colonial courts increased. By 1761 the use of general search warrants, considered an unlawful invasion of privacy by colonists, was in effect in Massachusetts, and a Boston lawyer, James Otis, had gone to court to argue that writs were "against the Constitution" and thus void, an argument he made more compellingly in his provocative pamphlet *The Rights of the British Colonies Asserted and Proved* (1766).[95] Despite general colonial reluctance to consider separation from England, Parliament's Stamp Act of 1765 and the rebellious riots by the Sons of Liberty in Boston that year underscore an increasing willingness by some colonists to resist British tyranny—a willingness that quickly solidified after the Boston Massacre of March 5, 1770.

A pattern of ideological and rhetorical influence becomes apparent when one compares the political discourse and emphases in "An Indian ORATION" to the December 2, 1773, notice or call to arms in Boston newspapers that reads:

> "FRIENDS! BRETHREN! COUNTRYMEN! The worst of plagues, the detested TEA, shipped for the Port by the East-India Company, is now arrived in this Harbour; the Hour of Destruction or manly Opposition to the Machinations of Tyranny stares you in the Face; every Friend to his Country, to himself, or to Posterity, is now called upon to meet In Faneuil-Hall, at Nine oclock THIS DAY (At which Time the Bells will Ring), to make a united, and successful Resistance to the last, worst and most destructive Measure of Administration.[96]

Beyond similarities in how the texts, for instance, address those assembled as "Friends," "Brethren," and "Countrymen," both "An Indian ORATION" and the newspaper call for arms appeal to a sense of country, or patriotism, and highlight the need to resist tyranny. That is, in addition to the ways in which both addresses recall classical conventions of address or in which alcohol and tea both become metaphors for disease and oppression, there is no mistaking the manner in which italicized references to those Creeks in "*assembly*" also reference colonists who, like the Creeks, face a "*Tyrant*" and oppressor in George III, and deliberate a particular course of political action. While the case for direct influence is not an easy one to construct, the "patriot" tone and import of the Indian oration fits into a tradition of patriotic Indian speeches and anticipates the patriotic impetus of Americans to resist English "Machinations of Tyranny" concerning imports in the 1770s.[97]

Similar ideological and rhetorical traces are even more evident, for example, in the *Royal American Magazine*, published and edited in Boston from January to June 1774 by Isaiah Thomas and from July 1774 to March 1775 by Joseph Greenleaf. As the first magazine in the colonies to use illustrations consistently and effectively, including a series of engravings by Paul Revere,[98] it also printed numerous articles, poetic essays, and such not only on British tyranny but also on American independence and "native genius." Even the title of the magazine, with its italicizing of the word *American* indicates a typographical attempt to emphasize political independence. To be sure, occasional stereotypes about the "barbarous manners" of Indians found its way in December 1774 into, for example, a "faithful narrative of the dangers, sufferings, and deliverance of Robert Eastburn, and his captivity among them."[99] But as the frontispiece for the magazine (an illustration of an Indian extending a peace pipe to an American), the "*annexed* Plate *of a conference held in the year 1764*," and various histories, Indian dialogues, and extracts illustrate, the American Indian had become more than a passing historical or scientific curiosity. This is underscored by the fact that the May 1774 issue of the magazine published a first of its kind—an "Indian Gazette," or iconographic "Account of one of their Expeditions."[100] The "print," says Thomas, "is engraved from an authentic copy, drawn by a *French* engineer, from an *American* original."

Of course, beyond the magazine's attempts to integrate material about or by American Indians, the language of ideological dissent and patriotism in Indian speeches such as "An American ORATION" resonates fully in the numerous political essays and other materials printed in the *Royal American Magazine*. Just as "A Christian" in the January 1774 issue laments the "hated *tyranny*" of British imperial policies and celebrates "the zeal and exertions of American patriots in defence of their rights and liberties,"[101] so a February 1775 poetical essay titled "Thoughts on Tyranny" denounces England's "Tyranny" and embraces "liberty" and the "pride of patriots" in the face of "monarchy and fear."[102] However, it is material such as John Hancock's March 5, 1774, commemorative "Oration" on the Boston massacre, which begins "*Men, Brethren, Fathers, and Fellow-Countrymen*," that recalls earlier instances of Indian oratory, particularly its resistance to unfair trade practices. Addressing "this great Assembly," Hancock expresses his "sincere attachment" to his "country" and her "liberties" at the same time, for instance, he publicly avows his "eternal enmity to tyranny."[103]

This same "Patriotism"[104] also manifests itself in texts like "The CHARACTER of an AMERICAN PATRIOT" (February 1774), where, unsurprisingly, American virtue and identity become aligned with a "native passion for glory" and "the productions" of a "native genius"[105] and in the June 1774 publication of "The Sentiments of an *Indian* on Venality and Bribery, delivered immediately before his death. In a remarkable history of the treatment of the *Spaniards* to the natives of *Florida*, after their conquest." Appealing to the fate of "oral traditions" and their instructive value for a "free and happy people," the narrator chronicles Spanish enslavement of Indians in Florida and their resistance, before being killed at the stake, to the tyranny and oppression of colonizing forces. In particular, the narrator appeals "to the heart of all whose own fortune it may be hearafter, to be placed in a like situation" and attempts to alert the reader, through speeches, to the guilt or remorse Indians feel because they allowed themselves to be overtaken by "tyrannic masters" and to lose their liberty.[106]

Like earlier representations of the Indian that focused on fierceness or noble qualities, such texts importantly delineate or underscore, as Elise Marienstras suggests, how the image of the Indian "became an integral part of the national culture and identity, providing a meaning and impetus to the new nations deeds and politics."[107] As the Indian, she argues, became more and more "a part of popular culture" or the national imaginary, especially after the War of 1812, the image had become naturalized,[108] allowing the early republic to "assert in front of the other nations of the earth that is was a nation quite like the others—with its own territory, its own past, and its own destiny."[109] Indeed, if as Philip J. Deloria argues, "the Pennsylvania Tammany societies almost eliminated the rhetorical boundaries between Indians and white colonists, creating an Indian hero virtually indistinguishable from the average patriot,"[110] imitation of Indian speech and actions during the Revolutionary period, especially incidents such as the Boston Tea Party, was central to how Americans constructed a sense of national identity.

Sandra M. Gustafson, in her recent study *Eloquence Is Power: Oratory and Performance in Early America* (2000), concurs. Citing Cadwallader Colden's *History of the Five Indian Nations* (1727) and his use of various treaty texts to illustrate "Iroquois eloquence and negotiating skill,"[111] she recounts how later editions were extracted in magazines and how Colden, who was critical of British imperial policy at the time, compared the speeches of Greeks and Romans with those of the Iroquois.[112] Suggesting that Colden's "description of Indian eloquence" echoed "the political discourse of classical republicanism that emerged into prominence with the publication in the early 1720s of the widely influential *Cato's Letters* of Thomas Gordon and John Trenchard,"[113] Gustafson then remarks how the ideas of classical republicanism stimulated an interest, on both sides of the Atlantic, in political oratory.[114] "Native Americans," she concludes, "and the peoples of the British Isles were linked in the rhetorical and political literature celebrating eloquence. . . . Eventually, the American colonies would use their own savage eloquence to speak back to the imperial center as oratory became the defining republican genre of the Revolution."[115]

In the end, the argument for seeing American Indian oratory, and its resistance to colonial "tyranny," as informing colonial American discourses of liberty and revolution rests on the notion that transcultural political and ideological exchange or, as Christopher Looby points out, the building of a nation ultimately relies on language.[116] Specifically, the Bakhtinian notion that language is heteroglot or dialogical speaks to how Native American oratory and the discourses of dissent during the Revolutionary period refract one another, thereby creating text that is not only centrifugal but also disruptive of imperial authority.[117] As such, the language and images of native protest, however they initially circulated in British colonial America, may also be seen as informing discursive gestures toward political independence and a uniquely American sense of national identity.

Postcolonial and Periodical Implications

For historians and literary cultural critics alike, the speeches of American Indians, whether real or fictitious, seem key to understanding the development and impact of Revolutionary–era discourses more fully. The discursive impact of Indian speeches, whether printed multiple times in magazine publications or only appearing once, has been underestimated by historians and literary critics. Such material, however, offers several provocative conclusions, some of which contemporary scholarship is already wrestling with and pursuing across interdisciplinary borders.

First, as Claudio Saunt has recently suggested, study of Creek history in the context of ignored primary sources—in this case, real or imagined translations of Indian speeches in eighteenth-century periodical literature—offers the possibility of more accurately historicizing Creek history and the "larger history of colonial expansion in North America."[118] The rhetorics or English, French, or Spanish empire, when contrasted with Creek or other resistance, further historicize patterns of cultural and ideological change. In addition, documents that appeared in periodicals like the *South-Carolina Weekly Museum* or that concerned Indian territory in South Carolina and Alabama argue for seeing Creek territory in the South as part of a "larger story of dramatic change and disruption" in colonial America.[119] If, as Saunt observes, "the rise of the new order of things in the Deep South is as much a part of the creation of the American republic as is the more familiar south history of the independence of the first thirteen states,"[120] then American periodical literature that reflects the South as a subject is also an important part of the historical and cultural record.

Second, although the argument for seeing American Indian oratory as disruptive of a colonial hegemony needs to be read more closely against popular sentimental discourses of the day—texts, for example, such as "The Humane Indian," Rev. J. Wharton's "The Dying Indian," and "The Victim, An Indian History"—it seems accurate to say that the presence of tales such as "Yonora" and American Indian "speech acts" such as Logan's in periodical literature offers alternative ways of seeing the "noble savage" trope and accounting for sentiment behind the "cult of vanishing Indian." Such material, along with speeches like "An Indian ORATION," strongly suggests evidence of previously neglected sources of colonial resistance, thereby enabling one to think about the contact literature, the repressed voice of the Other, and even a postcolonial ethos in more historically or culturally accurate ways.[121]

Insofar as European or transatlantic inquiry led to stereotyped representations of the American Indian, the increasing intercourse between an oral tradition and print culture contributes ironically, especially on the eve of the Revolutionary war, toward an American consciousness of Indian eloquence and—one night in Boston—to a symbolic performance of national identity. The discourses of sympathy and virtue not only blend the rhetoric of native resistance but also seem to have enabled early republicans to reflect on *their own* previous subject position and the manner in which the decolonization process with Britain was complicated—or contradicted—by the ideological forces of American imperialism. While discourse about the Indian and "heathen" remains a part of the cultural and textual record, it seems fair to say that essays such as "The Character of an American Patriot," which can be seen as equating American identity with Indian virtues or qualities such as "natural genius," "native genius," and so on, often blend such discourse with the rhetoric of patriot feeling or sentiment as part of an attempt to resist the political oppression or tyranny of the English.

Lastly, just as Gordon Sayre finds in the writings of Baron de Lahontan (1703) that "a satiric dialogue between Lahontan and a Huron interlocutor named Adario" offers a "unique innovation in colonial writing" and "anticipates major texts of the French Enlightenment,"[122] so one can suggest that certain instances of Indian oratory in eighteenth-century American periodical literature archive a hitherto-neglected layer or source of philosophical and political dissent. Beginning with the often neglected voice of the Other in Franklin's reprinted treaties and ending with instances of patriotic discourse in American Indian oratory and sentimental tales and stories, such texts actively critique, both directly and dialogically, the colonial status quo and contribute more fully than imagined, or previously acknowledged, to the construction of an American Revolutionary rhetoric and, ultimately, the discourse of republicanism.

That is, the manner in which the discourses of colonialism and liberation are *embedded* in patriotic Indian speeches, and vice-versa, complicates standard assumptions about the exclusive or monolithic origins of other counternarratives—antislavery discourses, writings sympathetic toward the domestic or political status of women, or various other treatises concerning issues of religious, economic, or political liberty. Like the more dominant Revolutionary era discourses of Thomas Jefferson and Thomas Paine, these countertexts may also derive part of their meaning or cultural cachet from American Indian oratory and resistance. As such, a reevaluation of these various rhetorical sites in light of Indian speech acts can potentially provide additional insight into the deep structures of canonical texts and how periodical writings circulated or, as was often the case, were appropriated to construct a national ethos or sense of identity.

Notes

1. Benjamin Woods Lebaree, *The Boston Tea Party* (New York: Oxford UP, 1964), 143.
2. Philip J. Deloria, *Playing Indian* (New Haven: Yale UP, 1998), 6.
3. Deloria 6. For a relatively recent study of American Indian oratory, speech, and translation, see David Murray's *Forked Tongues: Speech, Writing and Representation in North American Indian Texts* (Bloomington: Indiana UP, 1991).
4. Susan B. Brill de Ramirez remarks on the semiotics of the oral tradition in general and native autobiographies in particular, saying, "The past century of anthropological study of Native peoples in North America has yielded an enormously invaluable record. It now remains for scholars trained in literary and oral storytelling traditions to begin to unearth the stories within and behind the 'autobiographical' textual narratives. As Brumble importantly points out: 'It is perhaps fitting that, even embedded as we see them in written words, in books, these oral traditions have still the power to struggle against conventions of the dominant culture.'" See "The Resistance of American Indian Autobiographies to Ethnographic Colonization," *Mosaic* 32 (June 1999): 71.
5. Louis Owens, "As If an Indian Were Really an Indian: Native American Voices and Postcolonial Theory," in *Native American Representations: First Encounters, Distorted Images, and Literary Appropriations*, ed. Gretchen M. Bataille (Lincoln: U of Nebraska P, 2001), 13–14.

Complementing Owens's observation that "America never became postcolonial" (in the sense of indigenous inhabitants regaining control of territories), A. Lavonne Brown Ruoff asserts that "Postcolonial criticism offers insights into the impact of Western Europeans' perceptions of the Other on both them and those they marginalize." "In their speeches, oral stories, and writings," she argues, "Native Americans strongly attacked the hypocrisy of white Christians," revealing their "resistance to assimilation." See Ruoff's "Reversing the Gaze: Early Native American Images of Europeans and Euro-Americans," in *Native American Representations*, ed. Bataille, 199, 214.

6. On the relationship between Native Americans and the American Revolution, Colin G. Calloway remarks: ". . . with few exceptions, revolutionary revisionism and recognition of the far-reaching nature of the American revolution has not yet embraced American Indians. In general, historians of the Revolution have not been particularly interested in Indians, and scholars of Indian history have not paid much attention to the Revolution. Historians who have considered Indians in the Revolution have focused on the competition for tribal allegiances, the Indians' role in the fighting, their contribution to the outcome of the struggle for independence, and the symbolic significance of their involvement. They have considered Indians as military and political units, but rarely have they asked about experiences of Indian people caught up in the conflict, examined the effects of the war in the Indians' home front, or considered Indian groups as human communities. . . . The national mythology accords Indians a minimal and negative role in the story of the Revolution: they chose the wrong side and they lost. Their contribution to the outcome of the Revolution was therefore negligible, and their treatment after the Revolution justified. Because many Indians sided with the British, they have, from the Declaration of Independence onward, been portrayed as allies of tyranny and enemies of liberty." See *The American Revolution in Indian Country: Crisis and Diversity in Native American Communities* (Cambridge: Cambridge UP, 1995), xi–xiii.
7. See Burnham's introduction to *The Female American; or, the Adventures of Unca Eliza Winkfield* (Ontario, Canada: Broadview P, 2001), 10.
8. Tzvetan Todorov, *The Conquest of America: The Question of the Other*, trans. Richard Howard (New York: Harper and Row, 1984), 3.
9. William Penn, "A Letter of William Penn to His Friends in London," *Pennsylvania Magazine: or, American Monthly Museum* (March 1775), 107.
10. Anonymous, "To the Author of the *London Magazine*," *London Magazine* (September 1755).

11. Philip J. Deloria, *Playing Indian* (New Haven: Yale UP, 1998), 7.
12. William Clements, *Native American Folklore in Nineteenth-Century Periodicals* (Athens: Swallow/Ohio UP, 1986), 1.
13. David A. Copeland, *Colonial American Newspapers: Character and Content* (Newark: U of Delaware P, 1997), 43.
14. "Extract of a Letter from Virginia, June 4," *North-Carolina Magazine* (June 29–July 6, 1764).
15. Frank Luther Mott, *A History of American Magazines, 1741–1850* (Cambridge, MA: Belknap P of Harvard UP, 1966), 75.
16. Ibid.
17. Ibid., 77.
18. James Playsted Wood, *Magazines in the United States*, 3d ed. (New York: Ronald P, 1949), 10.
19. Ibid., 12.
20. "New York Indian Treaty," *General Magazine, and Historical Chronicle* (February 1741), 94.
21. Daniel K. Richter, "Rediscovered Links in the Covenant Chain: Previously Unpublished Transcripts of the New York Indian Treaty Minutes, 1677–1691," *American Antiquarian Society Proceedings* 92 (1982): 47.
22. Ibid., 47–48.
23. "New York Indian Treaty," *General Magazine, and Historical Chronicle* (February 1741): 88.
24. Wolfgang Hochbruck and Beatrix Dudensing-Reichel make a similar claim about "literary texts written in European languages by Native American authors" (1). In their essay "'Honoratissimi benefactores': Native American Students and Two Seventeenth-century Texts in the University Tradition," they contextualize and comment on two texts by students who attended Harvard's Indian College in 1665 and 1679. See Helen Jaskoski's *Early Native American Writing: New Critical Essays* (Cambridge: Cambridge UP, 1996), 1–14.
25. "New York Indian Treaty" 89.
26. Ibid., 90–91.
27. Ibid., 91, 93.
28. Ibid., 94.
29. Ibid., 95.
30. Ibid.

31. Ibid., 95–96.

32. Ibid., 96.

33. Ibid., 96.

34. Ibid., 96.

35. Ibid., 97.

36. Ibid., 98.

37. Eric Hindraker, *Elusive Empires: Constructing Colonialism in the Ohio Valley, 1673–1800* (Cambridge: Cambridge UP, 1997), xiv.

38. Philip Gould, "Remembering Metacom: Historical Writing and the Cultures of Masculinity in Early Republican America," in *Sentimental Men: Masculinity and the Politics of Affect in American Culture*, ed. Mary Chapman and Glenn Hendler (Berkeley: U of California P, 1999), 112.

39. Ibid., 117.

40. "A Few Strictures on Mr. Adet's late address," *South-Carolina Weekly Museum* (January 28, 1797).

41. The tale was published at least seven times under different titles such as "A Singular Instance of Magnanimity and Mercy in an Indian," in the *New Hampshire Mercury and General Advertiser* (May 17, 1786), and "Anecdote. The Christian Indian," in the *Christian's Scholar's, and Farmer's Magazine* (August–September 1790). See Edward W. R. Pitcher's *Fiction in American Magazines before 1800: An Annotated Catalogue* (Schenectady, NY: Union College P in conjunction with Antoca P in Lexington, KY, 1993).

42. Edward Watts, *Writing and Postcolonialism in the Early Republic* (Charlottesville and London: UP of Virginia, 1998), 2.

43. "Yonora; An Indian Tale," *South-Carolina Weekly Museum* (January 28, 1797): 109.

44. Ibid., 111.

45. Ibid., 110. As Joseph G. Tregle Jr. remarks, Le Page's *History of Louisiana* (1774 English translation) is sympathetic toward the Natchez despite British editorial bias toward Le Page's original French publication of 1758. In fact it contains speeches, in translation, that appear authentic and record native resistance to the French, as when Stung Serpent bluntly asks Le Page, "'Why did the French come into our country . . . at this day we are like slaves.'" See Tregle's introduction in *The History of Louisiana*, trans. from the French of M. Le Page du Pratz, ed. Joseph G. Tregle Jr. (Baton Rouge: Louisiana State UP, 1974), xxvii–xxix, xlii–xliii, lv.

46. "Yonora; An Indian Tale," 108.

47. In his article "Plotting the Natchez Massacre: Le Page du Pratz, Dumont de Montigny, Chateaubriand," Gordon Sayre examines the uprising and speeches of the Natchez in Le Page du Pratz's writings and remarks that the "figure of the vieillard precludes any heroic Natchez leader who might articulate principles of liberty and independence with the full rhetorical and political power that would soon be invoked by Indian tragic heroes such as Ponteach in Robert Rogers's play by that title, John Augustus Stone's Metamora, and revolutionaries like Patrick Henry." He concludes by saying that "French writers developed the 'plot' of the Natchez Massacre at first to help justify their reprisals against the tribe, then used it to invite a sympathetic identification with the Natchez, but finally the political dynamic of the conspiracy became subsumed in the histories of subsequent colonial wars and revolutions." See *Early American Literature* 37 (2002): 395, 407. Also see Laura Murray's "The Aesthetic of Dispossession: Washington Irving and the Ideologies of (De)Colonization in the Early Republic," *American Literary History* 8 (Summer 1996): 205–31.

48. To reiterate, it is toward the beginning of the tale, after we learn of Logan's marriage to an "affectionate woman" and his subsequent happiness with two daughters, where the story of Yonora blends the rhetoric of colonial resistance and sympathetic dissent:

> One of the Ichitimichas, perhaps more averse to their domination than the Rest, and guided by a vicious heart, perpetrated an act on one of those missionaries which involved their nation in a long and bloody war with the colony of Louisiana.

Although the tale continues, accounting less apologetically how M. de St. Come had fallen "victim" to some "unaccountable passion which agitated the breast of the Indian," the "genius" of Logan's tribe and their resistance to French Catholicism combines with his own physical resistance to the "vengeance of the French" to disrupt or challenge the totalizing narrative of French colonialism. See "Yonora; An Indian Tale," 108.

49. Michelle Burnham, *Captivity and Sentiment: Cultural Exchange in American Literature, 1682–1861* (Hanover and London: UP of New England, 1997), 3.

50. The speech appeared in magazines such as the *New-Haven Gazette, and the Connecticut Magazine* (May 3, 1787) and Noah Webster's *American Magazine* (January 1788).

51. Jay Fliegelman, *Declaring Independence: Jefferson, Natural Language, and the Culture of Performance* (Stanford: Stanford UP, 1993), 96–99.

52. Edward Watts, *Writing and Postcolonialism in the Early Republic* (Charlottesville and London: UP of Virginia, 1998), 1, 5.

53. "A Specimen of Indian Eloquence," *South-Carolina Weekly Museum* (March 4, 1797): 273, 274.

54. Ibid., 274.

55. Ibid., 278.

56. Anthony F. C. Wallace, *Jefferson and the Indians: The Tragic Fate of the First Americans* (Cambridge: Harvard UP, 1995), 5–6.

57. Ibid., 2.

58. "A Specimen of Indian Eloquence," 278.

59. Anthony F. C. Wallace, "'The Obtaining Lands': Thomas Jefferson and the Native Americans," in *Thomas Jefferson and the Changing West*, ed. James P. Ronda (St. Louis: Missouri Historical P, 1997), 28.

60. Thomas Jefferson, *Notes on the State of Virginia*, ed. William Peden (New York: W. W. Norton, 1954), 252.

61. Elizabeth Barnes, *States of Sympathy: Seduction and Democracy in the American Novel* (New York: Columbia UP, 1997), ix.

62. Ibid., x.

63. Benjamin Woods Labaree, *The Boston Tea Party* (New York: Oxford UP, 1964), 143.

64. Donald A. Grinde Jr., *The Iroquois and the Founding of the American Nation* (San Francisco: Indian Historian P, 1977). Bruce E. Johansen, *Forgotten Founders: Benjamin Franklin, the Iroquois, and the Rationale for the American Revolution* (Ipswich, MA: Gambit, 1982); Johansen, with chapters by Donald A. Grinde Jr. and Barbara A. Mann, *Debating Democracy: Native American Legacy of Freedom* (Santa Fe, NM: Clear Light, 1998), 18.

65. Johansen et al. 53.

66. Peter Mancall, *Deadly Medicine: Indians and Alcohol in Early America* (Ithaca: Cornell UP, 1995), 121.

67. Ibid., 121, 122.

68. Ibid., 122.

69. Introduction to "A Speech against the Immoderate Use of Spirituous Liquors, delivered by a Creek-Indian, in a National Council, on the Breaking out of a War, about the year 1748," *Universal Asylum, and Columbian Magazine* (June 1790): 367.

70. Introduction to "A Speech against the Immoderate Use of Spirituous Liquors," 367.

71. Robert Allen, qtd. in "Peter Wraxall." *American National Biography*, vol. 23, ed. John A. Garraty and Mark C. Carnes (New York: Oxford UP, 1999), 897.

72. Rev. J. Wharton published "The Dying Indian" in the *Literary Miscellany* (Philadelphia, 1795, vol. 1) and in the *Lady & Gentleman's Pocket Magazine of Literary and Polite Amusement* (New York, September 15, 1796). In the poem, the Indian speaker laments how Christians have despoiled the land and the tribe's virgins, and how he has not consorted with "those that eat their God" and bring disease. The speaker closes by rejecting the morality of "Christian cowards" and going because the "great COPAC . . . beckons" him.

73. Jason B. Jackson and Claudio Saunt generously assisted in distinguishing Creek and Iroquois speech patterns. I am indebted to Josh Piker for his identification of "Garangula" in an Iroquoian context. His remarks about the speech's possible Iroquois origins raises provocative questions about why the speech is attributed to the Creek. E-mails to author dated February 23, 24, and 28, 2000.

74. Gordon M. Sayre, *Les Sauvages Americains: Representations of Native Americans in French and English Colonial Literature* (Chapel Hill: U of North Carolina P, 1997), 41–42. See also Daniel Richter's explanation of "Otreouti" (the Iroquois name for Garangula) in *The Ordeal of the Longhouse: The Peoples of the Iroquois League in the Era of European Colonization* (Chapel Hill: U of North Carolina P, 1992).

75. James Parker printed and sold the *New-York Gazette, or Weekly Post-Boy* on Beaver Street, as is indicated, in part, by an address from "Civicus" to Parker in the February 6, 1748, issue of the paper.

76. "An Indian ORATION," *New-England Magazine of Knowledge and Pleasure* (March 1759).

77. Daniel H. Thomas, *Fort Toulouse: The French Outpost at the Alabamas on the Coosa* (Tuscaloosa and London: U of Alabama P, 1989), 2–3. The Henry Popple map of 1733 and the John Mitchell map of 1755, located in the Geography and Map Reading Room of the Library of Congress, designate British and French dominions in the Southeast during the eighteenth century. Also helpful in identifying likely tribal locations were reference materials on Alabama rivers.

78. Ibid., 4.

79. Ibid., 23.

80. David H. Corkran, *The Creek Frontier 1540 1783* (Norman: U of Oklahoma P, 1967), 4.

81. Ibid., 126–27.

82. "The Speech of a Creek-Indian, against the Immoderate Use of Spirituous Liquors" (London, 1754), in Peter C. Mancall's *Deadly Medicine: Indians and Alcohol in Early America* (Ithaca and London: Cornell UP, 1995), 189.

83. Ibid., 189–90.

84. Shirley Samuels, *Romances of the Republic: Women, the Family, and Violence in the Literature of the Early American Nation* (New York: Oxford UP, 1996), 16.

85. Sayre, *Les Sauvages Americains*, 44. Of this speech, Susan Castillo and Ivy Schweitzer remark, "the oration of the Onandaga leader Garangula (Grande Guele or Big Throat in French), delivered to the Governor of New France, Joseph Antoine Lefebre de La Barre, who had hoped that he could bluff the Iroquois into making substantial concessions, is a demonstration of native statesmanship, with its tone of elegant disdain and its awareness of the possibilities (and the limits) of political and military power." See *The Literatures of Colonial America: An Anthology* (Malden, MA: Blackwell, 2001), 348.

86. Sayre, *Les Sauvages Americains*, 42.

87. "Introduction; By the Translator," in "The Speech of a Creek-Indian, against the Immoderate Use of Spirituous Liquors," 183.

88. Ibid., 183–84.

89. Introduction to "A Speech against the Immoderate Use of Spirituous Liquors, delivered by a Creek-Indian, in a National Council, on the Breaking out of a War, about the year 1748," *Universal Asylum, and Columbian Magazine* (June 1790): 367.

90. "An Indian ORATION," *New-England Magazine of Knowledge and Pleasure* (March 1759): 15.

91. Ibid., 15.

92. Ibid.

93. Ibid., 16.

94. Ibid., 18–19.

95. John A. Garraty and Robert A. McCaughey, *The American Nation: A History of the United States* (New York: Harper and Row, 1987), 102.

96. Laurence Greene, *America Goes to Press: Headlines of the Past* (Garden City, NY: Garden City Publishing, 1938), 17.

97. In his study *The Patriot Chiefs: A Chronicle of American Indian Resistance* (New York: Penguin 1993), Alvin M. Josephy Jr. writes that Indian patriots from Hiawatha to Tecumseh, Osceola, Black Hawk, Crazy Horse, and Chief Joseph were to the Indians "'good and brave men,' their Nathan Hales, George Washingtons, and Benjamin Franklins," xiv.

98. See the *Index to the Reel Guide to the American Periodical Series of the 1700s*, vol. 2 (Indianapolis: Computer Indexed Systems, 1989), 8.

99. *Royal American Magazine* (December 1774): 449.

100. "Indian Gazette," *Royal American Magazine* (May 1774): 185.

101. "A Christian," *Royal American Magazine* (January 1774): 7.

102. "Thoughts on Tyranny," *Royal American Magazine* (February 1775): 67.

103. John Hancock, "Oration," *Royal American Magazine* (March 1774): 83–84.

104. Ibid., 85.

105. "The Character of an American Patriot," *Royal American Magazine* (February 1774): 45.

106. See the *Royal American Magazine* (June 1774): 215–18. In addition, see "An Account of the Indians at Carolina" in the *Boston Weekly-Magazine* (March 16, 1743), where Le Page, or another French traveler, gives an account of how Carolina Indians are "an industrious and laborious Nation; submissive to superior Powers but without being their Slaves; obeying without repining or grumbling their Sovereign's Orders: never minding their own particular Interests, when the Publick has need of their Service or Endeavours. . . ." Resistance to colonial tyranny and corruption is apparent in a speech that disrupts a colonial ethos when the native speaker posits, ironically: "'You wou'd (say they) have us becomes Christians? Well, to what End and Purpose? Is it to make us better than we really are, or is it not rather to make us wicked and vicious as your selves, to render us Adulterers, Whore-masters, Liars, Murderers, Robbers, without Faith, Honour, or Honesty, minding nothing but how to destroy you upon Pretence of Justice?"

107. Elise Marienstras, "The Common Man's Indian: The Image of the Indian as a Promoter of National Identity in the Early National Era," in *Native Americans and the Early Republic*, ed. Frederick E. Hoxie, Ronald Hoffman, and Peter J. Albert (Charlottesville and London: UP of Virginia, 1999), 262.

108. Ibid., 263, 295.

109. Ibid., 296.

110. Deloria 22.

111. Sandra M. Gustafson, *Eloquence Is Power: Oratory and Performance in Early America* (Chapel Hill and London: U of North Carolina P, 2000), 114.

112. Ibid., 115.

113. Ibid., 116.

114. Ibid., 117.

115. Ibid.

116. Christopher Looby, *Voicing America: Language, Literary Form, and the Origins of the United States* (Chicago and London: U of Chicago P, 1996), 1.

117. Mikhail Mikhailovich Bakhtin, *The Dialogic Imagination: Four Essays*, ed. Michael Holquist and trans. Caryl Emerson and Michael Holquist (Austin: U of Texas P, 1981), 321–24.

118. Claudio Saunt, *A New Order of Things: Property, Power, and the Transformation of the Creek Indians, 1733–1816* (Cambridge: Cambridge UP, 1999), 6.

119. Ibid., 7.

120. Ibid.

121. In *The Turn to the Native: Studies in Criticism and Culture* (Lincoln: U of Nebraska P, 1996), Arnold Krupat argues against using the term *postcolonial* with Native American texts, saying that "American literatures cannot quite be classed among the postcolonial literatures of the world for the simple reason that there is not yet a 'post-' to the colonial status of Native Americans" (30). While this has validity, a broader definition of *postcolonialism* not only acknowledges how speakers "assert [ ] themselves by foregrounding the tension with the imperial power, and by emphasizing their differences from the assumptions of the imperial center" but also records resistance to a colonial hegemony in more subtle ways (2). See *The Empire Writes Back: Theory and Practice in Post-Colonial Literatures*, ed. Bill Ashcroft, Gareth Griffiths, and Helen Tiffin (London: Routledge, 1989).

122. Sayre, *Les Sauvages Americains*, 31.

Robert D. Sturr

Civil Unrest and the Rhetoric of the American Revolution

Depiction of Shays's Rebellion in New England Magazines of the 1780s

During the two years that preceded the Constitutional Convention in Philadelphia, the newly independent United States experienced such political turmoil that many observers came to doubt the eventual success of the American experiment with republican government. Two periodicals were launched in New England during the first half of 1786 that directly addressed the political, economic, and social roots of the crisis and, in the process, demonstrated the potential of magazines to shape public opinion and offer new models of political discourse. Josiah Meigs and Eleutheros Dana's *New-Haven Gazette, and the Connecticut Magazine* and Isaiah Thomas's *Worcester Magazine* had both previously existed as newspapers and were continued as weekly publications. Lyon Richardson defines them as hybrids in his *History of Early American Magazines* because in their reporting of current events they retained the timeliness of newspapers. However, as magazines they featured a greater number of original essays on politics and culture, which made them unique and substantive vehicles for discussion, and debate of major events.[1]

With the closing of the *Boston Magazine* in October, they were also the only politically oriented periodicals operating in New England during the turbulent period of Shays's Rebellion.[2] That crisis forced reconsideration not just of the organization of government, but also of its function and legitimacy. Seeing what they perceived as failed leadership, Meigs and Dana constructed a magazine that they hoped would provide the clarity and vision that was missing from political life. In contrast, Thomas presented a range of opinions within the ongoing political debates—as though the magazine were a new agora, or forum—that, he believed, was superior to the contentious and insincere language of the state legislature. Although different in rhetorical mode and political orientation, both the *New-Haven Gazette, and the Connecticut Magazine* and the *Worcester Magazine* responded to the challenge posed by Shays's Rebellion by offering prescriptions for republican government at precisely the time when it seemed most vulnerable. In doing so, they enhanced the role of the periodical in the struggle to define the principles of sovereignty and representation in the early national period.

Shays's Rebellion and the Crisis of Representation

The immediate cause of Shays's Rebellion was the bursting of a credit bubble. After a period of heavy buying and borrowing directly after the Revolution, the new American confederation faced its first economic depression by the mid-1780s. New England was hit particularly hard. Wages fell, taxes increased, and punitive British trade policies crippled key segments of the economy.[3] English merchants demanded payment of debts in hard currency, thus creating a chain of debt as trading firms in Boston were forced to pass along the demand for specie to smaller, inland merchants. They in turn sought to collect debts (also in hard currency) from rural farmers, craftsmen, and other members of the yeoman class. Exacerbating this problem were efforts by state governments to raise taxes (again in specie) in order to discharge lingering war debts. Typically operating at the subsistence level, most farmers were unable to pay either their debts or taxes. The resulting epidemic of foreclosures and debt imprisonments spurred calls for the printing of paper money, the passage of tender laws, reduction of taxes, reorganization of state government to increase representation of backcountry interests, and other remedies. Throughout the spring and summer of 1786, yeomen across the state attended county conventions—a key tool used during the Revolutionary struggle—to express their grievances and demand reform.[4]

When those calls went unanswered, armed groups of farmers began closing courts to stop debt cases from being heard. The "regulation" movement began in late August of 1786 and quickly spread throughout Massachusetts and surrounding states during the two months that followed.[5] While the nascent uprising was quickly put down in the east, it grew to such an extent in central and western Massachusetts that a loosely organized military force arose in early December.

Daniel Shays, a former Continental Army officer, was among the commanders of this yeomen army and became its symbolic leader. For a time it even appeared as though the Shaysites might seize Boston and take control of the state government. Such talk quickly faded, however, when the insurgents were easily defeated in late January and early February of 1787 by a well-equipped and well-organized state force led by Gen. Benjamin Lincoln.[6]

Shays's Rebellion was rooted in economic trouble, but it revealed a much deeper crisis over political representation. To many of the former leaders of the Revolutionary struggle, the uprising confirmed their worst fears about the frailty of a republican form of government. One of the central rhetorical battles against monarchical power during the Revolutionary War involved disproving the axiomatic notion that America was too large and diverse to support representative government. However, after experiencing the chaos of the 1780s, some believed they had been too sanguine about the virtue of the people. "Shays's Rebellion," historian Gordon S. Wood has observed, "was received with excited consternation mingled with relief by many Americans precisely because it was an anticipated and understandable abuse of republican liberty."[7] From the perspective of the rebels and others frustrated by the economic decline, the apparent necessity of an armed struggle confirmed that their interests would never be represented in places such as Boston and other centers of power. The radical and unprecedented sense of equality that flowed from the American Revolution led to a pervasive sense that only those who were close to a particular segment of the population could in fact faithfully represent its views. As Wood has noted, "localist democracy" was a byproduct of the Revolution because "People felt so disconnected from one another and so self-conscious of their distinct interests that they could not trust anyone different or far removed from themselves to speak for them in government."[8]

This breakdown of political representation can be seen in the divergent attempts to name or represent linguistically the Massachusetts insurgents. The regulation movement was not centralized or well organized, and it never produced a truly unified fighting force or alternative governmental structures. Instead it was a broad coalition of disaffected yeomen who primarily wanted to defend a particular way of life and devise alternatives to their debt troubles. Although some talked of overthrowing the state government, at its core the uprising mainly provided an opportunity to express dissatisfaction over foreclosures and taxation. These were seen as abuses of legislative and judicial power similar to outrages by the royal administration in the 1760s and 70s. Accordingly, the Shaysites adopted familiar symbols of protest associated with the War of Independence. For example, many farmers wore sprigs of evergreen—the symbol of Massachusetts's Revolutionary struggle—in their hats as the rebellion got underway.[9]

Their opponents reacted in horror at the suggestion of a new revolution arising from the backcountry. The war against the British had required great sacrifice in Boston, and many in the east believed that this new uprising would ruin the glorious achievement of independence.[10] Accordingly, the rhetorical response was swift and angry. In a proclamation issued within two weeks of the initial court closings, Governor Bowdoin claimed that those responsible were seeking to "introduce universal riot, anarchy and confusion, which would probably terminate in absolute despotism, and consequently destroy the fairest prospects of political happiness that any people was ever favoured with."[11] Frustration ran so deep that Shaysites were thought to suffer from mental illness or character defects. Their illegal interruptions of courts and business transactions were, to trade-minded easterners, signs of insanity. To others extravagance was the problem, as the threat of mob violence was taken as proof that farmers were too lazy or immoral to pay the debts they had foolishly accrued. Conspiracy theories also abounded, as many believed that the British and a hidden cadre of Tories were using the crisis to reclaim lost colonies.[12]

From the outset the New England press was overwhelmingly opposed to the regulators and generally described the uprising as an "insurrection" rather than a reform movement or true revolution. The notion that the insurgents were akin to Revolutionary War soldiers was mocked and discounted despite the fact that perhaps as many as a third of the Shaysites had fought in the war. That certain former Continental Army officers led them was seen as evidence of an incipient dictatorship, and Daniel Shays was especially attacked as a potential tyrant.[13] Although he eventually came to the fore as the main military leader, he had little involvement in the beginnings of the regulation movement and apparently contributed little to its political demands. Shays was simply one among many indebted farmers who joined the cause because of his frustration and embarrassment at having been sued for debts. Nevertheless, it became important in press accounts to identify Shays as the central villain in the drama of insurrection. He was the pretender, the anti-Washington, who symbolized anarchy and a terrifying spirit of social leveling.

Virtually all of the contributors to both the *New-Haven Gazette, and the Connecticut Magazine* and the *Worcester Magazine* who commented on the armed rebellion emphasized their opposition to it. However, in those pieces, as well as the many more that spoke to the larger crisis, there are significant differences concerning the underlying causes of the new nation's troubles. Beneath these differences were competing perceptions of both public debate and the nature of the citizenry. To define and discuss civil unrest required a judgment—whether explicitly stated or not—about the composition and character of the people who might be participants in the rebellion.

Univocal and strident, the *New-Haven Gazette, and the Connecticut Magazine* sought to address the political problems of the day through the purging and ameliorative influence of satire. It is famous for publishing the mock-epic *The Anarchiad*, which attacked the Shaysites and urged ratification of the Constitution. Eager to adopt the visionary perspective of his friends in the Connecticut Wits poetic circle, Josiah Meigs, the intellectual force in control of editorial content in his partnership with Dana, defined the crisis atmosphere of 1786 in terms of arrested social development.[14] The people, he argued, could be too easily led into mob action and therefore needed strong and wise representatives to rein in their own selfishness and licentiousness. Yet the events in western Massachusetts could not be allowed to disprove the principle of representation or the broader theory of republican government. Therefore, the farmers following Shays had to be defined in a new way—not as citizens but as victims of madness or dupes of anarchy. The role of a magazine in such a situation was to serve as a central reference point and pedagogical tool—a textbook of government—to lend support to those seeking to educate and lead the people in the right direction.

As the furthest inland of the new American periodicals, the *Worcester Magazine* was at the center of the crisis, and thus Isaiah Thomas included a wider range of opinions. Instead of satire, he mainly published short essays and letters, often juxtaposing opposing positions within the same section of the magazine. Some contributors were harsh in criticizing not just the Shaysites but also the underlying reform movement. Others, while not expressing open sympathy with the rebellion, did seek to explain and address the root causes of discontent. Because so many in Worcester (particularly in the outlying areas of the county) took part in the uprising, Thomas could not afford to attack its aims openly; and indeed his own considerable irritation with the elite of Boston most likely led to a more balanced response. Contributors to the *Worcester Magazine* had to account for the fact that the insane and misled Shaysites described in some printed essays and letters might also be their relatives, friends, or neighbors. Thus, apologists for the yeomanry defended the common sense and wisdom of farmers at the same time that other writers questioned their characters and motives. Given the divisions within his readership, Thomas created a magazine that mirrored the debate in Worcester and that mimicked the role of a political body. The forum of the magazine, to an even greater extent than the deliberations of a legislature or convention, promoted both consideration of specific issues and reflection on the nature of political institutions themselves.

The *New-Haven Gazette, and the Connecticut Magazine*

When the *New Haven Gazette* was transformed into a magazine, Connecticut already had a highly competitive newspaper market, and so Meigs and Dana sought to distinguish their new venture by explicitly emphasizing its intellectual depth. They wrote in their initial proposal that "It has been a general complaint, that News-Papers are crouded with Advertisements, to the exclusion of those amusing or instructional articles, which subscribers generally expect." In response to that complaint, they promised that all advertising would be put into a supplement and that the magazine would be smaller and come with an index so that it could easily be bound and saved. This, they hoped, would induce "men of genius" to "be more willing to place their writings in a situation in which they will probably be preserved" rather than "lost as soon as read."[15] They were successful to the extent that other publications, including the fledgling *American Museum, or, Universal Magazine* in Philadelphia, liberally reprinted material from the *New-Haven Gazette, and the Connecticut Magazine.* Within a year, it achieved an impressive circulation of between nine hundred and one thousand copies for each weekly edition.[16]

The magazine was the product of the political and cultural values of New Haven, especially the students, teachers, and alumni of Yale. Meigs's close ties to the college, where he had been both a student and a tutor, likely provided an immediate base of subscribers. Meigs contributed his own writing and published the work of former classmates such as Noah Webster and Joel Barlow. Other members of the Connecticut Wits circle of poets, artists, literary critics, and political philosophers were featured, including Timothy Dwight, David Humphreys, and John Trumbull. As this list suggests, the magazine was strong in its literary offerings and expressed a conservative, federalist political agenda. The troubles of the postwar era had galvanized those who sought to contain the excesses of democracy through a strong national government. They argued for the immediate payment of war debt and vigorously opposed any proposal for paper money. They also railed against social ills such as excessive spending on luxuries, the lack of respect for religion, the decline of honest government, and the general disintegration of traditional systems of authority.

All of these sentiments appear in the *New-Haven Gazette, and the Connecticut Magazine.* Although some space was devoted to local Connecticut politics, including unrelenting satire aimed at antifederalists in the state legislature, most of the magazine's material was national; and at times some of the text was visionary in its scope. For example, selections from David Humphrey's optimistic poem, "On the Happiness of America," appeared in three different issues from the summer of 1786 to the winter of 1787. However, the majority of both the poetry and the prose was more in the vein of the jeremiad than the prospect poem. For example, Timothy Dwight contributed "The Trial of Faith," a poetic paraphrase of the first three chapters of the Book of Daniel. The poem dramatizes the prophet's unwillingness to bow down to the statue of King Nebuchadnezzar, suggesting a warning against the pursuit of political favor and influence for its own sake and offering encouragement to lone individuals who might speak out against the wishes of the majority.

Even before the outbreak of Shays's Rebellion, Meigs used the *New-Haven Gazette, and the Connecticut Magazine* as a vehicle for his concerns about the direction of the new nation. According to Lyon Richardson, he is most likely the author of a series of ten satirical essays that appeared during the magazine's first few months called "Observations on the Present Situation and Future Prospects of this and the United States." These essays attacked American self-congratulation and arrogance in the postwar years and warned about the lack of good men in public life. Meigs did this by adopting the voice of "Lycurgus," the Spartan lawgiver who, according to legend, devised the city-state's communal militaristic system. In Meigs's hands, Lycurgus symbolized the potential of a government, even one defined as a democracy, to create harsh and intrusive laws that destroy individual freedom under the pretense of upholding patriotism or ensuring equality. In the context the 1780s, this voice represented the leveling tyranny that might attend unchecked democracy. Accordingly, Lycurgus's proposals were delivered in an exaggerated, even humorous fashion that nevertheless hinted at the despotic power needed to enforce them. For instance, in the second essay Meigs's Lycurgus argues that everyone must be allowed to vote and hold office and therefore any attempt to create minimum standards for running for office or even to criticize corrupt or incompetent officeholders should be interpreted as a treasonous attack on the democratic state.[17]

In choosing the Spartan Lycurgus, however, Meigs also pointed to another figure: the Athenian Lycurgus of the third century B.C.E., who, as a statesman and orator, was known as a paradigm of virtue, patriotism, and public service. The cleverness of using the same name to signal Meigs's true feelings while still mocking his opponents would have appealed to a classically educated readership. It also reveals Meigs's most comfortable rhetorical mode: political instruction through satire and sarcasm. In the most aggressive of the series, which appeared under the subtitle of "The History of White Negroes," he purports to have discovered a race of "white negroes" in Africa who behave like the citizens of New England agitating for economic reform. He condemns the printing of currency and deferral of state debts as the first steps toward serfdom and feudal tyranny in America. According to Meigs, the transformation of free men into slaves involves three steps. First, those "chiefly among the lower classes of people" are duped into fearing "great men" and begin to be "proportionably fond of fools." Thereafter, "They begin to talk wildly of the vast and dangerous powers of Congress." Second, they "assemble in great numbers at taverns, town-meetings and conventions," which is similar to "several other orders of nature whom nature has formed to herd together." Finally, "They grow calm and industrious" as they agree to work under the heavy burden of state and personal debt.[18]

The "Observations" series was typical of many pieces in the *New-Haven Gazette, and the Connecticut Magazine* in its unrelenting hostility toward the issuing of paper money. To the satirical selections Meigs added a reprint of Thomas Paine's pamphlet against the practice, excerpts from Adam Smith's *Wealth of Nations*, passages from Benjamin Franklin's essay "Advice to a Young Tradesman," and selections from François Marie Arouet de Voltaire on economy and government. All of these appeared during the growing unrest in the spring and summer of 1786 and fulfilled the need of equipping readers with the best arguments against radical economic changes. The reproduction of pieces on the art of rhetoric, including reprints of Hugh Blair's lectures and an essay by Noah Webster, suggests that readers were being prepared to make a public case against radical reforms, particularly concerning paper money. While the magazine educated in a general sense, it was typically not dialogic in either the selection of material or the content of individual pieces. No space was devoted to arguments in favor of debt relief, paper currency, or legal reform.[19] To the extent that Meigs admitted that economic problems existed, they were defined almost entirely as a matter of greed, extravagance, and licentiousness on the part of debtors themselves.

When the "insurrection" was discussed following the Massachusetts court closings in September, references to the demands of Shays and his followers were entirely negative. Governor Bowdoin's initial proclamation condemning the rebellion was printed on September 14 and was followed a week later by a short satirical poem (reprinted from the *Hampshire Herald*) that mocked the insurgents as drunkards. A letter from Berkshire County complained that in closing the court "The people exhibited a striking specimen of the excess of absurdity and madness of which vulgar minds are capable when wrought into a state of fermentation by an unhappy delusion." Other accounts of the various court closings in Massachusetts expressed similar shock and derision. The first direct reference to Daniel Shays occurred in a piece from early October, "An Account of the Insurrections at Springfield, Given by the Gentlemen Who Were Present." He was described simply as "a deranged officer of the late army."[20]

During the later weeks of October and most of November, the *New-Haven Gazette, and the Connecticut Magazine* said little about the insurgency but focused instead on the actions of the Connecticut legislature, searching for any signs of sympathy with the Shaysites among the antifederalist faction. This pattern continued well into the later constitutional debates as the charge of Shayism was a rhetorical weapon used to great effect against the antifederalists.[21] By late December, personal attacks on Shays returned, especially as the military struggle in Massachusetts began to go in favor of state forces. "Anecdotes of Daniel Shaise" offered puns and mockery, describing him as a man "remarkable for subtilty and duplicity" and suggested that "his ambition is unbounded—and his fortune such as has sometimes urged men to desperation."[22]

The suppression of the rebellion during the winter and early spring of 1787 was documented in the *New-Haven Gazette, and the Connecticut Magazine* through short clippings drawn from other newspapers, magazines, government proclamations, accounts of legislative debates, and individual correspondents. This material was limited, however, as Meigs began to devote space to the mock-epic *The Anarchiad*, written in the style of Alexander Pope's *Dunciad*. It appeared sporadically in twelve installments from October 26, 1786, to September 13, 1787, as its authors (Joel Barlow, Lemuel Hopkins, David Humphreys, and John Trumbull) felt the need to offer warnings against localism, the leveling spirit, and excessive democracy. They mocked Shays's Rebellion in order to support the struggle for national union and later the ratification of the Constitution. Like other major satires or political pronouncements in the magazine, *The Anarchiad* was clothed in a humorous, scholarly frame.

In their first offering, which appeared when the regulation movement was nearing the peak of its strength, the authors describe the work of a "society of critics and antiquarians" who delight in investigating the ancient and natural history of America. They claim as their finest discovery an ancient epic poem, produced by a lost American civilization, that prophesies the rise of the figure of Chaos, who overwhelms a peaceful society by spreading ignorance, anarchy, and darkness:

> In visions fair the scenes of fate unroll.
> And Massachusetts opens on my soul.
> There Chaos, Anarch old, asserts his sway,
> And mobs in myriads blacken all the way:
> See Day's stern port—behold the martial frame,
> Of Shay's and Shattuck's mob-compelling name:
>
> . . . .
>
> Lo, THE COURT FALLS; th' affrighted judges run,
> Clerks, Lawyers, Sheriffs, every mother's son.
> The stocks, the gallows lose th' expected prize,
> See the jails open and the thieves arise.
> Thy constitution, Chaos, is restor'd;
> Law sinks before thy uncreating word. . . .[23]

The events are described in apocalyptic terms as Chaos rises up like an intellectual or political Antichrist to make reason (and therefore justice) impossible. Yet the image is also comic, as the leaders of the Rebellion—Luke Day, Daniel Shays, and Job Shattuck—are held up for ridicule as minions of Chaos. They are not serious figures but instead have learned how to conjure up the insurrection by striking stern or martial poses. The farmers of western Massachusetts are never described as anything but a mob, and even judges, sheriffs, and other officials of the state government are depicted as buffoons and cowards. The rebellion was thus explained as the result of intellectual deception and false rhetoric rather than as the result of true economic or political problems. Defined as a purely linguistic crisis, it required mainly a clarification and fixing of terms in order to set things right.

The poem was widely reprinted throughout the states and provided a new frame of reference for the disturbances in Massachusetts, painting the rebellion as the first incident in a long chain that might lead to the collapse of political liberty. To a greater extent than other publications, the *New-Haven Gazette, and the Connecticut Magazine* fixed Shays as the leader of the rebellion in the minds of outside observers, notwithstanding his limited control of the military struggle. Unlike the references to three different leaders in the first installment, the fourth one, printed in early January, identifies just Shays as the instrument of Chaos and imagines his future downfall and regret. The authors predict that he will someday feel "'T were better, thro' a furnace fiery red, / With naked feet on burning coals to tread; / Than point his sword, with parricidious hand, / Against the bosom of his native land." Even in March, more than a month after the rebellion had been routed, *The Anarchiad* continued to use it (and particularly Shays) as a symbol of general anarchy and imminent political dissolution. In attacking antifederalists in the Connecticut assembly, the authors suggest that Shays is their secret idol. Chaos declares: "Bid insurrections claim thy noblest praise, / O'er WASHINGTON exalt thy darling Shays; / With thy contagion, embrio Mobs inspire, / And blow to tenfold rage the kindling fire."[24]

The Anarchiad, along with the rest of the material that appeared in the *New-Haven Gazette, and the Connecticut Magazine*, was undoubtedly successful as part of the campaign to advocate the federal union and ensure that Connecticut ratify the Constitution. To establish the need for such a change, the magazine was apprehensive in late 1786 and early 1787 about the future of republicanism in America. Meigs and his contributors were fundamentally concerned about the breakdown of what they perceived as honest and rational political discourse. In a letter "To The Public" signed by "Cato," the writer contends that those who understand the true causes of the political and economic crisis have a "duty to inform the world, that there are still a virtuous few, who are solicitors for the honor and prosperity of their country, and that to this side belong the learning, the wealth

The *New-Haven* Gazette, *and the* Connecticut *Magazine.*

(VOL. I.) Thurſday, *January* 18, M.DCC.LXXXVII. (No 48.)

NON SIBI SED TOTO GENITOS SE CREDERE MUNDO.

NEW-HAVEN: Publiſhed by MEIGS & DANA, at the South Corner of the Green, fronting the Market. *Price 9ſ. per Ann*

TO THE PUBLIC.

IT has been the opinion of many learned as well as ignorant people, that a republican government was the moſt deſireable, ſafe and happy for the great body of a people. On this principle (true or falſe) was the late war taken up, and carried on in America: and when crowned with ſucceſs, we hoped to taſte the ſweets of civil and religious liberty; although every perſon who thinks properly of the intrigues and ambition of the human mind, muſt expect that it will be attended with jealouſy and watchfulneſs, otherwiſe they will be ſtolen from us by art and cunning.

I have been a ſpectator of the political exhibitions in the public papers of this ſtate: and amongſt other things, have obſerved ſeveral pieces which diſcover, either by ſatyric wit, or Hudibraſtic ſarcaſm, that the authors wiſh to bring every branch of republican government into contempt: and in ſome inſtances where their arts have failed, where their arguments have proved too light, by which they have been diſappointed in their views, have deſcended ſo far below the dignity of civiliſed gentlemen, as to undertake to proſtitute their learning, their wit, and the preſs, to the mean purpoſes of ſatyriſing, not the arguments (which they could not by fair reaſoning anſwer) but the places of abode, and (to uſe the celebrated poet's expreſſion), the Paunch, the viſage and the natural ſhape of the perſons who had fortitude enough to act their parts faithfully in oppoſition to them. This I am ſenſible deſerves no other anſwer than ſilence and neglect, as every candid obſerver will judge, whether ſuch authors do not merit the ſcorn and command the reſentment of every friend to humanity and lover of civility.

But when it appears (as in the Connecticut Magazine, *No.* 40.*), that ſome perſon under the ſignature of CATO, has the audacity to hold up to public view, that Connecticut has declared to the world, that ſhe will conſider herſelf detached from that union which ſhe has pledged her faith to ſupport and defend, that ſhe renounces all claims to national veracity and honour, and that ſhe will defraud with an open and unbluſhing countenance, her lawful creditors; that the requiſitions of Congreſs are vilely ſacrificed to the arts of a deteſtable and deſigning faction; and that there is but a virtuous few in the ſtate, claiming to be amongſt the patriotic and wiſe, whoſe voice is too gentle to be heard &c. proclaiming in the public papers. (becauſe it could not be otherwiſe known), that to his ſide belongs the Learning, the Wealth and Virtue of the ſtate; boaſting that many have ſuffered the ſarcaſtic ſeverity of wit, &c. undertaking as a patriot and friend to the public to point out a particular character as being an obnoxious, ignorant author of the impolitic, unjuſt and unfœderal meaſures aſſented to by both houſes of aſſembly, (pretending to have full knowledge of his heart) inſinuates, yea, has the* politeneſs *to ſay, that he is the perſon who in a former ſeſſion, took an active part in oppoſing the requiſitions of Congreſs on the ſubject of an impoſt, who with a duplicity inſeparable from a diſhoneſt heart, when he perceived himſelf incapable of effecting his purpoſe, diſowned uniformly in private converſation, the ſuffrage he had given in the houſe &c. warning the people to be no longer deluded by the pretenſions of* that man, *inviting them to place their confidence in thoſe who by their abilities and known integrity are worthy of it, (whoſe gifts by the bye have been concealed from the public eye, otherwiſe they would not have occaſion to beg the confidence of the people in the public papers) It ſeems when ſuch groſs miſrepreſentations are publiſhed, tending to diſcord, that the public ought to be informed, that after the report of the committee was accepted by both houſes of Aſſembly, acknowledging the debt of five pence on the pound in hard money, and ten pence on the pound in certificates for intereſt from the loan-office, by which the debt to the United States was fully acknowledged. The time of payment was the next and only thing to be determined, and after many ſerious and candid debates on the ſubject, it appeared that the arrearages of rates now lying on the people, the ſcarcity of proviſions and money at this time, rendered it impoſſible to collect a new tax if laid; and would tend to diſcourage even thoſe who were uſing their utmoſt endeavours to pay.*

Therefore it was thought by both houſes of aſſembly, that the juſtice

Title page from January 18, 1787, issue of Josiah Meigs's and Eleutheros Dana's the *New-Haven Gazette, and the Connecticut Magazine*. Combining the format and features of the newspaper and the magazine, Meigs's and Dana's periodical includes "To the Public," which references the "signature of Cato." The address underscores the ways in which a periodicals format responded to the issue of political "misrepresentations" in an emerging public sphere (as well as debates about private and public virtue) and how people openly contested the meaning and function of a "republican government" relative to state and personal interests. Courtesy of the American Antiquarian Society.

and virtue of the state." Satire, he asserts, is useful in attacking the "absurdities and ignorance" of those who have distorted the public good, but eventually, "in every honest bosom, indignation will take the place of sarcasm, when we reflect on the injuries they have done their country."[25] The purpose of a political magazine, then, was to combat the misuse and misrepresentation of language and ideas. The good citizen (and good political magazine) should embrace models of linguistic clarity and promote the sort of writing and speaking necessary for honest and virtuous republican government to succeed.

In his examination of the relationship between politics and language in colonial and early national culture, Thomas Gustafson has demonstrated that debates over the nature of government were typically accompanied by underlying attempts to fix the meaning of words more precisely and definitively. In seeking a political revolution that would overthrow British rule, the Revolutionaries of the 1770s also wished to correct the previous misuse of language by the Crown. Before a new government could be created, a nobler and more truthful political rhetoric must be established. Yet figures as diverse as John Adams and Thomas Paine were also acutely aware of the potential for chaos (both actual and rhetorical) inherent in any transfer of power. They feared what Gustafson calls the "Thucydidean moment," referring to the account—well known in eighteenth-century America—in Thucydides' *History of the Peloponnesian War* when factions at odds in the city of Corcyra created chaos because of their deceptive charges and counter-charges. The dream of Orphic order and clarity gives way in such moments to obfuscation, deceit, and manipulation. "Words," Thucydides wrote of Corcyra, "lost their significance." Consequently, "The pious and upright conduct was on both sides disregarded; the moderate citizens fell victims to both . . . the whole order of human life was confounded."[26] Steeped in classical learning and fearful of events in Massachusetts, the writers of the *New-Haven Gazette, and the Connecticut Magazine* sought to avoid such a fate. They saw potential in the political magazine, as they would later in the Constitution, to define and preserve the principles of honest and good government.

The *Worcester Magazine*

Unlike Meigs, who emphasized strong government, Isaiah Thomas expressed defiance toward the Massachusetts legislature in the first issue of the *Worcester Magazine*, which appeared in April of 1786. He was angry at the recent decision to impose a tax on newspaper advertising and had made the decision to transform his successful newspaper, the *Massachusetts Spy*, into a magazine primarily to avoid paying it. Thomas began publishing the *Spy* in 1770, and it eventually became the most aggressive patriot newspaper in Boston.[27] It was successful in the postwar period, but the *Worcester Magazine* was necessary, Thomas wrote, because the *Spy* had suffered "an attack upon its vitals by those who ought to have supported and protected it upon principles of honour and justice." Thomas asserted that his new magazine would undertake "nearly the same duty that was performed by the Spy," which mainly involved keeping a critical eye on the government. In another advertising notice, Thomas again relied on his reputation as a patriot to bolster his case against the new tax. He described having resisted both offers of patronage and threats of imprisonment from colonial governors in the 1770s and claimed that the *Spy* was a politically independent newspaper. The old slogan of the newspaper, "Open to all parties, influenced by none," was to be the guiding principle of the *Worcester Magazine*. A newspaper tax was anathema to Thomas not only because it hurt his business, but also because it had a tendency "to *destroy* those necessary vehicles of public information" and represented "an *unconstitutional restraint* on the Liberty of the Press."[28]

In defining the state government of Massachusetts as a potential oppressor—equal, in most respects, to the old colonial administration in its power to rob the people of liberty—Thomas took a different approach than Meigs did. Whereas Meigs worried that excessive liberty and leveling might lead the people to assert too much power and thus topple proper republican government in favor of mob rule, Thomas remained focused on the potential of government officials, no matter whether they were in a monarchical or republican system, to abuse their power and tyrannize the people. Worcester was also a quite different economic and political environment than New Haven, as currency, debt, taxes, and other issues were not just theoretical concerns but central to conducting everyday business. As one of the largest of the inland market towns, it served as a central artery for the movement of agricultural products and manufactured goods between the backcountry and the eastern seaboard. It was therefore diverse in the interests, backgrounds, and material condition of its inhabitants.

The county of Worcester was at the epicenter of the debt crisis, and as John L. Brooke has demonstrated, complex and interlocking factors such as religious affiliation, levels of education, types of debt owed, ethnic identity, class self-identification, and town loyalties all played a part in the decision of citizens either to support or to oppose the rebellion. Although definite patterns of participation can be determined, Brooke argues that predicting how certain individuals might have responded to the crisis is not a simple matter of assuming that farmer-debtors in rural areas were uniformly opposed to merchant-creditors in towns.[29] One might assume that readers of the *Worcester Magazine* were mainly drawn from the county's merchant class, but even if that were true, it would still not be an indication of uniformity of thought or reaction to the crisis. Given the complexity of the allegiances involved, Thomas could never assume that his readers would all agree, but he nevertheless sought common ground.

Such an attempt can be seen in the short, homiletic pieces that appeared in the spring and summer of 1786 that emphasized simple, homespun responses to hard economic times, such as the need for greater frugality and industry. These letters, anecdotes, and epigraphs suggested that the people were simply reaping what they had sown in spending so much during the postwar period and should return to a more virtuous lifestyle. "An Infallible Cure for Hard Times" included the assertion that "Industry and economy, will forever triumph over hard times" and "Therefore the general cry 'that we cannot pay taxes, and live,' is *absolutely false.*"[30] Troubling such advice was the fact that Thomas's magazine was supported by advertising designed to entice readers to spend money on new, imported goods. The *Worcester Magazine* sought to define cures for the times, but it was, by its location and very existence, a proponent of the new market economy which was making the people more acquisitive and less frugal. Also, while Thomas printed articles that defended higher state taxes, levied to dispose of the large public debt left over from the war, he continued to reprint his own arguments against the newspaper advertising tax.

The first serious attention paid to the agitation in the countryside occurred in the writing of "Tom Taciturn."[31] Appearing from April to September, these essays imitated the style of the *Spectator* and offered a vague and sometimes pretentious discussion of topics such as knowledge, religion, taste, virtue, and other general subjects. "Tom Taciturn" articulated the open philosophy of Isaiah Thomas's publication. He wrote that a magazine "is a place for every man to speak his mind," and that the *Worcester Magazine* could be favorably compared to the General Court "where every member has a right to speak his mind freely without being amendable in any other court whatsoever."[32]

In late August, Tom Taciturn tested his freedom to articulate unpopular views when he turned specifically to politics and forcefully defended efforts at political reform, especially the right of citizens to gather in county conventions. In the first week of September, he wrote that "We know it is an indication of a good constitution, when peccant humours break out in eruptions, and much safer than to have them remain in the blood. Then what right have we to complain of County Conventions? *Let them alone* I say." In this statement he unwittingly echoed Thomas Jefferson's famous assessment of Shays's Rebellion that "a little rebellion now and then is a good thing" and that "It is a medicine necessary for the sound health of the government." In the following week, Tom Taciturn wrote that the regulators who were closing down courts were truly "sensible people" who simply "do not *fully know*, and . . . are not *fully sensible yet*" about the best manner in which to reform government. This opinion was too much for at least one reader as a brief letter responding to the previous week's commentary appeared in the third week and read, in part, "Destroy your types, and office burn, / Or leave off printing Tom Taciturn." It was signed simply "S," and with this threat hanging over him, Tom Taciturn wrote only one more piece.[33]

The physical juxtaposition of opposing essays and letters was a favorite trick of Thomas, and despite the threat he did not stop printing a range of opinions. Unlike Meigs, he rarely revealed his own opinions and did not offer editorial commentary on behalf of the magazine. The only exceptions occurred when he pleaded for an end to hostilities and for mutual understanding. For example, in late September he called on fellow citizens to help calm the situation before military force was needed to put down the rebellion. Again, in January of 1787, he urged those in Worcester who had formerly been at odds over regulation to soften their differences. Writing as a "hand-servant to the publick," he claimed that in offering the *Worcester Magazine* during the crisis he had "studiously endeavoured . . . not to raise the boisterous passions of men of party" and that "he sincerely wishes, that all classes of men would divest themselves of prejudice, and join heart and hand in restoring that peace and good order, so essential to the well-being of the community, and without which, we cannot exist a sovereign and independent state."[34] His concern was not to clarify or even purify political thinking and rhetoric so much as he wished to create the proper framework—namely, the printed page and not the battlefield—for healthy discussion and debate.

The question of how and where the voice of the people might be heard was the central problem at the heart of Shays's Rebellion. Reformers and regulators believed that they had been betrayed by the legislature and that traditional places of authority, such as courts, had to be retaken in order to do the people's business. Central to that strategy were the ad hoc county conventions where protesters gathered, heard speeches, developed petitions, and planned strategy. Such gatherings had a long and successful history in Worcester and surrounding communities during the pre-Revolutionary agitation of the early 1770s and were again well attended and widely supported in the mid-1780s.[35] To supporters of the state government, conventions subverted the political process and undermined the duly elected legislature by attempting to settle questions in an extralegal manner. They also were thought to open the door for demagogues and dishonest men to stir up the passions of the people and lead them into actions directly contrary to those of the proper authorities.

These gatherings took place throughout the spring and summer of 1786, but the debate over their existence did not begin in the *Worcester Magazine* until September, after the actual armed uprisings had begun. Indeed, the debate continued into November and December even though most conventions had ceased and battle lines were drawn between Shays's army and Lincoln's troops. Perhaps this occurred because a debate over the conventions was safer and involved less exposure of allegiances than one over the more violent actions of the Shaysites. Isaiah Thomas printed both sides, and although the weight of opinion went against the legitimacy of conventions, a significant minority rose up to defend the right of the people to hold them. No one explicitly condoned the court closings, but some clearly laid the blame for the uprising on the government and not on the insurgents themselves. Fundamental to the exchanges in the *Worcester Magazine* was a debate over the nature of the ordinary citizens of the town, county, and state. Did yeomen have legitimate grievances, or were they too lazy in their work and lavish in their tastes? Could uneducated farmers gather in ad hoc political gatherings to discuss complex economic, legal, and political issues intelligently, or were they likely to be misled and duped by conniving and ambitious men bent on destroying the state's economy?

From September through November, twenty-six essays or letters (of at least ten lines or more) written specifically for the *Worcester Magazine* addressed the question of county conventions and, more generally, the debt crisis. Nearly two-thirds of them were strongly opposed to the conventions. "Citizen" stated firmly in early September that "County conventions are unconstitutional from the very nature of such assemblies." Writing two weeks later, "An Old Republican" granted that in theory some conventions might be constitutional if they were to limit themselves just to informing the public about issues, but then several paragraphs later he added that "they open a wide field for wicked and designing men, where the proper means of detecting their artifices is necessarily wanting." He feared that conventions would "excite a false alarm in the minds of the people" and they would be used to "perplex and embarrass government, by amusing and perverting the minds of many inattentive though honest people."[36] His concern was twofold: first, the people who attended the convention might be unable to unscramble and decipher poisoned messages, and, second, they would then become unthinking critics of the government. The implication was that to the extent to which the people are fragile in their understanding and education, then republican government is also a fragile institution that cannot stand heedless criticism or embarrassment.

The charge that the conventions provided a forum for dishonest and seditious talk was answered by less than a third of contributors, but their arguments were provocative enough to spark a lively debate. "A Member of the Convention" led the way when he asserted in early October that it is the duty of the people to express grievances and to complain about the government, which "will always chafe and fit uneasy, unless the body politick grows callous and insensible; then, to a generous mind, it would scarce be worthy the name of government." In other words, silent acceptance of government policies is an invitation to tyranny. Thereafter, "Member" focused on describing the plight of the yeoman and redefining the indebted farmer as a hardworking and thrifty figure who had been held down not by his own spending but by an unequal government that overtaxes and is too concerned with eastern interests. The following week, "A Freeman" reiterated the right of ordinary citizens to meet to question and even protest a republican government. He declared that if "meeting in Conventions is unconstitutional, it is high time the constitution was altered in this particular, as it takes from the subject a right rarely called in question in the most despotick government." Freeman also took pains to explain the relationship between conventions and regulation. "Our conventions had no hand in stopping the Courts of Justice," he wrote, and added that "The people, irritated and provoked, it must be confessed have acted imprudently, and taken a step that nothing but the most desperate circumstances could justify."[37] Rather than imply that ordinary citizens had gone mad or that they were under the influence of conspirators seeking to overthrow the government, Freeman pointed his readers once again to the desperate economic situation in the countryside.

In addition to the voices of clear partisans, Thomas published several pieces that offered analysis of the debate itself. "Admonisher," for example, complained of its harsh and uncivil tone. While these selections do not declare firmly for or against the conventions, they do argue for civility in discussing them. They also imply that debate within the magazine must be allowed to flow freely and without hindrance or threat. This was significant, in part, because some of the anticonvention writers had threatened Freeman and Member of the Convention with tarring and feathering. Other anticonvention contributors were more moderate. According to "A Son of Freedom," for example, Thomas's magazine had the credibility to publish a range of views. He asserted that "I justify the Printer in publishing some things, which, I am persuaded, that as a member of society, he could wish never to have seen, much less in his weekly Magazine."[38] This was a significant concession in such nervous times.

By December of 1786, published support for county conventions faded primarily because new laws, including a riot act and the suspension of habeas corpus, stopped almost all ad hoc conventions from being held. Even the most moderate expressions of antigovernment feelings were chilled. Thomas devoted much of the space in his December and January issues to publishing news of the victory of state forces, including letters and proclamations from both General Lincoln and Governor Bowdoin. The material dominated the magazine, but Thomas did not exult in the victory or suggest a sense of vindication even though he had previously said that he would welcome the end of the violence. Little serious or mocking writing on the personality of Shays or the drama of his defeat was printed. Mostly Thomas continued to create a forum that might improve a sense of civic unity. For example, a number of individuals who had previously been involved in the rebellion used the *Worcester Magazine* as a forum to publish letters confessing their participation and asserting their loyalty to the state. They had capitulated, of course, but letters in Thomas's magazine were not part of a larger pattern of public embarrassment or punishment. Rather, the magazine became an institution that could confer political credibility and the redemption of a public self that went beyond the power of judges and government officials to grant pardons.

In this way the *Worcester Magazine* helped to move the state forward and beyond the crisis. Although county conventions had been halted, Thomas continued to publish petitions, proclamations, and instructions to legislators produced by various towns in the county. The printing in the third week of January of a petition from the town of Holden serves as an example of the role the *Worcester Magazine* played in the emerging post-rebellion political discourse. The majority of the town petitioned Governor Bowdoin to liberate Job Shattuck, one of the leaders of the uprising, as well as everyone else who had participated. They also demanded that courts be closed until after the new elections in the spring, which was one of the regulators' key demands. An explanatory essay was added, but so too was a dissenting letter, signed by eleven progovernment men, requesting that the governor show no leniency in the prosecution of the recent rebels. This relatively balanced presentation was a prelude to the many essays, petitions, letters, and other documents devoted to the spring elections that surprisingly swept Governor Bowdoin out of office and brought in a more reform-minded government under John Hancock that promised more leniency toward the Shaysites. Thereafter, the *Worcester Magazine* played a leading role in the publication of arguments both for and against the ratification of the constitution, creating a series of well-known essays titled "The Worcester Speculator" that, to an even greater extent than the debate over the county conventions, offered a range of opinions on the proposed federal compact. While Thomas was more obvious in his support for the constitution, his magazine was open to writers from both camps.

Ironically, while so many contributors to the magazine in 1786 and early 1787 decried the role of county conventions in fomenting dissent and encouraging Shays's Rebellion, Isaiah Thomas's magazine functioned much like a convention. It provided a forum for discussion at a time when political divisions were widening to such a degree that the viability of the state and even nation were uncertain. Thomas's loyalties remained with the development of his own business interests and thus with the market economy that was changing forever the lives of the subsistence farmers who took part in the rebellion, so he was certainly not a disinterested or impartial observer. Nevertheless, he clearly did not conceive of his magazine as an instrument of persuasion to be wielded by any one person or party. The opposition of a majority of his contributors to county conventions, the regulation movement, and eventually Shays' Rebellion was clear, and yet he did not deny publication to those with more moderate or even opposing views. In Thomas's hands, the political magazine became a fluid instrument that forced the side-by-side evaluation of ideas. It assumed and embraced the existence of a diverse and often unpredictable readership.

The Evolution of the Political Magazine

The *New-Haven Gazette, and the Connecticut Magazine* and the *Worcester Magazine* were founded at a time of political and linguistic crisis, and so it is not surprising that they both ceased operation when government became more stable. By the middle of 1788, the Massachusetts legislature repealed the newspaper advertising tax, and so Isaiah Thomas returned to publishing the *Spy*, which was as successful as ever. The emphasis of the resurrected newspaper shifted, however, from debate to matter-of-fact presentation of political, economic, and cultural news. Josiah Meigs ceased the publication of his magazine in early 1789 after it was no longer financially viable. When the ratification of the Constitution was assured, the primary mission of the periodical had been achieved, and thus it surely had less appeal.[39]

Written reactions to Shays's Rebellion such as those found in these two magazines can be seen as part of the larger thrust in the 1780s toward the security and authority of a written constitution as the solution to the knotty problems of popular sovereignty and political representation. The function of a written constitution was, as Michael Warner has argued, to circumvent the endless appeals to the authority of conventions, meetings, and other political gatherings. The authority of "the people" could be made abstract and permanent within the lines of a single document. Warner writes that "It is the invention of the written constitution, itself now the original and literal embodiment of the people, that ensures that the people will henceforward be nonempirical by definition."[40] Literacy and the "printedness" of the Constitution were, Warner argues, key tools used to ensure the stability of law and society. The American form of government was given permanent authority beyond the reach of physical gatherings of the people who might make dangerous changes in the heat of the moment. This meant that the revolutionary appeal for "the people" to invoke their right to sovereignty could be deflected or moderated. Social change could occur, but only through existing republican structures. A written constitution created boundaries and rules for political rhetoric and reform, making uprisings like the rebellion of the Shaysites illegal, but also opening the door to the sort of political participation from underrepresented interests that they sought.

The political magazine was not as fluid, open, or democratic as physical gatherings of the people, nor was it as permanent and authoritative as a written constitution. Contributors to the *New-Haven Gazette, and the Connecticut Magazine* were eager to see an appropriate distance between the passions of the people and the deliberations of wiser and more sober legislators in properly constituted assemblies. The political magazine could, in their view, be an educating intermediary institution between the people and their representatives. The example of the *Worcester Magazine* both confirms and adds complexity to this model. While he had a stake in calming the population and protecting a stable government, Isaiah Thomas was unwilling to support state authority without question or dissent. He sought instead to bring the sort of give-and-take that might occur in the street, tavern, or convention within the framework of a periodical. The continued survival of his magazine depended on not allowing any particular voice to become too strong or to go unchallenged. The voice of the people (and its authority) could be expressed, but the efficacy of the magazine as an honest and reliable source of such perspectives would quickly be lost if it were to insist too much on one point of view. As Thomas envisioned it, a magazine should not just rationalize the political aims of established leaders or an influential clique; it should also communicate the divergent views of the populace (its readers) to those in power. The people did not speak with a single voice, and although governments sometimes needed to make decisions as though citizens were unified, there was no reason for a political magazine to act in the same way.

Notes

1. Lyon Richardson, *A History of Early American Magazines, 1741–1789* (1931; rpt. New York: Octagon Books, 1966), 237–39, 242–45, 258–60. The *New-Haven Gazette, and the Connecticut Magazine* (previously the *New Haven Gazette*) appeared in February and was reduced from four large pages to an eight-page quarto size. The *Worcester Magazine* (previously the *Massachusetts Spy*) was launched in April and was offered in octavo size on twelve to sixteen pages. Both cost nine shillings per year.
2. Richardson 237–39. The *American Musical Magazine* was also published in New Haven in 1786, but it did not focus on current events or politics.
3. Richard B. Morris, *The Forging of the Union, 1781–1789* (New York: Harper and Row, 1987), 130–42.
4. David P. Szatmary, *Shays' Rebellion: The Making of an Agrarian Insurrection* (Amherst: U of Massachusetts P, 1980), 19–36, 40–44.
5. Ibid., 58–59.
6. Alden T. Vaughn, "The 'Horrid and Unnatural' Rebellion of Daniel Shays," in *Riot, Rout, and Tumult: Readings in American Social and Political Violence*, eds. Roger Lane and John J. Turner (Westport, CT: Greenwood P, 1978), 60–66.
7. Gordon S. Wood, *The Creation of the American Republic, 1776–1787* (1969; rpt. New York: Norton, 1972), 412.
8. Gordon S. Wood, *The Radicalism of the American Revolution* (New York: Knopf, 1991), 245.

9. Alden T. Vaughn, "The 'Horrid and Unnatural' Rebellion of Daniel Shays," 62–65; Szatmary, *Shays' Rebellion: The Making of an Agrarian Insurrection*, 69.

10. William Pencak, "'The Fine Theoretic Government of Massachusetts Is Prostrated to the Earth': The Response to Shays' Rebellion Reconsidered," in *In Debt to Shays: The Bicentennial of an Agrarian Rebellion*, ed. Robert A. Gross (Charlottesville: UP of Virginia, 1993), 135.

11. *Worcester Magazine* 1, first week (September 1786): 279.

12. Stephen E. Patterson, "The Federalist Reaction to Shays's Rebellion," in Gross 104–6; Szatmary, *Shays' Rebellion*, 70–76.

13. Szatmary, *Shays' Rebellion*, 64–65, 74. Szatmary offers compelling evidence based on his analysis of selected groups of Shaysites for the one-third estimate; however, William Pencak has argued that such a claim is misleading because the service of many of those men was relatively brief and took place only within the militia. His point underscores the fact that while many western farmers were highly familiar with the symbols of the Revolution, they had not been involved sufficiently to feel great connection or sympathy with those in eastern counties.

14. Dana left the partnership in the second half of 1787.

15. *New-Haven Gazette, and the Connecticut Magazine* 1, (February 15, 1786): iii.

16. Richardson 244.

17. *New-Haven Gazette, and the Connecticut Magazine* 1, (March 9, 1786): 25-26.

18. *New-Haven Gazette, and the Connecticut Magazine* 1, (April 13, 1786): 66.

19. The only true debate featured in the magazine was the reprinting of an exchange on October 5 and 12 between two Yale students at the spring commencement exercises over the issue of sumptuary laws.

20. *New-Haven Gazette, and the Connecticut Magazine* 1, (September 28, 1786): 258; (October 12, 1786): 275.

21. Szatmary, *Shays' Rebellion*, 131–34; Patterson 116–18.

22. *New-Haven Gazette, and the Connecticut Magazine* 1, (December 21, 1786): 352.

23. Ibid., (October 26, 1786): 288.

24. Ibid., (January 11, 1787): 358; (March 15, 1787): 26.

25. Ibid., (November 30, 1786): 331.

26. Thomas Gustafson, *Representative Words: Politics, Literature, and the American Language, 1776–1865* (Cambridge: Cambridge UP, 1992), 70–71, 77.

27. Annie Russell Marble, *From 'Prentice to Patron: The Life Story of Isaiah Thomas* (New York: Appleton-Century, 1935), 49–63. Thomas moved in 1775 to Worcester, which was the home of the *Spy* until it was turned into the *Worcester Magazine* in 1786. He had previous experience publishing a magazine when he produced the *Royal American Magazine* for fifteen months from 1774 to 1775.

28. *Worcester Magazine* 1, first week (April 1786): 14; second week (April 1786): 24; Thomas's biographer, Annie Russell Marble, notes that he was certainly not neutral during the early 1770s and the Revolutionary struggle, but the evidence in the *Worcester Magazine* suggests that he held more closely to his old motto in the 1780s.

29. John L. Brooke, *The Heart of the Commonwealth: Society and Political Culture in Worcester County, Massachusetts, 1713–1861* (Cambridge: Cambridge UP, 1989), 192–229.

30. *Worcester Magazine* 1, third week (May 1786): 81.

31. Lyon Richardson has identified Edward Bangs, a leading citizen of Worcester, as the author of the series. Richardson 260–61.

32. *Worcester Magazine* 1, fourth week (April 1786): 46–47.

33. Ibid., first week (September 1786): 273; second week (September 1786): 286; third week (September 1786): 297.

34. Ibid., fourth week (September 1786): 314; fourth week (January 1787): 526.

35. John L. Brooke, *The Heart of the Commonwealth: Society and Political Culture in Worcester County, Massachusetts, 1713–1861*, 192–201.

36. *Worcester Magazine* 1, first week (September 1786): 275; third week (September 1786): 296.

37. Ibid. 2, first week (October 1786): 321; second week (October 1786): 336-37.

38. Ibid. 2, second week (November 1786): 304-05; fourth week (December 1786): 473.

39. Meigs eventually left publishing and, among other careers, returned to teaching. He moved south and in 1801 became an influential early president of the academy in Athens that would eventually become the University of Georgia. Although he had been a strong supporter of the Constitution, his politics shifted in the 1790s, and he became an outspoken Jeffersonian, which eventually caused him to leave his position in Georgia in 1811.

40. Michael Warner, *The Letters of the Republic: Publication and the Public Sphere in Eighteenth-Century America* (Cambridge: Harvard UP, 1990), 103.

Philip Gould

The African Slave Trade and Abolitionism

Rereading Antislavery Literature, 1776–1800

During the 1770s and 1780s, antislavery movements gained momentum in the British Atlantic world. Primarily concerned with abolishing the African slave trade, organizations such as the Pennsylvania Abolition Society, founded in 1775, and the English Society for Effecting the Abolition of the Slave Trade, founded in 1787, built upon the traditional base of Quaker humanitarians and contributed to the abolition of the African slave trade in Britain and the United States in 1807–8. The study of these early antislavery movements has produced an abundance of historical scholarship. Notwithstanding its nuances and complexities, it generally falls into three modes of interpretation: one cites the importance of the spread of political ideologies popularizing the discourses of natural rights and liberties informing revolutions in British America, France, and Saint Domingue; another emphasizes the cultures of sentimentalism and benevolence that refocused the plight of African slaves; the third argues for the direct relation between the concurrent rise of both antislavery movements and modern industrial capitalism.[1]

Literary scholarship generally has been less attentive to eighteenth-century antislavery culture—a puzzling fact in light of the abundance of antislavery writing published between the 1760s and 1810s. Early American periodicals provide an important discursive arena in which to consider both the aesthetic and ideological significance of antislavery writing. Though nothing like the print media that antebellum American abolitionists like William Lloyd Garrison marshaled against southern slavery, early American periodicals were an important venue for the rising sentiments against slavery and the slave trade. As many of the essays in this anthology acknowledge, early American magazines were designed to instruct morally, to entertain, and to cultivate the tastes and sensibilities of literate, bourgeois readers. The antislavery writings they published were meant to fulfill these cultural goals. The antislavery writing published in eighteenth-century magazines lacks the spirit of confrontation and the sustained moral outrage of nineteenth-century abolitionist journals such as Garrison's *Liberator.* Instead they demonstrate a more genteel approach that engaged audiences more on their own terms, satisfying their curiosity about foreign places, satiating their appetites for sentimental feeling, and fulfilling their self-images as enlightened and civilized Americans.

What, then, were the cultural stakes of the early antislavery literature that was originally published or reprinted in these magazines? One brief yet representative example begins to address this central question. In 1787 Mathew Carey's *American Museum, or, Universal Magazine* reprinted the Rhode Island antislavery statute, "An Act to Prevent the Slave Trade and to Encourage the Abolition of Slavery," enacted earlier that year. The law rhetorically framed ending the state's participation in the African slave trade in the following terms: "Whereas the trade to Africa for slaves, and the transportation and selling of them in other countries, is inconsistent with justice and the principles of humanity, as well as the laws of nature, and that more enlightened and civilized sense of freedom which has of late prevailed."[2] Such language registers several important features of early antislavery writing: its general emphasis upon the abolition of the slave trade rather than the immediate emancipation of slaves; its appeal to natural law and natural principles of justice; the embellishment of such principles with the (modest) tones of sentimental humanitarianism; and the assumption of a moral and cultural position ("that more enlightened and civilized sense of freedom") that participating in the African slave trade severely jeopardizes.

This language also begins to suggest that the slave trade threatened cultural assumptions connecting commerce to the refinement of manners—a term that recently has gained increasing scholarly importance in eighteenth-century studies.[3] As J. G. A. Pocock has argued, commercial societies historically evolved in conjunction with ideologies meant to legitimate changing social and cultural relations. In this context, manners (or "moeurs") signified

> a complex of shared practices and values, which secured the individual as social being and furnished the society surrounding him with an indefinitely complex and flexible texture; more powerfully even than laws, manners rendered civil society capable of absorbing

> and controlling human action and belief. . . . Commercial society, characterized by the incessant exchange of goods and services, moral and material, between its members, was that in which "manners" and "politeness" could reign undisturbed, and philosophy was perceived as the sociable conversation which Enlightenment sought to make it.[4]

Although never a dominant literary form within the periodical genre, the antislavery literature published in eighteenth-century magazines registers ongoing considerations of the relations between commerce and manners. Prose and verse attacks on the African slave trade (an "iniquitous" and "savage" trade) were founded upon the assumption Pocock articulates above: that commerce civilized and socialized human beings. One way of viewing this literature's critique of slave trading is to see it actively engaged in trying to secure this cultured equation which "civilized" European and American slave trading belied. That is why antislavery literature thematizes two forms of enslavement simultaneously, often with varying moral and racial effects: the bodily enslavement of African slaves mercilessly transported across the Atlantic and the cultural enslavement of those Europeans and Americans who bought and sold them—and those who bought the goods produced by them.

Transatlantic Print Culture

Early magazine literature about slavery demonstrates the overlapping positions of the proslavery and antislavery writers.[5] Both emphasized the need to improve the conditions of American slaves, and both were founded on hierarchical assumptions about American society that necessitated the need to control Africans themselves. The *New American Magazine*'s proslavery essay "On the Use and Abuse of Negro Slaves," for example, argued that slavery maintained the divine "mode of subordination, whereby men are by the wisdom of providence placed under one another in a chain almost infinite," and urged American slaveholders to "act as Christians themselves in their treatment of them."[6] Similarly, many conservative antislavery writers later employed this ideology of benevolent subordination when exposing the abuses on West Indian plantations. Religious and evangelical magazines in particular emphasized this necessity by thematizing the priority of spiritual over physical freedom. Hence, religious periodical pieces against slavery ideologically coincided with proslavery apologies that religious conversion was the most important means of improving slave conditions. Each side viewed conversion in terms of social and racial management of Africans themselves. One religious magazine, for example, published "An Account of the Experience of an African" in 1796, which makes much more of "poor Camba" and his morphology of conversion than it does his prospects for escaping the plantation, concluding that "We may see by this narration, how God justifieth the heathen, and by what simple means he blesseth the conversion of a sinner."[7]

The emphasis on virtue and feeling that developed in antislavery literature marks the convergence of didactic projects of the magazine genre and antislavery politics. Each was premised largely on the virtues of sympathy and benevolence; each fed the other, in other words. Scores of prefaces to early American magazines set out the terms for promoting, for example, "the immutable basis of *Virtue* and *Religion*,"[8] which appealed to the ability of the magazine to cultivate enlightened sensibilities and thereby bolster the patronage of "Friends and Benefactors" often necessary to commercial publication itself. This trope of cultivation was far-reaching and densely coded with important cultural meanings. In 1786 the *New Jersey Magazine and Monthly Advertiser*, for example, likened itself to the Ovidian Garden of Flora, a place where "what Time and Industry shall collect, may be disposed with Grace and Elegance."[9] Such pronouncements, however, also suggest the danger in publishing antislavery materials, for magazines, while cultivating the virtue of benevolence, generally avoided the passionate partisanship characteristic of this era's newspapers.[10]

Even though American magazines cast the cultivation of virtue in national terms, the tension between national virtue and transnational publishing begins to reveal important connections between American and British antislavery movements. During this era American magazines still relied significantly upon British writers and literary materials. Some, like Robert Aitken, the editor of the *Pennsylvania Magazine: or, American Monthly Museum* tried to deny it. He claimed that America's political growth from infancy to manhood necessitated the particular kind of cultural independence that avoided the "foreign vices" and "voluptuousness" of the British magazines.[11] Haunted by the specter of cultural dependence, post-Revolutionary American magazines repeatedly celebrated the "Republic of Letters," and those such as the *New-York Weekly Magazine; or, Miscellaneous Repository* and the *Massachusetts Magazine; or, Monthly Museum of Knowledge and Rational Entertainment* included frontispieces allegorizing the future greatness of American liberty. Yet if editors such as Isaiah Thomas called for literary originality in the name of national honor, just as many were forced to acknowledge the necessity of reprinting British and Continental European materials. In his introduction to the *American Magazine*, for example, Noah Webster intended to publish as much original American writing as possible but reluctantly admitted editorial realities: "In this new world, a thousand subjects present themselves for discussion, which in Europe, are almost exhausted. Our predilection for foreign productions, among other causes, has operated to discourage undertakings of this kind; but while we allow foreign publications all their merit, it must be conceded that none of them can be wholly calculated for this country."[12]

Notwithstanding national loyalties, the widespread reprinting of British antislavery materials reveals the transatlantic nature of both antislavery movements and early American magazines. Many of them reprinted as many British and French as American antislavery works—a fact that makes problematic the very rubric of an "American" literature during this period. Prominent British antislavery writers such as Thomas Clarkson were widely republished eighteenth-century American magazines. Works such as *An Essay on the Slavery and Commerce of the Human Species* (1786) developed an American life all their own.[13] Or editors would reprint antislavery excerpts from European works about America, such as Brissot de Warville's *New Travels in the United States of America, Performed in 1788* (1791), part of which appeared, for example, in Philadelphia's *Universal Asylum, and Columbian Magazine* (1792). Prominent British antislavery poets such as William Cowper, Thomas Day, Hannah More, Robert Southey, and Ann Yearsley also appeared widely in American magazines, accompanying other canonical British writers such as John Milton, Alexander Pope, and James Thomson. In this context of transatlantic print culture, the most popular antislavery poem was Cowper's "The Negro's Complaint" (1788), which was widely republished in America for many of the same reasons it was sung aloud in the streets of London. The poem was a concise, sentimental lament of an African family ruined by the slave trade. Reprinted, for example, in Carey's *American Museum* in 1791, the poem succinctly put the issues of race and slavery in the mouth of an African speaker: "Slaves of gold, where sordid dealings / Tarnish all your boasted powers, / Prove, that *you* have human feelings, / Ere you proudly question *ours.*"[14]

Many important black Atlantic writings that appeared in American magazines were also reprinted from British sources. One should note that their appearance did not always coincide with antislavery politics—rather, the contexts for reprinting early black writing varied widely. For example, parts of *The Letters of the Late Ignatius Sancho* (1782) were republished in the *Gentlemen and Ladies Town and Country Magazine* (1784), which did emphasize the injustice of African slavery. "Of all my favourite authors," Sancho informed Lawrence Sterne, "not one has drawn a tear in favour of my miserable black brethren, excepting yourself, and the humane author of *Sir George Ellison.*"[15] Yet Sancho's example extended beyond antislavery politics. If he dramatized the capacity of Africans to possess civilized manners, he also provided a model for a kind of cultural refinement that resonated favorably for British American readers far removed from the metropolitan circles of London. The republication of Sancho in American magazines could even avoid antislavery politics, or at least approach it obliquely. The reprinting of two of his letters ("From the CRITICAL REVIEW") in the *Boston Magazine* (1784), for example, focused on Sancho's belief in the "wonders of immensity" that elicited one's necessary gratitude to the "Divine Architect."[16] The religious theme here embeds its antislavery message indirectly. It works on the lowest—and least contentious—frequencies, for it suggests the universal context for humanity that was most often expressed in antislavery writing in Acts 17.26: "And hath made of one blood all nations of men for to dwell on all the face of the earth."

Savage Trade

The preoccupation with the slave trade demonstrates the dual concerns of this topic in American magazines: the physical enslavement of Africans and the cultural enslavement of British Americans who bought and sold them. Rhetorically these dual concerns work reciprocally; each needs the other in order to express itself fully. The sympathy this literature produces for African slaves facilitates further considerations of the effects of such "heartlessness" and "brutality" for supposedly civilized Christians. Consider, for example, Ann Yearsley's popular antislavery poem, "On the Inhumanity of the Slave Trade" (1788), which was reprinted widely in the early republic. Parts of it appeared almost immediately in Noah Webster's *American Magazine* after its British publication. The extract's opening passage demonstrates the easy confluence between the mutual didacticism of anti–slave trade writing and the periodical genre:

> I know the crafty merchant will oppose
> The plea of nature to my strain, and urge
> His toils are for his children: the soft plea
> Dissolves my soul—"but when I sell a son,
> The God of nature, let it be my own!"
> Behold that Christian!! See what horrid joy
> Lights up his moody features, while he grasps
> The wish'd-for gold, purchase of human blood!
> Away thou seller of mankind! Bring on
> Thy daughter to this market! Bring thy wife![17]

In "Lactilla," the unlettered milk-woman of Bristol, Yearsley creates a persona built around moral sincerity, which easily facilitates the occasion for offering broader critiques of British commercial society. The above passage's bitter irony arises from the slave trader's transparent hypocrisy—the discrepancy between the "crafty merchant" and the "Christian" he claims to be. The love story that the poem recounts about Luco and Incilanda exists only to fulfill this larger design. Specifically, the disruption of the African family measures the depravity of this kind of trade. The exposure of such hypocrisy goes far in establishing the sentimental equivalence between British and African families.

American magazines targeted the barbarity of the slave trade by contrasting the "clamours of Self-interest" with the "dictates of Humanity."[18] The slave trade divorced moral feeling from profits, civility from exchange, commerce from manners. It was no better than the other kinds of illicit activities used as tropes for slave trading: notably piracy, prostitution, and gaming. To distinguish, then, between civilized and barbaric forms of commerce, antislavery writing invokes the category of "Christianity" in the broadest possible terms. The very epithet "Christian" all but loses its theological moorings and now signifies moral and cultural status. As the *American Magazine* put it, "It was not till Christianity influenced the manners of men, and introduced a spirit of mildness and justice in our dealings with others, that slavery received its first check. Civilization, or rather the reflection of Christianity upon the human mind, showed slavery in its true colors, and taught us to pay a proper respect to our species."[19] Connecting manners and morals in this way now places the burden of sympathy upon early American readers. "Where is the human being," the author of "Remarks on the Slave Trade" asked in the *American Museum* in 1789, "that can picture to himself this scene of woe, without at the same time execrating a trade which spreads misery and desolation wherever it appears? Where is the man of real benevolence, who will not join heart and hand, in opposing this barbarous, this iniquitous traffic?"[20]

This kind of cultural critique extended to consumption as well. Beginning in the 1780s, British antislavery campaigns to boycott West Indian goods, particularly the "blood sugar" raised there, became more prominent. The issue was of course part of much larger cultural changes—and anxieties—about norms of consumption over the course of the long eighteenth century.[21] In America antislavery denunciations of slave-grown sugar and coffee echoed the nonimportation movements against Britain itself during the Revolutionary war. In 1797 the *American Moral & Sentimental Magazine*, for example, published "The Negro-Trade: A Fragment," which attacked the slave trade by foisting guilt on those who continued to luxuriate in West Indian products that were invested with material and moral meaning. Employing the antislavery convention of the anonymous narrator/voyeur witnessing the horrors of slavery, the piece in this case portrays a ship captain listing the deaths of white mariners. The thematic turn—the idea that slave trading destroys British American as well as African families—was common enough: Thomas Clarkson, for example, emphasized it in *An Essay on the Impolicy of the African Slave Trade* (1789). Its conclusion, however, implicates consumers in the barbarity of the slave trade and makes consumption a matter of maintaining civilized identity. "And why is this cruelty practiced?" the narrator demands, "That we may have Sugar to sweeten tea, which debilitates us: Rum to make punch, to intoxicate us: And Indigo to dye our clothes. In short, myriads are made wretched, nations are dragged into slavery, to supply the luxuries of their fellow creatures."[22]

The cultural equation between suffering in the West Indies and decadent consumption in British America easily produced all sorts of popular (and sometimes bad) poetry in American magazines. Poems such as "On Sugar" connected chattel and cultural forms of slavery and ultimately made Americans themselves culpable for sustaining the West Indian slave economy. Here the trope of blood sugar makes consumption a form of cannibalism:

> Go guilty sweet seducing food,
> Tainted by streams of human blood!
> Emblem of woe and fruitless moans,
> Of mangled limbs and dying groans!
> To me thy tempting white appears
> Steep'd in a thousand Negroes' tears![23]

Poems like this one—and there were dozens and dozens published in periodicals during the 1790s—evoke sympathy simply for the "moans" and "groans" of the West Indian plantation. Philip Freneau's better-known poem, "To Sir Toby," which first appeared as "The Island Field Negro" in 1791 and was soon reprinted in magazines such as the *American Museum*, had done the same thing. Personal choices become political choices filled with moral ramifications. Yet a poem such as "On Sugar" also demonstrates the greater rhetorical complexity of this antislavery motif by making slavery a matter of consumption and consumption a matter of seduction. Goods themselves can excite the passions and seduce consumers into moral peril. Uncannily, then, slave-grown sugar is thus the emblem of both sympathy and corruption—it contains the slave's tears and the slave's blood, and it registers the corrupted tastes of seduced consumers.

Antislavery Sympathy

The thematic connections between commerce and manners in antislavery literature thus reinforce the early American magazine's didactic project of cultivating the sensibilities of its readers. Antislavery writings presumably helped to teach readers how to feel—how to feel in the right way. Historians have long been suspicious of the role of sentimental feeling in antislavery movements, questioning, as Winthrop D. Jordan has done, the authenticity of sympathy for "poor Africans."[24] Early American magazine literature commonly belies the self-indulgent and self-reflexive potential of sentimental antislavery. For instance in "The African's Complaint," which appeared in the *New-York Weekly Magazine; or, Miscellaneous Repository*, the conventional man of feeling overhears "a slave's "voice that seemed to pierce through [his] inmost soul."[25] A few years before, in 1787, the *American Museum*'s short piece "The Slave—A Fragment" culminated in the narrator's effusions of feeling in the face of a slave owner now emancipating his slaves: "It was enough. I was amply paid, and felt a more exquisite sensation, than if the Indies had been added to my estate. O ye sons of affluence! Ye children of prosperity! Listen and be wise!"[26] Moments like these tend to shift the subject of sentimental feeling from suffering object (the African) to vicariously suffering subject (the British American).

Simply writing off this language, however, misses the important relations antislavery reveals between sentimental and capitalist economies. Antislavery magazine writings demonstrate the multiple levels of meaning for the very idea of human value during this era. A good example of the relation between sentimental and market economies complexity is the antislavery fable "Selico: An African Tale," which appeared in 1793 in the *Lady's Magazine; and Repository of Entertaining Knowledge.* It recounts the trials of Selico—"the blackest, the best made, and the most amiable" man in the kingdom of Juida along the Guinea Coast.[27] Invaded by the king of Dahomia, the inhabitants are forced to flee their homeland, and Selico and his brothers "plunge into the woods" to save themselves and protect their ill mother, Darina. Soon the family begins to starve, and the three sons decide to draw lots to see which one will sell himself into slavery in order to raise the revenue to buy food and supplies to save their poor mother. Grieving for his beloved Berissa, whom he believes has been killed during the conquest, Selico volunteers to sacrifice himself for his family.

Selico's plan highlights the intimacy between sentimental and capitalist registers of value—the ways in which feeling and the market are inextricably connected. The tale is founded on an apparent ontological paradox: the moral value of Selico's humanity rises the very moment he agrees to turn himself from a free man into a slave—a commodity. As the tale progresses, the king of Dahomia offers a lucrative reward of four hundred ounces of gold to whoever furnishes the "young negro" who supposedly has "violated" his seraglio, and Selico alters the original plan to assume the role of criminal in order to—literally—gain more wealth for himself. Hence, both his monetary value (four hundred ounces of gold) and his sentimental value (as the tale's paragon of benevolence) appreciate concurrently. The tale reaches a climax by several turns of plot: Berissa is alive, she and Selico recognize one another, and her father publicly confesses to the king that it was he who came to see her the night before. When the king learns of Selico's misfortune and his plan to save his mother, the tyrant is moved to tears. "Such is the charm of virtue, that barbarians themselves adore it!"[28]

The king's sympathy for Selico only highlights the ongoing thematic tensions over the source and nature of human value. Turning to the European slave traders, the king asks,

> "You, to whom wisdom, experience, and illumination of a long civilization, have so long taught what is the specific value of a man, of how much value think you is this?" A young Frenchman more bold than the rest, exclaimed, "Ten thousand crowns of gold!" "Which shall be given to Berissa," said the king, "with this she shall purchase the hand of Selico."[29]

The scene may suggest the necessity of sympathy for the plight of slaves, but it notably refrains from displaying the abolition of slavery. Instead it models—through the king—the need to imbue feeling into all of our commercial transactions. Selico's benevolence, moreover, has a market value assigned to it; his virtue produces the capital necessary to purchase him within the structure of a slave economy that ultimately remains intact. What complicates the matter even further is that this market transaction is the means by which Selico's virtue is finally preserved. Sentimental and market economies, in other words, work reciprocally, not in opposition. The sentimental economy in "Selico"—located in the value of Selico's benevolent heart—exists inextricably with its market economy—located in the value of Selico's body.

This tale's equivocal position on antislavery was not uncommon during this era and within the magazine genre. Yet its plot and thematic concerns derive from the central narrative figure in antislavery literature: the African family in ruins. The motif of the destruction of the family by the African slave trade forced magazine readers to engage antislavery politics domestically and sympathetically. In "The Negro," for example, published in 1798 in the *General Magazine, and Impartial Review, of Knowledge and Entertainment*, the English speaker laments the fate of the enslaved African: "Curse on European avarice that deals in cargoes of wretchedness, and thrives by the traffic of despair. . . . Perhaps, said I, this child of sorrow has been torn from a father,—a mother. Nature must have pleaded very loudly against his captivity; for I thought I could perceive the tears of affection standing in his eyes."[30] The sentimentalization of the African family, however, immediately engendered a new set of racial and cultural stereotypes: the imagery of domestic and pastoral bliss in Africa, the figure of the "noble African" forced from his or her homeland, the deceitful European slave trader, and the melancholia culminating in the slave's suicide. Mixing antislavery sympathy with an exoticism about "primitive" Africa, in other words, antislavery literature validates African humanity only finally to resubmerge it within Enlightenment-based hierarchies.

No better instance of this exists than the antislavery literary convention of the dying African. The popularity of Thomas Day's poem "The Dying Negro" (1773), for example, derived largely from the convenient pathos of the slave suicide.[31] A good example of this is "The Slave," which appeared in Isaiah Thomas's *Massachusetts Magazine* in 1789:

> O, Christians! Fiends to our unhappy race,
> Why do we wear these ensigns of disgrace?
> Did nature's God create us to be slaves,
> Or is it pride, that God's decree outbraves?
> Had he design'd that we should not be free,
> Why do we know the sweets of liberty?

He could no more. But mounting on a rock,
Whose shaggy sides o'erhung the silver brook—
Whence tumbling headlong down the steepest side,
He plung'd determin'd in the foaming tide.
His mangled carcass floated on the flood,
And stain's the silver winding stream with blood.[32]

Poetic laments such as this succinctly display the genre's structural pattern of captivity, melancholia, and suicide. The trope of the dying African offers both the critique of "civilized barbarians" and the eventual displacement of the agency of that critique—through the slave's suicide. The Jeffersonian overtones of the African's lament (in the reference to the phrase "nature's God," which comes from the *Declaration of Independence*) draws on enlightened political rhetoric to condemn slavery. In doing so, however, traditional hierarchies are in danger of collapsing—"Christians" and "heathens" lose their traditional places. Only the slave suicide contains this unsettling process, as this kind of popular and sentimental antislavery poetry typically reestablishes those hierarchies by default. Once the slave's voice has done its work, it safely disappears. All that remains is that speaker's "mangled carcass."

The sentimental antislavery writing in American magazines generally makes little effort at cataloguing ethnographic detail. Instead it makes "Africa" a set of conflicting social ideas. It is the place of very real familial attachments; it is also the place of presumably uncivilized social and political conditions, an argument that ironically overlapped with the proslavery position. These dual imperatives run through "The Wretched Taillah: An African Story," which appeared in 1793 in the *New Hampshire Magazine or the Monthly Repository of Useful Information*. Here the love story between Taillah and Tildah arises from the barbarity of ongoing African tribal wars—those very wars that proslavery apologists claimed were the source of slaves in the first place. As the daughter of an African prince "of fierce and cruel disposition" in Gambia, Taillah eventually engineers the escape of both herself and her lover from her father's inhumane kingdom.[33] The refuge of private feeling, however, becomes untenable. Besieged by slave traders, the two lovers escape and eventually save an American sea captain, who eventually betrays them and their children to American slave traders. "O God!" the narrator concludes, "why slept thy thunders and crushed not the execrated heads of such monsters of ingratitude and humanity!"[34]

Such a lament suggests the importance of the dynamic between gratitude and humanity to preserve stable social relations in the post-Revolutionary United States. As Gordon S. Wood has argued, traditional hierarchical relations in colonial British America, based on systems of patronage and dependence, became sentimentalized during the Revolutionary period as a way of preserving old hierarchies according to new cultural forms of benevolence and gratitude around which republican society would now cohere.[35] In this context, then, the sentimental allegory of American ingratitude suggests much more than the legacy of the "noble African" popularized in British culture as far back as Oronooko and Othello. Yet the antislavery thematic of benevolence and gratitude was just as often put to socially conservative purposes that contained the place of "free" Africans in American society. In "Zimeo: A Tale," published in Samuel Bradford's *Desert to the True American* (1798), the story of a slave rebellion in Jamaica is resolved by the reunification of the African family made possible only by the benevolence of Paul Wilmot, the Quaker planter there. In "The Slaves," published in the *New-York Weekly Magazine* (1796), the conventional romance between Ala and Area culminates in their being sold to a benevolent planter in Jamaica who "endeavored by all possible means to make the lives of those that were under him as easy as possible."[36] Granting them freedom after hearing their story, he allows them the opportunity to remain with him as wage laborers "and be treated as his children": "They fell down and embraced the feet of this 'one in a thousand,' and sobbed out their thanks." The exchange of benevolence and gratitude does not merely deploy racial stereotypes of the African as child; rather, it provides the symbolic resolution to the social problem of "free" labor populations, which, as the historian David Brion Davis has emphasized, was at the ideological core of the rise of antislavery movements. "The Slaves" does not stop at exposing the iniquity of the slave trade that violates the African family; it considers the prospect of "free" Africans living in British American societies, and it finds literary solutions to quell social and political fears about such a prospect.

Antislavery Satire

The most popular alternative literary form to sentimentalism was antislavery satire. American magazines include numerous satirical anecdotes and sketches that debunk the slave trade and chattel slavery while entertaining readers with rather facile comic stereotypes of Africans and African Americans. In this sense antislavery satire presents the same representational problems found in early "local color" writing—the reliance on types, predictable manners, and stilted forms of dialect. These comic pieces range from simply burlesque performances, with little or no antislavery value, to gentle kinds of satire whose humorous effects often overshadow the antislavery message. An instance of the former mode is the "Anecdotes of Two Negroes" that appeared in Carey's *American Museum*: "Two negroes meeting in a dram shop called for a bowl of grog—after it was made, one fellow takes the bowl, and after drinking two thirds of the contents, cries 'hem! hem! Massa dis here too trong: do put a little more water here.' 'Tay mate,' says the other one: 'no be in sitch dam hurre—let me cry hem too.'"[37] In other cases, satire more ably conveys much more serious antislavery messages. "A Dispute between an Indian and a Negro, Respecting the Natural Right of Pre-eminence," for example, creates the absurd scenario where the two stock figures meet on a narrow bridge, each refusing to give ground, and each claiming racial superiority to the other. The sketch immediately parodies the proslavery biblical exegesis of Genesis 9—the story of Noah's curse upon Ham and Canaan, which, as the common proslavery argument proceeded, justified the perpetual enslavement of the African race. In Indian pidgin, the story seems all the more ridiculous:

> Now when he awake up, they tell him what his matchet boy [the wicked Ham] had done, old man he lay it up, so when he come to make his will, he call his boys together and he tell his oldest boy, you shall be good Englishman; his next boy he tell, you shall be good Indian; but when his matchet boy come, he tell him you shall be devilish Negro; so you see Indian are above Negroes.[38]

Such a comic debunking, however, of proslavery's biblical arguments belies the similar use of low types to make the antislavery argument. While deflating the biblical rationale, the burlesque trades in racial and cultural humor arising from the absurdity of Native Americans and African Americans engaged in serious debate. The humor itself all but consumes their presumed humanity and, at the very least, secures them along the bottom rungs of social and racial hierarchy.

Notwithstanding the cheap humor often produced by this kind of antislavery satire, it too offered trenchant critiques of both the slave trade and chattel slavery. Sometimes satire effectively cut through the learned conundrums and semantic ambiguities of the slavery debates. One of the major tenets, for example, that antislavery movements consistently embraced was the ethical incongruity between Christianity and slavery. Many learned antislavery writers, such as James Ramsay, Samuel Hopkins, and Thomas Clarkson, cited scores of scriptural references to win this point, but the overall ambiguity of biblical evidence—including references to Exodus, Leviticus, Matthew, Paul's epistles, among others—made this line of argument difficult to win. In such cases antislavery satire wielded the rhetorical capacity of reducing arcane ambiguities to common—and comic—sense. For example, a little-known Maryland magazine, the *Key*, published a satirical sketch in 1798 that crystallized the hypocrisy of slavery in just such terms. "A Negro, not long since, was transported from the Rev. Mr. R—'s parish to Carolina, for sale. Mr. R— was soon accosted by one of the African fraternity, 'Massa, an't you shepherd?' 'Yes, if you have a mind to call me so.' 'Why a d—l en don't you take care black sheep as well as white?'"[39]

Antislavery satire, however, just as often offers counter-narratives to its central argument about the universal nature of humanity. For example, in 1791 the *American Museum* published a satirical sketch emphasizing the common antislavery argument that human beings could not be reduced to property. In doing so, however, it raised the troubling possibility that enslaved Africans were just another kind of commodity:

> A Negro fellow being strongly suspected to have stolen goods in his possession, was taken before a certain justice of peace in Philadelphia, and charged with the offense. The fellow was so hardened as to acknowledge the fact, and, to add to his crime, had the audacity to make the following speech: "massa justice, me know me got dem tings from Tom dere—and me tinke Tom teal dem too—but what den, massa? Dey be only a picaninny cork-screw and a picaninny knife—one cost sixpence and tudda a shilling—and me pay Tom for dem honestly, massa."
>
> "A very pretty story truly—you knew they were stolen, and yet allege in excuse, you paid honestly for them—I'll teach you better law than that, sirrah! Don't you know, Cesar, the receiver is as bad as the thief? You must be severely whipt, you black rascal you!"
>
> "Very well, massa—If de black rascal be wipt for buying tolen goods, me hope de white rascal be wipt too for same ting, when me catch him, as well as Cesar." "To be sure," rejoined his worship. "Well den," says Cesar, "here be Tom's massa—hold him fast, constable, he buy Tom as I buy de picaninny knife and de picaninny cork-screw. He know very well poor Tom be tolen from his old fadder and mudder; de knife and the cork-screw have neder."
>
> Whether it was that his worship, as well as Tom's master, were smote in the same instant with the justice or the severity of Cesar's application, we know not: but after a few minutes pause, Cesar was dismissed, and the action discharged.[40]

There is the immediate syntactic difficulty of reading the crucial phrase "to have stolen goods": Does this mean that the "Negro fellow" possesses stolen goods, or that he stole them previously? This forecasts the ambiguity that will ultimately serve to reassign guilt from Cesar to Tom's master. This reassignment is consistent with and dependent on the antislavery opposition between positive law and natural justice. Indeed, the potency of the word *justice* stems from the contrast between the silly constable and natural justice in the abstract. If Cesar's voice is crucial to debunking the proslavery claim to property rights, the cultural authority of that voice is still questionable. On the one hand, the sketch espouses the antislavery message of racial equivalence, since, really, both Cesar and Tom's master are guilty of the same thing. But just as the passage humanizes the African American—the "piccaninny" knife has no parentage—it simultaneously withdraws that claim by equating slave and knife. This crucial tension in antislavery thinking rhetorically expresses itself in the African American's language, which itself creates the dialogue between "picaninny" black dialect ("massa" and "dem tings") and conventional English (the common humanity of "as well as Cesar" and "Hold him fast, constable").

The literature of antislavery in late-eighteenth-century American magazines never reached the popularity that it would during the antebellum era. But the periodical antislavery literature published in the era between the 1770s and 1810s does provide an important connection between Revolutionary American antislavery and antebellum abolitionism. Consider that in 1776 the Declaration of Independence assails the slave trade as "piratical warfare, the opprobrium of INFIDEL powers, is the warfare of the CHRISTIAN King of Great Britain." Less than a decade before the outbreak of the Civil War, *Uncle Tom's Cabin* (1852) similarly begins with a scene displaying the slave trade as a form of commerce that brutalizes whites as it destroys the African American family. Early American magazines published pieces against slave trading that talked about two kinds of enslavement simultaneously: the persecution of African captives and the cultural depravity of supposedly civilized British Americans. Both were enslaved to a particular set of social and commercial conditions. By distinguishing between virtuous and vicious—or "free" and "enslaving"—kinds of trade, this literature negotiated the ideological relations between commerce and manners. The subject of either sentimentally abused or satirically comic Africans and African Americans provided a medium in which early American readerships could also contemplate themselves.

Notes

1. For the first approach, see Gary Nash, *Forging Freedom: The Formation of Philadelphia's Black Community, 1720–1840* (Cambridge: Harvard UP, 1988). For a critique of antislavery sentimentalism, see Winthrop Jordan, *White over Black: American Attitudes toward the Negro, 1550–1812* (Chapel Hill: U of North Carolina P, 1968). The seminal, though highly revised, work about capitalism and antislavery is Eric Williams, *Capitalism and Slavery* (Chapel Hill: U of North Carolina P, 1944). The work of David Brion Davis, particularly *The Problem of Slavery in the Age of Revolution, 1770–1823* (Ithaca: Cornell UP, 1975), emphasizes the attempt by a new industrial order to target the injustice of "slave" labor as a way of legitimizing (and socially controlling) "free" wage labor in British factories. The responses to Davis, as well as to his refinement of

his earlier work, may be found in Thomas Bender, ed., *The Antislavery Debate: Capitalism and Abolitionism as a Problem of Historical Interpretation* (Berkeley: U of California P, 1992).

2. *American Museum; or, Repository of Ancient and Modern Fugitive Pieces* 2 (1787): 503. Its subtitle was later changed to "*or, Universal Magazine.*"
3. This body of work derives from that of Norbert Elias completed decades ago: See, for example, Richard Bushman, *The Refinement of America: Persons, Houses, Cities* (New York: Random House, 1992); Lawrence Klein, *Shaftesbury and the Culture of Politeness* (Cambridge: Cambridge UP, 1994); and David S. Shields, *Civil Tongues and Polite Letters in British America* (Chapel Hill: U of North Carolina P, 1997). The argument here is part of the critical revision of the place of "liberalism" in eighteenth-century culture. The importance of the paradigm of manners for the literature against slave trading is that it resists the imposition of nineteenth-century ideologies of individual rights upon eighteenth-century texts. For this critical revision, see, for example, James Kloppenberg, *The Virtues of Liberalism* (New York: Oxford UP, 1998).
4. J. G. A. Pocock, *Barbarism and Religion: Narratives of Civil Government* (Cambridge: Cambridge UP, 1999), 19–20.
5. Before the 1770s, American magazines published roughly as many proslavery as antislavery writings. The writings against slavery were scant at best. Philadelphia magazines such as Mathew Carey's *American Museum, or, Universal Magazine* later published a good deal of antislavery literature but during the mid–eighteenth century showed virtually no interest in it. See, for example, the *American Magazine, or General Repository* (Philadelphia, 1769) and the *American Magazine and Monthly Chronicle for the British Colonies* (Philadelphia, 1758).
6. *New American Magazine* (January 1760): 25.
7. *Experienced Christian's Magazine* 1 (July 1796): 84. It would be misleading to represent all religious magazines in this light. The "Articles of Faith" preceding the *Free Universal Magazine*, for example, refused this easy formula of the fortunate fall and took a much stronger position against the slave trade. One of its "Recommendations" reads, "We believe it to be inconsistent with the Union of the human race in a common Saviour, and the obligations to mutual and universal love, which flow from that Union, to hold [any] part of our fellow creatures in bondage. We therefore recommend a total refraining from the African trade, and the adoption of prudent measures for the gradual abolition

of this slavery of the Negroes in our country." See the *Free Universal Magazine* 1 (New York, 1793): 51.

8. See the "Preliminary Address" to the *American Moral & Sentimental Magazine* (July 3, 1797): n.p.
9. *New Jersey Magazine and Monthly Advertiser* (New Brunswick, 1797): n. p.
10. Consider, for example, the address "To Our Patrons and Correspondents" in the *Massachusetts Magazine* 1 (Boston, 1789): "BRUTUS writes warmly—but we wish not to scorch ourselves by a political fire." Some periodicals, like newspapers, were extensions of political partisanship, especially in the tumultuous decade of the 1790s. Charles Brockden Brown noted the dilemmas facing magazine editors in a mock-epistle, "On Periodical Publications." If editors published mildly supportive opinions about either France or Britain, some constituencies were likely to complain of political bias. "If you drop politics altogether, matters will be worse still; you will not be criticized indeed, but, then, you will not be read." See the *Monthly Magazine and American Review* (April 1799): 2.
11. "To the Publisher of the *Pennsylvania Magazine*," *Pennsylvania Magazine: or, American Monthly Museum* 1 (January 1775): 10.
12. *American Magazine* 1 (December 1787): 4.
13. See, for example, "A Fancied Scene in the African Slave Trade," in the *New-York Magazine; or, Literary Repository* 1 (August 1790): 464–67, and "A Summary View of the Slave Trade" in the *Methodist Magazine* (April–May 1798): 164–67, 213–17. Another important seminal British text that was excerpted in American magazines was James Ramsay's *On the Treatment and Conversion of the African Slaves in the British Sugar Colonies* (1784), which appeared, for example, in the *Boston Magazine* (July 1786): 302–4. Ramsay's story of Quashi, the wronged slave who is forced to murder his brother-master before taking his own life, also appears in different form as "The Desperate Negro" in the *American Museum, or, Universal Magazine* (December 1789): 433–34.
14. Some American versions of Cowper selectively edited out the most radical portions of the critique of white avarice by the African speaker. See, for example, the version published in the *American Moral & Sentimental Magazine* 1 (December 1797): 381–82. Other magazines published antislavery poems using African speakers under the title of "The Negro's Complaint," which was likely a result of Cowper's popularity. See the *American Magazine*, for example, 751. This was not the only poem that saw reprinting in American periodicals; Cowper's "Charity," for example, was excerpted in the *Christian's, Scholar's, and Farmer's Magazine* (1789): 120.

15. *Gentleman and Lady's Town and Country Magazine* (August 1784): 137.

16. *Boston Magazine* 1 (June 1784): 328–30. See also the serialization of James Gronniosaw's *Narrative* in the *American Moral & Sentimental Magazine* in 1797.

17. *American Magazine (August 1788):* 673.

18. "A Brief Historical Account of the Rise, Progress, and Present State of the African Slave Trade," *Universal Asylum, and Columbian Magazine* (November 1790): 295–96.

19. "On the Treatment of Slaves"*American Magazine* (July 1788): 561.

20. *American Museum* (1789), 429.

21. For cultural debates over consumption, see, for example, John Brewer and Roy Porter, eds., *Consumption and the World of Goods*, (London: Routledge, 1993), and Neil McKendrick, John Brewer, and J. H. Plumb, eds., *The Birth of a Consumer Society: The Commercialization of Eighteenth-Century England* (Bloomington: U of Indiana P, 1982).

22. *American Moral & Sentimental Magazine* (September 1797): 182.

23. Ibid. (August 1797): 159.

24. For Jordan's critique of the self-indulgence of antislavery sentimentalism, see his *White over Black*, 365–72.

25. *New-York Weekly Magazine; or, Miscellaneous Repository* (May 1797): 353.

26. *American Museum* (January 1787): 46.

27. *Lady's Magazine; and Repository of Entertaining Knowledge* (May 1793): 284.

28. Ibid., 291.

29. Ibid.

30. *General Magazine, and Impartial Review, of Knowledge and Entertainment* 1 (June 1798): 25.

31. This genre allowed some flexibility and variation. In "The Negro Boy," the speaker is an African prince now in England, who confesses his sin of selling "a blooming Negro boy" to British slave traders for "a simple toy." "I doom'd the hopeless youth to dwell / A poor forlorn insulted slave, / A beast that Christians buy and sell." See the *Philadelphia Monthly Magazine* 1 (January 1798): 46.

32. *Massachusetts Magazine* (June 1789): 387.

33. *New Hampshire Magazine* 1 (June 1793): 53.

34. Ibid., 56.

35. Gordon S. Wood, *The Radicalism of the American Revolution* (New York: Knopf, 1991), 95–109, 213–225.

36. *New-York Weekly Magazine* (January 1796): 212.

37. *American Museum* (1790): 20–1.

38. *Boston Magazine* 1 (Nvember 1784): 564.

39. *Key* 1 (January 1798): 16.

40. *American Museum* (1791): 332–33.

THE EARLY REPUBLIC AND THE 1790s

According to historian Steven Watts, a wealth of evidence suggests that beginning in the post-Revolutionary years, the 1790s in particular, a "massive, multifaceted transformation away from republican traditions and toward modern liberal capitalism" took place.[1] The explosion of periodical publication underscored the liberal market economy, the extraordinary acceleration of print culture, and the rise in literacy in the United States. The rise of commerce, anti-Federalist rhetoric, and print deeply influenced public and private debates centered on how to define the political, legal, and social aspects of this emerging nation; indeed, what constituted the new nation itself was open for debate.[2]

Every forum imaginable—congressional debates, political pamphlets, legal cases, town-square lectures, dinner-table and tavern discussions—became a venue for examining what republicanism would mean, what the requirements of citizenship were, and how these changes would affect social dynamics in the new nation. Beyond the legal construction of nationhood, then, was the far more arduous and compelling task of how to conceptualize a new kind of republic in the minds and lived experiences of its citizens. The eighteenth century's focus on a new liberalism—emphasizing individual liberty of body and mind—penetrated all political, cultural, and scientific debates of the period. From the early challenges to and by liberalism (see, for example, Mulford's essay in Part I) to the flourishing of liberalism in the 1790s, periodical literature embraced these debates as a means for public exchange—and influence—in the diverse challenges inherent in redefining political orders and concepts of the sociopolitical contract between citizens and their government.[3]

As the essays in this section reveal, periodicals were a force in these intellectual debates, both from the perspective of editors who wished to advocate certain ideologies and from the perspective of readers who could express their support or difference through subscriptions, written responses to the editors, and increasingly by contributing their own thoughts for publication. In political terms, there was both the literal sense of nation building—truly to form a union out of state entities with diverse and sometimes conflicting interests and needs—and in the conceptual sense of understanding the often-difficult and unexpected challenges of independence. Citizens as well as political leaders had to come to terms with the uniqueness of being "Americans" while also recognizing that they shared a political and social history in common with England. The decision by editors of emerging periodicals to include numerous selections from British and European sources was rooted in both economics *and* an understanding of the need to maintain a transatlantic dialogue to ensure both a status of independence and mutuality. While this transatlantic exchange of print culture proliferated, so, too, did original publications for U.S. newspapers and magazines. Increasingly the periodicals became known for their interest in developing native talent and in defining particularly "American" themes and identities.

Periodicals were also central to the arduous emergence of distinct political parties in the new republic. Perhaps no aspect of cultural influence has been so overlooked in periodical literature as the ways in which these newspapers and magazines helped shape public opinion about political affiliations. Most often termed "factionalism" by those concerned with how heated the debates were becoming in the 1780s and 90s, the specific interests of political suasions—Federalists, anti-Federalists, Democratic-Republicans, and so on—were promoted or denigrated in a wide range of periodical literature before and after the crafting of the Constitution. Some editors were becoming so concerned about factionalism that they sought to warn against the idea of "party spirit," as when the editors of the *General Magazine, and Impartial Review, of Knowledge and Entertainment* included an essay "On Party" in their June 1798 issue. "A party spirit," the anonymously authored essay asserts, "is as great a curse to society as can befall it; it makes honest men hate each other, and destroys good neighbourhood. It rends a government into two distinct people, says mr. Addison, and makes fellow citizens greater strangers and more averse to each other than if they were of two distinct nations."[4] Periodicals themselves, as the essays in this collection demonstrate, were either founded to promote a particular political party view or soon felt the pressure to take sides. Trying to negotiate the terrain of shifting political party developments in this period was not an easy task for an editor who wished to remain "impartial."

Equally important in terms of the public debates played out in periodical literature of the period—and certainly linked to political party formations—was the idea that newspapers and magazines could shape the makeup of the new citizen. In conjunction with defining "republicanism" in this volatile moment, the idea of an educated populace became increasingly important and the majority of periodicals saw education as a key element of their mission. Although by definition intended for a literate audience, the periodicals sought to advance their readers' educations in politics, belle-lettres, and science. Deeply embedded in the debates about what this new political order would entail was the emerging idea of the importance of (white) women writers and readers as integral to the new nation's political, social, and cultural development. Women writers were important—and necessary—to the production of material for many of the early periodical editors, especially those who wished to include historical and literary texts within their pages. Equally important, as subscription lists demonstrate, was the impact of women as readers of periodicals.[5] But the tenuousness of women's status, both as citizens and as voices in these public debates, was inseparable from the debates of what constituted a citizen. As Linda Kerber has noted, "'Citizen' is an equalizing word" and the American Revolutionary leaders "produced a new and reciprocal relationship between state and citizen . . . . any free person who had not fled with the British or explicitly denounced the patriots was a citizen."[6] While the new nation granted white women some rights and many obligations of citizenry, they were never treated with the same sense of citizenship as men, and, it is important to note, "the United States absorbed, virtually unrevised, the traditional English system of law governing the relationship between husbands and wives," thus limiting women's rights to independence and full citizenship.[7]

Susan Branson has noted that the periodical was a unique publishing venue for women: "It was magazines, more than any other medium, that helped to develop an American public discourse on gender roles and gender relations in the early republic."[8] As several of the essays in this section reveal, negotiating this imbalance between newfound independence and traditional obligations of dependence marked many women's writings and, just as often if not more so, the many essays—pro and con—concerning women's changing status that appeared in periodical literature of the period. Periodicals proved to be a major force in the rise of women's public political voices.

"Exhibiting the Fair Sex: The *Massachusetts Magazine* and the Bodily Order of the American Woman," by Beverly J. Reed, analyzes how the *Massachusetts Magazine* (1789–96) participated in the cultural discussion regarding the construction of the American woman in the new nation and asserts that in whatever social relationship a woman found herself—single, married, widowed—there were bodily standards that cut across these roles and applied to all women, standards that were based on scientific theories of race and gender and that in turn determined perceptions of a woman's capacity for self-control and her subsequent position in the new nation. Important to this process was the idea of placing U.S. national identity in dialogue with international scientific discourse. Thus, these standards were instrumental, Reed argues, in crafting cultural types such as the Republican Mother and Republican Wife within the construct of whiteness while undesirable traits were marked by the nonwhite Other. The result was that the institutionalization of racial identity became literally and figuratively a part of the anatomy of national identity.

Frank Shuffelton's "Thomas Jefferson, Francis Hopkinson, and the Representation of the *Notes on the State of Virginia*" also elaborates a facet of these debates by examining the history of extract publications from the letterpress editions of Jefferson's *Notes on the State of Virginia* until about 1795, by which time American printings of the complete text had begun to appear. Periodical literature was instrumental in creating a new national identity that claimed both participation in the Atlantic culture of the British empire and a recognition of the importance of shared differences from the British model of culture and literature. Tracing the extract publications of Jefferson's *Notes on the State of Virginia* offers a prime example of how this changing national identity was formulated. Shuffelton clarifies the model of friendship that supported Jefferson's and Hopkinson's initial conception of the text but also argues that publication of the extracts contributed to the peculiar first structuring of party interests, and history thereof, and illuminates the understanding of serialized publication of public and private documents.

Lisa M. Logan's "'The Ladies in Particular': Constructions of Femininity in the *Gentlemen and Ladies Town and Country Magazine* and the *Lady's Magazine; and Repository of Entertaining Knowledge*" (1789–90 and 1792–93, respectively) addresses questions of gender and print culture by examining two early monthly magazines devoted in part or wholly to women. She explores the ways that reading—particularly of various prose genres, such as the serialized novel, advice columns about relationships between the sexes, and letters to the editor—establish paradigms for gender relationships in the new republic. In addition to exploring the role of engraved illustrations and the serialization of early fiction, she points to how issues of "taste" and women's authorship were influenced by a variety of factors, including class, education, and locale.

Like Shuffelton's essay, Seth Cotlar's "Reading the Foreign News, Imagining an American Public Sphere: Radical and Conservative Visions of 'the Public' in Mid-1790s Newspapers" offers yet another view of the means by which "party spirit" was played out in the early republic and society sought to restructure itself. He examines how Irish, English, and French radicalism in Europe affected laboring-class utopianism in America. By focusing on the writings of Painite "democrats" such as DEMOCRITUS in *Greenleaf's New York Journal* (1796) and how they absorbed foreign accounts of popular political action, Cotlar historicizes the neglected role of nonelected citizens and "public opinion"—what he identifies as "radical publicity"—in the formation of democratic institutions. Understanding how democratic editors, their readers, and their political opponents interpreted European events and politics, developments of which were often more democratic or progressive than those in America, reframes the context, argues Cotlar, for understanding early republican political discourses of the early to mid-1790s. It asks us to rethink how we understand not only the role and impact of oppositional print, particularly in newspapers and pamphlets, in rural and urban areas, but also the formation and history of laboring-class political clubs and societies relative to the emergence of electoral politics.

Last, Sharon M. Harris's "The *New-York Magazine:* Cultural Repository" traces the means by which the editors of one of the longest-lived periodicals in the eighteenth century (1790–97), Thomas and James Swords, sought to establish its political and cultural voice. Focusing on the periodical's emphasis on serial history and current political debates such as the French Revolution, she argues that, in addition to further documenting the history and formation of political parties, the nationalistic republicanism embraced in the magazine quickly takes on a transatlantic flavor, reflecting the international movement toward republicanism. Within this context, the magazine's negotiation of how to address the "woman issue" in the new nation while at the same time promoting several women writers, most notably Ann Eliza Bleecker and Margaretta Bleecker Faugeres, demonstrates that the struggle for an equalized citizenship was inseparable from other political debates of the period. Equally important is the way in which the publishers' emphasis on republicanism was shaped by popular opinion, demonstrating that the fluidity of "republicanism" was influenced by readers as well as editors and publishers of periodicals.

The conjunction of the political, the social, the cultural—and the gendered nature of these concepts—suggests many avenues for further exploration of periodical literature. Scholars have yet to examine fully how party politics and political debates were shaped by newspaper and magazine coverage, and they have barely begun to tap into the significant body of periodical writings by women in the early period.

Notes

1. Steven Watts, *The Republic Reborn: War and the Making of Liberal America, 1780–1820* (Baltimore: Johns Hopkins UP, 1987), xvii.
2. See Saul Cornell's *Other Founders: Anti-Federalism and the Dissenting Tradition in America, 1788–1828* for further explanation of how a "dissenting public discourse about politics and constitutionalism" emerged (Chapel Hill: U of North Carolina P, 1999), 8.
3. For a more complete discussion of eighteenth-century liberalism, see Steven Watts, *The Republic Reborn: War and the Making of Liberal America, 1780–1820* (Baltimore: Johns Hopkins UP, 1987), especially 7–16; and Gilliam Brown, *The Consent of the Governed: The Lockean Legacy in Early American Culture* (Cambridge: Harvard UP, 2001), especially 8–9, 15–17.
4. "On Party," *General Magazine, and Impartial Review, of Knowledge and Entertainment* (June 1798): 24.
5. While individual periodical subscription lists are difficult to locate, access exists to subscription lists of periodical literature that was subsequently published in book form. Many of these subscribers undoubtedly first read the material in magazine form. Judith Sargent Murray's "The Gleaner" essays, for example, first appeared in the *Massachusetts Magazine*, and when these essays were published in book form, almost 20 percent of subscribers were women. So, too, with *The Posthumous Works of Ann Eliza Bleecker*, largely drawn from the periodical publications of Bleecker and her daughter (and editor of the volume), Margaretta V. Bleecker Faugeres; in this instance, the women constituted roughly 14 percent of the subscribers.
6. Linda K. Kerber, *No Constitutional Right to Be Ladies: Women and Obligations of Citizenship* (New York: Hill and Wang, 1998), xx.
7. Ibid., xxiii.
8. Susan Branson, *These Fiery Frenchified Dames: Women and Political Cultural in Early National Philadelphia* (Philadelphia: U of Pennsylvania P, 2001), 23.

Beverly J. Reed

Exhibiting the Fair Sex

THE *MASSACHUSETTS MAGAZINE* AND THE BODILY ORDER OF THE AMERICAN WOMAN

> . . . a Magazine, so judiciously constructed and executed as to gain the attention and gratify the curiosity and taste of a discerning public. Such a publication on a good plan, supported by men of ability, supplied by men of genius, and erudition, would answer many valuable purposes.
>
> —"On the Utility of Well Regulated Magazines," *The Massachusetts Magazine,* January 1789

> What fine proportions, what nicely moulded features, what expressive eyes, what delicate complexions . . .
>
> —Dr. Langhorne, "On the Fair Sex," *The Massachusetts Magazine,* January 1790

In the April 1790 issue of the *Massachusetts Magazine: or, Monthly Museum of Knowledge and Rational Entertainment,* an engraving and story titled "Adelaide; or the Lovely Rustick" appeared. As is typical of a pastoral tale, Adelaide is placed within an idealized Arcadian landscape, living in harmony with nature "far . . . from the haunts of fashion or the giddy maze of polite amusements":

> the lovely rustick awoke from the slumbers of virtue, and walked forth to inhale the breezes of morn. Already the choral songsters tuned their mattins on the budding spray; the little lambkin frolicked amid the verdant mead; and finny tribes held gambols in the refluent pool.[1]

An industrious individual, she awakes early to start her day when "Scarce the first gleam of light [had] silvered the mountain's brow" and maintains a "living converse with the god of nature in his ample volume, writ by Deity's fine pencil"; at the end of the day, "the beauteous maiden [seeks] the cool retreat: the valley bounded by a circling hill; the tufted glade . . . arched with shadowy elms."

Adelaide: or the Lovely Rustick.

"Adelaide; or the Lovely Rustick," from Isaiah Thomas's *Massachusetts Magazine.* As the first and therefore predominate engraving in the April 1790 issue, this visual representation of Adelaide underscores the importance of the pastoral ideal and the proper racial and gendered position for women in the new nation. Samuel Hill contributed this engraving, along with all signed and unsigned plates for the 1789–96 run of the *Massachusetts Magazine*. Courtesy of the American Antiquarian Society.

The corresponding engraving underscores this depiction of a "second Eden": Adelaide is depicted living in harmony with her surroundings, her lambs looking benevolently toward her (see page 228).

In addition to tending her flock, Adelaide fulfills her womanly duties through completing her domestic chores and by virtuously influencing others. After completing her "daily routine of domestick duty [which] employed an allotted part of [her] time," Adelaide spends "vacant hours" reading "elegant and instructive authors" and serves as the "protectress of [her] sex" by instructing others to act virtuously.[2] For example, when the curiosity of a young man, Amintor, is "awakened to a pitch of enthusiastic inquiry" in reaction to her physical appearance, she rebuffs him with a reaction evidenced in her body: her "looks beamed [the] dignity of innate worth," and a "rising blush announced [her] enkindled indignation." Adelaide rebukes him for his inappropriate attentions since he is already promised to another woman, Myra. Labeled the "Queen of Rural Innocence," Adelaide reunites the chastised Amintor with Myra, and the "village maidens [who meet] her at the hall of Virtuous Pleasure . . . [robe] her in a mantle of flowing muslin, whiter than the snowy fleece," crowning her "Adelaide, the Lovely Rustick."[3]

While on the surface level the narrative of Adelaide appears to be a simple pastoral story, a deeper analysis of its cultural signifiers reveals that this story and engraving function as an exemplary "exhibition" through their display of the desired racial configuration for women in the new nation. The "fair and virtuous" Adelaide not only manifests a form that is compared to "the flower that opens to the sun," her beauty is equated with the ideal of racial whiteness: her skin rivals "the lily of the vale," and her blush resembles the roses of nature.[4] The accompanying engraving reinforces this view: Adelaide displays bodily whiteness with a countenance that bespeaks refinement and gentility. As will be shown, this exhibition, along with others within the pages of the *Massachusetts Magazine*, is informed by the ways in which contemporary scientific theories of race and gender classified a woman's identity, theories manifested in both the new American nation and within the pages of this illustrated magazine.[5] Indeed, inextricably woven within the display of national ranking found in the magazine's exhibits portraying moments of national pride, specimens of American natural history, and signs of civilizing progress, the *Massachusetts Magazine* provided exhibitions that established its citizens' racial identity within a global stratification. This ranking was especially important since the new nation saw itself as a body politic; its relative position among enlightened nations was not only signified through the display of an ordered and civilized landscape, its national identity was literally based on the racialized and regulated bodies of its citizens, bodies symbolic of a desired national order.

This cultural discussion regarding the racial identity of citizens in the new nation was embedded within the need to establish America's national status alongside that of other enlightened nations while still maintaining a separate and distinct national identity.[6] To these ends, the *Massachusetts Magazine* provided numerous displays of scientific and cultural progress that served as visible signs of the order being imposed upon the wild and chaotic landscape of the new nation. In "Reflections on America," an article in the December 1795 issue of the *Massachusetts Magazine*, "Philoenthusiasticus" addressed this progress, describing America's transformed appearance by comparing late-eighteenth-century America with its appearance to Europeans three hundred years before: to the early settlers, the country had been a "howling wilderness" filled with "Ferocious beasts and unnumbered tribes of savages." But by 1795 the new nation not only "had risen to the zenith of celebrity" by taming the wilderness in which "beasts and barbarians have fled before the sons of Europe as dew before the sun," it had caused the "arts and sciences, philosophy and religion . . . [to] flourish with immortal vigour."[7]

The *Massachusetts Magazine* exemplified this civilized order through the display of government buildings, such as the Federal Building in New York (June 1789) and the Salem Court House (March 1790); churches, such as the Providence, Rhode Island, Baptist Meeting-House (August 1789) and Christ's Church in Boston (July 1792); educational institutions, such as Dartmouth College (February 1793) and the Colleges at Cambridge (June 1790); and residential estates, such as Hancock's home (July 1789) and Meredith's home near Philadelphia (October 1792). The magazine also provided plans for future structures and cities, including the engraving and description of the "Plan for the City of Washington" (May 1792), and displayed the latest technological innovations, among them the completed Mystic River Bridge (September 1790), all providing evidence of how the new nation ordered and controlled the "howling wilderness."

Within this context of ordered national progress, the *Massachusetts Magazine* employed visual and verbal elements to provide a racial foundation for the ideal American woman, which in turn contributed to the determination of her position in the new society. Indeed, whatever situation a woman found herself in—single, married, widowed—there were bodily standards that cut across these roles and applied to all women and in fact provided a scientific basis on which to build such cultural types as the "Republican Mother" and "Republican Wife."[8] This display of womanhood has a curious dynamic: while the magazine's readers were taught to scrutinize and classify the body of the nonwhite "Other," white women were simultaneously displayed in a positive light in order to reinforce the desirability of the dominant race and its inherent degree of civilization. Indubitably these observations, filtered through the lens of the preeminence of national whiteness, controlled the way in which an individual was read and interpreted: undesirable traits were projected onto a nonwhite negative Other, and positive qualities were associated with racial whiteness. These observations in turn provided bodily standards internalized by the magazine's readers, supplying not only a basis for the racial superiority of the nation's founders but for the country's ranking within a global hierarchy.

Magazines, Museums, and the "Exhibitionary Complex"

As an illustrated periodical, the *Massachusetts Magazine* was linked with other scientifically informed eighteenth-century institutions in what Tony Bennett has termed the "exhibitionary complex." This complex, according to him, included institutions, such as museums and international expositions, that "played a pivotal role in the formation of the modern state and [were] fundamental to its conception as . . . a set of educative and civilizing agencies."[9] While these institutions did not work together consciously, their common dissemination of knowledge, informed and authenticated by scientific discourse, worked to establish power relations in the new nation. These interrelated institutions utilized exhibits in order to provide "object lessons of power—the power to command and arrange things and bodies for public display." Institutions within the exhibitionary complex utilized "new technologies of vision" whereby individuals could become, through "seeing themselves from the side of power, both the subjects and the objects of knowledge, knowing power and what power knows, and knowing themselves as (ideally) known by power." It is from this vantage point that individuals would internalize the power of the gaze "as a principle of self-surveillance and, hence, self-regulation."[10] In his application of this concept to the institution of the museum, Bennett demonstrates the ways in which these establishments participated in cultural signification: collections within museums "mediate[d] the visitor's or spectator's access to the realm [of signification] by making it metonymically visible and present."[11] But the "correct" way to view these exhibits was not self-evident; spectators were shown how to "possess the appropriate socially-coded ways of seeing—and, in some cases, power to see—which allow[ed] the objects on display to be not just *seen* but *seen through* to establish some communion with the invisible to which they belong[ed]."[12]

Although Bennett does not include them in his formulation, nevertheless illustrated magazines were similarly linked to other institutions in the exhibitionary complex as a result of the way in which the exhibitions' visual and verbal elements intersected to disseminate knowledge to the readers. In fact, the designations of "museum" and "magazine" were linked semantically at the end of the eighteenth century. According to the *Oxford English Dictionary*, a "museum" was defined in the late eighteenth century as "a repository for the preservation and exhibition of objects illustrative of antiquities, natural history, fine and industrial art, or some particular branch of any of these subjects" and is also "applied to the collection of objects itself." Similarly, the *OED* not only defines a "magazine" as a "periodical publication containing articles by various writers" but also as a "storehouse of information on a specified subject." The connection between these two terms is also evident in the title of the *Massachusetts Magazine:* not only is it a "magazine," but it is also a "*Museum of Knowledge and Rational Entertainment*"; as an illustrated magazine, its exhibits were much like those found within the walls of a museum.[13] In addition, these periodicals fulfilled a special role within this complex. While the exhibits in a typical museum were most often fixed at a singular location, requiring individuals to travel to its collections, the displays within an illustrated magazine were "portable"; their exhibits traveled to the reader, and indeed the magazine itself served as a "traveling exhibition show"—reaching not only the subscribers but also other readers/viewers.[14]

Similar to the exhibitions within the pages of the *Massachusetts Magazine*, late-eighteenth-century museum exhibits demonstrated the need for order. Previously museums were "cabinets of curiosities," collections kept by the aristocracy in an enclosed space and organized according to their physical similarities and dissimilarities in order "to present a circular, harmonious representation of the world."[15] According to Susan M. Pearce, eighteenth-century collections reflected a "shift from a concentration on the rare and curious among which esoteric resemblances might be sought, to that of the normal and regular through which recurrent and reliable patterns might be perceived." While specimens in previous collections were "displayed together to demonstrate the variety and richness of the world," artifacts in the late eighteenth century were viewed through a classifying gaze that "searched for difference, based on measurable surface features. Old confusing elaborations were cut away to reveal individual singularities."[16] The reason for this change in the organization of material artifacts gleaned from exploration and travel was that scientists had begun to classify them into an organized schema of the world and publicly display them for the education of the general public.

One such eighteenth-century museum in the new nation was Charles Willson Peale's American Museum, which was located in Philadelphia. Not only does this museum reflect the growing desire for order in the late eighteenth century, it can also provide a paradigm for the exhibits displayed within the pages of the *Massachusetts Magazine*. In the magazine's January 1789 issue, an article titled "Curiosities" listed the latest contributions to Peale's museum: natural history artifacts included a live rattlesnake, a "fine correl tree," sixty-three young snakes, and a "tyger cat of South America" (whether it was dead or alive is unknown); articles of clothing and accessories included a Mandarin dress, a "Chinese lady's shoe," "sundry specimens of clothing made from bark," a "curious spear," and a "Mandarin pipe"; and geological specimens included minerals and fossils from Great Britain and polished lava from Mount Vesuvius.[17] These "curiosities" represented the miscellany that formed collections at the end of the eighteenth century. But Peale, unlike previous collectors, organized and carefully labeled his exhibits according to Carolus Linnaeus's scientific classification system. In his *Scientific and Descriptive Catalogue* (1796), Peale emphasized the importance of Linnaeus's system and the accurate adherence to it in his museum: "[we are] directed by the precepts of Linnaeus . . . in whose steps we are ambitious to tread, we will not fail to correct errors as soon as they are discovered."[18]

Through his Linnaean classificatory gaze, Peale sought to create a museum that would represent the "world in miniature." According to Christopher Looby, the world that Peale scientifically presented reflected the "perfect visual order of the Linnaean pattern" with the "top of the hierarchy" occupied by two rows of Revolutionary War heroes portraits, who presided "over the rational order of things, of which they were the superior extension."[19] Indicative of the Linnaean classification of man in the upper echelons of the "Great Chain of Being," Peale strategically placed "busts of physicians, scientists, and generals sculpted by William Rush and Jean Antoine Houdon" to look down at patrons from wall mounted shelves.[20] Below these portraits and busts, Peale placed glass-covered cases that displayed birds and animals in "positions that replicate[d] their living postures" and included landscapes of Germantown, Pennsylvania, and his country house, Belfield, along the walls.[21] Not only did Peale order his natural history specimens to reflect the Linnaean classification system, he also ranked men according to their racial classification. Besides the portrait paintings and sculpted busts, Peale provided his visitors with displays of life-size wax figures of men. In addition to including a wax figure of himself, which startled many a museum visitor, Peale created figures to represent the different races of the world. In a September 30, 1797, announcement in the *Aurora*, Peale states that the "waxen figures of men, large as life, (some of them casts from Nature) are here dressed in their proper habits, and placed in attitudes characteristic of their respective nations. Here may be seen the North American Savage, and the Savage of South America—a labouring Chinese, and the Chinese Gentleman,—the sooty African, . . . with some Natives of the South Sea Islands."[22]

Peale's display of "the full range of natural and artificial productions from around the globe" provided what David Brigham calls a "dynamic social site" in which citizens of the new nation were not only shown where their country ranked among nations but how their racial identification fit on a global scale.[23] This vision for a public museum differed from that of the newly formed museums of Europe, which at this time excluded the great mass of people from viewing their collections. In order "to fulfill a particularly American and republican goal" of creating a "universally educated public," he "extended the museum's hours into the evenings [and] similarly scheduled evening readings of his natural history lectures to reach audience members who worked during the day."[24] According to John C. Greene, Peale also "had a vision of the service a popular museum of natural history could render to the progress of science and the scientific education of the public."[25] To these ends, "Peale cultivated an image of the museum as a serious educational enterprise"[26] and in fact employed "contemporary ideas about . . . public school curriculum that would advance useful knowledge."[27]

Peale's belief in the advancement of "useful knowledge" is not only reflected in other late-eighteenth-century institutions, such as the American Philosophical Society and the University of Pennsylvania, but was also shared with magazines. Editors and leaders alike believed that magazines, like museums, could also help to produce "a universally educated" citizenry. In his 1788 letter to Matthew Carey, editor of the *American Museum, or, Universal Magazine*, reproduced in the magazine's July 1788 issue, George Washington articulated the importance of magazines in the new nation by asserting that they were "eminently calculated to disseminate political, agricultural, philosophical, and other valuable information." He also ventured "to pronounce . . THAT A MORE USEFUL LITERARY PLAN HAS NEVER BEEN UNDERTAKEN IN AMERICA, OR ONE MORE DESERVING OF PUBLIC ENCOURAGEMENT." Not only did Washington believe that the "merit of [Carey's] Museum" will become "well known . . . [in] this continent," he also maintained that it would also gain fame in "some countries of Europe."[28] Washington further emphasized the important role that all periodicals played in the new nation:

> For my part, I entertain a high idea of the utility of periodical publications: insomuch that I could heartily desire, copies of the Museum and Magazines, as well as common Gazettes, might be spread through every city, town, and village in America. I consider such *easy vehicles of knowledge*, more happily calculated than any other, to preserve the liberty, stimulate the industry, and meliorate the morals of an enlightened and free people. (emphasis added)[29]

Washington was not alone in this estimation of magazines; John Dickinson, Benjamin Rush, and Ezra Stiles in the same issue of the *American Museum* praised these "easy vehicles of knowledge," arguing that they were useful for the dissemination of "valuable information" in a "very advantageous manner."[30]

While Isaiah Thomas, the founder and driving force behind the *Massachusetts Magazine*, also advocated the role of magazines in the promotion of knowledge to the general public, he proposed in his preface to its first bound volume (1789) that this knowledge should be informed by science: "The Editors, perfectly sensible, that their *abiding place* must be the *Temple of Science*, earnestly entreat her benevolent votaries, to furnish gratuitous assistance, and guide them along the paths of knowledge."[31] This emphasis on "The Temple of Science" not only occurs in his editorial writings but is also underscored by its use as a recurring motif in the magazine's frontispieces. The frontispiece to the first volume depicts a woman, who symbolizes the "Hope" of the new magazine, as being assisted by Apollo within the "abiding place" of the temple of "Heaven born science." Thomas's preface works in tandem with this engraving by providing a directed "reading" of it: "no remission of the most sedulous attention to matter and manner, will ever be permitted, lest a failure. . . discourage *Hope* from any farther attendance—extort an indignant frown from the smiling *Apollo*—and wrest the *prophetick scroll* from the hand of *Fame*."[32] Similarly, the 1793 frontispiece for volume 5 continues the alignment between magazines and scientific knowledge in its display of a woman who represents the "Genius of the Massachusetts Magazine," kneeling at the feet of "Science" and soliciting its assistance in her endeavor, and in its depiction of the necessary tools for the acquisition of "knowledge and rational entertainment": a globe, books, paints, music, and musical instruments (see page 236).

In order to create scientifically informed exhibits that would educate and entertain its readers, the *Massachusetts Magazine* utilized both visual and verbal texts. The visual elements used to portray a "world in a miniature" were engravings that depicted cities, bridges, government buildings, estates, American natural history, portraits of notable men, and fictional scenes. Altogether this periodical published ninety-five copperplate engravings, one to two engravings per issue, with Samuel Hill responsible for all of the magazine's engravings.[33] In its construction of exhibitions, it combined these engravings with the an eclectic collection of natural history, biographical sketches, essays, short stories, serialized stories and novels, literary and dramatic criticism, and poetry. Written under pseudonyms such as "The Gleaner" or "The Philanthropist," essays chosen for publication often commented on the manners, fashion, and social life of readers, incorporating different characters and tales to make their point. Fiction usually consisted of character sketches, sentimental tales, and Oriental tales; poetry emulated the classical forms of ode, pastoral, elegy, and satire along with poetic tributes to other contributors to the magazine. Biographical entries focused mainly on domestic and foreign men and were often accompanied by an engraving: American biographies included tributes to Washington and Franklin, and foreign biographies featured heroes of the American and French Revolutions,

"The Genius of the Massachusetts Magazine, soliciting the patronage of Science." As in this 1793 issue, the *Massachusetts Magazine* repeatedly employs a woman as a representative figure for the collective efforts of the magazine. For example, the engraving that served as the frontispiece for the first volume of the magazine uses a woman to symbolically represent the "hope" of the new enterprise. Courtesy of the American Antiquarian Society.

such as Lafayette and Necker. The magazine also featured political and religious articles that followed controversial topics of the day, such as the nation's position toward France and the defense of deism, and published articles informing the public about archaeological discoveries in the new nation, historical accounts of the recent American Revolution, and reviews of both foreign and domestic books and plays.

Reading the Body, Reading Gender

In addition to this promotion of scientific knowledge in both the visual and verbal elements of the magazine, it is essential to note not only that Hill chose a woman to symbolize the hopes and dreams of the magazine's editors in his frontispiece engravings but that the body of this iconic woman reflects the preeminence of whiteness in contemporary scientific discourse regarding race and gender. By scrutinizing the body through a racialized gaze, eighteenth-century scientists assumed the superiority of European and British American whiteness and sought to contain nonwhite races through their analyses. Indeed, according to Mary Louise Pratt, eighteenth-century scientists examined and classified races through the lens of a "planetary consciousness," whereby bodies were organized and described in terms of a "global-scale [of] meaning."[34] Viewed as an object of scientific inquiry and a site for the acquisition of knowledge, this body was systematically classified and ranked within a racial hierarchy that covered humanity from every corner of the Earth and in which the Caucasian body was deemed to have the ideal form, shape, and color. Although this system was presented as objective, it was not; the scientist's value judgments shaped his findings. In alignment with the environmentalist argument that asserted that climate directly affected the body, these scientists associated enlightened civilization with temperate climates and savagery and its attendant unregulated passions with both frigid and torrid climates.

From these assumptions, scientists sought to measure the signs of racial difference and their attendant degree of civilization. One such individual was Petrus Camper, a Dutch physician, naturalist, and professor of anatomy and surgery at the Athenaeum Illustre of Franeker and the University of Groningen. Camper, known for his concept of the "facial angle," which allowed him to rank his collection of skulls from the monkey to the sculptures of Apollo and Venus de Medici, continued to be highly influential in nineteenth-century measurements of race. In the formation of the facial angle, Camper dissected skulls in order "to define the lines of the countenance, and the angle of these lines with the horizon," which in turn led him to establish a maximum and minimum angle: "I began with the monkey, proceeded to the Negro, and the European, till I ascended to the countenances of antiquity, and examined a Medusa, an Apollo, or a Venus de Medicis."[35]

Although Camper worked to establish a configuration of "national physiognomies" based on the structure of skulls, it was Johann Friedrich Blumenbach who formulated the classification system whereby humanity was placed into five different races, a classification that dominated the field of anthropology until the end of the nineteenth century. Known as "the father of Anthropology," Blumenbach, faculty member at the University of Göttingen, was a physiologist, anthropologist, and comparative anatomist.[36] Blumenbach worked out his classification system in *On the Natural Variety of Mankind*; in his first edition (1776), Blumenbach divided humanity into four races, and in the 1781 edition he formulated the highly adopted division of the Caucasian, Asiatic, American, Ethiopian, and Malay races. Indeed, this publication came to be the major authority on the subject of racial classification. Based on the human "variety from Mount Caucasus," Blumenbach formulated the term "Caucasian" as the classificatory term for racial whiteness. Not only did his selection of this particular "variety" result from the fact that this area "produces the most beautiful race of men," Blumenbach also believed that Caucasians were the original race since "it is very easy for [white skin] to degenerate into brown, but very much more difficult for dark to become white."[37]

Although he characterized the Caucasian physiognomy as "that kind of appearance which, according to our opinion of symmetry, we consider most handsome and becoming," Blumenbach was not satisfied with mere surface appearances and sought a more foundational basis for his classification system.[38] Such a basis was found in his examination of the human skull "because when stripped of the soft and changeable parts [skulls] exhibit the firm and stable foundation of the head, and can be conveniently handled and examined, and considered under different aspects and compared together."[39] Although he believed that the appearance of individuals within a racial classification can differ to some degree, Blumenbach argues that "there is in [the skulls of different nations] a constancy of characteristics which cannot be denied and . . . has a great deal to do with the racial habit, and which answers most accurately to the nations and their peculiar physiognomy."[40] Predictably, Blumenbach declares the skull of the Caucasian to be predominant and preeminent since it not only "displays . . . the most beautiful form of the skull, from which, as from a mean and primeval type," but that all "others diverge by most easy gradations on both sides to the two ultimate extremes [of the Mongolian and the Ethiopian]."[41]

The classification systems of Camper and Blumenbach were further bifurcated in scientific writings regarding the standard for an "ideally perfect female body," a standard aligned with Greek and Roman models of beauty reflected in classical sculpture and the neoclassical replication of them. Similar to the eighteenth-century neoclassical artist who sought to create ideal figures that would represent high principles and unblemished beauty, the German anatomist Samuel Thomas Von Soemmerring compared his representation of the female skeleton with both the Venus de Medici and the more delicate Venus of Dresden.[42] But Soemmerring was not the only anatomist and physiologist who used classical models for comparison. According to Londa Schiebinger, Godfried Bidloo's anatomical plates, published by William Cowper in 1697, "were drawn not from life but from classical statues" with "Bidloo claim[ing that] these figures exhibited 'the most beautiful proportions of a man and woman as they were fixed by the ancients.'"[43] William Cheselden, the first English anatomist to draw a female skeleton (1733), continued the Bidloo tradition by comparing the proportions and attitudes of his male figure with the Belvedere Apollo and those of his female figure with the Venus de Medici.[44]

Even though eighteenth-century anatomists and physiologists sought to investigate the differences between the sexes in an objective, scientific manner, their assumption that men and women have "a distinct telos—physical and intellectual strength for man, [weakness and] motherhood for woman"—affected the outcome of their research.[45] In addition to aligning beautiful physical characteristics to the dominant Caucasian race, Blumenbach associated the physiology of women's bodies with their inferior role in society. He finds that the "general conformation of the female body" consists of "tenderness" and "softness," in stark contrast with man's superior "athletic and robust body," and shows the "most striking" difference between the sexes.[46] In addition, the nervous system of women is "much greater than in males," making their "propensity to commotions of the mind . . . more prompt and spontaneous" and giving scientific foundation to the belief that women were ruled by their emotions rather than reason, thus making them fit only for a lesser role in the power structure of society.[47] Blumenbach also locates gender differences in the foundational structure of the skeletal system: the different "external habits . . . that characterise the two sexes is . . . observable in the bones themselves" since they "are evidently much more smooth and round in females than in males" and woman's "cylindrical bones, in particular, are more slender and delicate, and the plane ones more attenuated or thin."[48] Furthermore, Blumenbach found that the sex organs themselves are evidence of "natural" gender roles: "As the male organs of generation are naturally calculated to *give*, so are the female to *receive*, and in the two sexes these organs are, in a general point of view, widely different from each other." Female genitalia are described independently but in comparison to a male norm: "the *clitoris*, which lies concealed in the superior commissure of the labia, resembles the male penis in more respects than one."[49] And indeed a woman's sexual organs determine her morality:

> Over the very threshold or entrance of the vagina is expanded a weblike production denominated the *hymen.* This is a membrane, the existence of which in an unlacerated condition, is considered as a sure badge of spotless virginity—a membrane bestowed exclusively on the female of the human species.[50]

According to Blumenbach and others, a woman's hymen was a physical manifestation of her moral role. Like their unique physical components that were presumed to "guard" against sexual immorality, women were required to serve as "guardians" of sexual propriety between men and women. Indeed, the regulation of a woman's moral role was founded in her body since it could offer substantive physical evidence of her pure (or impure) moral character.

Although the works of these scientists did not directly appear in the *Massachusetts Magazine,* excerpts from the works of Johann Caspar Lavater were frequently reprinted. This Swiss scientist and minister was greatly influenced by current scientific theories and incorporated them into his own published works. Originally published as "Male and Female" in his *Essays on Physiognomy* (*Physiognomische Fragmente,* 1775–78), Lavater's "General Remarks on Women" appears in the January 1794 issue of the magazine and exemplifies his major concern regarding the configuration of the body of woman and his connection to the larger scientific debate on the differences between the sexes. Much like his scientific contemporaries, Lavater asserts that a woman's physical form reflected her innate capabilities and character. In this selection, Lavater states that the "primary matter" that constitutes a woman's body is "more flexible, irritable, and elastic, than that of man." In fact, a woman's body is "formed to maternal mildness and affection" and her "organs are tender, yielding, easily wounded, sensible, and receptible." A woman's form, in other words, fits her function since her physical appearance confirms her proper place within the domestic sphere. In his published work, Lavater reads the countenance of one woman as indicative of the "most accurate female housewifery" and assumes that his reader will agree with him in his judgment that her whole face reflects her femininity and domesticity: her forehead is "entirely feminine," her nose is "indicative of household discretion," and, as with any good housewife, her eye is "sharply attentive" and her mouth is "strictly economical."[51] Even the wrinkles on this woman's face "express good sense" and confirm the scope of her interests as "confined within a small domestic circle."[52]

In *Essays on Physiognomy,* Lavater also provided physiognomical readings of female silhouettes and agreed with Camper and Blumenbach that the reading of skulls provided "the only certain foundation of physiognomy," basing his "true" readings of gender on them. According to his readings of the physical evidence, he aligns a skull's profile with the inner qualities of its once-living owner. In one such reading, he finds that a particular woman's skull indicates that she "must [have] by nature . . . had a taste for the minute, the neat, and the punctilious." In a reading of a second skull, he classifies it as that of a male skull since a "female skull [never] has such *sinus frontales*" that ascribe the living owner with the "truly masculine" traits of being "open, candid, [and] intelligent."[53] Indeed, Lavater explicitly connects the outer appearance of a skull with the individual's inner character since "the countenance is the theatre on which the soul exhibits itself" and affirms that it is here that "its emanations [must] be studied and caught." In addition to finding the "noble spotless maiden . . . superior to all the powers of description" since "her angelic form" is equal to "the mild and golden rays of an autumnal evening sun," he further elaborates on the connection between this ideal description and a woman's inner character. Lavater's ideal of a "noble spotless maiden" has an inner character that is visible in a "large arched forehead," a "gentle-outlined or sharpened nose," and "pure and efficient lips," which all speak to her qualities of "refined taste," "sympathetic goodness of heart," and "humility and complacency."[54] These readings worked together to underscore Lavater's belief that gender differences are visible on two levels: while the outer fleshly appearance is aligned with the foundational skeletal system, a woman's external appearance in turn corresponds to her internal qualities.

Within this larger scientific discourse regarding a woman's body, the visual/verbal exhibitions within the *Massachusetts Magazine* underscore this connection between a woman's outer appearance and her inner character. While the display of "Adelaide; or the Lovely Rustick" fulfills the bodily standard with her classically defined body and skin of a whiteness that rivals "the lily of the vale," a close reading of Adelaide's racial markers take on additional importance since the "spotless purity" of her outer appearance "informs her soul."[55] The author of "The Accomplished Female Character" (April 1792) also asserts that the countenance of "Sally, beautiful Sally" with its "rosy cheek, . . . ruby lip and sparkling eye" serves as "a faint emblem" for the "beauties of her mind."[56] Not only does her face reflect "the traits of sincerity" and "the traces of rectitude," it also evidences the "internal dignity and nobleness of [her] soul" and her "flexibility of disposition."[57] According to the perspective of Dr. Langhorne in the January 1790 article, "On the Fair Sex," a woman was made for the pleasure of man; her body was created by God "to make her amiable in [men's] eyes," and her appeal is found in her "soft and gentle graces" and "obedient blush of modesty" that are inscribed on her body's "fine proportions," "nicely moulded features," and the "expressive eyes" and "delicate complexion" of her countenance. Indeed, this outer appearance reflects the "finer ornaments of [her] mind" and her desire to "practice . . . every moral and social duty."[58]

This connection between a woman's appearance and its effect on a male observer is also described and analyzed in William Alexander's "On the happy Influence arising from FEMALE SOCIETY" (July 1795), an excerpt from the 1784 edition of his two-volume *The History of Women*. Like Linnaeus's classification of racial varieties, Alexander divides the "human genus" into two sexes since "the Author of nature has placed the balance of power on the side of the male, by giving him not only a body more large and robust, but also a mind endowed with greater resolution, and a more extensive reach." A woman's power, on the other hand, resides in her ability "to bend the haughty stubbornness of man" through her use of an "insinuating word, . . . a kind look, or even a smile." According to Alexander, this power has "conquered Alexander, subdued Caesar, and decided the fate of empires and of kingdoms" and further asserts that the two sexes form a complementary relationship on "nearly . . . equal footing" since "the Author of our being" is not a "partial parent" and has given to each sex "its different qualifications."[59]

For Alexander, these gender distinctions are based in the body, maintaining that a woman's body is "naturally" "weak, timid, and defenceless," while a man's "robust" body is endowed with "courage and bravery." Accordingly, a woman's "chiefest excellence" lies in her body's "beauty [and] chastity," along with its "softness and delicacy," while a man's superior physical strength serves "to defend [women] from the assaults that may be made on their bodies." Alexander also finds that a man's "enterprising and robust" nature is complemented by "female softness"; her "lenient balm of endearment . . . [smoothes his] rugged nature" and blunts "the edge of corrosive care."[60] This description of a woman's "qualifications" indicates that although she may have power over men, it is an *indirect* power. Whereas men act directly on the conditions around them, women need to become objects of beauty and softness in order to manipulate men into providing for their needs and wants and are in fact dependent on a man's inclination to do so. Indeed, Alexander finds that "it is by the arts of pleasing only, that women can attain to any degree of consequence or of *power;* and it is by pleasing only, that they can hope to become *objects* of love and affections" (emphasis added).[61] A woman's power therefore is channeled through her subservient bodily display for men; and her "soft nature" serves to refine a man's "rough nature."

In his classification of the "human genus" into the two sexes, Alexander also ranks individuals within a hierarchy of national types, whereby each is classified by its degree of "civilization." The barometer that Alexander employs to measure a society's degree of civilization is its treatment of women. He asserts that the social interaction between the sexes in European societies, with its use of women's "civilizing power," is much preferable to Eastern societies in which the sexes are kept separate and that do not allow for a woman's "softening influence." Accordingly, he ranks British society at the height of civilization and Eastern societies at the other end of the scale since "jealousy, that tyrant of the soul" rules "the present state of mankind in the East" and excludes "all the joys and comforts of mixed society." As a result, Eastern men are "gloomy, suspicious, cowardly, and cruel" and "divested of almost all the finer sentiments that arise from friendship and from love." This lack of "mixed society" has a pernicious effect: without the "company and conversation of women" a "roughness and barbarity have settled their empire, and triumph over the human mind," resulting in a lack of all "social virtues" and "sentimental feelings."[62]

Subsequent to Alexander's description of women in non-European countries, "where so much of our colouring has been employed to paint the vicious and the disagreeable," he focuses on European societies, finding them to be "polished and refined," as men spend time "in conversation [with] their women." In fact, the "advantages resulting from [a man's social interaction] with the female sex" influence "every custom and every action of social life."[63] In *The History of Women,* Alexander elaborates further on this contrast and asserts that in Eastern societies,

> where women are kept as the miser does his gold . . . the passions of men are so raised by partial glances, by brooding over the thoughts of ideal beauty, and ideal happiness, in the enjoyment of it, and so inflamed with almost insurmountable obstacles to that enjoyment, that if they ever happen to find a woman alone, they attack her in the most licentious manner.[64]

The sexual purity of women in less civilized countries is also "disarmed" through "the romantic ideas they entertain of the happiness they would derive from [men]," which in turn causes them to "fall an easy prey to the first rude invader." Alexander also asserts that "in spite of cautious parents, and jealous husbands, of locks, bars, and eunuchs," the chastity of these women is "less secure" than in European societies "where the sexes live free and easy together."[65]

Whereas the "spotless purity" of a white woman's skin was linked to the potential to nurture the desired qualities of "delicacy and modesty," which in turn could positively influence men, the *Massachusetts Magazine* frequently portrayed a nonwhite woman as a "negative Other," an individual regarded as being incapable of fostering such traits because of the assumptions about the innate qualities of her racial classification. A manifestation of this negative attitude can be seen in "Description of the Moorish Women," published in the October 1795 issue. According to this anonymous author, Moorish women "are not in general very reserved" since they are often offered as sexual favors to travelers. Consequently, the author links this loose sexuality with their racial identity and invokes the contemporary scientific theory of environmental determinism: "Climate has a vast influence on the temperament of the body; and licentiousness [in torrid regions] is . . . more general and less restrained." This climatic theory also substantiates the assertion that "females in warm countries sooner arrive at puberty" and that "polygamy has been generally adopted in such climates."[66] This projection of negative qualities on to a "negative Other" is also seen in "The Family Economy and Employments of the Gypsies" (November/December 1790). "Grellman," the author of this account, aligns the savagery of this race with the bodies and behavior of its women. Since Gypsies are "still the unpolished creatures that rude nature formed them; or at most, have only advanced one degree towards humanity," they appear no better than "wild beasts"; in fact all family members share the same room, where "the father and mother lie half naked [and] the children entirely so."[67] Not only do Gypsy women lie around half naked, they also "frequent brothels, or let their persons out, in some other way, for hire." In order to earn money, these "savage" women do not work industriously but dance in "the most disgusting [manner] that can be conceived, always ending with the most fulsome grimaces, or the most lascivious attitudes and gestures, uncovering those parts, which the rudest and most uncultivated people carefully conceal."[68]

The Necessity of Bodily Regulation

While nonwhite women supposedly lacked the ability to regulate their bodies, a number of contributors to the magazine asserted that it was essential for a white woman to be placed under surveillance and thus be regulated since her body could affect not only her own life but also that of others. The exhibition of Adelaide emphasizes this "natural" power to affect men. In her chastising of Amintor and the resultant reuniting of the betrothed couple, "the Lovely Rustick" demonstrates her innate ability to influence men and serves as an example to other young women. Further, the anonymous writer of "Essay on Female Charms" (July 1793) draws a connection between a woman's appearance and its effect on those observing it: when a woman's "finest features, ranged in the most exact symmetry, and heightened by the most blooming complexion" are "animated," they strike the observer and cause a physical reaction. Indeed, the writer asserts that there is a direct relationship between the type of "passions . . . they [the features] express" and the reaction of the observer.[69] When a woman's features, for example, reflect "the dead calm of insensibility," they will cause an emotionless reaction, and "if they do not express kindness, they will be viewed without love." Since her appearance has this power, a woman must regulate the display of her countenance, especially since it could be the cause of her own downfall: if a woman wears a "wanton aspect," she will excite in a man a "desire . . . that [is like a] savage for his prey," seeking "the destruction of [his] object."[70]

This perceived need for the regulation of a woman's body is especially evident in the exhibition of "The New Pygmalion," an engraving and story published in three installments of the *Massachusetts Magazine* in 1790. This "New

Pygmalion," a young man named Mr. De M—, first scrutinizes the body of Louisa Passementier and then imposes order upon it, all to serve his own needs and desires. In his reading of her body for racial signifiers that would indicate her potential for improvement, he views her as an object that needs to be molded and shaped into the ideal woman who will serve as a counterpart to him.[71] The accompanying engraving, "I am an Orphan, Sir," captures this moment of surveillance whereby Mr. De M—'s benevolence is aroused by what he views (see page 246). Indeed, while walking down the street, Mr. De M— is "*struck* with the appearance of a beautiful little creature" picking up cinders and finds her to be an "uncommon . . . object" for his benevolence. In the engraving, Louisa turns her face up to him and exhibits "the symmetry of her features" veiled under a "disfigurement" of dust. This young woman has the power to incite benevolence since her body fits the acceptable racial- and gender-specific configuration. Although not permanently disfigured by dark skin and nonwhite features since the layer of surface dust can be washed away, Louisa does assume a subordinate and demure position that is gender assigned. On the basis of this initial encounter, Mr. De M— judges that Louisa's "person might make her fortune," and he sets out to "clothe and instruct [her] in some business." This judgment is later confirmed when he observes her after the grime has been removed and her "tatters" have been replaced with "decent" clothes; Mr. De M— believes he has found "a valuable diamond [that has been] incrusted with dirt."[72]

The engraving also graphically exhibits Louisa's subordinate position, which is representative of the position of women within the dynamic of gender relations in the eighteenth century. Mr. De M— assumes the powerful stance of an observer, looking down on the upturned face of Louisa, who displays the inferior position of an object under scrutiny. Unlike Pygmalion, who looks up at the statue that he has placed on a pedestal, Mr. De M— gazes downward at Louisa, his inferior both in terms of gender and social ranking. Within the engraving, the repetitive vertical lines of the crowded buildings along narrow streets suggest an atmosphere of confinement and enclosure, thereby emphasizing Louisa's lowly placement in both the spatial configuration of the engraving and the power relations of gender and social status.

These power relations are in turn evident in the ways in which Mr. De M— provides training for his charge. Rather than encouraging her to take an active role in her own "creation," her education and training instead focus on his desires, on the qualities and abilities appropriate to her passive role as a woman. Since he does not believe that women ever need to make rational decisions, Mr. De M— provides only the basic education in reading and writing and concentrates on molding her into an industrious contributor to society.[73] To these ends, he places her with a number of craftswomen who gradually train her in

"I am an Orphan, Sir," an engraving from the October 1790 issue of the *Massachusetts Magazine*. This illustration accompanies the lead story for the issue, "The New Pygmalion," and points to the desire to regulate a woman's body by graphically depicting Louisa's subordinate position and the sexual tension that exists between Louisa and Mr. De M—. This story continues in the November and December issues without illustrations. Courtesy of the American Antiquarian Society.

skills appropriate to her rising social rank. And as Louisa improves her social rank, this progress is visible on her body. Under Mr. De M——'s scrutiny, he finds that she has "acquire[d] an air, which [renders] her pretty face still more interesting," and her show of "modesty in seeing her benefactor, [gives] her additional charms." But this progress is not attributed to Louisa's hard work and Mr. De M——'s response confirms the power relations between the two: "Mr. De M—— could not help exclaiming to himself, happy Pygmalion! The gods [have] animated thy statue."[74]

The verbal and visual elements in this story also underscore the underlying sexual tension between Louisa and Mr. De M——. Although the text depicts Louisa as a naive, asexual being who blindly makes her way through potentially threatening sexual situations, the engraving portrays her as a sexual being: her low-cut dress reveals a cleavage much more appropriate to an older woman than a young girl of twelve. The body indeed seems more like that of Louisa at fifteen, when it causes a "forcible impression" on Mr. De M——, who feels its "power" and its "consequences."[75] The fact that Louisa remains oblivious to either her own sexuality or any sexual threat also makes her "irresistibly seductive" to him. Since she has not received a rational education, Louisa is unaware of any threat to her reputation. As a man of experience, Mr. De M—— takes charge of the situation. Viewing her as a "poison," a "fever," and a "disorder" in need of treatment, he goes through a desensitizing process of frequent visits to Louisa, whereby he learns how to resist her seductive body. For her part, Louisa retains her bodily regulation throughout the story and in the end becomes "what every woman ought to be, the pupiless, the friend, the sensible and accomplished companion . . . the counterpart of her husband."[76]

Through the utilization of its visual and verbal elements, the *Massachusetts Magazine* fulfilled its role as an "easy vehicle" for the dissemination of cultural knowledge to its readers. Embedded with the larger narrative regarding national identity and informed and authorized by contemporary scientific theories of race and gender, its visual and verbal exhibitions provided readers with displays that prescribed regulated bodily whiteness as the desirable racial identity for women in the new nation.

Notes

1. "Adelaide; or the Lovely Rustick," *Massachusetts Magazine* 2 (April 1790): 195.
2. Ibid.
3. Ibid., 196.
4. Ibid., 195.

5. For further information on *Massachusetts Magazine*, see Edward E. Chielens, "The Massachusetts Magazine," *American Literary Magazines* (New York: Greenwood P, 1986), 244-50 and "Periodicals and the Development of an American Literature," in *Making America/Making American Literature*, eds. A. Robert Lee and W. M. Verhoeven (Amsterdam: Rodopi, 1996), 93-103; Frank Luther Mott, "The Massachusetts Magazine," *A History of American Magazines, 1741-1850*, vol. 1 (New York: Appleton & Co., 1930), 108-11; and Lyon N. Richardson, *A History of Early American Magazines, 1741-1789* (New York: Thomas Nelson and Sons), 354-61.
6. Two recent studies offer additional information and insight into this connection between the creation of a national identity and the racialized bodies of its citizens: Jared Gardner, *Master Plots: Race and the Founding of an American Literature, 1787-1845* (Baltimore: The John Hopkins UP, 1998) and Pauline Schloesser, *The Fair Sex: White Women and Racial Patriarchy in the Early American Republic* (New York: New York UP, 2002).
7. "Reflections on America," *Massachusetts Magazine* 7 (December 1795): 559.
8. For further information regarding the role of American women in the eighteenth century, see Ruth H. Bloch, "American Feminine Ideals in Transition: The Rise of the Moral Mother, 1785-1815," *Feminist Studies* 4 (1978): 101-26; Nancy Cott, *The Bonds of Womanhood* (New Haven: Yale UP, 1977); Cathy Davidson, *Revolution and the Word* (New York: Oxford UP, 1986); Linda K. Kerber, *Women of the Republic: Intellect and Ideology in Revolutionary America* (New York: W. W. Norton, 1980), "The Republican Mother: Women and the Enlightenment—An American Perspective," *American Quarterly* 28 (1976): 187-205, and "'I Have Don . . . much to Carrey on the Warr': Women and the Shaping of Republican Ideology after the American Revolution," in *Women and Politics in the Age of the Democratic Revolution*, eds. Harriet B. Applewhite and Darline G. Levy (Ann Arbor: U of Michigan P, 1990), 227-57; Jan Lewis, "The Republican Wife: Virtue and Seduction in the Early Republic," *William and Mary Quarterly* 44 (1987): 689-719; Margaret Nash, "Rethinking Republican Motherhood: Benjamin Rush and the Young Ladies' Academy of Philadelphia" *Journal of the Early Republic* 17 (1997): 171-191; Mary Beth Norton, *Liberty's Daughters* (Ithaca: Cornell UP, 1980) and "The Evolution of White Women's Experience in Early America," *American Historical Review* 89 (1984): 593-619; Carroll Smith-Rosenberg, "Subject Female: Authorizing American Identity," *American Literary History* 5

(1993): 481-511; and Rosemarie Zagarri, "Morals, Manners, and the Republican Mother" *American Quarterly* 44 (1992): 192-215.

9. Tony Bennett, "The Exhibitionary Complex," in *Culture/Power/History: A Reader in Contemporary Social Theory*, eds. Nicolas B. Dirks, et al (Princeton, NJ: Princeton UP, 1993), 129. While Bennett focuses on mid to late nineteenth-century institutions, I believe that the "exhibitionary complex" is in fact a phenomenon that commences in the late eighteenth century.
10. Bennett, "The Exhibitionary Complex," 126.
11. Bennett, *The Birth of the Museum* (London & New York: Routledge, 1995), 35.
12. Ibid. A number of recent studies have focused on the ways in which "new fields of vision" and "specular relations" operate in eighteenth-century American and British novels. For further information see Julia Stern, *The Plight of Feeling: Sympathy and Dissent in the Early American Novel* (Chicago: U of Chicago P, 1997); Kristina Straub, "Reconstructing the Gaze: Voyeurism in Richardson's *Pamela*," *Studies in Eighteenth-Century Culture* 18 (1988): 419–31; and David Waldstreicher, "'Fallen under My Observation': Vision and Virtue in *The Coquette*," *Early American Literature* 27 (1992): 204–18.
13. Although he focuses on the literary rather than the illustrated magazine, Jared Gardner also aligns contemporary museums with early American magazines. See Gardner's "The Literary Museum and the Unsettling of the Early American Novel," *English Literary History* 67 (2000): 743–71.
14. In the July 1794 issue of *The Massachusetts Magazine*, Judith Sargent Murray suggests in her "Gleaner" series one of the ways in which readers other than the original subscriber would view the exhibits within this magazine. In the embedded narrative of Margaretta, it is through his perusal of this magazine in the home of an acquaintance that her father finds out that Margaretta is alive and is able to be reunited with her. For information on the reading public in the late eighteenth century, see Cathy Davidson, "The Life and Times of *Charlotte Temple:* The Biography of a Book," in *Reading in America: Literature and Social History*, ed. Cathy Davidson (Baltimore: Johns Hopkins UP, 1989), 157–79, and *Revolution and the Word* (New York: Oxford UP, 1986); William J. Free, *The Columbian Magazine and American Literary Nationalism* (The Hague and Paris: Mouton, 1968); Mary Kelley, "Reading Women/Women Reading: The Making of Learned Women in Antebellum America," *Journal of American History* 83 (1996): 401–24; Edward Larkin, "Inventing an

American Public: Thomas Paine, the *Pennsylvania Magazine*, and American Revolutionary Political Discourse," *Early American Literature* 33, no. 3 (1998): 250–76; David Lundberg and Henry F. May, "The Enlightened Reader in America," *American Quarterly* 28 (1976): 262–93; Frank Luther Mott, *A History of American Magazines, 1741–1850*, vol. 1 (New York: D. Appleton, 1930); David Paul Nord, "A Republican Literature: A Study of Magazine Reading and Readers in Late Eighteenth-Century New York," *American Quarterly* 40 (1988): 42–64; Rosalind Remer, "Building an American Book Trade: Philadelphia Publishing in the New Republic," *Business and Economic History* 23, no. 1 (1994): 1–6, and *Printers and Men of Capital: Philadelphia Book Publishers in the New Republic* (Philadelphia: U of Pennsylvania P, 1996).

15. Eilean Hooper-Greenhill, *Museums and the Shaping of Knowledge* (London and New York: Routledge, 1992), 139–40.
16. Susan M. Pearce, *On Collecting: An Investigation into Collecting in the European Tradition* (London and New York: Routledge, 1995), 121.
17. "Curiosities," *Massachusetts Magazine* 1 (January 1789): 56.
18. Charles W. Peale, *A Scientific and Descriptive Catalogue of Peale's Museum* (Philadelphia: S. H. Smith, 1796), iii–iv.
19. Christopher Looby, "The Constitution of Nature: Taxonomy as Politics in Jefferson, Peale, and Bartram," *Early American Literature* 22 (1987): 267.
20. David Brigham, *Public Culture in the Early Republic: Peale's Museum and Its Audience* (Washington, D.C.: Smithsonian Institution P, 1995), 46. Fortunately Peale left an illustrated and written record of how he arranged his museum: in two paintings, "The Long Room" (1822), a work begun by him and finished by his son, Titian II, and "The Artist in His Museum" (1822); and in two of his publications, *Guide to the Philadelphia Museum* (Philadelphia: Museum P, 1806) and the unfinished *A Scientific and Descriptive Catalogue of Peale's Museum* (Philadelphia: S. H. Smith, 1796).
21. Brigham 46.
22. Qtd. in Charles Coleman Sellers, *Charles Willson Peale* (New York: Scribner, 1969), 285.
23. Brigham 1.
24. Ibid., 5.
25. John C. Greene, *The Death of Adam: Evolution and Its Impact on Western Thought* (Ames: Iowa State UP, 1996), 26.
26. Brigham 13.

27. Ibid., 18.

28. "Letter," *American Museum* (July 1788): n.p.

29. Ibid.

30. "Preface," *American Museum* (July 1788): n.p.

31. "Preface," *Massachusetts Magazine* 1 (January 1789): n.p. For further information on Thomas, see Lyon N. Richardson, *A History of Early American Magazines, 1741–1789* (New York: T. Nelson and Sons, 1931); Mott, *A History of American Magazines, 1741–1850*, vol. 1; Clifford K. Shipton, *Isaiah Thomas: Printer, Patriot and Philanthropist, 1749–1831* (New York: Leo Hart, 1948); and Terry Hynes, "Isaiah Thomas," *American Newspaper Journalists, 1690–1872*, vol. 43 of the *Dictionary of Literary Biography* (Detroit: Gale Research, 1985), 435–49.

32. Ibid.

33. These signed and unsigned copperplate engravings used the intaglio technique of recessed line engraving dating from the fifteenth century, which allowed ink to fill its lines in order to produce a fine line image. *The Massachusetts Magazine* was not the only late-eighteenth-century illustrated magazine to use copperplate engravings; *The Universal Asylum, and Columbian Magazine* (1786–92) contained 97 engravings, and *The New-York Magazine* (1790–97) had 101. According to Benjamin Lewis, "Hill engraved all of the signed plates . . . from 1789 to 1796 and probably did all the unsigned ones also" for *The Massachusetts Magazine* (207). Hill was an active engraver and copperplate printer in Boston from 1789 to 1803. In addition to the work he did for this magazine, Hill was also known for his engraved Bible plates for the New York publisher William Durell, and he supplied the engravings for the first American edition of Johann Caspar Lavater's 1794 *Essays on Physiognomy*, trans. Thomas Holcroft, 4th ed. (London: Thomas Tegg, 184?)

34. Mary Louise Pratt, *Imperial Eyes: Travel Writing and Transculturation* (London and New York: Routledge, 1992), 15.

35. Qtd. in Lavater 353–4.

36. Greene 222.

37. Johann Friedrich Blumenbach, *The Anthropological Treatises of Johann Friedrich Blumenbach*, trans. Thomas Bendyshe (Boston: Longwood P, 1978), 269. This degeneration of skin color was a highly discussed topic both in the scientific and in the general population at the end of the eighteenth century. In the new nation, this debate often focused on the bodies of "white negro" "anomalies of nature," which blurred the boundaries

between blacks and whites and required scientific explanation as to its cause. One of these "white negroes" was exhibited in *The Massachusetts Magazine* on December 1791. For further discussion of "white negroes," see Jared Gardner, *Master Plots*, 1–24; Winthrop D. Jordan, *White over Black: American Attitudes toward the Negro, 1550–1812* (Chapel Hill: U of North Carolina P, 1968); Joanne Pope Melish, "Emancipation and the Em-bodiment of 'Race': The Strange Case of the White Negroes and the Algerine Slaves," in *A Centre of Wonders: The Body in Early America*, eds. Janet Moore Lindman and Michele Lise Tarter (Ithaca: Cornell UP, 2001), 223–36; and Beverly J. Reed, "Reading the Traveling Exhibition Show: *Massachusetts Magazine* and the Visual/Verbal Construction of the American Woman" (Ph.D. diss., Purdue University, 2000), 67–86.

38. Blumenbach, *Anthropological Treatises*, 265.
39. Ibid., 234.
40. Ibid., 235.
41. Ibid., 269.
42. Ludwig Choulant, *History and Bibliography of Anatomic Illustration* (New York: Hafner, 1945, 1962), 306.
43. Londa Schiebinger, *The Mind Has No Sex? Women in the Origins of Modern Science* (Cambridge: Harvard UP), 184–85.
44. Ibid., 195. Chelselden's anatomical works were widely published in the United States. For example, see his 1796 *Anatomical Tables of the Human Body* published by Manning and Loring in Boston.
45. Schiebinger 190–91.
46. Johann Friedrich Blumenbach, *Elements of Physiology*, trans. Charles Caldwell (Philadelphia: T. Dobson, 1795), 111. This text was translated by a Philadelphia physician who later became the editor of the *Port Folio* magazine after Joseph Dennie's death.
47. Ibid., 113.
48. Ibid., 111–12.
49. Ibid., 133.
50. Ibid., 135.
51. "General Remarks on Women," *Massachusetts Magazine* 6 (January 1794): 20.
52. Lavater 459.
53. Ibid., 249.
54. Ibid., 399.

55. "Adelaide; or the Lovely Rustick," *Massachusetts Magazine* 2 (April 1790): 195.

56. "The Accomplished Female Character," *Massachusetts Magazine* 4 (April 1792): 223.

57. Ibid., 222.

58. "On the Fair Sex," *Massachusetts Magazine* 2 (January 1790): 55.

59. "On the Happy Influence arising from FEMALE SOCIETY," *Massachusetts Magazine* 7 (July 1795): 222.

60. Ibid., 220.

61. Ibid., 221, emphasis mine.

62. Ibid., 220.

63. Ibid., 221.

64. William Alexander, *The History of Women, from the Earliest Antiquity* (1782; rpt. Bristol: Thoemmes P, 1995), 492–93.

65. Ibid., 493.

66. "Description of the Moorish Women," *Massachusetts Magazine* 7 (October 1795): 420.

67. "The Family Economy and Employments of the Gypsies," *Massachusetts Magazine* 2 (November/December 1790): 679–80.

68. Ibid., 721

69. "Essay on Female Charms," *Massachusetts Magazine* 5 (July 1793): 389.

70. Ibid., 390.

71. In 1762, Rousseau composed a libretto titled "Pygmalion" with Horace Coignet providing the orchestral accompaniment. "Pygmalion" was first given as a private performance in 1770 in Lyon and "enjoyed several highly successful revivals in Italy and in German-speaking lands," as well as a performance in Paris (Jean-Jacques Rousseau, *Pygmalion* [Milan: Casa Ricordi, 1996], lxxvi). Coignet's score was replaced with one by Franz Aspelmayr for the Vienna production in 1772, and the libretto was published that same year. Although it is unknown whether or not Americans knew of Rousseau's libretto, it is interesting to note the popularity of the Pygmalion story in contemporary Europe.

72. "The New Pygmalion," *Massachusetts Magazine* 2 (October 1790): 579.

73. While it is interesting to note (both within and without *The Massachusetts Magazine*) that Judith Sargent Murray advocated a much more rigorous type of education for women, she also emphasized the need for bodily surveillance and regulation. Indeed, as already noted, she

advocates an educational system that focuses equally on a *social* and a rational education for women—a system that emphasizes "new technologies of vision" that would enable women to read others correctly—thus avoiding costly mistakes in judgment. See Reed dissertation, 151–211.

74. "The New Pygmalion," 580.

75. Ibid., 649.

76. Ibid., 720.

Frank Shuffelton

Binding Ties

Thomas Jefferson, Francis Hopkinson, and the Representation of the *Notes on the State of Virginia*

I

In the 1780s the crucial issue for the new United States was union, how to preserve and strengthen the connections between the states, loosely held together by the Articles of Confederation. With the successful termination of the War for Independence, the thirteen states had no external enemy to force on them a compelling need for joint defense, but by the end of the decade delegates from the states had met in convention and drafted a constitution that, once ratified by nine states, authorized a new government to begin operation in the spring of 1789. The story of how this happened has been told and analyzed often, but the tenuous, contingent nature of the new constitutional union is less often noted in popular, celebratory accounts.[1] When the new Congress assembled in March and April of 1789, for example, Rhode Island still had not made up its mind to ratify the Constitution and subscribe to the new distribution of power and political ties; it would come into the union only in late May of 1790, after Congress, now with representatives from the twelve ratifying states, threatened to embargo all trade with Rhode Island. Opponents of the constitution might have sensed in all this a confirmation of their fear, portrayed satirically in 1787 by federalist Francis Hopkinson, that the constitutional roof over the states was framed to "stand independent of the walls; and that in time the walls might crumble away, and the roof remain suspended in air, threatening destruction to all that should come under it."[2] The anti-federalists, however, missed a cultural shift that Hopkinson, who was not only a signer of the Declaration of Independence but a poet, composer, and journalist, recognized more clearly in the post-Revolutionary years.

The constitutional union of 1789 was a political and legal achievement that accompanied and in many ways subtly depended on the ongoing process of creating a common civic understanding that might be understood, to use Jack P. Greene's phrase, as "the intellectual construction of America."[3] In the course of the eighteenth century, a variety of cultural phenomena reached across boundaries as the individual colonies, quite different in their seventeenth-century foundings, became more and more alike. The colonies came to identify themselves as participants in the British empire, and they sought to create within their own domains a culture modeled on the values of the metropole.[4] When it came time to resist British dominion, as John Murrin has pointed out, "public life in America was so thoroughly British, the colonists resisted Britain with all the available weapons of eighteenth-century politics—ideology, law, petitions, assembly resolves, grassroots political organizations, disciplined crowd violence."[5] The periodical press was one important medium, perhaps the most important medium, through which the colonies participated in the Atlantic culture of the British Empire and also shared with each other their emerging cultural self-understanding. The spread of newspapers and magazines supported a shared sense of Britishness, in part by allowing Americans to share the experience of magazine reading that was becoming a hallmark of gentility and in part by reprinting material that had originally appeared in British magazines. At the same time, however, the spread of periodical literature fed a growing recognition of shared American differences from the British model as editors sought to speak to an increasingly national readership.[6]

These differences became more powerful as they were identified with affection, with feelings identifying with local landscapes, local communities, and family. If the British Empire was mostly a grand idea for most residents of the thirteen colonies, America was right outside the door, where people lived and died. The Revolution itself intensified feelings of Americanness as men and women experienced the whole range of consequences of independence—at the same time, many of those most committed to the imperial model left the country as loyalist exiles. The Declaration of Independence, which had forthrightly asserted, on rather flimsy grounds and all too brief experience, the existence of the United States, in its last words had promised the support of the signers as individuals based on their "Lives, Fortunes, and our sacred Honor." By the end of the 1780s, John Jay, writing as Publius in the *Federalist*, could imagine the union as "an inheritance so proper and convenient for a band of brethren, united to each other by the strongest ties."[7] The United States evolved from textual fantasy and legal fiction because of the lived experience of many Americans but also because of the elaboration of it as a political, factual possibility in the writings that appeared in pamphlets and periodicals. And, as Jay's language suggests, this evolution accompanied the development of public affections that were based on private feelings of individuals.

The periodicals were in a privileged position to elaborate the new national identity for at least three reasons: first, they expressed the continuity of colonial and early national culture as also a continuity of essentially British literary and social values. No American magazine publisher or editor was unaware of the models laid down by Addison and Steele, Johnson, and the *Gentleman's Magazine*, and republican politeness reflected the values of the world represented in British periodicals. They were business projects intended to show a profit, although few ever did, and often were editorial collectives of writers who appeared in public as individuals but shared ties of friendship in private. Second, they acted out one of the crucial roles of independence: to take part in the affairs and in the imagination of the larger world. European anecdotes and oriental tales were an expression of American independence, implicitly asserting the right, as the Declaration of Independence had claimed in its first sentence, of a people "to assume among the Powers of the earth, the separate and equal station to which the Laws of Nature and of Nature's God entitle them." An equal people has the same rights to be curious and knowledgeable about the rest of the world as that world has to be curious about it. Finally, American periodical publications devoted considerable space to local creations, to travels, histories, ethnographies, political debates, and literary productions that in their various ways defined America for the reader.

One of the notable local creations in the 1780s was Thomas Jefferson's *Notes on the State of Virginia*, which carried America's case to the scientific world of Europe and also argued for crucial reforms yet to be accomplished in the American states. It envisioned a future at once full of economic promise and expanding liberty, yet in perhaps in his most quintessentially American move Jefferson undermined the largest dimensions of his republican vision with racist language that contradicted his call for the end of slavery. Focused on the particular situation of Virginia, Jefferson wrote synecdochally about America at large, and his work captured the attention of readers on both sides of the Atlantic. His original intention had been to seriously restrict the circulation of *Notes on the State of Virginia*, but it escaped into the public domain with a British edition in 1787 and an American edition in the following year. Previous to the 1788 American printing in Philadelphia by Prichard and Hall and just after, significant sections of the book had been extracted in American periodicals. If Jefferson's text seemed impersonal and objective in its form and tone, it grew out of intense emotional upheavals in his own life. And just as many magazines reflected the work of groups of literary friends, Jefferson's text developed by means of epistolary inquiries shared among friends and acquaintances, and its first presentation to the American public in the form of extracts printed in periodicals was sponsored by a friend. The initial appearance of an extract from *Notes on the State of Virginia* came out of a friendship at once deeply personal in its implications for author, editor, and public in its enlightened cultural dimensions for its citizen readers. Jefferson's *Notes on the State of Virginia*, in other words, came out of a milieu of private feeling to become a moment of national self-definition. It is worthwhile to explore the modulation from private to public in Jefferson's life, and the role of American magazines in the late 1780s in mediating this as a model of citizenship.

II

The decade of the 1780s opened with political and personal catastrophes for Thomas Jefferson. In 1780 he had been elected to a second term as governor of Virginia, but in late December a British army under the command of Benedict Arnold invaded the state. The Virginia militia was unable to put up an effective resistance because of a shortage of men and supplies, and on June 4, 1781, two days after his term as governor had expired, Jefferson had to flee Monticello itself, only minutes ahead of Banastre Tarleton's troops. Eight days later the Virginia House of Delegates voted to conduct an inquiry into the actions the former governor Jefferson and his council took or failed to take in the face of the British invasion. Although the legislature in December 1781 unanimously voted "to obviate and remove all unmerited Censure" for his conduct as wartime governor, the charges of administrative incompetence were a serious and embarrassing blemish on Jefferson's record, one that Federalist opponents would throw in his face in later elections.[8] Although the charges did not seriously harm his standing with his fellow Virginians, Jefferson was clearly pained by the assault on his public self and temporarily withdrew from public life, partly in order to nurse his wounded self-esteem, partly to encounter a much more threatening family crisis.

The Virginia legislature's inquiry of 1781 merely challenged his public persona, but he suffered a much greater hurt in September 1782, when his wife died, following a difficult childbirth in the preceding May. Jefferson plunged into a grief so deeply felt that it occasioned concern among family and friends.[9] In the months before and after his wife's death, he wrote far fewer letters than usual; relieved from the demands of office, he found occasion to write scarcely a handful of letters on public business in 1782, and he was apparently too taken up with his wife's illness to carry on an extensive personal correspondence.[10] One of the few important letters in this period was a lengthy diatribe on public ingratitude that he sent to James Monroe on May 20 in which he claimed, "I examined well my heart to know whether it were thoroughly cured of every principle of political ambition, whether no lurking particle remained which might leave me uneasy when reduced within the limits of mere private life. I became satisfied that every fibre of that passion was thoroughly eradicated."[11] But if he had turned his back, as he professed, on public life, an act of public imagination still had its hold on his private consciousness.

Sometime in the latter half of 1780 Jefferson had received from François Marbois, the secretary of the French legation in Philadelphia, a list of questions concerning conditions in Virginia. He had begun to think about these queries by November 1780, when he informed a correspondent, "I am at present busily employed for Monsr. Marbois . . . and have to acknolege to him the mysterious obligation for making me much better acquainted with my own country than I ever was before."[12] When Benedict Arnold's invasion of Virginia began a month later, Jefferson was forced to set aside this project, which he took up again only in the following summer after his term as governor had expired. Working under the shadow of possible public disgrace, Jefferson completed a first draft of his answers to Marbois in the seclusion of Poplar Forest, the estate in Bedford County that later became his customary refuge when he felt Monticello was too crowded with family and visitors. On December 20, 1781, he sent off the manuscript of what had become *Notes on the State of Virginia*, although as he explained to the legation secretary, it was "very imperfect and not worth offering but as proof of my respect for your wishes."[13] Jefferson, however, invited Marbois to show the manuscript to Charles Thomson, the secretary of Congress and a member of the American Philosophical Society, to which Jefferson had recently been elected. On the same day he also wrote to Thomson, explaining that as a recently elected counselor, it had occurred to him that some of the material he had written up for Marbois "might, if more fully handled, be a proper tribute to the Philosophical society." He went on ask Thomson as an old friend to look over the manuscript and send on his opinions as to its suitability. The day before writing to Thomson and Marbois, Jefferson had sent off a note to George Rogers Clark asking for teeth from the great animals whose remains had been found in Kentucky, and a few days after this he wrote to Isaac Zane in search of information on a variety of other subjects. James Madison wrote in the following April, "I intreat you will not suffer the chance of a speedy and final determination of the territorial question by Congress to affect your purpose of tracing the title of Virg[ini]a to her claims . . . [For] it is proper to be armed with every argument and document that can vindicate her title."[14] As Jefferson developed his argument in *Notes on the State of Virginia*, however, he went far beyond Madison's parochial interest in legitimating state boundaries, and he constructed an argument for America at large against the pretensions of European history and science. *Notes on the State of Virginia* would thus ultimately reach out to a national community, but it nevertheless gestated within a circle of Jefferson's mostly Virginian friends who were concerned both with issues of knowledge and science and also with their participation as informed citizens of the new nation.

Although Jefferson wrote little in the summer of 1782, during his wife's final illness, he was receiving answers to his inquiries for further information, and he began to revise and enlarge his manuscript in the months after her death. His "Advertisement" placed at the head of the 1787 London edition of *Notes on the State of Virginia* quietly alludes to his troubled state of mind; regretting the imperfect treatment of many of the subjects, he concludes, "To apologize for this by developing the circumstances of the time and place of their composition, would be to open wounds which have already bled enough."[15] But the surviving letters of these months show Jefferson coming out of his grief and self-doubt as he took up again the imaginative demands of expanding the text of *Notes on the State of Virginia*. He informed the marquis de Chastellux on November 26, 1782, "your friendly letters. . . found me a little emerging from that stupor of mind which had rendered me as dead to the world as she was whose loss occasioned it. Your letter recalled to my memory, that there were persons still living of much value to me." Travel consequent on his recent appointment by Congress as one of the peace commissioners would bring him to Philadelphia, he said, where he looked forward "to learn the result of your observations on the Natural bridge, to communicate to you my answers to the queries of Monsr. de Marbois, to receive edification from you on these and on other subjects of science, considering chess too as a matter of science."[16]

In his bitter letter of May 20 to James Monroe, Jefferson had somewhat melodramatically claimed that his political misfortunes "had inflicted a wound on my spirit which will only be cured by the all-healing grave." Yet six months later, on the same day as the letter to Chastellux, he wrote in a different spirit to George Rogers Clark, who had sent him information on fossil bones in the West. Jefferson opened his letter with a paragraph on his scientific interests and his desire for information on the American West, but in the second half of the letter he addressed Clark's sensitivity to political criticism. Jefferson had by now been able to turn his own experience into consoling wisdom. "I perceive by your letter you are not unapprised that your services to your country have not made due impression on every mind. That you have enemies you must not doubt, when you reflect that you have made yourself eminent. If you meant to escape malice you should have confined yourself within the sleepy line of regular duty."[17] Jefferson's commitment to his *Notes on the State of Virginia* helped bring him back to the world of persons still living, to the world of intellectual friendship, of political reality. If the *Notes on the State of Virginia* would be recognized at the time of its publication three years later as salve for a wounded national self-esteem, smarting under the scientific critiques of Buffon and Raynal, at the time of its writing it was a means of comfort and therapy for Jefferson's own anguish over the death of his wife and the possible loss of political and civic credibility with the citizens of his own state.

III

Jefferson's troubled movement from public life to private reflection and then back to public involvement was mirrored by his uncertain and shifting opinions about the desirability of gaining a wide audience for the *Notes on the State of Virginia.* His initial audience was one man, Marbois, but he almost immediately thought of the whole membership of the American Philosophical Society as another possible audience. By January, 1784, he was cautioning Chastellux, "distrust information from my answers to Monsr. de Marbois' queries. I have lately had a little leisure to revise them. I found some things should be omitted, many corrected, and more supplied or enlarged. They are swelled nearly to treble bulk. Being now too much for M. S. copies, I think the ensuing spring to print a dozen or 20 copies to be given to friends, not suffering another to go out."[18] By the time he had arrived in Paris and arranged for the first printing by Philippe-Denis Pierres in 1785, he had enlarged his sense of his audience again and ordered two hundred copies; he had even begun, he wrote to Madison on May 11 of that year, to consider the idea of providing copies for the students of William and Mary College, "as well on account of the political as the physical parts."[19] Not even a month later, however, he was writing to Chastellux in a more cautious tone: "I am not afraid that you should make any extracts you please for the Journal de physique which come within their plan of publication. The strictures on slavery and on the constitution of Virginia are not of that kind, and they are the parts which I do not wish to have made public, at least till I know whether their publication would do most harm or good."[20]

Jefferson's vacillation about the appropriate audience for the *Notes on the State of Virginia* suggests an author unsure of his standing with his native society, his audience in its broader sense as opposed to the more-restricted audience that might be controlled by a private, limited distribution of his book. This seems to be an author unsure of his imaginative and moral authority because the material he wishes to limit to a select circle of readers relates to questions that he thought might be still open for consideration in the Virginia legislature. Jefferson obviously feared that his arguments for a new, more republican constitution might hinder efforts in that direction because his support might be as likely to provoke opposition as agreement; similarly his desire to repress his criticism of slavery points to a belief that something might be done in that regard as well. At the same time, the 1785 letter to Chastellux points toward a possible way to introduce his text to a wider readership by allowing extracts to be printed in a periodical, assuming that he can control which passages might be chosen. Despite Jefferson's anxieties about his audience at home, he would nevertheless find a wide and appreciative readership in the years before he left Paris, and by the time he arrived back in America he would have felt there was a recovery of his civic authority not simply in Virginia but in the nation at large. This recovery was certainly grounded in his work in Congress before he left and in his career as minister in Paris, but it was also furthered by recognition of his *Notes on the State of Virginia* as an American book and not merely as a book about Virginia. The interest from the *Journal de Physique* points toward a wider interest in Jefferson's text, and his recognition in America would be significantly encouraged by the publication of extracts from his book in American periodicals.

Just as Jefferson's creation of *Notes on the State of Virginia* drew on his epistolary community of friends, so in the distribution of his text friends would play a significant role. When he began to send out copies of his new book, he wrote nearly the same inscription on each flyleaf. A typical example written early in July 1785 reads, "Th. Jefferson having had a few copies of these notes printed to offer to some of his friends, and to some other estimable characters beyond that line, takes the liberty of presenting a copy to Mr. Hopkinson as a testimony of the esteem in which he bears him. Unwilling to expose them to the public eye, he asks the favor of Mr. Hopkinson to put them into the hands of no person on whose care and fidelity he cannot rely, to guard them against publication."[21] Francis Hopkinson, the recipient, was a Philadelphian, a fellow signer of the Declaration, a poet, a composer, a lawyer, an inventor, and a member of the American Philosophical Society. Jefferson had been on friendly terms with Hopkinson since 1776, but he had actively corresponded with him only since December 1783. When Congress moved to Annapolis in that year, Jefferson needed someone to care for his daughter Polly, who had been staying with him, and the Hopkinsons took her into their own home. Sharing his daughter with the Hopkinson family established a new level of intimacy and friendship that revealed itself in the correspondence between the two men.

The ensuing correspondence between the two men brimmed over with their shared interests in music, science, literature, and politics. On January 4, 1784, Hopkinson sent off a high-spirited missive, reading Buffon's system of astronomy as political allegory and including a "Literary Christmas Gambol," a whimsical experiment in picture writing. Jefferson responded with a bit of whimsy of his own, speculating about the revolutionary possibilities of balloons as a possible means for Congress to move about the country. The closeness of the two men at this time is suggested by Hopkinson's apparent awareness that Jefferson was thinking about Buffon's application of natural history to human populations and by Jefferson's willingness to give a rare flash of humor in a letter. A year later Jefferson, by then in Paris as the U.S. minister, wrote to Hopkinson, complaining of "the dearth of American intelligence in which we live here. I had formed no conception of it. We might as well be in the moon."[22] Their further correspondence in the years in which Jefferson was in Paris cover a variety of topics such that if one indexed them, they might seem to resemble the contents of one of the magazines of the time. Hopkinson had invented an improved method for quilling harpsichords, and he was eager for Jefferson to assist him in introducing the idea to European harpsichord makers. Other correspondence from Hopkinson included political news, information about the doings of the Philosophical Society, and the health of their mutual friends Benjamin Franklin and David Rittenhouse, and it occasionally accompanied packets of recent newspapers.[23] Taken all together, the Jefferson-Hopkinson correspondence began to resemble the contents of a magazine, which would appeal to shared cultural interests of readers dispersed in space, unlike those of a newspaper who more typically shared an interest in a locality.

Hopkinson was not the only American friend to whom Jefferson lamented his "dearth of American intelligence," and the letters and newspapers represented only a minor strand in the epistolary network Jefferson acquired during his stay in France. Correspondents such as Hopkinson, however, represented an important means through which Jefferson was able to reassert his presence in American intellectual and political life. Hopkinson, moreover, performed an important service in seeing that the *Notes on the State of Virginia* gained a wider audience. In his letter acknowledging receipt of his copy of the book, he assured Jefferson, "I shall be careful to observe your Instruction in the blank leaf of your Notes." Jefferson's inscription did not forbid private circulation of the volume, however, and on December 31, 1785, Hopkinson remarked, "I have lent your Notes on Virginia to some friends, under the Restrictions you prescribed. They have been instructed and improved by them, and speak highly in Commendation."[24] Gratifying as this praise might have been to Jefferson, if he still wished to restrict the circulation of *Notes on the State of Virginia*, he might have been made somewhat anxious by Hopkinson's subsequent letter, which suggested that copies be sent to the Philosophical Society and the Philadelphia library in order to make it available to a wider audience. Hopkinson's was not the only voice raised in praise of the *Notes on the State of Virginia;* interest was growing, and in September 1785, Jefferson wrote Madison, "I have been obliged to give so many of them here that I fear their getting published."[25] Early in 1786 he learned that his fears were all too real; the French bookseller Barrois had obtained a copy and planned an unauthorized translation. He managed to regain some control over his text by agreeing to their translation by the Abbé Morellet, a friend of Franklin's and the translator of Beccaria. Unsatisfied with Morellet's version, however, and aware that control of his text was slipping away from him, he agreed at last to an English edition to be published in 1787 by the London bookseller John Stockdale.[26]

Hopkinson had at about the same time become interested in a pair of monthly magazines published in Philadelphia, the *Columbian Magazine: or, Monthly Miscellany* and the *American Museum, or, Universal Magazine.* He edited the *Columbian Magazine* briefly in 1787 and was on close terms with Mathew Carey, whose *American Museum* published four pieces by him in its first number.[27] In November 1786 he sent Jefferson the first two numbers of the *Columbian Magazine,* mentioning that he had taken out a subscription for him. Carey may have been one of the friends who had borrowed Hopkinson's copy of the *Notes on the State of Virginia* because in the March 1787 issue of the *American Museum* the anonymous author of an essay on American genius praised Jefferson's refutation in the *Notes on the State of Virginia* of theories of American degeneracy, urging that "His observations particularly on the writings of the abbe Raynal, and the count de Buffon, relative to America, deserve publication."[28] In the same month Hopkinson, now beginning his short term as editor of the *Columbian Magazine,* began to publish selections from *Notes on the State of Virginia,* thus breaking with Jefferson's request not to publish extracts and opening the way to further publication in most of the other major American magazines of the time.

Hopkinson took his authorization to print on assumption rather than by request, for he did not inform Jefferson about his actions until April 14, 1787. Even then, he was tacitly evasive about what he had actually done, telling Jefferson that he had become the editor of the *Columbian Magazine* and that in the April issue, "I shall take the Liberty of giving an Extract from your valuable Notes on Virginia, respecting the Comparative Size of European and American Animals. I hope this will not displease you."[29] In fact, the first extract had already appeared in the March issue, reprinting all of Query V under the title "Account of Remarkable Cascades and Caverns in the State of Virginia; from a Work not yet Published." Hopkinson, to his credit, did not attach Jefferson's name to the work until the April issue, by which time he had managed to get his letter of explanation on the way. By mid-June of 1787 Joel Barlow, another recipient of a presentation copy of *Notes on the State of Virginia* was writing to Jefferson, "Your Notes on Virginia are getting into the Gazettes in different States, notwithstanding you request that they should not be published here." Nevertheless, Barlow went on to say, "We are flattered with the idea of seeing ourselves vindicated from these despicable aspersions which have long been thrown upon us and echoed from one ignorant Scribbler to another in all the languages of Europe."[30] By that time extracts from *Notes on the State of Virginia* had appeared in the *New-Haven*

Gazette, and the Connecticut Magazine (May 3, 1787) and a second selection in the May issue of the *Columbian Magazine.* Further magazine selections would appear in the months to come, suggesting or establishing a market for a larger publication; in the following year the first American edition appeared in Philadelphia. Jefferson's private work of collecting knowledge in order to assuage his grief became at this point fully public, a sign identifying him to an American readership as much as it was the intervention into the public sphere for which he had perhaps all along secretly hoped.

IV

Barlow's pleasure in feeling vindicated from European aspersions on America echoed the feelings of many of Jefferson's other American readers. Jefferson was the first American of genuine intellectual standing to offer a full-length refutation of the degeneracy theory of European natural historians.[31] Like the anonymous author in the *American Museum* noted above, his countrymen responded gratefully to his reasoned attack on the theories of De Pauw, Raynal, and Buffon concerning the degeneration of all natural forms, including man, in the New World because of the supposedly unhealthful environment. A desire to assert the grandeur of American landscape and American nature guided Hopkinson and other magazine editors when they chose which sections of the *Notes on the State of Virginia* to extract. Thus, the first extract in the *Columbian Magazine* included the now-famous description of the Natural Bridge, and the April 1787 issue reprinted the passage on the comparative sizes of European and American animals from Query VI, "Productions, Mineral, Vegetable, and Animal," including Jefferson's speculations on mammoths.[32] the *New-Haven Gazette, and the Connecticut Magazine* for April 26, 1787, opened with the description of the passage of the Potomac River through the Blue Ridge at Harper's Ferry and also added the description of the Natural Bridge and part of the passage on animal sizes. A week later it offered more on animals, the speech of Logan, and Jefferson's defense of American genius in the persons of Washington, Franklin, and Rittenhouse.[33] Out of the sixteen extracts from *Notes on the State of Virginia* printed before Jefferson returned from France in 1789, nine came from Queries IV, V, and VI, where he is most obviously countering degeneration theorists, and most of these came from the long, densely factual Query VI.

By the time Joel Barlow wrote to Jefferson about the gazette appearances of the *Notes on the State of Virginia,* there were seven instances of extracts, and all were from the queries on natural history. Extracts appearing later in 1787 as well as in 1788 and 1789 were more often drawn from six other queries dealing with subjects other than natural history. The *Columbian Magazine,* now under the editorship of Alexander James Dallas, continued to extract passages from the natural history queries in the issues for May, July, and August. During these same months the Constitutional Convention, called to address the by-now-obvious failure of the Articles of Confederation, met and deliberated in secrecy. The extracts asserting American power, grandeur, and strength were obviously appropriate for a readership anxious about national weakness, fragmentation, and decay and waiting expectantly to hear what the convention would produce. The *American Museum* author of March 1787, after praising Jefferson's refutation of Buffon, had gone on to editorialize, "The time has come, to explode the European creed, that we are infantine in our acquisitions, and savage in our manners, because we are inhabitants of a new world lately occupied by a race of savages."[34] In the inaugural issue of the *American Museum* two months earlier, Benjamin Rush had contributed a notable essay "On the Defects of the Confederation." There he had proclaimed, "The American war is over: but this is far from being the case with the American revolution . . . It remains yet to establish and perfect our new forms of government: and to prepare the principles, morals, and manners of our citizens, for the forms of government, after they are established and brought to perfection."[35] Rush's opening shot in the struggle to create a new and revolutionary form of government for the United States in effect argued that the Articles of Confederation had to be discarded because they were undeveloped, appropriate to the childhood of a society and not to its maturity. In a word, they were "infantine," the term of European derogation the *American Museum* essayist two months later was so pleased to see Jefferson reject.

After the convention concluded its business in September and proposed the new constitution for ratification by the states, the extracts tended to reflect concerns about national defense, the presence of racial Others, and constitutional issues, all concerns central to the problem of constructing and preserving a nation. In November 1787, however, the *Columbian Magazine* extracted a passage from Query XXII regarding issues of defense and calling for a small naval force that would be sufficient to meet "an European enemy."[36] Two months later Noah Webster's *American Magazine* printed under the title "Eloquence of the Natives of This Country!" Jefferson's account of Logan and his speech and appended an editorial comment on Logan's rhetoric that admired its expression of "natural sentiment."[37] This extract perhaps reflected Webster's interest in native eloquence, but it also may have had implications for national defense by touching on anxieties relative to the contemporary threat posed by the Indians in the Ohio country. Material more directly related to constitutional questions included the *American Museum*'s reprint in November 1787 of the "Act for establishing religious freedom in Virginia," which had also appeared as an appendix to the 1787 edition of *Notes on the State of Virginia*. The *Columbian Magazine* for

February 1788 echoed Webster's editorial interest in native Americans in the January *American Magazine* by publishing two passages describing Jefferson's excavation of an Indian mound, and it also seconded the *American Museum*'s concern for individual rights by publishing all of Query XVII, "Religion," where Jefferson argued vigorously for the rights of conscience.[38] In the same month Webster in the *American Magazine* came back to Jefferson and *Notes on the State of Virginia* with "Mr. Jefferson's Arguments in favor of an Unalterable Constitution considered," although he seems to have somewhat misread Jefferson's Query XIII, "Constitution." Jefferson had argued that the Virginia Constitution was defective because it could be altered at the will of the legislature, thus potentially putting inordinate power in the hands of a relatively small number of men who might compose a quorum. Jefferson in fact had criticized the notion of an unalterable constitution, but Webster the federalist tried here to cast Jefferson as a member of the antifederalist camp of prominent Virginians such as Richard Henry Lee, George Mason, and Patrick Henry, further pointing out that the Virginia Constitution was "not shackled with a Bill of Rights."[39] The more important target for Webster in 1788 was Jefferson in the act of criticizing any constitution, Virginian or national, for the one was identified with the other, and Jefferson's thrust in Query XIII was to persuade Virginians to reject their 1776 constitution and draft a fully republican document.

Webster's strictures on Jefferson and the *Notes on the State of Virginia* signaled a new phase in its publication history and in the reconstruction of Jefferson as a public person. Where earlier extracts from the *Notes on the State of Virginia* were accompanied with praise for its author that represented perhaps the earliest contributions to the image of Jefferson as national icon, Webster welcomed him to the hurly-burly of a national public sphere that was contentious, divided, suspicious of motives. Jefferson had initially been hailed as the author of a national consensus, but Webster exposed the possibility of disruptive misreadings generated out of different perspectives. By focusing on Jefferson's ideas about constitutions, not the clearest chapter in *Notes on the State of Virginia* by any means, he at the same time targeted a site of contradiction and incompletion in Jefferson's own thinking that would trouble scholars and biographers in the future.[40] An additional site of Jeffersonian contradiction was unintentionally revealed in March 1788, when the *Columbian Magazine* printed "A Comparative View of the Faculties of Memory, Reason, and Imagination of Negroes," comprising some of the more racist paragraphs from Query XIV in *Notes on the State of Virginia*.[41] Nineteen months later when the *Massachusetts Magazine* printed passages from Queries VIII, XIV, and XVII, grouped under the title "Extracts on the Slave Trade. By request to the Editors to aid the cause of humanity," Jefferson was by contrast represented as a spokesman for the abolition of slavery.

The editors of the magazines that introduced Jefferson's *Notes on the State of Virginia* to the American reading public thus represented fragments that appeared to be increasingly contradictory and troubling as more and more of them appeared. Their selections on the one hand exposed rifts and aporias in Jefferson's self-construction as the author of *Notes on the State of Virginia*, but on the other hand they simply fulfilled the generic expectations of magazines that by their very nature printed in any given issue fragments and selections of quite different kinds of material. Heteroglossic collages that they were, these magazines at once expressed the eighteenth-century bourgeois public sphere in which any citizen could find a voice and also intimated the modernity that was emerging from the Revolutionary moment with its sense of exhilarating possibility and threatening alienation and disruption. The magazines curiously enough made the public image of Jefferson the author of *Notes on the State of Virginia* by unmaking him. He had assembled his text out of the fragments of information he had gleaned from his extensive library and from an array of citizen informants who corresponded with him. Beginning as fragments that Jefferson had to bring into order, *Notes on the State of Virginia* first appeared before the American public as a series of fragmentary extracts, as treasures from the Jefferson museum that signified a multiplicitous subject behind it.

The Thomas Jefferson represented by the varied extracts of his work that were published in the magazines emerged as the figurative first citizen of the republic. Washington, the universally respected figure of virtue and wisdom, admirably filled the role of an idealized father of his country, a role that demanded him only to be benignly visible and do nothing. Chair of the Constitutional Convention by acclaim, unanimously elected first president, he lost the aura lent by reputation and distance and became subject to criticism and dissent only when as president he was forced to speak out on issues and take sometimes unpopular actions. Jefferson as represented in the magazines became the first citizen by acting out in *Notes on the State of Virginia* and in the editor's selections from them the contradictions, possibilities, and fantasies of the citizen readers of the periodical press. Washington represented to Americans a fantasy of their own virtue, but Jefferson represented to them their very real uncertainties, possibilities, and endless variety. Ironically, Washington, the man of action, became in the popular imagination the passive republican version of the Patriot King, patriotic because of his reluctance to interfere in the legislative body. Jefferson, the man of books, became a chief agent in the intellectual construction of America by representing the possibility of a democratic individual to continually reinvent himself.[42]

V

When Jefferson was severely criticized for his management of the Virginia governorship in 1781, he threatened to withdraw from public life, but in the years after 1789 he faced down political attacks and slanders, although as his letters show controversy and invective continued to pain him. He was at the center of increasingly tense political struggles in the 1790s, and as president he faced continuing hostility from Federalist politicians, clergy, and press. He maintained an equanimity that had been difficult for him earlier in part because of the new public self that he had first constructed for himself as author of *Notes on the State of Virginia* and that the editors of the magazines had in turn constructed for him.[43] Certainly, Jefferson's successful conduct of his ministry in France had gone far to repair any political damage that might have attached to his conduct in the governor's office, but the dissemination of the *Notes on the State of Virginia* played a significant role in restoring his imaginative and moral authority as a leader by identifying him as the author of his text at a time when the nation's other great political authors were taking an anonymous stand behind the text of the Constitution.

Both *Notes on the State of Virginia* and the new constitution announced to the world that the United States signified an expansive and not a degenerate society, or so Hopkinson and other readers of the *Notes on the State of Virginia* took them to be. However, Jefferson's later poise in public office when attacked by political enemies resulted from successfully grounding his one published book in circles of private friendship that fed the text in its beginnings and guided its representation as it became known to a wider public. With *Notes on the State of Virginia* and its insertion into the world of liberal discourse represented by the magazines, Jefferson created an organic relationship between his private and public selves that mirrored a mature understanding of the limits of human life. His vision of self and text appeared in the well-known letter of September 6, 1789, when he responded to the proposed constitution in a letter to James Madison by contending "that the earth belongs in usufruct to the living," that no generation of men has the power to bind the next to come.[44] Jefferson had produced the text of *Notes on the State of Virginia* out of private emotional distress, nourished it through the intimacy of friendship, and finally maintained and then relinquished control of his literary property as befitted an individual citizen of the republic he wished to construct. Grief that brought his world to a stop became a recognition of the horizons of a man's life, of a generation's power. The dissemination of his text through the magazines' extracts mediated and facilitated his coming to terms with entanglements between the intimate world of love and friendship and a contentious public life.

To read the *Notes on the State of Virginia* as a quasi-constitutional docu ment, or for that matter as one whose central interest was in refuting Buffon, important as that was to Jefferson, is then subtly to misread it by reducing it to an uncomplicated text whose ultimate "message" is in its content rather than in its mode of presentation. Misreading a text such as *Notes on the State of Virginia* in this fashion is ultimately a failure to consider contexts, to read without considering the tensions and contingencies of the text but also without considering the larger arc of the author's life. The editors of the magazines who extracted Jefferson's *Notes on the State of Virginia*, and in the process brought it more widely to public attention, also were guilty of encouraging such misreading by implicitly allowing each diverse fragment to stand for "Mr. Jefferson's opinion." The magazines' procedure of extracting, taken as a whole over the period between the *Columbian Magazine*'s first selection and the American publication of the full text in book form, managed to present some of the discursive possibilities of *Notes on the State of Virginia*, but on an issue-by-issue basis the magazines falsified a revolutionary text by incorporating it into the rites of upper middle class culture that they embodied. Jefferson's *Notes on the State of Virginia* simultaneously performed self-construction, an act of private friendship, and a public service, and Jefferson refused to have his intellectual liberty constrained by being forced to choose a single voice or an uncomplicated position that merely satisfied polite (or not so polite) expectations.

Francis Hopkinson, for example, was in a favored position to give a sophisticated reading of *Notes on the State of Virginia*—he was an important member in Jefferson's circle of friends who were involved in producing the text—but even he missed the complexity of *Notes on the State of Virginia* because he assumed it and the man behind it had a relatively simple position to stake out that was not all that different from his own. Himself a supporter of the new constitution, he was pained to hear reports that Jefferson had become an anti-federalist; Jefferson replied by asserting, "I am not a Federalist, because I never submitted the whole system of my opinions to the creed of any party of men whatever in religion, in philosophy, in politics, or in anything else where I was capable of thinking for myself. Such an addiction is the last degradation of a free and moral agent. If I could not go to heaven but with a party, I would not go there at all. Therefore I protest to you I am not of the party of federalists. But I am much further from that of the Antifederalists."[45] Having thus proclaimed his intellectual independence, however, Jefferson went on to explain his thoughts on the Constitution and to measure the distance between his opinions and those of his countrymen on some issues. He concluded, however, that the whole text be kept fluid and changeable, although "since the thing is established, I would wish it not to be altered during the life of our great leader, whose executive talents are superior to those I believe of any man in the world, and who alone by the authority of his name and the confidence reposed in his perfect integrity, is fully qualified to put the new government so under way as to secure it against the efforts of opposition. But having derived from our error all the good there was in it I hope we shall correct it the moment we can no longer have the same name at the helm."[46] Writing to a former editor, Jefferson, who once chafed visibly as Congress revised his Declaration of Independence, seems to have fully imbibed the editorial spirit, that is, that all texts can be revised, recut, improved.

As it turned out, the only correction to the Constitution that came during Jefferson's presidency resulted from the circumstances of his own election in 1800. When he and his running mate Aaron Burr received the same number of electoral votes, the decision was thrown into the House of Representatives, and only after thirty-six ballots was the election decided in his favor. The Twelfth Amendment, ratified in 1804, provided for separate ballots for president and vice-president and prevented future confusion of this sort. The next correction to the Constitution, the Thirteenth Amendment, which abolished slavery, was not ratified until December 1865. It corrected both a national contradiction and one inherent in *Notes on the State of Virginia* that the editors of the magazines had exposed when in separate extracts they printed Jefferson's racist speculations and his opposition to slavery. In the years after the 1788 printing of the full text of Jefferson's book and after his return to the United States in 1789, his position as a public figure was assured, and magazines and newspapers blossomed with selected bits from *Notes on the State of Virginia* and his other writings. Earlier appearances in the press tended to emphasize his role as governor of Virginia and as a transmitter of information, as with the *United States Magazine*'s printing in June 1779 of his report on George Rogers Clark's victory at Vincennes. Later extracts and quotations were used for more political, ideological purposes by allies and opponents alike. Thus, an extract from Jefferson's letter of December 20, 1787, to James Madison criticizing features of the new Constitution, particularly the failure to limit the president's time in office, appeared under the title of "Remarks on the Constitution of the United States" in Philadelphia's *Universal Asylum, and Columbian Magazine* of October 1792. Whether inserted by Jefferson himself or by Madison as another example of politics grounded on friendship, the point of the 1792 publication was to criticize the growing tendency toward what Jefferson called monarchism that he ascribed to the emerging Federalist party. Surely an index of the increasingly tense partisan atmosphere of the 1790s, this extract and others like it signal the presence on the national scene of Jefferson the citizen, whose private opinions had possible public significance. If citizenship is primarily exercised in the political sphere, it can also be, and in Jefferson's case was, a creation of the public sphere of print.[47]

If the publication and dissemination of *Notes on the State of Virginia* helped lead Jefferson back into American public life, he never gave up his grounding in privacy and intimacy, although he significantly reinterpreted his life there. He concluded his letter of March 13, 1789, to Hopkinson, the first American who broke his restrictions on publication of *Notes on the State of Virginia*, by remarking, "My great wish is to go on in a strict but silent performance of my duty; to avoid attracting notice & to keep my name out of newspapers, because I find the pain of a little censure, even when it is unfounded, is more acute than the pleasure of much praise."[48] Where silence and retreat had marked his near breakdown after the death of his wife, silence now became the scene of creativity, where his most important work was given its ultimate shape in a reconstructed private self. *Notes on the State of Virginia* is a preliminary sketch for an empire of liberty with its rich appreciation of the expansive, liberating possibilities of American life, but it is an empire of individual agents linked in webs of public duty and private affection.[49] Jefferson never criticized Hopkinson for ignoring his request to keep *Notes on the State of Virginia* among friends, never reprobated him for mistrusting him as merely another Virginian antifederalist, but his corrective to Hopkinson's misreading of him and of his text was guided by his friendship for him. A year later, after Hopkinson had suffered a minor stroke and began to think of his own mortality, his own final silence, Jefferson received the ultimate reward of publication in a remarkable expression of intimacy. Hopkinson wrote, "Be assured that I sincerely love and esteem you, and will tell you so more at large when I shall have recovered the use of my Pen. I have but few words to spare. If I had but Six left three of them should be spent in saying I love you."[50]

Notes

1. Standard accounts of constitutional formation that reveal its complexity include Jack N. Rakove, *Original Meanings: Politics and Ideas in the Making of the Constitution* (New York: Knopf, 1996) and Gordon S. Wood, *The Creation of the American Republic, 1776–1787* (Chapel Hill: U of North Carolina P, 1969). Susan Manning's *Fragments of Union: Making Connections in Scottish and American Writing* (New York: Palgrave, 2002) explores the issue of fragmentation and unity as a persistent theme in American culture.
2. Francis Hopkinson, "The New Roof," in *Comical Spirit of Seventy-Six: The Humor of Francis Hopkinson*, ed. Paul M. Zall (San Marino: Huntington Library, 1976), 190. In this essay lowercase *federalist* denotes supporters of the Constitution of 1788, while uppercase *Federalist* indicates supporters of the party that emerged in the 1790s in opposition to the Jeffersonians.
3. Jack P. Greene, *The Intellectual Construction of America* (Chapel Hill: U of North Carolina P, 1993).

4. The work of David S. Shields has been exemplary here, particularly for the pre-Revolutionary era. See his *Oracles of Empire: Poetry, Politics, and Commerce in British America* (Chicago: U of Chicago P, 1990) and *Civil Tongues and Polite Letters in British America* (Chapel Hill: U of North Carolina P, 1997). See also Richard Bushman, *The Refinement of America: Persons, Places, Houses* (New York: Knopf, 1992), for the period of the early republic.

5. John Murrin, "A Roof without Walls: The Dilemma of American National Identity," in *Beyond Confederation: Origins of the Constitution and American National Identity*, ed. Richard Beeman, Stephen Botein, and Edward C. Carter II. (Chapel Hill: U. of North Carolina P, 1987), 340.

6. For further discussion on how American periodicals sought to distinguish themselves from their European counterparts, see Mark Kamrath, "*Eyes Wide Shut* and the Cultural Poetics of Eighteenth-Century American Periodical Literature," *Early American Literature* 37 (2002): 497–536.

7. John Jay, Federalist no. 2, in *The Federalist*, ed. Jacob Cooke (Middletown, CT: Wesleyan UP, 1961), 9.

8. Dumas Malone, *Jefferson the Virginian* (Boston: Little, Brown, 1948), 361–69, covers the investigation and its later consequences.

9. Malone suggests (397–98) that Jefferson's personal grief swallowed up his sense of injury over the outcome of his governorship and made him the readier to return to public life. But see Fawn Brodie, *Thomas Jefferson, an Intimate History* (New York: Norton, 1974), and Andrew Burstein, *The Inner Jefferson: Portrait of a Grieving Optimist* (Charlottesville: UP of Virginia, 1995), on the depth of Jefferson's grief.

10. The authoritative edition of Jefferson's writings includes only eight letters from him in the second half of 1782. He did not start his Summary Letter Journal until 1783, so there may have been a few that did not survive. See Julian Boyd, Foreword, *The Papers of Thomas Jefferson*, ed. Julian Boyd et al. (Princeton: Princeton UP, 1950–), 6:vii–x.

11. *Papers of Thomas Jefferson*, 6, 184.

12. Ibid., 4:168.

13. Ibid., 6:142.

14. Ibid., 6:142, 139, 143–44, 176.

15. Jefferson, *Notes on the State of Virginia*, ed. Frank Shuffelton (New York: Penguin, 1999), 2.

16. Jefferson, *Papers*, 6:203.

17. Jefferson to Monroe, *Papers*, 6:185; to Clark, *Papers*, 6:204–5.

18. Jefferson to Chastellux, *Papers,* 6:647.

19. Jefferson to Madison, *Papers,* 8:147.

20. Jefferson to Chastellux, *Papers,* 8:184. In this letter he spells out more specifically his plans for distributing the book to the students but decides to wait.

21. Coolie Verner, "Mr. Jefferson Distributes His *Notes:* A Preliminary Checklist of First Editions," *Bulletin of the New York Public Library* 56 (1952): 159–86.

22. Jefferson to Hopkinson, *Papers,* 7. 602.

23. On Hopkinson's correspondence with Jefferson, see George Everett Hastings, *The Life and Works of Francis Hopkinson* (Chicago: U of Chicago P, 1926), 341–56.

24. Hopkinson to Jefferson, *Papers* 8:562; 9:132.

25. Jefferson to Madison, *Papers,* 8:462. For Hopkinson's letter suggesting placement in libraries, see 9:320.

26. On Morellet and his translation, see Dorothy Medlin, "Thomas Jefferson, André Morellet, and the French Version of *Notes on the State of Virginia,*" *William and Mary Quarterly* 35 (1978): 85–99.

27. For Hopkinson's publications in these magazines, see Hastings 434–35; for his involvement with the *Columbian,* see William J. Free, *The Columbian Magazine and American Literary Imagination* (The Hague: Mouton, 1968), 28–31.

28. *American Museum, or, Universal Magazine* 1 (March 1787): 206. The same issue also printed diplomatic correspondence to and from Jefferson.

29. Hopkinson to Jefferson, *Papers,* 11:289–90.

30. Barlow to Jefferson, *Papers,* 11:473. Barlow here implies newspaper publication as well as magazine appearances, but the latter is the principal concern.

31. Edwin T. Martin, *Thomas Jefferson: Scientist* (New York: H. Schuman, 1952), 162. For the history of degeneracy theory, see Antonello Gerbi, *The Dispute of the New World: The History of a Polemic, 1750–1900* (Pittsburgh: U of Pittsburgh P, 1973).

32. *Columbian Magazine: or, Monthly Miscellany* 1 (April 1787): 366–69. This passage occurs in *Notes,* 43–48.

33. *New-Haven Gazette, and the Connecticut Magazine* 2 (April 26, 1787): 73–75, prints passages from *Notes,* 20–21, 23, 25–27, 43–47. The issue for May 3, 1787, 81–83, prints passages from *Notes,* 47–48, 67–68, 69–70.

34. *American Museum, or, Universal Magazine* 1 (March, 1787): 206.

35. Ibid. (January, 1787): 8–9.

36. *Columbian Magazine: or, Monthly Miscellany*, 1 (November, 1787): 767, quotes *Notes*, 181–82.

37. *American Magazine* 1 (January 1788): 106–08.

38. On Indians and mound builders and the Jeffersonian connection, see Gordon Sayre, "The Mound Builders and the Imagination of American Antiquity in Jefferson, Bartram, and Chateaubriand," *Early American Literature* 33 (1998): 225–49.

39. *American Magazine* 1 (February 1788): 137.

40. See on Jefferson and constitutions David N. Mayer, *The Constitutional Thought of Thomas Jefferson* (Charlottesville: UP of Virginia, 1994), especially 295–319. The earlier extracts had already presented implicitly contradictory versions of Jefferson as romantic nationalist and as objective observer and scientist.

41. Unintentional because the *Columbian* probably shared racist views; it had previously published from Edward Long's *History of Jamaica* an extract titled "Observations on the Graduation in the Scale of Being between the Human and Brute Creation" (vol. 2 [February 1788]: 70–75).

42. See Jared Gardner, "The Literary Museum and the Unsettling of the Early American Novel," *English Literary History* 67 (2000): 743–71, for a similar argument about the potential of magazine editorial practice to construct new models of citizenship.

43. This is not to deny the anger or rage that Jefferson could entertain against perceived enemies such as the British, Federalists, or Aaron Burr, but he typically expressed these feelings in private correspondence and almost always in language that requires careful analysis in order to discover the depth of feeling behind it. Conor Cruise O'Brien would disagree. Also, in spite of Jefferson's injured self-esteem, he was clearly respected by his contemporaries who gave him important work to do in Congress in 1783–1784 and who appointed him to his diplomatic mission.

44. *Papers of Thomas Jefferson*, 15, 393.

45. Ibid., 14:650.

46. Ibid., 14:651.

47. A ProQuest search of American periodicals before 1810 turns up 1,009 hits for "Jefferson," a fact for which I am indebted to Mark Kamrath, who also pointed me toward the two occurrences cited in this paragraph.

48. Jefferson to Hopkinson, *Papers*, 14:651.

49. On the empire of liberty, see Peter Onuf, *Jefferson's Empire: The Language of American Nationhood* (Charlottesville: UP of Virginia, 2000).

50. Hopkinson to Jefferson, *Papers*, 16:422.

Lisa M. Logan

"The Ladies in Particular"

Constructions of Femininity in the *Gentlemen and Ladies Town and Country Magazine* and the *Lady's Magazine; and Repository of Entertaining Knowledge*

With the following addresses to readers, the editors of two late-eighteenth-century periodicals, the *Gentlemen and Ladies Town and Country Magazine: Consisting of Literature, History, Politics, Arts, Manners, and Amusements, with Various Other Material* and the *Lady's Magazine; and Repository of Entertaining Knowledge*, attest to the central role that women readers, writers, and subjects play in the literature of the new republic:

> . . . the Ladies in particular, are earnestly entreated to patronize a Work, the major part of which, will ever be dedicated to their instruction, or amusement; and confident that feminine abilities, are not congenial with European climates alone, may the future pages of this Magazine, rival the elegant diction of a SEWARD, and the luxuriant fancy of a WILLIAMS.[1]

> But, the best return we can make [the Ladies of Philadelphia] is, (we presume) to render the *Ladies Magazine*, sufficiently interesting and instructive—to present them with the most *lively prose*, and *pathetic verse:* in a word, to lay at *their* feet, the *first fruits* of our *literary labours*, that they may smile upon them, and cherished by *their smiles*, grow up into ripened maturity. . . . In short, it is the province of *female excellence alone*, with the beams of intellectual light, which

illuminates the paths of literature, to diffuse the glowing warmth of genial affection; and by a lively combination of sweet perfections, *add charms*—even to the native beauties of the most brilliant production.[2]

Such statements call to mind extant studies of early American fiction, which have consistently examined the intimate links between the novel and women. Such fine studies as Cathy Davidson's *Revolution and the Word* (1986), Julia Stern's *Plight of Feeling* (1997), Michelle Burnham's *Captivity and Sentiment* (1997), and Shirley Samuels's *Romances of the Republic* (1996) examine from various perspectives the importance of gender to the rise of the novel in the late eighteenth and early nineteenth centuries. This body of groundbreaking work demonstrates that approaches to early American fiction must attend to the ways that writers and texts conversed with their audiences about gender, constructing women in ways that at once presented them as literary and political subjects and limited their possibilities.

As the editorial statements of these eighteenth-century periodicals quoted above make clear, one important purpose of these publications is to teach and delight the "ladies."[3] Given this stated purpose, a deeper understanding of early American fiction develops from considering how these two magazines participated in the construction of femininity. Like novels, periodicals operated as instruments of reform, education, and often cultural critique. However, unlike novels, statements of editorial policy, letters from readers, news items about people and events, and the broad and diverse range of materials included in periodicals provides unique information about their audiences' expectations and assumptions. Correspondence, essays, illustrations, and fiction from the *Gentlemen and Ladies Town and Country Magazine* and the *Lady's Magazine* provide valuable insight into the magazines' construction and circulation of images of women. While this analysis emphasizes the presumed likes and dislikes of readers of these specific magazines, the regular inclusion and discussion of fiction throughout their pages, especially the serialization of the blockbuster novel *The History of Constantia and Pulchera* in the *Gentlemen and Ladies Town and Country Magazine* (June 1789 through January 1790), suggest that such a study bears on early American fiction in more general terms and perhaps the so-called rise of the American novel in the early republic.[4] A consideration of constructions of femininity in these two periodicals can inform the growing understanding of what eighteenth-century readers found when they read texts by, for, or about women.

The *Lady's Magazine; and Repository of Entertaining Knowledge*

Published from June 1792 through May 1793 by W. Gibbons of North Third Street in Philadelphia for "a Literary Society," the *Lady's Magazine* addressed itself to the "*fair daughters* of Columbia; with the fond, but pleasing hope, of *its* meeting with *their* kind approbation and support" [5] The first issue alludes to "the extraordinary marks of applause, with which the Ladies of Philadelphia received the proposals for this work," suggesting the presence of a real or ostensible society of learned ladies in that city of the new nation for whom the editors labor.[6] Such editorial statements mark the magazine as a specifically American publication, one that attempts to meet the needs of a literate female population who might describe themselves as or aspire to be "ladies."[7]

In keeping with this emphasis, the frontispiece shows two female figures, the genius of the *Lady's Magazine* and the genius of Emulation, approaching the female figure Liberty, who bears a star-spangled shield and reaches out for a copy of the "Rights of Woman," which her two supplicants present.[8] With this plate, the editors link in positive ways literature by, for, and about women, and, specifically, their magazine (that is, the two geniuses) with the image of the new nation (Lady Liberty) and its values of virtuous citizenship. Through this image, the editors cast "female patronesses of literature" in a positive light, noting that they "discover an understanding, in the fairest part of intelligent Creation, to distinguish works of real merit, from the false glare of empty profession" and "shed a luster on the amiable qualities which adorn the minds of the fair."[9] Not only do these patronesses accurately assess literature; in doing so they reflect well on the "fair sex" in general. As the quotation at the head of this essay suggests, they also bring a specifically female character and intellect to the "paths of literature." Hence, the editors suggest that "ladies" might be viewed as able writers and readers—at least by other members of their sex.

Its original plan, published in the same issue, promises a "selection of miscellaneous pieces, taken from the works of the most entertaining and instructive writers that have appeared in the present century, whether in Europe or America."[10] Such a miscellany might include a "general review of polite literature": "Essays, calculated to regulate the taste, form the judgment, and improve the mind, will constitute its chief ornament, and it is hoped, recommend it to the notice of a judicious public."[11] In other words, by offering models of polite behavior and thought, its instructive contents are appropriate for consumption by "ladies." Promising a regular mix of "Sentiment, wit, and humor," the editors initially planned two volumes per year, appearing "in a handsome large octavo volume, of at least 300 pages, ornamented with an elegant frontispiece, and marble cover."[12] With such elegance, the editors proclaim their work above the level of monthlies, which are "*stuffed* with that disgusting and worn-out expression '*to be continued.*'" Such disdain appears to be a shameless bid for readership, as the following paragraph claims that "PERSONS of ERUDITION and LEARNING" believe the book could be

> universally recommended in all boarding-schools throughout the continent—as it is to *contain every thing* requisite to disseminate the knowledge of real life, portray virtue in the *most amiable* point of view—Inspire the FEMALE MIND with a love of religion, of patience, prudence, and fortitude—In short, whatever tends to form the ACCOMPLISHED WOMAN, the COMPLETE ECONOMIST, and that greatest of all creatures—a GOOD WIFE.[13]

Such claims that the development of the female mind is in consonance with "religion," the virtues of "patience, prudence, and fortitude," and that most important role for women, wife, clearly echo and/or anticipate the strategies of early feminists such as Judith Sargent Murray, who argued that improved education would only make women better and more companionable wives to their husbands.[14]

The editors express perhaps a normal level of trepidation about the reception of this "first attempt of the kind, made in this country" at a time when magazines might begin and end publication within the space of the same year.[15] They hope to be "secure from the attacks of envy, or malevolence," and argue that, "since it is devoted to the fair sex," perhaps "every lover of the ladies, will stand forth as a champion in defense of a work, peculiarly calculated for the instruction and amusement *of the lovely.*"[16] In championing the magazine, "lover[s] of the ladies" will legitimize not only women's reading but their writing as well, since women's "correspondence is respectfully requested, in either poetry or prose." The editors note that the "elegant productions of *their pen* have hitherto adorned the most valuable libraries, and it is expected, the FEMALES of Philadelphia are by no means deficient in *those talents.*"[17] The editors thus put in place the image of a community of learned female readers and writers with similar concerns about and interest in dominant cultural ideas about taste, behavior, and judgment.[18]

While asserting the legitimacy of women's writing, the editors devise for the inaugural issue a demonstration of the diversity of readers' opinions.[19] For example, one young correspondent "rejoice[s]" at the dedication of a magazine solely to the ladies, claiming that parents are "afraid to give us improper books, and do not know what are or are not proper," while another demands that the editors "give us articles that are calculated for the gentlemen . . . to omit many things that are of the feminine kind, and give us such articles as may suit the scholarship and genius of men . . . [who comprise] [m]ore than one half of your SUBSCRIBERS."[20] This dispute suggests that the public perceives a marked discrepancy between what constitutes typical reading material for men and women but also that this publication, by insisting on certain undefined literary qualities that include instructiveness, taste, sentiment, wit, and humor, can deliver a product that pleases both. The voices of "discordant counselors" continue, as "Miranda" grows impatient with satires on "the continual reprehensions of our dress," and "Matrona" begs that the "follies and foibles of the fair sex will appear in their true colours. Nothing can better deserve your attention, than the outrageous modes of dress, which are becoming more and more ridiculous."[21] Again, the editors' selection of (real or imagined) correspondence identifies a gap in the desires and perspectives of its intended reading public, in this case between matrons and young unmarried women. This distance persists in a letter from Mary, Lydia, and Rebecca, who ask "to let us know all the new novels and plays that are published, for we have but a miserable library here, and nothing in it but old stuffy Spectators."[22] Hannah Motherly counters their request: "The indispensable object of a periodical work like your's, ought to be to caution the fair sex against reading improper books; and let me say, sirs, that of improper books, the most distinguished, and what you ought to be particularly severe against, are novels."[23] Scholars of early American novels will recognize the pattern of conflict between older and younger generations of women, a conflict that the editors clearly aim to mediate through periodical literature and the placement of the *Lady's Magazine* in boarding schools throughout the nation.[24]

This attentiveness to the propriety of and the materials for women's education confirms a larger ongoing discussion in the new republic; in bringing forth their publication, the editors seem to capitalize on a growing need for literature by, for, and about women. Certainly, each issue offers readings that would seem to correspond to what parents in the new republic might find appropriate for daughters at boarding schools. As Linda K. Kerber and Nancy Cott have observed, the number of schools for women grew dramatically from 1790 to 1830, and regular curricula included reading, writing, English grammar, composition, and geography, as well as more traditional subjects, such as needlework, music, and dancing.[25] Monthly tables of contents of the *Lady's Magazine* point to a strong editorial consciousness of arguments that women's education could unfit them for the traditional roles of wives and mothers. Therefore, and in keeping with curriculum for girls recommended by thinkers such as Murray and Benjamin Rush, monthly issues regularly ran nonfiction prose, especially didactic essays on conduct or descriptive and travel essays and correspondence, and poetry. Brief news items and marriage and death notices would seem to keep women informed, in a basic way and in consonance with their proper sphere, of community events. One selection of fiction per issue at most is billed as such (demarcated by "the story of" or with the amendment to the title, "a tale"), although fiction is often presented in "anecdotes" or as parts of letters. Readers could expect the following regular features: letters to the editor, essays on particular virtues and vices (that is, on happiness, prudence, female authorship, parental authority, love, matrimonial obedience, coquetry, ambition, and so on), "Select letters, or specimens of Female Literature," "The Essayist," "Poetical Essays," "Interesting and Pleasing Reflections," "The Ladies Friend," "Anecdotes," "Letter from a Brother to a Sister at a Boarding School," "New Publications," "Curious Account[s] of . . ." various non-European peoples, "Foreign News," "Domestic News," "Marriages," and "Deaths."

In its devotion to women—as regular consumers and producers of literature and as people who deserve to be educated but, also and emphatically, as somehow different from men[26]—the *Lady's Magazine* fulfills a growing cultural (and market) need and participates in constructions of femininity that are at once traditional and reformist.[27] Further, as Shevelow contends, such audience-based constructions of femininity resulted in the formation of a "text-based" community of readers who, perhaps because of shared class backgrounds or even in spite of class differences, commonly desired similar kinds of advice and information.[28] Therefore, in addressing itself to the monolithic category "ladies," the periodical would seem to be in the business of regularizing female behavior in an economically and ethnically diverse nation, a regularization that elides class differences in favor of naturalizing the category "female" through its conflation with the term "ladies."[29] In addition to its attention to codifying moral behavior through didactic essays on virtue and vice, the *Lady's Magazine* throws itself into the concern which the nation and especially women ostensibly share: marriage.[30] In its single-minded focus on "ladies'" concerns, including education, moral conduct, and reform in the service of wise marriage, the *Lady's Magazine* distinguishes itself from its New England peer, the *Gentleman and Lady's Town and Country Magazine* and its successor, the *Gentlemen and Ladies Town and Country Magazine.*

The *Gentleman and Lady's Town and Country Magazine* (1784) and the *Gentlemen and Ladies Town and Country Magazine* (1789–1790)

Published in Boston as a monthly from June through December of 1784 and then again from February 1789 through January 1790, the *Gentle-man and Lady's Town and Country Magazine; or, Repository of Instruction and Entertainment,* as its title suggests, was less explicitly directed at but nevertheless attentive to women.[31] First printed and sold by Job Weeden and William Barrett at E. Russell, Essex Street, and at W. Green, Shakespear's Head, the title was resumed by Nathaniel Coverly, who printed and sold it from his office at Back-street as the

Gentlemen and Ladies Town and Country Magazine: Con-sisting of Literature, History, Politics, Arts, Manners, and Amusements, with Various other Matter. Under Coverly's direction, each month's issue featured an engraving, usually of a scene from one of the fictional pieces included.

In June 1784 and then again in February 1789, the magazine included editorial statements that shed light on its relationship to the reading public. In June 1784, Weeden and Barrett promise one engraving at the close of the year, a list of "Births, Deaths, Marriages, &c." from Boston and "neighbouring Towns," contents "more agreeable to the general Taste" than "Meteorological Observations" after the fact, that is, "the account of Snow-Storms after the Sky is serene, or the history of North-Westers when the Wind is South-East."[32] Instead they ask for public submissions from the "Learned and Ingenious" and vow that "All pieces of Merit will be carefully noticed, and those which are refused, neither blasted by indelicate Censure, or solemn Criticism."[33] They hope for a wide public readership: "their wishes center in the Esteem and Confidence of ALL, from the most brilliant character in the Republic of Letters, to the Child of Science in the value of Obscurity."[34] In so saying, the editors address the work to an apparently literate nation of people, rich and poor, urban and rural.[35] Finally, they solicit "The Ladies in particular," [who] are requested to patronize this Work, by adding the elegant polish of the female Pencil, where purity of sentiment, and impassioned Fancy, are happily blended together."[36] As with the *Lady's Magazine*, the editors register the assumption that a woman's writing, imagination, and sentiment are somehow unique because of her gender; that is, women are "naturally" different from or other than men.

Coverly's editorial statement in February 1789 mirrors his predecessors in hoping that "every Son of Science, and Daughter of Genius, [will] favour him with their generous assistance" and that "all communicated advice will be received with pleasure, considered impartially, and respectfully acknowledged." Like Weedon and Barrett, Coverly addresses "The Ladies in particular," to whose "instruction, or amusement" he dedicates "the major part" of the volumes. Moreover, he emphasizes the Americanness of the magazine and argues that "feminine abilities are not congenial with European climates alone." These editors' hopes for their works' reception suggest that a perusal of their contents might reveal crucial information about women as readers, writing subjects, and objects of literary representation in late-eighteenth-century America.

Similar in content to the *Lady's Magazine*, the 1784 edition of the *Gentleman and Lady's Town and Country Magazine* offered its monthly readers a miscellany of essays and letters of advice, description, and philosophy, foreign and domestic news items ("Monthly intelligencer"), notices of baptism and death (but interestingly omitting marriages), "poetic essays" (moral or philosophical poems), occasional or "amusing and instructive questions," didactic or quirky "anecdotes," and one or two pieces of fiction. Issues under Coverly included all of the above elements as well as Boston and London "Price Currents," marriage notices, a fuller roster of foreign and domestic news, and, increasingly, short tales and serialized fiction. The cover of each issue, with two exceptions, featured an engraved illustration of a selected fictional piece within,[37] including "The Wronged Wife" (March), "Conjugal Infidelity detected" (April), "Faithful though at Liberty" (May), "The Story of Constantius and Pulchera" (June), "The Fatal Concealment" (August), "Lucinda and Leonora" (November), "The Patriotic Lover" (December), and "The Friar's Tale" (January 1790). Despite the diversity of its contents, Coverly's printing practices consistently foregrounded fiction for the reading and buying public.

Constructions of Femininity

In the October 1784 issue of the *Gentleman and Lady's Town and Country Magazine*, Judith Sargent Murray, under the pen name "Constantia," published "Desultory thoughts upon the Utility of encouraging a degree of self-complacency, especially in female bosoms." Noting the presence of themes from Murray's later essays, Sheila L. Skemp summarizes this work as follows:

> . . . it emphasized women's innate rationality and the need for women to value themselves if they were to achieve their full potentials. Women who had no confidence in their own abilities . . . were likely prey for wily seducers or unworthy husbands.[38]

Murray's piece also insisted on the importance of improving women's educations, and her editors registered their approval by clamoring for more of her submissions.[39] "The History of Miss Hortensia Melmoth" (May 1789) echoes Murray's views; Miss Hortensia's seduction is attributed to her education at a London boarding school, "where instead of that strict regard being paid to the morals, and proper care taken to implant the love of virtue and goodness in the breasts of the fair pupils . . . the grand and only object is to make them accomplished in those external qualifications which serve to catch the eye, but seldom win the affections."[40] In the *Lady's Magazine*, the writer of "Thoughts on Women" concurs: "sound judgment cannot be formed but by continual exercise, and frequent comparisons. It is impossible for a woman to have these advantages; and thence, I believe, the principal cause of the inferiority of their judgments" is lack of education.[41]

Similar in spirit to Murray's "Desultory thoughts" is W.J.'s essay "On the Virtues of WOMEN," which claims that "Genius has no sex."[42] Although the writer emphasizes women's essential difference from men by locating her particular "point of honour" in modesty, while men's lies in "strength of mind and bodily courage," he or she argues that "it is in [women's] power to give either a good or a bad turn to society; and to make men take whatever shape they think proper to impose."[43] The author stresses as natural to women the admittedly laudable but dangerous qualities of sentiment and sensibility as well as their constancy, fidelity, and integrity, all of which are best put into the service of influence, particularly over men. The key point here is that women's virtues are best exercised in private—"behind the stage"—but that, according to W. J., such exercise is by no means at odds with their distinction as writers, historians, philosophers, and political subjects. W. J. affirms the idea that even an educated woman's proper place is in the private sphere. Of course, the security and maintenance of such a position requires a husband or father who makes a private home—and the leisure of the women in it—possible.

Repeatedly, the *Gentleman and Lady's Town and Country Magazine* and its successor, the *Gentlemen and Ladies Town and Country Magazine*, uphold the model of what scholars have called "sentimental" marriage, a union based on affection and compatibility rather than a purely economic partnership.[44] As one essayist avers, "without Love the very best of all good qualities will never make a constant *conversation*, easy and delightful."[45] Similarly "On the Choice of a Wife" suggests that men seek "congeniality of sentiment" and "virtuous conduct, good temper, discretion, regularity, and industry" in building a happy and felicitous home.[46] The brief essay "Courtship and Marriage" reiterates that "Of all disparities, that in humour makes the most unhappy Marriages."[47] Despite such advice and instruction, however, the fiction published in the *Gentlemen and Ladies Town and Country Magazine* suggests that, in the words of the author of "The Fatal Concealment," "people in love have never all their wits about them."[48]

The *Lady's Magazine* concerns itself with the relationship between women's education and marriage as well, but in ways that consistently focus on issues of power. "The Matrimonial Creed," for example, takes as its theme the word *obey*, arguing with tongue in cheek that "whosoever would be married, before all things it is necessary that they hold the conjugal faith. Which faith, unless they keep whole and undefiled, without doubt there will be scolding continually . . . it is necessary for matrimonial subordination, that we also believe rightly the infallibility of the wife."[49] By contrast, a more serious-minded "Matrimonial Republican" writes to "object to the word *obey* in the marriage service . . . because it is a general word, without limitation or definition. My dictionary tells me what it is *to obey*, and the word in our marriage service, admits of no exceptions."[50] To include the word *obey*, she maintains, is to construct marriage "as a contract between a superior and an inferior," a view that is at odds with her "republican" opinion of marriage as "a reciprocal union of interest, an implied partnership."[51] Further, the writer states quite boldly that "there is no woman born to be a slave, and no woman whose understanding is so very barren, but that she may at sometimes take the lead in command, with a better effect, than her husband."[52] Appealing to the "laws of our country," the essay builds the case that "the wisdom of our constitution has provided, that we have no laws to obey but what are just and good, and for the welfare of society."[53] Matrimonial Republican's emphasis on women's power and rights contrasts dramatically with "Singular Resolution in a Married Lady," printed in the *Gentleman and Lady's Town and Country Magazine*, in which a woman, raised by a maiden aunt, insists on separate beds and is shocked by her husband's savage "violation" of her request. The misogynist editors dismiss her concerns about her situation, "At present very lamentable to her [but which] will no doubt, in a short time wear a more favorable aspect."[54]

Expanding ideas about the necessity of women's confidence presented in Murray's "Desultory thoughts," "Amelia" claims a "lively imagination, but little ardour of sentiment; a heart susceptible of transient emotions, and a great deal of self-love and vanity."[55] Her self-love enables her to "escape from [her lovers] like Prometheus" and enjoy "more power than the most important personage," knowing that "profound sentiment, ardent and lasting, is a chimera."[56] She concludes that "for some time [her detractors] believed that I was wanton; at present, the world does me more justice, and the man whom I seem to distinguish, cannot be a coxcomb at my expense."[57] Amelia's transgressive claims to women's power outside of marriage invite censure yet spare her hurt feelings and ultimately spare her the possibility of seduction.

The object of myriad moral tales and essayists' rants throughout the pages of these two periodicals, seduction (and its social consequences for women) is consistently treated as a symptom of cultural and legal inequities. An "Observer" in the *Lady's Magazine* proposes that, in stigmatizing the double-standard of men's public behavior instead of trivializing seducers as "wild, gay, young, fellow[s]," women could "discourage all such behaviour as an insult offered to themselves—an insult offered to the married state, and a tacit avowal of principles."[58] Rather, the seducer should be viewed as "a cool, deliberate villain, who thought he bought pleasure cheap, at the expence of the infamy and ruin of some misguided and unsuspecting female."[59] "The History of Henrietta (Written by Herself)" is even more damning. The educated daughter of tender parents, Henrietta disobeys her parents and succumbs to her seducer, who laughs when her pregnancy is revealed.[60] Abandoned by her father and her lover, Henrietta offers her story, like *Charlotte Temple* or *The Coquette*, as a warning to young women of the folly of giving in to temptation, breaking their parents' hearts, and "ruining themselves." However, this familiar moralizing gives way to a diatribe against masculine values:

> Why is it that men, who profess to have the highest regard for the principles of honour, and would take it as an high affront to be suspected of not looking down with sovereign contempt on a base or

> vile action, men who would scorn to defraud their neighbour of the value of a shilling, yet at the same time will practice every art in their power to seduce female virtue, and do an injury which it is not within the compass of their power to make compensation for—can unfeelingly behold the miserable, contemptible objects, which they by their insidious arts, unwearied solicitations, and *Stanhopean* wiles, have precipitated from the fair walks of virtue into the infamous gulph of pollution and disgrace, and perhaps smile too at the horrid and heart-breaking spectacle.[61]

The incensed writer, hotly aware of the impossibility of her own social redemption, demands that these "remorseless monsters" be hanged for their crimes, not the least of which is that they continue to "tread the ground" and "breath the air."[62]

As these examples show, women and their particular situation in early national culture are central to the literature of these periodicals, which attempt to instruct them properly about how best to negotiate their positions as women in a patriarchal culture. These magazines use textual representations of and literature by women to mediate cultural debates about women's power, especially in relation to education, seduction, and marriage.

Serialized Periodical Fiction and the Construction of Early American Heroines: "Original Letters" between Frederick and Felicia

From the summer of 1789 through its final issue in January 1790, the *Gentlemen and Ladies Town and Country Magazine* presented two of its longest-running pieces of fiction, "Original Letters" between Frederick and Felicia and "The Story of Constantius and Pulchera." These pieces stand out for their sustained depictions of women characters and can serve as a lens for viewing the work of serialization in relation to constructions of femininity.

If the project of early national periodicals is to instruct women in reading, writing, behavior, and taste—that is, to standardize and regulate ideas about femininity, the elegant, accomplished, and virtuous Felicia is a perfect model. In a series of thirteen letters exchanged between Felicia and her beau Frederick, readers learn of her impeccable character and admirable habits of reading and writing. The effusive Frederick consistently remarks her goodness, virtue, and "exquisite taste and sensibility."[63] Her letters in return evince an easy conversance in ancient Western philosophy that sets the stage for one of the series' most crucial themes: education.[64] Obviously a member of the leisure class, Felicia censures the tradesman who "give[s] his children that sort of education which may fit them for those spheres of life in which they are never likely to appear; an education which renders the mind like a toy-shop, full of very pretty and very useless things, leaving the hand idle, the heart vacant of principle, and the soul a prey to dissipation." Felicia proposes that

> there are species of mental acquisition adapted to every different situation in life; and can anything be more ridiculously absurd than giving a tradesman's daughter the education of a Countess?—Such, however, is the prevailing folly of this 'enlightened age,' and robs the middling, that is, the most respectable part of the community, of solid comfort, fills the metropolis with a sort of splendid misery, and the Gazettes with bankrupts.[65]

Such comments seem peculiar in a magazine apparently circulated widely among women of middle-class status; but the passage in some ways affirms the usefulness of the knowledge purveyed in the pages of the *Gentlemen and Ladies Town and Country Magazine.* It assumes a community of readers who would admire Felicia and wish—insofar as they have the means—to regulate their tastes and judgments according to hers. Frederick concurs with her views as he launches the story of Anna D., a family friend whose involvement with one Captain B. has distracted him from writing letters to his beloved more regularly. It seems that Anna "received a village education; that is to say, she went to school with many others, to the clerk of the parish; and, instead of modern books of amusement, was taught to read in the bible; her copies were maxims of morality; and pious mottos formed the subjects of her samplers." Frederick expresses approbation for this "plebeian mode of education" because it instills "veneration and love for the Deity, and a consequent dread not only of vice, but even the appearance of it; this is more especially requisite for the female mind."[66] As she repels the less than honorable advances of the libertine Capt. B., her education serves Anna well, offering her the language to remark on his deliberately ambiguous promises and the wisdom to consult her friends. Nevertheless, her naïveté and village education cannot prepare her for the sophisticated machinations of Captain B., who lures her into a secret and false marriage. Here Frederick takes another moment for cultural critique, condemning the "deficiency in our laws, which inflict no punishment on a crime of this magnitude" and ensure that a man who steals a horse will be hanged, while a man who seduces a woman goes unpunished.[67]

Significantly, although the cause of Anna's fall is linked to improper education in accordance with her class, her salvation turns on the importance of letter writing and publishing, particularly as it is deployed by a middle-class woman. Anna's mistress, a milliner, suspecting that all is not well, "inserted in the news-papers" the report that Capt. B. has in fact married Miss Anna D.[68] An angry Capt. B. spurns his falsely acquired "wife," but Mrs. —— implements her pen once again, this time conveying in a letter the whole story to Capt. B.'s wealthy father, who receives Anna as a daughter and rights his son's wrongs.[69] While the female pen is centrally and persistently present here, it is the man of means, the benevolent father, who is empowered to save the day. Not coincidentally, Felicia confesses to being in love with the father and, perhaps as her readers are expected to do, overlooks the role of both women in the story (except to condemn the education of them above their class).

Not only do plots revolve around reading, writing, and the consumption of literature; Felicia herself has much to say about these matters, especially the question of novels. In response to Frederick's enclosure of a novel in one of his letters, Felicia writes, "Nothing but your desire could have tempted me to the perusal of it." Most contemptible in the modern novel is the "affectation of sensibility which pervades all these effusions of insipidity." The number of subscriptions to novels, she continues, might suggest that "our noblesse were the most humane, compassionate people in the world," but such literature lacks "true" and "real sensibility" and substitutes its representation for religion. Concluding that "when one is read, all are read" and that "in reading two volumes, you have read two thousand," Felicia begs that Frederick "Send me no more novels."[70]

This tension between real and apparent sensibility persists in Felicia's critiques of early American theater as well.[71] Felicia wonders if a new play is above the generality of "belles and beau" in attendance and considers that they would have to be "wonderfully improved in knowledge and sentiment, and particularly in their language, before this comedy can be said to be a representation of nature, or even of what you very justly call artificial life." The discrepancy between "sentimental plays," which she terms "sermons in dialogue," and the language of actual verbal communication troubles her, but she believes that "they shew, at least what life itself ought to be." Nevertheless, she fears their result will be that people will merely "assume a virtue, though we have it not."[72] Frederick refers to this quality as "insensible sensibility," a quality possessed by his friend Frank, whose artifice prevents the representation of his true self. His "heart is hid in clouds of darkness" that defend "his bosom from those arrows of delicacy that so deeply wound a heart of feeling."[73]

This concern with real versus feigned sentiment is the locus of many early American novels, including *The Power of Sympathy*, *Charlotte Temple*, *The Coquette*, and *Female Quixotism*, each of which traces the fates of emotionally susceptible women who succumb to the false sentiments of their seducers.[74] Although Felicia's sense of superiority would seem to argue for the advancement of women's roles, these letters bring into dialogue class, education, and woman's place in ways that emphasize traditional roles and preserve class hierarchies.

"The Story of Constantius and Pulchera"

Published serially from June 1789 through January 1790, "The Story of Constantius and Pulchera" was so popular that, according to Cathy Davidson's count, it was published in eight English editions between 1794 and 1802 and translated into German for readers in Pennsylvania.[75] Describing the work as "bizarre," Davidson explains that it is "virtually unreadable today or readable only as a parody of itself."[76] While one can concede the bizarre and even absurd nature of this story, it not only can be read but it is useful to do so because of what the text reveals about constructions of gender in late-eighteenth-century America. Examination of the text within the trends of gender construction in these two late eighteenth-century periodicals that are addressed deliberately to women (in part or in whole) extends Davidson's consideration of the work of the early American novel as a literature of the margins. That is, like the novels that Davidson studies, this story raises questions about the intertwined roles of marriage, women's legal, economic, and personal power, and female literacy and literary representation in the new republic.

Set during the Revolutionary War and beginning in Philadelphia, the story spotlights Pulchera, a "most beautiful lady of sixteen," whose engagement to the "adorable Constantius" has been broken by her British father's ambitious decision to marry his daughter off to Monsieur Le Monte, "only son and heir to a rich nobleman in France."[77] Held captive in her father's home until her ship's departure, Pulchera escapes with her lover, who "straightway conveyed her to his chamber where the remainder of the night was spent in a far more agreeable manner than the former."[78] After these few brief hours of bliss, her father's men seize Constantius and carry him off, at which Pulchera beats her breast, tears her hair, curses her fate, and is confined again, this time more securely, to await her conveyance to the French monarch's court. Meanwhile she reads in a newspaper a report of her lover's death and resigns herself to the inevitable. Her journey to Europe is similarly complicated, as she endures a series of wartime battles that result in her captivity, cross-dressing, shipwreck, near cannibalism, arraignment in England for piracy, and not a little letter writing. The resilient and resourceful Pulchera survives it all and finally arrives intact in France, where she orchestrates a reunion with the very much alive Constantius.

Citing elements of romance and its "strained language," Davidson's analysis considers the book as an early example of the American picaresque novel and in terms of "narrative transvestism or emotional role reversal." She writes,

> The novel focuses on Pulchera's prowess and adventures, and Constantius, consistent with the passive connotations of his name, is finally reduced, rhetorically, to the role traditionally occupied by a woman, that of the grateful heroine overwhelmed by good fortune

and the capable attentions of another. One almost expects the fellow to swoon.[79]

Davidson's reading places the text squarely in the tradition of the early American novel, a genre that permits women only "in crossdressing or captivity" to "find something of the same full freedom that the picaresque regularly grants to its male protagonists." Furthermore Davidson adds, such freedom is "conditional and temporary, and definitely not for domestic consumption."[80] In other words, Pulchera breaks "virtually every imaginable restriction placed upon the eighteenth-century American woman" because she is *"forced"* to, but "her exhilarating trials all end in the domesticity she would have entered on page 1 except for the intervention of her parents."[81] Davidson's reading allies Pulchera with Deborah Sampson, who, dressed as a man, fought in the Revolutionary War, and with America itself—both Pulchera and America fight a war for independence.[82] In addition, Davidson's characterization suggests the ways that the story anticipates Tabitha Tenney's picaresque cross-dressing novel *Female Quixotism* (1801). Cross-dressing and Pulchera's writing and speaking voice at once challenge and conserve dominant cultural constructions of femininity. While Davidson focuses on how the ending of the text undermines those moments of transgression that Pulchera's cross-dressing creates, also of interest is how Pulchera's character enables sites of subversion.

When read against the consistent concern with women's roles and economic, legal, discursive, and personal authority that these periodicals evince, these moments of gender transgression generate a kind of counter-text to canonical representations of women in early American novels of the 1790s. That is, unlike Tenney's Dorcasina, Foster's Eliza, or Rowson's Charlotte, Pulchera chooses rightly and against the wishes of her family (represented by her father) a lover with whom she evidently has sex before the marriage ceremony. While she certainly suffers, Pulchera neither dies in childbirth like Charlotte and Eliza nor is she rendered ridiculous and unmarriageable like Dorcasina. Rather, readers are asked to identify with a young woman who is at once emotional and reasonable, capable of action and thought, and the mistress of her own self-construction in deed and word. In the mostly forgotten (by literary critics) spaces of eighteenth-century periodicals lie heroines who are "written beyond the ending" of more canonical traditions of writing represented by Charles Brockden Brown or Hannah Webster Foster, whom Julia A. Stern has argued wrote increasingly from conventional public perspectives.[83]

At first glance "The Story of Constantius and Pulchera" seems a typical romance; Pulchera, "clad in a long white vest, her hair of a beautiful chesnut colour hanging carelessly over her shoulders," utters her fair share of romantic heroine discourse ("O cruel fortune!" and "Alas!"). This traditional romance discourse is complicated, however, as Pulchera's predicaments are rendered consistently in the language of legal and economic discourse. For example, our heroine describes the "flood of transport" she felt upon "surrendering [her] heart to him, and took delivery of his in exchange, and called on Heaven to register the indissoluble contract."[84] In light of representations of women's views of and concerns about marriage published in the periodical literature considered in this essay, such language bears exploring. By registering the marriage "contract" with a heavenly rather than an earthly authority, and by representing the transaction as an even "exchange," Pulchera's statement embraces ideas about marriage as a union between coequal partners and opposes the antirepublican views represented by her father. Further, Pulchera's remonstrations to her father appeal not to his sense of love and affection but to his reason through the language of contracts and rights. She cites his initial "free and voluntary consent" to his daughter's union with Constantius as evidence for *his* breach of contract. In building her case, Pulchera argues,

> . . . but I am not my own—At your special leave and request I have in a most solemn manner given myself to Constantius, and am no more my own—he took full possession of my heart when I gave him my promise, and I have neither power or inclination to take it back. You, Sir, was present, and ratified our contract by your most explicit approbation thereof; and therefore, cease to possess the right or power of disposing of me again.[85]

Thus, Pulchera constructs her position not as rebellious but obedient. At the same time, she effects this obedient self-positioning not through the language of sentiment or sensibility, but by appropriating the legal language that underpins patriarchy. Lacking legal self-ownership, she can only consign herself to the wishes of first her father and then her husband, both of whom are bound by law to protect her. In presenting the argument in the language of the father, Pulchera (unsuccessfully) displaces the responsibility for her current dilemma onto her "cruel parent" and begs him to respond in a way that honors the "contract."

Her father, however, refutes her attempts to speak the language of law and power: "Poor silly creature, your folly would be your utter ruin, had you not a father living to bridle your giddy passions: But to reason with a person void of rationality is no part of my business. Remember you are under my government, and that my will is your law."[86] In a sense, her father takes her literally at her word, refuting her authority not only to choose her own partner but to interpret the workings of contracts and rights that determine men's *and* women's fates. Readers are clearly expected to identify with Pulchera and to interpret her father's views of his daughter and, by extension, women in general, as tyrannical, unsympathetic, and wrong, the primary cause of the protagonist's woes.[87] Once Constantius is reported dead, Pulchera, grasping the patriarchal paradigm of male ownership of women, finds herself again "under parental disposal . . . and that *that* religion which she the day before spoke so highly of, made it her duty now to submit to the dictates of her father."[88] Despite this language, she is not so easily defeated and, in a tableau moment of Revolutionary independence, against the background of the receding American shore, she warns her future husband that "tho' he had the power over her body, yet her mind was, and should continue free—and that she would never give him her hand or heart, and that he might rest assured he would never have the satisfaction of being her husband—that even the crown of France was too trifling a toy to have any effect on her mind."[89] Her rhetoric accepts his ownership of her body but maintains her own right to her hand, heart, and mind, which I read respectively as her will, affections, and intellect. In this passage, Pulchera resists the characterization of woman as a sentimental creature ruled by her heart that emerges in women's novels of this period and that the contemporary periodicals under discussion here sometimes support explicitly even as they present arguments for women's literacy and education that clearly militate against that view.

The consideration of Pulchera's cross-dressing in the context of literary representations of women in the *Gentlemen and Ladies Town and Country Magazine* invites further complication of Davidson's reading. Davidson maintains that the constant reminders of the necessity of men's clothing for the preservation of Pulchera's safety and chastity compromise the radical potential of the work.[90] Moreover, she contends, readers no doubt presumed that Pulchera finished with a man's wardrobe once she retrieved and married Constantius in France. This reading suggests that domesticity (or perhaps even Constantius) rescues the heroine from an unseemly wardrobe. Within the pages of this periodical, however, Pulchera's cross-dressing clearly—if fleetingly—participates in the rupturing of those traditional constructions of femininity that the magazine would seem to endorse. These constructions—and their rupture—are especially important to consider within a larger history of cultural perceptions of the gendered body. For example, Thomas Laqueur argues that the eighteenth-century saw a gradual replacement of an earlier "one-sex" model of gender and biology with a "two-sex" model. That is, he argues, "The dominant, though by no means universal, view since the eighteenth century has been that there are two stable, incommensurable, opposite sexes and that the political, economic, and cultural lives of men and women, their gender roles, are somehow based on these 'facts.'"[91] The *Lady's Magazine* and the *Gentlemen and Ladies Town and Country Magazine* at once support and resist this emerging two-sex view of gender by addressing women readers and writers as essentially different from men.

Women are often represented as having naturally endowed qualities that men do not, such as a preponderance of feeling, virtue, or modesty. Many instances cited here indicate that women's seeming lack of judgment or quality of mind is linked to their lack of education. These magazines under consideration evince a tension between the one- and two-sex models of gender and biology, mirroring a broader, pseudo-scientific conversation about what kind of creatures women actually are. The presence of such tension in literary constructions of women within the space of the same (or a similar) publication, especially insofar as Pulchera's cross-dressed figure represents women to readers, points to what Marjorie B. Garber has called a "category crisis . . . one of the most consistent and effective functions of the transvestite in culture." That is, like Deborah Sampson or the Female Marine, other cross-dressed figures of the late eighteenth and early nineteenth centuries, Pulchera "call[s] attention to cultural, social, or aesthetic dissonances" in cultural constructions of gender.[92] Following Garber's and Laqueur's lead, scholars of the early national period have read female cross-dressing as a response to a tightening of gender categories.[93]

Pulchera's cross-dressing would seem to signal if not a crisis then at least a dissonance in literary representations of women in the late eighteenth century. Abandoned by the crew of a sinking vessel and washed ashore atop a piece of hatch, Pulchera, "with a voice as loud as her enfeebled situation would admit" hails a passing ship. Facing capture, she dons Capt. M's "neat suit of red regimentals, a gold-laced hat, and a sword by her side" and assumes the name Valorus; even the narrator refers to her by this name until story's end. Thus clad, she weathers a host of shipwrecks and storms, the cold, and wilderness without discovery. Her adventures with fellow shipmates on a deserted island suggest to readers that women are no less capable than men in the techniques of survival. In this liminal space outside of civilization, the crew makes group decisions and cares for their beloved Valorus when "he" becomes ill. At one point, Pulchera/Valorus becomes so despondent that "he" "half resolved to unbosom herself to her comrades; but reasons of policy forbid the measure."[94] The choice of the word *unbosom* to describe the revelation of her true biological sex is especially pointed, since it marks the linguistic link between the body and gendered identity. Furthermore, this language links woman's identity closely to her gendered body. Pulchera perseveres as a man, serving as prizemaster on a privateer, suffering in irons in a Halifax prison, and escaping through a sewage drain. Finally, still posing as a man (in a newly purchased clean suit), she makes her way to France to wait out the war. Through Pulchera's adventures, the story in many ways resists the very assumptions on which the magazine is based—that women are somehow basically different from men. Moreover, although Davidson's reading emphasizes Pulchera's extenuating circumstances as compelling her male dress, her cross-dressing is consistently rendered as a conscious choice, an optional strategy that she adopts because it yields positive results.

In the story's final installments, Valorus/Pulchera, in France seeking other Americans, comes upon Constantius in the act of reading a manuscript.[95] Wisely she keeps both her own counsel and her male identity, for her hard work must continue even now; Constantius, who has long since given up on Pulchera, is poised to marry Le Monte's sister. Disguised as Valorus, Pulchera wrangles her former lover's true feelings into the open. Satisfied with his answer and suitably motivated, Valorus, dressed as Pulchera, posts a letter informing Constantius of her whereabouts. Resuming the garb of Valorus and hopeful of a rendezvous, she then hurries to the named location, where she once again dons the garb of and resumes her identity as Pulchera, "decked in all the magnificence which the city of Bourdeaux could afford."[96] An overjoyed Constantius reunites with his beloved but is vexed with the problem of his current fiancée. At a loss, he confesses his dilemma to Le Monte, who, through legal and contractual discourse, assures him that he may not make "a second conveyance of [him]self to one woman before [he is] discharged from the other."[97] This argument reverses the gender roles but maintains the premise of self-ownership that Pulchera earlier presented to her father. It is important to note that Constantius makes his decision only after seeking Le Monte's clarification in resolving the linguistic and legal dilemma. That is, he distrusts his own capacity to interpret the contractual rhetoric that Pulchera, a young woman still in her teens, navigates so ably throughout the story.

The story's ending links in significant ways acts of cross-dressing with scenes of writing and public behavior that are clearly and emphatically gendered. Cross-dressing is here a choice rather than an imperative (although employed in the service of ultimate domestic happiness). For Pulchera cross-dressing operates as a strategy of textual and cultural authority, enabling her self-positioning as a writer and speaker who achieves autonomy and agency in a world that yields her neither. Each time Valorus/Pulchera adopts a pen—once when facing death by starvation and exposure on a deserted island and again in writing to Constantius—she writes as Pulchera, thus figuring forth for readers the image of a woman dressed as a man and writing as a woman.[98] Such scenes of cross-dressing would seem to locate, to use Garber's phrase, a category crisis in the scene of writing itself. The very notion of writing and its close relationship to gender in the eighteenth-century is destabilized by the layers of gendered crossing that Pulchera enacts. Perhaps the text means to demonstrate that a woman wielding a pen is less strange than a woman dressed as a man, or a woman dressed as a man wielding a pen. The confluence of these images—woman, man, pen— may have ruptured normative cultural constructions of femininity in readers' minds. At least the image of a man writing is destabilized by our knowledge that he is in fact a woman (and a better "man" at that).[99]

So what of the "ladies in particular"? The *Lady's Magazine* and the *Gentlemen and Ladies Town and Country Magazine* evince many of the same concerns expressed widely in early American novels, including the importance of women's education, the problem of seduction, and ambivalent views of marriage. They do so in a context that provides another framework for understanding women as readers and writers, as subjects in, of, and to literary representation. This context suggests that, even as these periodical editors ostensibly wished to purvey advice and instruction about culturally acceptable behavior and thinking to women, their range and variety of materials appearing in juxtaposition resulted in the circulation of ambivalent and often contradictory constructions of femininity. This material is vital to the development of any history of the American novel, its traditions and readers. At the very least, the work of these periodicals deepens the sense that women in particular are at once a crucial and enigmatic force in the literature of early America. However, this study also suggests that the relationship of women to literature requires more exploration. The *Lady's Magazine* and the *Gentlemen and Ladies Town and Country Magazine* were available and addressed to women in the urban centers of Boston and Philadelphia. Their consideration of "women" as an essential category elides differences in class, ethnicity, and geographic location that are vital to understanding the relationships among early American novels, culture, and politics. To what extent did the novel serve as a democratic, radical, or conventional tool for women readers and writers in the new republic? The body of information these periodicals yield about women readers raises questions that challenge any single answer. The absence of certain voices and narratives from these periodicals underlines the importance of considering magazines and newspapers from less urban regions or from cities in the American South. Other genres, such as women's autobiographies, diaries, memoirs, and commonplace books, can assist us in avoiding the fallacy of essentialism early periodicals' editors sometimes perpetuated. To memoirist Abigail Abbot Bailey of Haverhill, New Hampshire, married to a husband who committed incest with their sixteen-year-old daughter, and mother of seventeen children, these magazines may have been as remote and unrealistic as *Cosmo* is to most working women today. The *Gentlemen and Ladies Town and Country Magazine* and the *Lady's Magazine* remind one that the work of recovery is critical—and unfinished.

Notes

I thank Sharon M. Harris and Mark L. Kamrath for their wisdom, generosity, and patience in working with me on this essay.

1. *Gentlemen and Ladies Town and Country Magazine* (Boston), February 1789, n.p.
2. *Lady's Magazine; and Repository of Entertaining Knowledge* (Philadelphia, June, 1792–93): i–ii.

3. Kathryn Shevelow argues that new periodicals in eighteenth-century Britain commonly "apostrophize[d] the 'Fair Sex'" in early issues. See *Women and Print Culture: The Construction of Femininity in the Early Periodical* (London and New York: Routledge P, 1989), 23.
4. This observation concurs with Shevelow's wish to avoid the construction of an "explicit or implicit hierarchy of intellectual interest assumed by most treatments of the periodical as a precursor of a more important literary form" (18).
5. *Lady's Magazine* (June 1792), i. According to the original plan, subscriptions would be sold for two dollars per year through the publisher and booksellers in Boston, Albany, New York, Baltimore, Richmond, Charleston, and Savannah, suggesting that the magazine, while attending specifically to its Philadelphia readers, has broader implications for the construction of femininity in the early republic. David Paul Nord states that a normal salary for a workingman in New York at this time was fifty cents per day and suggests that subscriptions were therefore most prevalent among the artisan and merchant classes. However, as Nord observes, readership and subscription should not be confused, and perhaps shopkeepers made their magazines available to their customers. See David Paul Nord, "A Republican Literature: Magazine Reading and Readers in Late Eighteenth-Century New York," in *Reading in America: Literature and Social History*, ed. Cathy N. Davidson (Baltimore: Johns Hopkins UP, 1989), 119–20.
6. Branson reviews the "new and more engaged relationship" of late-eighteenth-century American women to print in *These Fiery Frenchified Dames: Women and Political Culture in Early National Philadelphia* (Philadelphia: U of Pennsylvania P, 2001), 21–53. Moreover, the recent recovery and publication of *Milcah Martha Moore's Book* attests to the existence of a vital manuscript culture in the latter half of the eighteenth century among Philadelphia's socially elite women. Editors Catherine La Courreye Blecki and Karin A. Wulf find that of the 126 entries, which include poems, a travel journal, and correspondence, 100 are authored by women, including Susanna Wright, Hannah Griffitts, and Elizabeth Graeme Fergusson. Preface to *Milcah Martha Moore's Book: A Commonplace Book from Revolutionary America*. (University Park: Pennsylvania State UP, 1997), xii. In her introductory essay to the volume, Wulf observes that Fergusson regularly held a literary salon for men and women in her family home near Philadelphia and that circles of women with mutual literary interests mirrored men's societies of the time. See "*Milcah Martha Moore's Book:* Documenting Culture and Connection in the Revolutionary Era," *Milcah Martha Moore's Book*, 1–58.

7. David Paul Nord contends that "magazine reading in this era seems to have been a more broadly democratic activity than has usually been supposed." Nord, "A Republican Literature," 115.
8. The "EXPLANATION OF THE FRONTISPIECE" is as follows: "The Genius of the Ladies Magazine, accompanied by the Genius of Emulation, who carries in her hand a laurel crown, approaches Liberty, and kneeling, presents her with a copy of the Rights of Woman." *Lady's Magazine; and Repository of Entertaining Knowledge* 1 (Philadelphia, 1792): v. *Lady's Magazine* reprinted several excerpts from Wollstonecraft's *Vindication of the Rights of Woman* (1792) and was one of the few American periodicals to review the tract positively. See Anonymous, "New publications. A Vindication of the Rights of Woman: With Strictures on political and moral subjects." *Lady's Magazine; and Repository of Entertaining Knowledge* 3 (September 1792): 189–99. For a discussion of differences between this image as it appeared in the British versus the American *Lady's Magazine*, see Branson 39. While Branson notes the plate's emphasis on "marital, social, and possibly political roles for American women," this essay emphasizes the relationships among women and literature in the new nation.
9. *Lady's Magazine; and Repository of Entertaining Knowledge* 1 (June 1792): ii.
10. Ibid., iv.
11. Ibid. See Nord 125 for a discussion of the miscellaneous character of American and British magazines of this period, including a contemporary review of what eighteenth-century magazines were expected to accomplish.
12. *Lady's Magazine; and Repository of Entertaining Knowledge* 1 (June 1792): v. However, the magazine was issued monthly.
13. Ibid.
14. See especially Murray's essay "On the Equality of the Sexes," *Massachusetts Magazine* 2 (March–April 1790): 132ff. Murray is careful to emphasize the close relationship between woman's traditional domestic duties and the necessity of developing her mind. Wulf has effectively countered the belief that all women were expected to marry. In her study of colonial Philadelphia women's manuscript culture, Wulf concludes that, beginning in the mid–eighteenth century, "both New England and the Delaware Valley show a strong trend toward lower marriage rates." See her *Not All Wives: Women of Colonial Philadelphia* (Ithaca: Cornell UP, 2000), 18. Wulf's scrutiny of women's commonplace books reveals "a broader range of options and ideals for women outside of marriage than generally has been recognized. Spinsterhood. . . was not only accepted as an alternative life course for women (and men), but in some cases celebrated. In the minds of colonial Philadelphians, and on the pages they read, singleness

could be a respectable choice." *Not All Wives*, 31. For discussions of the intimate link between marriage and republican values, especially the notion of marriage as a microcosm for the new nation, see Linda K. Kerber, *Women of the Republic: Intellect and Ideology in Revolutionary America* (Chapel Hill: U of North Carolina P, 1980); Nancy Cott, *The Bonds of Womanhood: "Woman's Sphere" in New England, 1780–1835* (New Haven: Yale UP, 1977); Ruth H. Bloch, "American Feminine Ideals in Transition: The Rise of the Moral Mother, 1785–1815," *Feminist Studies* 4 (1978): 101–26; and Jan Lewis, "The Republican Wife: Virtue and Seduction in the Early Republic," *William and Mary Quarterly* 44 (1987): 689–719.

15. *Lady's Magazine; and Repository of Entertaining Knowledge*, 1 (1792): v. Nord writes that the longest run of any American magazine of this period is eight years (118).
16. *Lady's Magazine; and Repository of Entertaining Knowledge*, 1 (1792): ii–iii.
17. Ibid., iv.
18. In using the magazines' term *ladies*, one should not elide the particularly vexing problem of exactly which women were included in this category. As Nord points out, these periodicals circulated among more than just the elite through venues such as social and circulation libraries and among customers at shops in urban centers (119–20). However, other evidence by women writers themselves, especially those living in rural areas, including Abigail Abbot Bailey, whose husband's incestuous abuse of their daughter occurred around this time (1788–90), suggests that not all women were equally caught up in magazine reading. Bailey reports her reading as limited to the Bible. See Ann Taves, ed., *Religion and Domestic Violence in Early New England: The Memoirs of Abigail Abbot Bailey* (Bloomington: Indiana UP, 1989). Other evidence of women's reading and writing practices occurs in the gallows crime confessions of Rachel Wall, a farmer's daughter from Carlisle, Pennsylvania, who was hanged in Boston for robbery, and Elizabeth Wilson of rural Chester County, Pennsylvania, hanged for the murder of her twin infants in Chester. Again, these women, caught up in the day-to-day challenges of economic survival, seem less concerned with the niceties of conduct, even as their stories evince the need for the nation to address women's position in patriarchy. See Daniel E. Williams, ed., *Pillars of Salt: An Anthology of Early American Criminal Narratives* (Madison: Madison House, 1993). Bailey took her abusive husband to court and won a property settlement, and Wall and Wilson, who protest their innocence, blame the impossibilities of poverty for their situations. Indirectly, then, these narratives, written by rural and less socially elite women who probably did not read the magazines under

discussion regularly, nevertheless mirror from a different class perspective the ongoing dialogue occurring in periodicals addressed to more urban and socially elite women.

19. In considering readers' correspondence, one must be well aware of the problem of these letters' authenticity. However, Shevelow observes that, since they are "*represented* as the work of the periodical's readership . . . [they] project an image of a community of readers mutually engaged in the production of the text" (38). These letters provide valuable clues to social constructions of women as readers and writers and to the cultural values that editors and readers would find appropriate within this particular community.

20. *Lady's Magazine; and Repository of Entertaining Knowledge* 1 (June 1792): 9–10.

21. Ibid., 10.

22. Ibid.

23. Ibid.

24. The editors' desire is reasonable. According to Wulf, women and girls kept commonplace books regularly, in which they copied passages that pleased them from almanacs, novels, the Bible, religious tracts, and the widely available periodical. Moreover, copying was also an assigned school activity. See *Not All Wives*, 26. Furthermore, as Linda Kerber observes, interesting materials for girls' curricula was in short supply, and "founders of girls' academies were often driven to prepare their own collections or to write their own teaching materials" (215). It seems logical that those same women who frequently copied favorite passages from the manuscripts of friends and literary magazines might also use these resources in the teaching of girls.

25. Kerber discusses differences among recommended curricula by advocates for women's education(210–14).

26. Of eighteenth-century British periodicals, Shevelow writes, "The periodicals' characteristic attention to women and 'women's concerns' (the editorial policy that Swift sneeringly labeled 'fair-sexing it') served an emerging ideology that, in the act of making claims for women's capabilities and social importance, constructed women as essentially—that is, both biologically and socially—'other' than men" (1–2).

27. Branson argues that the *Lady's Magazine* was alone in featuring pieces that favored "expanding women roles and opportunities" but that the number of articles that argued for women's remaining in traditional roles far outnumbered such content (27). Despite this statistic, by presenting a dia-

logue and emphasizing women not merely as objects of representation but as purveyors of aesthetically and morally valuable texts worthy of emulation, the *Lady's Magazine* participates, although not always explicitly, in discursive practices that disrupt dominant cultural constructions of women. The "reforming" of ideas about women's traditional roles should not be confused with behavioral "reform" on the part of women. Shevelow's study of eighteenth-century British periodical literature concludes that the boundaries between this kind of reform and learning were hopelessly blurred and that, ultimately, these texts conflated knowledge with "behavior modification" (4).

28. Shevelow 49–50.

29. Wulf writes that populations of New York, Pennsylvania, and New Jersey are especially heterogeneous in their "urbanity, their economic structure, and their religious diversity." See *Not All Wives*, 19. While the address to the "ladies" would seem to target elite and leisured audiences, it is likely that the accessibility of periodicals and the inclusion of readers in their pages led to their wide circulation among women who perhaps considered themselves outside of upper-class spheres. Further, as Kerber notes, women's education was often deployed to advance the upwardly mobile; that is, an educated girl might have more (and "better") choices of a husband (209–10).

30. Wulf writes that the "contemporary problems of marriage are suggested by the regularity with which marriage and marital status were topics of literary representation in the most accessible publication, almanacs, and literary magazines." According to Wulf, "Even after they had determined to marry, women questioned the costs of marriage. In particular, they repeatedly mourned the loss of personal freedom that marriage entailed." See *Not All Wives*, 32, 42.

31. In *Women and Print Culture*, Shevelow claims that such address was a common practice in British periodicals at mid-century (1–2).

32. *Gentlemen and Ladies Town and Country Magazine* 1 (June 1784): 3.

33. Ibid.

34. Ibid.

35. Nord notes the "widespread American belief that diffusion of knowledge was beneficial for republican government and for the virtue of its people" (130).

36. Ibid.

37. The July 1789 issue featured a plate of "Fidelity" from the essay "The Passions, and their Effects, exemplified in a variety of incidents," and the

September issue included a plate of a scene from Thomas Gray's *Elegy Written in a Country Churchyard.*

38. See Sheila L. Skemp, "Judith Sargent Murray" in *American Women Prose Writers to 1820,* ed. Carla Mulford et al., vol. 200, *Dictionary of Literary Biography* (Detroit: Gale Research, 1999), 257.
39. As Skemp notes, the magazine folded soon after, and Murray continued to publish in the *Massachusetts Magazine; or Monthly Museum,* which carried her poetry and perhaps her best-known essay, "On the Equality of the Sexes." See "Judith Sargent Murray," 257. For another discussion of Murray's 1784 essay, see Branson 33–35.
40. *Lady's Magazine; and Repository of Entertaining Knowledge* 1 (Philadelphia, May 1789): 164.
41. *Lady's Magazine; and Repository of Entertaining Knowledge* 1 (August 1792), n.p.
42. *Gentlemen and Ladies Town and Country Magazine* (December 1784): 337.
43. Ibid.
44. See note 6.
45. *Gentlemen and Ladies Magazine* (March 1789): 85.
46. Ibid., 147.
47. *Gentlemen and Ladies Town and Country Magazine* (June 1789): 245.
48. *Gentlemen and Ladies Town and Country Magazine* (August 1789): 339. "The Matron," a column appearing in the *Gentlemen and Ladies Town and Country Magazine,* reinforces the pervasive problems women experienced in marriage, including a faithful wife's contraction of venereal disease from her husband. Letters to the editor also included the query of an overly passionate wife, whose unruly emotions the editors advised she curb, and a woman who, abandoned by a husband who has since married another, wonders about the legalities of marrying another husband.
49. *Lady's Magazine; and Repository of Entertaining Knowledge* 1 (January 1792): 37.
50. Ibid., 64.
51. Ibid., 66.
52. Ibid., 66–67.
53. Ibid., 65. Branson mentions this essay in her study but emphasizes its post-Revolutionary context and references to "mutual" obedience (13).

54. *Gentlemen and Ladies Town and Country Magazine* (November 1784): 290–91.
55. *Lady's Magazine; and Repository of Entertaining Knowledge* (July 1792): 77.
56. Ibid., 78.
57. Ibid., 79.
58. *Lady's Magazine; and Repository of Entertaining Knowledge* (June 1792): 24.
59. Ibid.
60. The fiction in the *Lady's Magazine* consistently presents parents as being owed obedience. In contrast, the *Gentlemen and Ladies Town and Country Magazine* portrays parents as tyrannical, lacking in sentiment, and motivated by ambition.
61. *Gentlemen and Ladies Town and Country Magazine* (September 1789): 432.
62. Ibid.
63. *Gentlemen and Ladies Town and Country Magazine* (July 1789): 306.
64. In the *Gentlemen and Ladies Town and Country Magazine*, education is consistently linked to class.
65. *Gentlemen and Ladies Town and Country Magazine* (August 1789): 354–55.
66. *Gentlemen and Ladies Town and Country Magazine* (September 1789): 402.
67. *Gentlemen and Ladies Town and Country Magazine* (October 1789): 463.
68. Ibid., 464.
69. This turn of plot marks one of the few instances in the *Gentlemen and Ladies Town and Country Magazine* in which a father's control over his progeny and their mates operates for the powers of good. By contrast, "The Story of Constantius and Pulchera," "The Story of Alcander and Rosilla," and "The Two sisters, or Lucinda and Leonora," like Rowson's *Charlotte Temple*, hinge on fathers' tyranny and opposition to marriages of affection.
70. *Gentlemen and Ladies Town and Country Magazine* (November 1789): 527.
71. Felicia's views echo those expressed by Eliza in *The Coquette*. Following her fall from social grace, Eliza reveals that the "imaginary" grief contained in novels and plays tempers her enjoyment of them. See Hannah

W. Foster, *The Coquette*, ed. Cathy N. Davidson (New York: Oxford UP, 1986), 210–14.

72. *Gentlemen and Ladies Town and Country Magazine* (January 1790): 624.

73. Ibid., 625.

74. Jay Fliegelman discusses this phenomenon in terms of eighteenth-century philosophers Adam Smith and Benjamin Rush. Smith argued that sympathy was an "active" virtue, enabling humans, through "moral projection," to "feel another's woe." By contrast, Fliegelman argues, Rush pathologized sympathy, as it made one vulnerable to disease and the petitions of the self-serving. See *Prodigals and Pilgrims: The American Revolution against Patriarchal Authority, 1750–1800* (Cambridge: Cambridge UP, 1982), 231–32.

75. See Cathy N. Davidson, *Revolution and the Word: The Rise of the Novel in America* (New York: Oxford UP, 1986), 182. Despite its short length (some editions are only twenty-five pages long), Davidson considers the book as a novel.

76. Davidson, *Revolution and the Word*, 182.

77. *Gentlemen and Ladies Town and Country Magazine* (June 1789): 227–28.

78. Ibid., 229.

79. Davidson, *Revolution and the Word*, 184.

80. Ibid., 185.

81. Ibid., 184–85.

82. Under the name Robert Shurtlliff, Sampson enlisted, fought, was wounded in battle, and, years later, successfully petitioned the U.S. government for a pension for her service. For an extremely well researched study of Herman Mann's fictionalized biography of Sampson, see Judith Hiltner, "'She Bled in Secret': Deborah Sampson, Herman Mann and *The Female Review*," *Early American Literature* 34 (1999): 190–220.

83. Rachel Blau DuPlessis formulated the concept of writing "beyond the ending," or writing women into texts in ways that defy conventional plots in *Writing beyond the Ending: Narrative Strategies of Twentieth-Century Women Writers* (Bloomington: Indiana UP, 1985). Joanna Russ discusses the problem with relation to contemporary fiction in "What Can a Heroine Do? or Why Women Can't Write," *Images of Women in Fiction: Feminist Perspectives*, ed. Susan K. Cornillon et al. (Bowling Green, OH: Bowling Green U Popular P, 1972), 3–20. In *The Plight of Feeling: Sympathy and Dissent in the Early American Novel* (Chicago: U of Chicago P, 1997), Julia A. Stern argues that early American women novelists place women in the

public sphere but fail to question the parameters of that sphere in ways that could significantly change ideas about women's roles.

84. *Gentlemen and Ladies Town and Country Magazine* (June 1789): 228.

85. *Gentlemen and Ladies Town and Country Magazine* (August 1789): 349.

86. Ibid., 350.

87. In order to parse the dynamics of cross-dressing, this reading deliberately plays down the rather obvious interpretation that, as with Susanna Rowson's *Charlotte Temple* and Hannah Webster Foster's *The Coquette*, the text uses Pulchera to represent a youthful America brutalized by its tyrannical father, England.

88. *Gentlemen and Ladies Town and Country Magazine* (August 1789): 351.

89. Ibid.

90. In his introduction to *The Female Marine* (1814), historian Daniel A. Cohen argues that late-eighteenth- and early-nineteenth-century audiences were perfectly comfortable with women donning men's clothes, since they viewed gender as largely performative. See Daniel A. Cohen, ed., *The Female Marine and Related Works: Narratives of Cross-Dressing and Urban Vice in America's Early Republic* (Amherst: U of Massachusetts P, 1997), 1–45.

91. Thomas Walter Laqueur, *Making Sex: Body and Gender from the Greeks to Freud* (Cambridge: Harvard UP, 1990), 6.

92. Marjorie B. Garber, *Vested Interests: Cross-Dressing and Cultural Anxiety* (New York: Routledge P, 1992), 16.

93. See, for example, Susan Juster, "'Neither male nor female': Jemima Wilkinson and the Politics of Post-Revolutionary America," in *Possible Pasts: Becoming Colonial in Early America*, ed. Robert Blair St. George (Ithaca: Cornell UP, 2000), 357–79.

94. *Gentlemen and Ladies Town and Country Magazine* (November 1789): 522.

95. Constantius has not seemed to lift a finger since fighting a duel with Le Monte on a ship. By contrast, Pulchera's incessant activity is suggestive of the labor required to resist dominant cultural representations of women. One imagines that readers by this point grew weary for her and prayed that she find asylum—even in domesticity.

96. *Gentlemen and Ladies Town and Country Magazine* (January 1790): 629.

97. Ibid.

98. This image seems to convey the complication of narrative cross-dressing for readers of a periodical addressed to "ladies" but edited presumably by men who publish essays ostensibly written by women as well as by men or by writers whose gender is not marked.

99. For a fuller discussion of cross-dressing and its relationship to eighteenth-century authorship, see Lisa Logan, "Columbia's Daughters in Drag; or, Cross-Dressing, Collaboration, and Authorship in Early America," unpublished essay delivered at Omohundro Institute for Early American History and Culture, 7th Annual Conference, University of Glasgow, Scotland, July 11, 2001.

Seth Cotlar

Reading the Foreign News, Imagining an American Public Sphere

Radical and Conservative Visions of "the Public" in Mid-1790s Newspapers

In late 1794, the public career of Thomas Greenleaf, the editor of New York's leading opposition newspaper, was in serious jeopardy. The most powerful men in the country were determined to destroy both him and the political club of which he was a leading member, the Democratic-Republican Society of New York. George Washington's November message to Congress blamed such "self-created societies" for the recent Whiskey Rebellion in western Pennsylvania. Rumors circulated that Congress intended to outlaw political clubs, and to encourage this action Federalist newspapers across the nation vilified the clubs as bastions of infidelity and anarchy. Greenleaf responded to this situation by filling his *New York Journal* with examples of well-known reformers from the recent past who had formed political associations to further the cause of liberty and equality. Indeed, the columns of his newspaper in late 1794 read like a roll call of the standard, democratic heroes of British America's late eighteenth century—Joseph Gerrald, Thomas Muir, Joseph Fyshe Palmer, William Skirving, Maurice Margarot, Thomas Hardy, Daniel Iaaac Eaton, John Thelwall, Robert Watt, David Downie, Archibald Hamilton Rowan, Napper Tandy, and John Horne Tooke. Greenleaf's regular readers would have recognized the names and known the stories of these British and Irish radicals who had been prosecuted for treason by the Pitt administration in 1794,[1] yet the same could probably be said for only a few contemporary scholars of American history or literature. This speaks volumes about both the transatlantic nature of American print culture in the 1790s and the dearth of transatlantic scholarship on that decade.

Indeed, most recent interpretations of the Democratic-Republican Societies frame them as a resurgence of American Revolutionary–era practices and ideologies.[2] Greenleaf's transatlantic defense of his political activities, however, urges us to rethink the solely American focus of such interpretations. When forced to justify their political activities in 1794, newspaper editors and Democratic-Republican Society members such as Greenleaf, Benjamin Franklin Bache (Philadelphia *Aurora*), Thomas Adams (Boston *Independent Chronicle*) and John Bradford (Kentucky *Gazette*) only rarely trotted out the American pantheon of Samuel Adams, John Hancock, the Committees of Correspondence, the Sons of Liberty, and the like. Instead they wrote glowing accounts of the French Jacobin clubs, memorialized the British and Irish martyrs listed above, and reprinted column after column of declarations from the organizations that these European radicals had formed—the London Corresponding Society, the Sheffield Society for Constitutional Information, the United Irishmen, and many others. Democratic editors, their readers, and their political opponents interpreted this foreign news, and those interpretations shaped the American debate over the role of the public in general and the Democratic-Republican Societies in particular.[3]

What those editors chose to see when they looked across the ocean were ordinary citizens using the mechanisms of print and public meetings to construct a more radically democratic polity. In the brief utopian moment of the early- and mid-1790s, self-described "democrats" throughout the Atlantic world explored some of the most radical implications of popular sovereignty—a widely accepted political doctrine that legitimated both the American and British political regimes.[4] In its most simple formulation, the notion of popular sovereignty held that political institutions should not be regarded as a cherished and inviolable inheritance, but rather as elaborate artifices constructed by the people who lived under them. This vision of politics raised the difficult question of when the process of political construction and reconstruction should stop. Where should the line be drawn between the role of the sovereign citizenry and that of their designated rulers? Once "the people" had theoretically crafted the constitutions under which they lived, should they then regard themselves as politically passive between election days? If certain portions of the citizenry disagreed with the actions of their representatives, how could the political system be constructed so as to incorporate their opinions into the decision making process? Or did the mere act of voting encompass the full exertion of their sovereignty? In forcing such questions to the fore, the Atlantic world's democrats pushed the political project of the Enlightenment to some of its most radically inclusive and participatory extremes. While all could agree that the people were sovereign, it remained to be seen what that theory would look like in practice.

In the late 1770s and 1780s, in the process of forming their state constitutions, a few Americans had explored some of the more radical implications of popular sovereignty. After the perceived crisis of the confederation period, however, many American leaders sought to limit the potential meanings of popular sovereignty and thus to bring that period of experimentation to an end. Jeremy Belknap, for example, noted in a letter to a friend: "Let it stand as a principle that government originates from the people, but let it be taught . . . that they are not able to govern themselves."[5] Benjamin Rush likewise perceived danger in the sentiment that "the sovereign and all other power is seated in the people." Rush stressed that the people "possess it only on the days of their elections. After this, it is the property of their rulers."[6] To a great extent, the Constitutional Convention of 1787 was an attempt to reinforce the boundary between the rulers and the ruled and thereby restrain the "excesses" of popular sovereignty, excesses that had legitimated popular movements and uprisings in several states as well as the pro-debtor policies that these groups had demanded.

The French, British, and Irish popular radicalism of the 1790s worked at counter-purposes to America's constitutional settlement, making it easier for democrats to reopen the conversation about popular sovereignty and consider new meanings for three concepts that were intimately related to it—representation, public opinion, and citizenship. In the 1790s, as unprecedented numbers of ordinary citizens in the Atlantic world joined political groups and created a market for political newspapers and pamphlets aimed explicitly at non-elites, they rendered plausible the radically active and inclusive visions of "the public" (or "the people") that pro-French Revolutionary writers such as Thomas Paine espoused. In the early 1790s, buoyed by the initial success of Europe's democratic revolutions, Painite democrats saturated the world of print with utopian ideas about how political representation could be made more actual and authentic, how public opinion could play a larger role in the day-to-day decision making of politics, and how citizens could exert their sovereignty in between elections. Where the voluntary political organizations that had emerged during the American Revolution (such as the Sons of Liberty and the Committees of Correspondence) framed themselves as temporary, defensive actions intended to fight off corruption, the political groups of the 1790s (and the democratic newspapers that supported them) began to see themselves as potentially permanent features of the political system. British radical David Williams captured this new aspect of popular political action in 1791, when he noted that even though modern philosophers such as John Locke and Jean-Jacques Rousseau had discovered some of the key truths of political theory, they had stopped short of engaging with "the problem most important to the happiness of mankind"—that is, the problem of "governing all by all."[7]

For the democrats of the 1790s, public opinion (or what one might call an active political public sphere) promised to solve the problem of how that first, unified "all" could authentically represent that second, polyvocal all. At the center of this emerging variety of democratic theory lay the utopian idea that the unified voice could never legitimately exclude any portion of the populace. As one New York democrat put it in 1796: "every attempt [to] silence the speculative voice of any small part of the people on subjects relating to the public interest, upon the ground of their being but a minority, is . . . a treasonable attempt to stifle the voice of the sovereign whole."[8] Painite reformers sought to bolster institutions such as the free press, voluntary organizations such as the Democratic-Republican Societies, and public education in the hopes of making the process of public-opinion formation as open and inclusive as possible. Most important, public opinion appealed to these reformers because it was capable of both changing along with the times and providing a unifying center to the nation. It lent the actions of the governing body a contingent authenticity, thus keeping the government in a state of what Paine called "constant maturity."[9] It was the process of approaching authentic representation that counted, and a rich public sphere served as the institutional embodiment of this process.

This attempt to theorize a more substantive role for nonelected citizens in the daily work of politics—an intellectual tradition that can be referred to as "radical publicity"—has dropped out of modern accounts of 1790s American political thought. Gordon Wood's brief discussion of public opinion in *The Radicalism of the American Revolution*, for example, acknowledges that Americans in the 1790s regarded it as the "vital principle underlying American government, society, and culture." Although it was an important concept, Wood argues that no one ever seriously thought about public opinion; rather, it "was like vegetation, it was like sunshine: no one knew how it worked." This fits neatly into Wood's depiction of "democracy" as an untheorized, anti-intellectual, individualistic, and essentially amoral impulse.[10] The democrats of the 1790s, according to Wood, had abandoned the orienting, unified republican vision of the common good for a liberal, laissez-faire pursuit of their own, various goods. In contrast to that account, this essay argues that many democrats did consciously seek to bring order out of the chaos of proliferating self-interests; however, they looked to an active public sphere (comprised of institutions like widely disseminated and affordable political newspapers and the DRS), rather than to supposedly disinterested leaders, to define the common good. "Citizen" Richard Lee, a radical émigré from Britain who began publishing the *American Universal Magazine* soon after his arrival in Philadelphia, pithily captured the essence of these democrats' intellectual project with this question: "The general will is always good . . . but by what sign shall we know it?"[11] Indeed, for those many Americans who, like Lee and others in his cohort of international radicals, had rejected the republican ideal of rule by a virtuous elite, it was precisely the vague but inspiring notion of public opinion (the "sign" by which the general will could theoretically be known) that held out the possibility of putting the doctrine of popular sovereignty in its most literal sense into operation.

1790s Visions of Radical Publicity in the Democratic-Republican Societies and the Opposition Newspapers

In 1793 and 1794, groups of disgruntled Americans in some forty localities formed political clubs dedicated to discussing and making public their opposition to the domestic and foreign policies of the Washington administration. These Democratic-Republican Societies[12] were composed of white men from across the ethnic and socio-economic spectrum—artisans, farmers, mechanics, laborers, professionals, landed elites, and a few merchants. Joined together by committees of correspondence and frequent intervisitation, these societies, in both their public meetings and the innumerable declarations and lists of toasts they published in newspapers across the country, articulated a vision of politics in which citizens played a more substantive role than merely electing representatives, where public opinion would have a greater impact on the shaping of political policies, and where opinion formation would be more open, inclusive and rational. In their most optimistic moments, Democratic-Republican Society members imagined a nation comprised of radically active citizens who contributed to the country's governance through their participation in local, public meetings and through their actions as readers of and contributors to the nation's burgeoning print culture. Although many historians (like the opponents of the Democratic-Republican Societies in the 1790s) have interpreted these societies as cynical forms of partisanship intended to do little more than replace current leaders with new ones, many advocates of these societies regarded them as a far more fundamental challenge to the way politics would be conducted in the new nation. Politics, as these democrats conceived of it, would no longer consist of the actions that leaders took inside the halls of formal power; rather, it would become the vocation of innumerable reader-citizens who regarded their periodicals of choice as powerful mediators between their private opinions and the world of public politics. To eighteenth-century critics (and many modern observers), this radically inclusive and decentralized vision of politics seemed threateningly anarchical. Caught up as they were in the excitement over the revolutions sweeping the Atlantic world in the 1790s, however, the democrats under investigation here saw only boundless possibilities in their new conceptualizations of print, public opinion, and politics.

A good example of these more radical visions is a 1796 essay written by DEMOCRITUS for *Greenleaf's New York Journal.* He began his summary of the "FUNDAMENTAL PRINCIPLES" that should govern "REPUBLICAN SOCIETY" with the uncontestable assertion that all power flows from the people and should be exercised for their "impartial benefit." According to DEMOCRITUS, the continued exercise of popular sovereignty in the strictest sense was "impracticable" because of the "numbers, local diffusion, &c." of the people. Yet, despite these obstacles, he insisted that the "general political will is necessarily impartial and incorrupt" and thus should not be thought wanting just because it must exercise its power through representatives "who may have a sinister bias." Whenever the general will did "deviate from the pursuit of the common good," it resulted only from "want of further or more general knowledge; hence appears the necessity of a thorough diffusion of information in a state, and of research, vigilant inspection, and communication." According to DEMOCRITUS, the best means "for calling forth the declaration of the popular sentiment [were] small assemblies of citizens, frequently combining their researches on subjects relating to the public good, and publishing the result of their deliberations for approbation or correction. . . The more generally such social combinations are distributed in a state, the more impartial and efficacious will be the operation."[13] What DEMOCRITUS imagined here was an inclusive, participatory politics that was both embodied (in the form of public meetings) and disembodied (in the form of printed accounts of those meetings). While his essay may read today as an abstract, rather vague paean to the people, it would have appeared to readers of the revolutionary 1790s as part of a broader plan to construct the concrete mechanisms of the political public sphere. The failure of his radical vision has made it difficult for modern observers to recapture the charged political valence he lent to a range of relatively uncontroversial terms that have since come to have far less radical connotations.

Take "public opinion," for example. In this essay DEMOCRITUS put to new, controversial use the widely held assumption that all governments relied upon public opinion for their stability and legitimacy. DEMOCRITUS's radical appropriation of public opinion differed significantly from the way moderates such as James Madison used the term in the 1790s. Madison, like David Hume before him, argued that "public opinion sets bounds to every government."[14] His point was a pragmatic one. Nations could no longer rely on physical force to extract loyalty from their citizens. Rather, rulers must pay some respect to "the sentiments of the people" and maintain their power by crafting policies that excited voluntary admiration and allegiance in the citizenry. In this Madisonian model, public opinion played a constraining rather than a constitutive role in governing the nation. A few delegated rulers did the constructive work of generating laws and policies to govern the nation, while the role of the general public was to vote their rulers into office and occasionally express their approval or disapproval of the political decisions worked out inside the houses of Congress. Only in times of crisis, when the government seriously infringed on the peoples' rights, could the broader public legitimately take on an active, shaping role. DEMOCRITUS, in contrast to Madison, imagined a public that was continually active and deliberating. The public imagined in his essay—and scores of others like it in the opposition press of the early 1790s—sought to do more than merely agree or disagree with governmental acts. It claimed the right to shape them.

DEMOCRITUS's editorial must also be read in the context of an ongoing debate about how to avoid the antidemocratic possibilities inherent in a government based on representation. Should yearly elections provide the only means through which the people expressed their sovereignty? Were electoral results, in other words, an authentic sign of the general will? DEMOCRITUS was just one among many in the 1790s who answered no to these questions.[15] For such thinkers, only a vocal, deliberative public could ensure that the representation of the people that ruled over them would be as accurate and authentic as possible. Having rejected a vision of society in which the few decided for the many, 1790s democrats followed David Williams's previously mentioned suggestion that "the only skill and knowledge of any value in politics, is that of governing All by All."[16] In this conception of politics, elections functioned as a necessary but imperfect means to discern the general will. This cardinal principle for early 1790s democrats departed significantly from the theorizing of most American leaders during the founding era. In *Federalist No. 10*, for example, Madison framed the election of representatives not as a necessary evil, but as a useful mechanism that could "refine and enlarge the public views by passing them through the medium of a chosen body of citizens."[17] Indeed, in *Federalist No. 63* Madison argued that the superiority of the American constitution over ancient republics lay in its "total exclusion of the people in their collective capacity" from the process of lawmaking. This skepticism about the possibility of public reason informed much of the opposition to radical theories of publicity. For DEMOCRITUS the vision of a rational republic where every person had a right to shape the laws under which they lived made the necessity of what Paine called "representation ingrafted upon democracy" palatable.[18] His opponents reversed this formulation, arguing that the "refining" and "enlarging" function of representation tempered the more radical, destabilizing possibilities of a government of the people.

In Billerica, Massachusetts, several hundred miles from New York, William Manning, a farmer and tavern keeper who was an avid reader of the opposition press, put forward a strikingly similar theory of radical publicity in an unpublished, 1797 manuscript titled *The Key of Libberty*. Manning's essay explored how the few had managed to maintain their power over the many in the new republic, despite the fact that Americans had just fought a revolution against such unjust political arrangements. For Manning the problem was that elites had a highly developed network of social, professional, and literary clubs that knit them together, while the many remained divided because no institutions existed that could enable them to pool their knowledge and opinions. Thus, the only way the humble majority could counter the power of the exalted few and establish a more truly democratic government was by forming a national system for the dissemination of political information to ordinary citizens. Manning mapped out a detailed plan for a national "Society of Laborers" broken down into state, county, and town divisions. Membership was open to "all the free male persons in the United States who are twenty-one years of age, who labor for a living" as well as "all persons of any other denominations, provided they subscribe to its funds and submit to the regulations of the society." Each division would be supplied (ideally at the federal government's expense) with copies of the organization's monthly magazine and would then periodically meet to read and discuss it along with other political texts. The ultimate goal of the society was "to establish as cheap, easy, and sure conveyance of knowledge and learning for a laborer to have as possible."[19] Although his arguments did not start from the same universalistic principles as DEMOCRITUS's, Manning came up with a similar solution—the formation of political societies of nonelected citizens throughout the nation bound together through print—to the same problem—the limitations of the representative system.

While most historians regard Manning as a product of a uniquely American style of politics, the specifics of his plan echo all of the key themes of the transatlantic discourse of radical publicity. In one of the few lengthy, modern analyses of Manning's work, Sean Wilentz and Michael Merrill cite two sources of inspiration for his Laborers Society, the Committees of Correspondence of the 1770s and the Methodist's regional, national, and international method of organization. While these sources were undoubtedly influential, Manning's essay can also be read as an extended engagement with the uniquely cosmopolitan, oppositional print culture of the 1790s.[20] His newspaper of choice, Boston's *Independent Chronicle*—with its excerpts from the Atlantic world's other, leading democratic papers (such as DEMOCRITUS's *New York Journal*) as well as its sympathetic accounts of English, Scottish, Irish, and French radicals' attempts to operationalize democratic theories of popular sovereignty—functioned as a primer of sorts for the political public sphere. Like Manning, the *Independent Chronicle*'s editor Thomas Adams sought to marshal opinion against power, a vocal public against elites who thought themselves uniquely qualified to govern. And like DEMOCRITUS and other democrats throughout the Atlantic world, Manning sought a solution through small, popular associations that could use the expanding institutions of popular print culture to channel local opinions into a national, public discussion.

The editors of the three most influential and frequently excerpted democratic papers of the 1790s—Benjamin Franklin Bache of Philadelphia's *Aurora*,

Thomas Greenleaf of the *New York Journal*, and Thomas Adams of Boston's *Independent Chronicle*—shared DEMOCRITUS and Manning's vision of an increasingly democratized public sphere.[21] All three editors were leading members of their local Democratic-Republican Societies, and their readership was composed of those Americans most likely to sympathize with current European and American political innovations. Through their daily presentation of foreign events, these editors crafted a compelling narrative of the relationship between their own associational activities and the actions of their democratic compatriots in Europe. As they printed story after story about the successes of European political associations as well as reports of the governmental persecution that they and their members faced, these editors used Europe as a mirror in which Americans could see various, future incarnations of themselves. Vehemently pro-French, the editors presented readers with what seemed like an easy choice. They could imagine themselves as stifled Britons banding together to protect their rights from a war-hungry, unresponsive government or as free French citizens experimenting with institutions and policies that would create a more just and egalitarian society.

Advocates of radical publicity appropriated the language and method of Enlightenment science in order to reimagine the state as a constantly deliberative, more literally self-governing entity. Where the editor of the conservative *Gazette of the United States* thought that his allotted role was to "conciliate the minds of our citizens, to the proceedings of the Federal Legislature,"[22] opposition editors argued that newspapers should do much more than elaborate on the ideas worked out inside the halls of Congress. As one writer put it in Philip Freneau's *National Gazette*, "The action of laws upon public opinion, and the re-action of that opinion upon government, is the criterion, by which to judge of the wisdom, the policy, or the folly of political measures." In the age of democratic revolutions the government was no longer the only pro-active political entity. The key problem was to rethink the impact "of the government upon the people, and of the people upon the government," or, in other words, how these two separate but intimately connected entities could shape each other yet not be dissolved into one entity.[23] It was this perceived dilemma that drove many Americans to begin thinking about concrete institutions that could serve the function of collecting and articulating the opinions of those people who did not happen to occupy an official position in the government.

In America the first public call for the formation of explicitly political voluntary societies appeared in 1792 on a day that was becoming increasingly symbolic for democrats and increasingly disliked by Federalists, July 4.[24] A correspondent of the *National Gazette* observed that political societies had been formed in Britain, and he sent along an extract "from a London publication" illustrating the principles of one of them, the Friends of the People. In defense of their entrance onto the public stage, this British group declared that "equal active citizenship, is the unalienable right of all men—minors, criminals, and insane persons excepted." With this open-ended, French-inflected rhetoric of citizenship they situated themselves firmly in the utopian present: "We contemplate with pleasure the progress which this nation, and mankind in general, are now making in the hitherto mysterious science of government. We see a spirit of calm rational enquiry arising and diffusing itself among all orders of people, of a nature totally different from the tumultuous malevolence of party, and the artful policy of statesmen." They thus distinguished their project from the way politics had traditionally been conducted by a constricted governing elite. Although their claim that they were not a party was standard fare in eighteenth-century British politics, their alternative vision of how the nation should be governed departed significantly from the arguments traditionally adopted by opposition groups. They did not simply frame themselves as the politically pure "outs" who saw the "ins" as irretrievably corrupt. Instead they called for a structural transformation of British politics that would permanently render it more inclusive and participatory. In pursuit of this new politics, they announced their desire to unite "with several societies already formed in various parts of the nation" and went on to "CALL UPON OUR FELLOW CITIZENS OF ALL DESCRIPTIONS, TO INSTITUTE SIMILAR SOCIETIES, FOR THE SAME GREAT PURPOSE, and we recommend a general correspondence with each other."[25] The American who submitted this extract shared their enthusiasm, recommending "that societies should be formed in every county of the United States upon similar plans." Making the link between French, British and American politics even more explicit, he ended by suggesting that "the 14th day of July would be a good time for annual meetings of those Societies."

A few weeks later, editor Philip Freneau included in the same paper two more pieces that used foreign events to justify a call for the creation of political societies in America. After reprinting yet another address from the Friends of the People in London, one of Freneau's correspondents noted that "From the spirit and tenor of the above address, it is most presumeable . . . that the late proclamation of the British king, against what are termed seditious publications and associations, is . . . pointed at the friends of the people, and other societies now forming in England." The following article provided an American democrat's gloss on this news, suggesting that the repression of an emerging British public carried lessons for American democrats: "at the dawn of the present glorious revolution in France, political clubs frequently met at the coffeehouses; the king issued an edict prohibiting such meetings—The kings of Europe are at this moment using every effort to prevent their subjects from investigating the principles of religion or government: And a junto of American aristocrats, influenced by the same spirit, are pursuing similar measures." Even worse, the proadministration papers in America (such as the *Gazette of the United States*) were contributing to this backlash and acting much the same way as the antidemocratic prints in Europe. "A venal press, considered as a necessary appendage to the general government, is constantly employed in bestowing fulsome commendations on the most unwarrantable acts of government; and in abusing those free citizens who presume to come forward with their opinions on public measures."[26] That writer thus framed the political present, in Europe and America, as a battle between two forces: the "people," who were increasingly demanding a greater role in politics, and those who opposed the new forms of publicity being expressed in voluntary societies and newspapers throughout the Atlantic world.

With such stories, opposition newspaper editors used news from Europe to define their political vision against what they defined as a British model of politics, a model that denied that the nonelected public had any role in the process of law and policy formation. On a daily basis, opposition newspaper editors such as Bache, Greenleaf, Adams, and Freneau offered up inspiring accounts of European democrats who were forming institutions dedicated to the discussion of political issues. They wove this foreign news into an analysis of domestic politics, framing the Democratic-Republican Societies as an American expression of an international movement on behalf of the people and framing the societies' enemies as part of a similarly transatlantic, British-led effort to turn back the tide of popular politics. The future of the newly forming American public, in other words, was intimately bound up with the future of the various European publics struggling into existence against the resistance of the world's monarchists and aristocrats.

This transatlantic narrative saturated the public pronouncements of the Democratic-Republican Societies.[27] These clubs rarely linked their efforts to their American Revolutionary predecessors like the Sons of Liberty or the Committees of Correspondence, choosing instead to identify with their fellow democrats across the ocean.[28] In 1794, for example, a writer who identified as "A DEMOCRAT" credited the French Revolution for reinvigorating American popular politics. "It is well known that, after the adoption of the federal constitution, a general negligence of their political affairs seemed to pervade almost every class of citizens. It appeared as if they had said . . . 'our constitution is formed and adopted, and our general government established; let the respective officers of it act as they please, as for us, we will give ourselves no further trouble. . . .' Had not the French revolution commenced, we know not to what lengths this spirit might have been carried. But that glorious revolution has awakened us from our stupidity."[29] This narrative of the French Revolution enabled American democrats to frame themselves not as dangerous innovators, but as participants in a virtuous political movement that had begun in America in the 1770s, had dissipated in the late 1780s, but now had been resuscitated in Europe. When Americans across the new nation raised their glasses to the ubiquitous 1790s toast

"The Democratic Societies throughout the world,"[30] they declared their allegiance to an international movement that sought to expand the political role and power of ordinary citizens.

Almost every week between the June 1792 and late 1794 regular readers of the opposition press would have encountered stories that portrayed the active citizens of Europe debating political matters in voluntary societies and communicating their opinions to other, like-minded groups. Bache informed his readers on April 20, 1793, for example, that "The Irish newspapers we have received by the late arrivals, contain in every page spirited resolutions of a political nature entered into by numerous associations throughout the country."[31] The examples of these resolutions that he parceled out over the following weeks probably met with many receptive readers. Pennsylvanians had formed their first Democratic-Republican Society and issued its first "spirited resolution" only one month before these pieces had appeared, and the state's most influential society emerged only a few weeks after it. Bache's compatriot in New York, Greenleaf, also found the resolutions of foreign political clubs repeatedly newsworthy. On February 19, 1794, for example, he informed his readers that he had just received a cache of British newspapers. Significantly, the pieces that struck him as being most worthy of republication on that day were several laudatory stories about the London Corresponding Society.

Opposition editors used such accounts of foreign events to do more than simply demonstrate that Europeans were forming political societies like the ones emerging in the United States. They also discussed in concrete terms how these societies experimented with innovative political ideas, many of which were more democratic than those currently dominant in America. On February 19, 1794, for example, Greenleaf reported that "a CONVENTION of delegates from certain [British] societies [met in Edinburgh] for the purpose of obtaining a REFORM of . . . Parliament on the principles of universal suffrage." The manifesto that had outlined the goals of this convention was widely available in America, as was the radical French constitution of 1793 that inspired it.[32] In these documents—which all opposition editors advertised for sale—American democrats read about plans to divide the nation into small, primary assemblies in which citizens could debate and suggest amendments to proposed laws. These documents teemed with ideas and concrete models of how to politicize the people by disseminating cheap pamphlets, holding public meetings, and organizing reading and debating societies for laborers. American readers also found in these documents a compelling rhetoric of radical popular sovereignty that conjured up a world in which the people would be "joint sovereigns" and where they would be subject to no laws that they had not had a hand in constructing. Thus, in the newspapers and bookshops of Democratic-Republican Society leaders such as Greenleaf and Bache, Americans encountered an inspirational (and highly selective) picture of ordinary European citizens voluntarily banding together to create a political and social system that would enable "the people" to govern themselves in a far more literal sense than in any other nation in recent history, even America.

The utopian and experimental political atmosphere of the early 1790s made it relatively easy for the Democratic-Republican Societies to legitimate their innovative organizations. They claimed to advocate nothing more than the rights of rational citizenship and argued that those who opposed their project must be Burkean elitists. In May 1794, for example, one defender of the societies sarcastically suggested that the Federalists hated them only because they encouraged a critical attitude in a populace that was supposedly "well disposed to submit to any thing that they were told was for their good." This author confidently mimicked the Federalists' disdain for those ordinary citizens who admired the French revolutionaries: "The people are running crazy with the idea of citizen, and citizen implies the right to think, and the right to think implies an analysis of governmental doctrines and measures, and oh! horrid to relate, an analysis of this sort."[33] Federalist fear of the societies, this democrat argued, was nothing more than fear of having their actions exposed to the people at large. The societies thus claimed to advocate openness, not revolution as their enemies charged. Repeatedly, American democrats played the role of the innocent inquirer, seeking only to "banish mystery from politics, open every channel of information, call for investigation, [and] tempt a discussion of measures." They defended such public inquiry and discussion on the seemingly unobjectionable basis that in the ideal republic "the public sentiment will be the best criterion of what is right and what is wrong in government."[34] As the Canaan Democratic Society stated in its constitution: "the political happiness of every enlightened people depends on their observance of the Democratical form of republican government, which is untenable without social union and communication." The societies claimed to reject crass partisanship, arguing instead that their purpose was merely to provoke public discussions of political matters to make the "real public opinion known, as much as possible, by those in power."[35]

With this rhetoric about the legibility of government and the desire to collect and articulate public opinion, the societies described themselves as utterly unthreatening to any legitimate government. A writer in the (Boston) *Independent Chronicle* of September 15, 1794, asked, "Why are these people so alarmed at these societies? Are they afraid to have measures of government considered by the citizens? Do they wish to keep all public transactions within a particular circle[?]" George III's repression of similar political societies provided ample ammunition for those American democrats who sought to resist Federalist criticisms. When Congress began debating whether the Democratic-Republican Societies should be censured or outlawed, the German Republican Society of

Pennsylvania drew attention to "The most extraordinary fact . . . that *patriotic societies were the objects of denunciations in the same year, in Great Britain, France and the United States of America!!"* The society framed these denunciations as an attempt to squelch one of the key aspects of any legitimate polity, freely formed public opinion. "Men are the creatures of opinion, and it is by means of opinion alone that laws in all well regulated societies can and ought to be enforced." Opinion was so important because representatives could never be entirely trusted: "rulers have no more virtue than the ruled, the equilibrium between them can only be preserved by proper attention and association; for the power of government can only be kept within its constituted limits by the display of a power equal to itself, the collected sentiment of the people. . . . To obtain a connected voice associations of some sort are necessary, no matter by what names they are designated."[36] While later political actors could use the term *public opinion* as if such a thing already existed and as if they had uniquely authentic access to it, the democrats of the early 1790s recognized, at least to some extent, the complexity of how public opinions were formed. For this reason, one of the centerpieces of their political project was the formation of concrete institutions in which substantive opinions could be formed, collected, and articulated. Publics could not merely be evoked; they had to be constructed and sustained.

What made this idealized radical Enlightenment vision appear even more inspirational and heroic was the violent resistance it met from British authorities. Throughout the summer of 1794, Greenleaf described for his readers how the Edinburgh Convention was broken up by authorities and its leaders transported to Botany Bay. Greenleaf deluged his readers with almost daily updates on the latest monarchical attempts to squelch reform, and he lost few opportunities to draw a parallel between the actions of the British government and those of Americans who opposed the Democratic-Republican Societies. In July 1794, for example, Greenleaf reprinted George III's message to the House of Commons that vilified the seditious practices "*carried on by certain societies in London, in correspondence with societies in different parts of the country.*" He italicized this line so that readers would not overlook the connections between British and American opposition to political clubs. In another section of that same paper, Greenleaf noted that the leaders of several political societies in England had been arrested, and he followed this news with the sarcastic comment "How sweet is English liberty!" By printing story after story about the repression of British political societies, Greenleaf crafted a nightmarish picture of a British politics that had essentially outlawed the Atlantic world's emerging practices of democratic self-rule, practices that he had been eagerly participating in and describing for his readers over the past few years.[37]

A group of Greenleaf's readers in Canaan, New York—a group that called themselves the "democratic society"—obviously found his cosmopolitan call to domestic political action compelling. Their constitution, which Greenleaf inserted in his paper in March 1794, claimed that they had formed a society "for elucidating and establishing . . . the Rights of Man . . . because a powerful combination in Europe seem now desperately bent on the extermination of liberty; while in these States the growing establishment of pride, formality, inequality . . . and a baneful and servile imitation of. . . corrupt nations . . . justly awaken the solicitude of the true patriot." According to these Canaan democrats, the present provided the best moment "to give force and effect to reformation, principles and regulations, in favor of the equal Rights of Man . . . because, the glorious revolutions of America and France, have now, more than ever, disclosed the true objects of society and free government." They ended their constitution with a list of abstract, Painite political principles that they wished to see better implemented in the new United States. Significantly, they did not identify these ideas or their group with any particular nation; rather, they proudly claimed to have rejected all "prejudice[s]," "religious, national and political." Here was Greenleaf's interpretation of the link between domestic and foreign events, appropriated by a group scores of miles from New York City, utilized as a justification for local political action, and then dispatched back to the city for publication and circulation among the area's other, as yet unorganized, democrats.

While these arguments about collecting the peoples' voice enabled the Democratic-Republican Societies to appear both constitutional and innocuous, the Whisky Rebellion in western Pennsylvania in the spring of 1794 raised some difficult problems for them. The Whiskey rebels shared the societies' critique of the Washington administration, and Federalist newspapers immediately attributed their armed resistance to the influence of the Democratic-Republican Societies. This widely disseminated charge forced American democrats to explain how their criticisms of the government differed from outright rebellion. In December 1794 a Democratic-Republican Society member tried to defend the group's actions, arguing that "a great distinction lays between opinion and action, should any citizen really and conscientiously believe that any particular act of government was either oppressive or injurious to the public good, he has an unquestionable right to publish that belief to his fellow-citizens, but at the same time it would be criminal in him to take up arms and forcibly resist the operations of a constitutional law."[38] Institutions dedicated to the exercise of public reason, in other words, differed widely from groups that used physical violence.

At the same time American democrats made this argument, however, the news from France was beginning to suggest that the Jacobin clubs, one of the models for the American societies, had been responsible for the widespread violence of Robespierre's Terror. Thus, on the same day that the above article distinguishing opinion from physical violence appeared in *Greenleaf's New York*

Journal, editor Thomas Greenleaf had to respond to reports in the Federalist press claiming that the French government had declared the Jacobin clubs a threat to the nation and had outlawed them. Greenleaf defensively argued that "The National Convention have asserted, and we pledge our reputation to prove it, that the *Popular Societies* have saved the Republic of France; they have also said that these Societies, are among the main pillars of the revolution; and . . . that they will never suffer these societies, or any other to *govern* the Convention; nor on the other hand shall they be suppressed by any means whatever."[39]

As it turned out, Greenleaf was wrong about events in France, but his defense of the societies reflects a key aspect of the emerging argument about how such clubs fit into the American political system. The combination of the Whiskey Rebellion and the Jacobin Terror forced the American Democratic-Republican Societies to stress their private or nonpolitical nature. They had to emphasize, in other words, that they did not seek to govern. Yet this diminution of their ability to effect change worked at counter-purposes to their goal, which was indeed to influence the process of political decision making. Thus, there was a key ambiguity at the heart of the emerging discourse of radical publicity—the societies were private, voluntary, and not an official part of the governing structure, yet they publicized their actions and explicitly sought to bring about concrete political changes. This contradiction had remained fairly hidden until the Whiskey Rebellion and the French Terror brought it to public attention.

Constructing an American Alternative to Radical Publicity

Until early 1794, opponents of the Democratic-Republican Societies had difficulty crafting legitimate arguments as to why they should be discouraged or outlawed. The societies were exercising their right to assemble and publish their opinions for others to read. How could that be dangerous? Furthermore, only the tyrannical British sought to squelch the expanding power of public reason, while French social and political advances testified to its benefits. This narrative was difficult to contradict in 1793 and early 1794, when public support for France and hatred of Britain remained strong. But two events in early 1794 raised difficult problems for the defenders of the Democratic-Republican Societies: the Whiskey Rebellion in western Pennsylvania and the increasingly dire news of the Jacobin Terror in France. Much has been written on how the Federalists successfully blamed the violence in Pennsylvania on the Democratic-Republican Societies, but the impact of the French Terror on American politics has received far less attention. Although it occurred thousands of miles away, the Terror transformed American political discourse by rendering visions of radical publicity highly susceptible to attack. As the brief moment of French-inspired political experimentation passed, advocates of radical democracy such as Greenleaf and DEMOCRITUS found their case harder to make in public forums.

Opponents of the Democratic-Republican Societies such as Noah Webster used accounts of the Terror in France to demonstrate that political clubs were effective only in undermining, not exercising, authority and that such clubs inevitably sought to take over the government and, when in power, tended toward tyranny. The guillotine provided just the latest evidence of this undeniable fact. Webster applied this analysis of France to the American scene in a series of essays on the French Revolution that was reprinted in Federalist newspapers throughout the country and eventually collected into a pamphlet.[40] Bache and Greenleaf countered Webster's attack on political clubs by emphasizing the distinction between French ideas, which were good, and French practice, which may have temporarily strayed off course as result of the pressures of war and the influence of a few corrupted men.[41] The Democratic-Republican Societies, they contended, fought only with "the weapons of reason"[42] that were incapable of inspiring physical violence. They charged that Webster wanted to turn America into Pitt's Britain, where they had suspended habeas corpus and essentially outlawed extraparliamentary political action. Trying desperately to triangulate their own project against the twin specters of French violence in the name of the people and British repression in defense of the government, the defenders of the Democratic-Republican Societies ironically had to emphasize the innocuous nature of their project to institutionalize public reason. Their attempts to defend the distinction between French principles and French practices, collective reason and collective violence, however, were no match for Webster's persuasive interpretation of the French Revolution.

Beginning in the summer of 1794 and continuing for the rest of the decade, the Federalist press eagerly exploited French news about the violent potential of popular political clubs and used it as a means to argue for their abolition. One writer in the *Gazette of the United States* asked incredulously whether "the Constitution countenances, much less acknowledges, that any set of men . . . shall *set themselves* up, as umpires between the people and the government the people themselves have established?" Unlike representatives who periodically returned to the general public, the democratic societies were permanent entities that threatened to "act with more energy and effect, and thereby encrease the momentum of their influence." According to that writer, the "good sense of the people" had until recently acted as a shield against the democratic societies and they were "not yet sufficiently strong to assume the powers of government openly." The future did not look promising, however, for the Jacobin clubs, which had provided "the MODEL" for the American societies, had changed the

French form of government four times in recent years. This demonstrated that these clubs were inconsistent with a "fixed form of government." While the writer admitted that "clubs may answer excellent purposes in destroying a bad government, . . . they were enemies to a settled state of things. . . . If our government is to be overturned, these societies are the best instruments to effect the work, they can answer *no other* purpose."[43]

In his widely disseminated and excerpted (New York) *Minerva*, Noah Webster consistently rang the changes on this same theme, printing almost daily pieces devoted to the idea that the salvation of the American political system lay in rejecting the French example. In October 1794, for example, he noted gleefully that "The hall of the Jacobins in Paris" had "been found equally inimical to the liberty of the people, as the Bastile." He suggested that the key to their meeting place "be sent to the celebrated WASHINGTON" and placed "beside that of the Bastile," which Washington had received from Lafayette in 1790. Just as Lafayette's celebrated gesture had symbolically linked the American and French Revolutions at the outset of the decade, Webster used the downfall of the Jacobins in 1794 to argue that Americans should learn from French failures and sever any remaining ties of political sympathy. Where the French Revolution had simply replaced the "despotism of absolute monarchy" with "the despotism of the Jacobin Clubs," Americans had the opportunity to avoid this fate as long as they shunned the political clubs that Webster claimed had done so much damage.[44] Indeed, one of the central themes of Webster's 1794 newspaper pieces on the French Revolution and the Democratic-Republican Societies was that such movements, built upon the fantasy of public reason, could easily fade into the catastrophe of collective violence. Over the course of the next several years, this initially controversial argument about the inevitable destructiveness of political clubs would become one of the central, unquestioned conventions of American political debate.

The most trying moment for America's advocates of radical publicity came in November 1794, when President Washington denounced the Democratic-Republican Societies in his address to Congress. Washington blamed "certain self-created societies" for the Whiskey Rebellion, describing the clubs as "combinations of men, who, careless of consequences . . . have disseminated . . . suspicions, jealousies, and accusations, of the whole Government." In past years Congress had simply echoed the president's words back to him in their formal response, but in the House of Representatives James Madison, who was chairman of the committee responsible for drafting the House's reply, sought to avoid any mention of "self-created societies." When Representative Thomas FitzSimons of Pennsylvania protested this omission, he began a debate that was to last almost a week. Something about these clubs struck a nerve inside the halls of Congress, and within days the congressional deliberations became the focus of innumerable newspaper and tavern debates throughout the country.[45]

In their opposition to the clubs, Federalists avoided the difficult question of whether these clubs were lawful and instead began crafting an argument for why these clubs posed a dangerous threat to the new nation's political system. Fully aware that the newspaper-reading public would be following their debate, Federalist congressmen used the occasion to explain why their fellow citizens should reject the forms of radical publicity that their democratic opponents advocated. Their appeal rested heavily on a new set of arguments (most forcefully and prominently articulated by Noah Webster in his newspaper articles and pamphlet on the French Revolution) about the uniqueness of the American situation: "In France, where a Despotism, impregnable to public opinion, had reigned—where no channel opened a sympathy by Representation with the great body of the nation—[political clubs] were admirably adapted to break down and subvert the old bulwark of habitual authority. But in America the case was widely different." Political societies may have been useful during the Revolutionary era, this congressman granted, but under the present constitutional order "the whole country is full of well-constituted organs of the People's will. . . . It would not be easy to organize the nation into a more multifarious shape."[46] The formal structures of the American government, in other words, accurately represented the people's will; thus, the Democratic-Republican Societies' attempts to imagine ways to gather public opinion more accurately and fully were entirely unnecessary.

Another Federalist, Fisher Ames, took this point one step further, arguing that the Democratic-Republican Societies' vision of public reason was philosophically incoherent and little more than a smokescreen for their sinister plans to undermine "the social order and the authority of the laws." According to Ames, the only way "this great people, so widely extended . . . could form a common will and make that will law" was by temporarily resigning their sovereignty to their chosen representatives. The democrats seemed to imagine their national network of political societies as "a substitute for representation," and according to Ames such visions of a truly self-governing nation were absurd: "shall the whole people be classed into clubs? Shall every six miles square be formed into a club sovereignty?" In their most utopian moments, Democratic-Republican Society members such as Greenleaf or his correspondent DEMOCRITUS may have answered yes to these questions, but they would not have agreed with Ames's claim that a nation populated with such institutions of public reason would inevitably succumb to either tyranny or anarchy. Where defenders of political clubs emphasized the inevitable gap between the will of the people and the government that was temporarily to represent it, Ames saw the election of representatives as the primary, if not only, active political duty of American citizens. The election of representatives "puts [the people] into full possession of the utmost exercise of . . . their rights." In this vision of American politics, there were only two operating entities, the people (in their individual capacities as voters) and the government. An active politicized public, that nebulous community that the Atlantic world's democrats had sought to call into more forceful existence, had no place. Even worse, those who sought to strengthen it threatened the survival of the nation. "If the clubs prevail, they will be the Government."[47]

This critique of the dangers posed by the Democratic-Republican Societies was supplemented in the mid-1790s by a series of pamphlet and newspaper pieces that lampooned the attempts of plebeian democrats—Greenleaf's target audience—to educate themselves on political matters and voice their opinions publicly. J. S. J. Gardiner's *Remarks on the Jacobiniad* (1795), for example, offered his well-educated readers an elaborate, quasi-Augustan satire of the Boston Democratic Society. Gardiner portrayed their debates as ludicrous exercises in rhetorical posturing and mutual misunderstanding, unfavorably comparing these democrats' futile efforts to form substantive opinions on complicated political matters with the sober and judicious behavior of the men who comprised Washington's administration. According to Gardiner, popular politics was undesirable because it encouraged ordinary people to act in a manner not suited to their station in life. Thus, after pointing out that "the former president of [Boston's] *jacobin* club was a *cobbler*," Gardiner went on to note that "however well qualified such a person may be, for *mending shoes*, we cannot think him equally well qualified for *mending laws*." While a "cobbler may doubtless be an honest man and useful citizen," the "prudent" working man "will leave the task of legislation and reformation, to more skillful *workmen*."[48]

If 1795 had witnessed an initial flurry of pamphlets and newspaper essays such as Gardiner's that were critical of radical publicity, this stream turned into a flood during the war scare of 1798–99 as Federalist orators and printers churned out increasingly hysterical accounts of the supposedly tyrannical designs of the nation's democrats. Convinced that the French were poised to invade, Federalists framed all opposition to the nation's chosen leaders as treason. Orator after orator insisted that obedience, rather than critical engagement, was the primary duty that all citizens owed their government. Not surprisingly, in virtually all of these performances the Democratic-Republican Societies and the newspapers that supported them played the role of the critical foil, the model of citizenship that Americans should avoid if they wanted their nation to survive. Thus, in one oration Hezekiah Packard both lauded the unique virtues and extreme piety of the nation's current leaders and reminded his auditors that "citizens have a place and a sphere in which to act as well as their rulers." He lamented "the conduct of those men who wontonly undertake to decide upon the constitutionality of laws and treaties" when the constitution itself had provided an appropriate "tribunal for such trial and decision."[49] In Wrentham, Massachusetts, Nathanael Emmons echoed this sentiment, insisting that "The People have nothing to do, in the affairs of government, but merely to chose" their leaders. Indeed, Emmons argued that the more active a nation's citizens were the more unstable it would be. "Just so far as any civil constitution allows the people to assist or control their Rulers; just so far it is weak, deficient, and contains the seeds of its own dissolution."[50] Because their auditors feared that American democrats would join the French in overthrowing the Adams administration, Federalists were able to make increasingly explicit arguments about passive citizenship and the unavoidably exclusionary nature of American politics, yet without appearing to advocate a return to an aristocratic system. As they called on their fellow citizens to protect the American republic, they also sought to legitimate a more nonparticipatory and exclusive vision of that republic's political system.

The least-subtle argument against radical publicity that appeared in 1798–99 framed it as an American outcropping of the Bavarian Illuminati's international conspiracy against all government and religion. John Robison and Abbe Barruel's reactionary accounts of Europe's secret clubs of radicals were imported to America in late 1797 and early 1798 and appeared in American editions almost immediately. American Federalists embraced these texts, one Scottish and the other French, as useful tools for understanding the American political societies. Robison's and Barruel's lengthy descriptions of the Jacobin international suggested that plebeian political organizations should not simply be mocked as Gardiner had done, for these European works seemed to prove that these clubs were part of a well-knit conspiracy with a clear goal. Federalists saw in the Democratic-Republican Societies what Barruel saw in the Illuminati: every tyrannical manifestation of the French Revolution "was foreseen and resolved on . . . they were the offspring of deep-thought villainy, since they had been . . . produced by men, who alone held the clue of those plots and conspiracies, lurking in the secret meetings, where they had been conceived, and only watching the favorable moment of bursting forth."[51] Barruel's work enabled American Federalists to frame political clubs not as forums where ordinary citizens rationally discussed political and philosophical matters, but as breeding grounds for treason.

Federalists such as Timothy Dwight eagerly used the European example to explain why Americans should curtail their practices of radical publicity and give unqualified obedience and affection to their chosen rulers. Indeed, the primary lesson that Dwight drew from Barruel's text was that "existing rulers must be the directors of our public affairs, and the only directors." America's system of "universal suffrage" rendered passive citizenship even more necessary, because each person possessed so much "personal consequence" and thus posed a greater threat to the stability of the nation than a degraded subject of a monarchy. Thus, Dwight simultaneously overstated the democratic nature of the American nation—universal suffrage—and diminished the role of ordinary citizens, claiming that the American government, more than any other, particularly depended upon "the harmonious and cheerful co-operation of the citizens" and "the hearty concurrence of the community." His work neatly encapsulated two of the main threads of the case against radical publicity—America was already a thoroughly democratic country in no need of further reformation by political clubs, yet what made the American political system work was the voluntary refusal on the part of ordinary citizens to criticize their leaders publicly and to meddle in formal politics.[52]

Just as Federalists redescribed conceptions of active citizenship as subversive rather than patriotic, they also argued that unregulated public opinion often functioned as a dangerous infection polluting American politics. In this way they countered the democrats' claim that public opinion served as a uniting force that could render the nation's politics more inclusive and authentically representative. Fears of international conspiracy lent much credence to the Federalists' negative evaluation of public opinion. The threat of foreign invasion made opposition newspaper editors and political organizers appear as more than just selfish demagogues; they could now plausibly be seen as foreign agents out to deceive the people and destroy their government. These new fears about the infectious danger of public opinion legitimated the Sedition Act's efforts to outlaw criticisms of the nation's leaders. As Hezekiah Packard put it, those who disseminated opinions critical of the actions of the legislature and "our beloved President" were extremely "poisonous to our American soil." Where democrats saw public opinion as the fluid that would sustain the legitimacy of the government and allow ordinary citizens to play a political role, Packard drew on the work of Barruel to demonstrate how "evil communications corrupt good governments."[53]

The crisis of 1798–99 generated a final, relatively new genre of text that functioned as a critique of radical publicity—the morality tale that sought to shame citizens into relinquishing their political aspirations. William Brown's *Look before ye Loup; or, A Healin' sa' for the Crackit Crowns of Country Politicians, by Tam Thrum, an Auld Weaver* encapsulated many of this genre's key themes. This text had first appeared in Edinburgh in 1793 in an effort to combat the political clubs that had formed there, and in the political climate of 1798 printer Richard Dobson found it appropriate to offer such a production to an American audience. Where Federalists such as Gardner had simply mocked the actions of plebeian democrats in 1795, pamphlets such as this one foregrounded characters who offered a more attractive alternative. The narrator, Tam Thrum, for example, attends a meeting of the local political club, only to find himself utterly unpersuaded by their efforts to turn ordinary people into political activists. "To be plain wi' ye, lads, you have ta'en us aw frae our ploghs, our shuttles, an' our needles, to mak' constitutions, an' mend governments; you've deprived us of our innocence, our happiness an' contentment." In his thick Scottish brogue, Tam called for his fellow laborers to "Renounce Tam Paine, and a' his seditious crew, an' tell common fo'k to gae hame, be dilligent, an' industrious, an' thank their Maker for the blessin's they enjoy beyond ony people i' the warld." Throughout the pamphlet, wise commoners chastise their compatriots for abandoning their duties to their wives and children in pursuit of something that is beyond their ken. Harry Heeltap's "rusty-cat" wife, Jenny, for example, intrudes into one of his political meetings, asking him to come home and make money to help support his starving family: "leave your speeches an' your nonsense about the rights o man to them that can afford to fool awa their time in sic a way. Come awa home, an' mind your family."[54]

Texts such as this one framed domestic bliss as the more virtuous alternative to radical publicity. Where earlier criticisms of the political activity of ordinary citizens had focused solely on the foolishness or dangerousness of these activities, tracts such as *Tam Thrum* argued that plebeian political activity served to distract men from their duties as fathers and husbands, as providers for those who were dependent upon them. Such portrayals offered ordinary citizens an important role to play in preserving social harmony and national prosperity, only that role was a profoundly nonpolitical one. The collective life envisioned in these texts involved the family and the church. When men strayed into other venues—the tavern, the coffee house, or the political club—they risked being pulled into a world where they could become the tools of powerful demagogues and where their productive energies would be channeled in irresponsible, socially disintegrative directions. Indeed, this argument—that experimentation with theories and practices of equal, active citizenship threatened to undermine all "natural" forms of social order—provided the primary, clinching argument against radical publicity in virtually every Federalist newspaper and oration produced in 1798. While Federalism as a partisan persuasion was nearing the end of its effective life, these Federalist attacks on radical publicity became a central component of American political discourse for years to come.

By the late 1790s, a compelling narrative about the unique merits of American politics began to structure public political discourse: unlike Britain, America had had its democratic revolution; but unlike France, America had seen fit to end its revolution. This narrative left no space in American politics for the visions of radical publicity espoused by democrats such as Greenleaf and DEMOCRITUS. Although the Federalists failed to pass an official censure of the Democratic-Republican Societies, their contention that political clubs were effective only in destroying, not supporting, political authority became a veritable truism in American political debate. In the midst of the war scare of 1797–98, the particular form of democratic political culture that radical Enlightenment reformers had advocated came to appear more than unnecessary: it was dangerous. Events in Europe seemed to lend credence to the Federalists' claim that America possessed an ideal constitutional order, one that enabled citizens to go about their private affairs and leave politics to the only legitimate "organs of the public will," their chosen representatives. So rather than continuing to think about the insufficiency of representation and the need for institutional arrangements that could make the process of public opinion and policy formation more inclusive and fully deliberative, Americans who shaped mainstream political discourse in the late 1790s used spurious histories of the Jacobin menace to demonstrate that such avenues of thought were inherently and inevitably conducive to upheaval and tyranny.[55]

While this move away from utopian visions of radical publicity throughout the Atlantic world was in hindsight a predictable by-product of the failure of the French Revolution, the Americans of the late 1790s did not experience this political transformation as an inevitable process. Indeed, DEMOCRITUS and William Manning formulated their ideas at least a year after news of the Terror had reached America, and even into the early nineteenth century few Americans believed that the battle was over. Federalists continued to demean working-class activism and plebeian forms of political and religious organization as Jacobinical threats to the American nation. At the same time, working-class radicals and deists continued to form debating clubs, publish their own newspapers, and sponsor public lecture series. Over time, however, talk of American Jacobins came to appear increasingly hysterical and ungrounded. Soon after Jefferson's election it became clear that fears about his Jacobinical tendencies were unfounded as he distanced himself from the most radically democratic elements in his electoral coalition. Meanwhile, the Painite radicals who had once seemingly posed such a great threat to national stability were pushed further and further outside the mainstream of American political discourse. Mainstream democrats continued to imagine more active and inclusive conceptions of politics, yet these visions departed significantly and intentionally from the heights of democratic aspiration articulated in the early and mid-1790s by the Democratic-Republican Societies and their compatriots in Europe.

In fact, where radical democrats such as DEMOCRITUS and Greenleaf had imagined the dispersed institutions of radical publicity as the mediating force between the people and their government, the majority of rank-and-file Jeffersonian Democrats imagined a much more concrete and pragmatic mediating mechanism—the political party.[56] The creation of a well-organized system of party organization in the years preceding the election of 1800 drew unprecedented numbers of ordinary citizens into the political process, especially newly arrived Irish immigrants. While the party made politics more inclusive, it tended to constrict the meaning of citizenship. The primary goal of the party was to win elections; thus, it framed voting as the ultimate expression of citizenship. Partisan competition gave political leaders an incentive to extend the franchise, and it gave citizens the ability to choose between candidates in an increasing number of contested elections. But by defining popular politics as electoral politics, parties rendered illegitimate a wide range of other definitions of citizenship that had emerged in the 1790s. Talk of institutional transformations to ensure greater citizen participation in the day-to-day process of governing ended as citizens were encouraged to look to election day as the primary moment when they had an active role to play in the nation's politics.

Partisan competition had a similar effect on the role of public opinion, both expanding its importance and constricting its meaning. As parties competed for voters through an increasing number of newspaper essays and pamphlets, more and more political issues were hashed out before the tribunal of public opinion. The two-party system, however, polarized and thus delimited the parameters public debate. As newspapers became mouthpieces for one party or the other, party leaders gained more power to define what issues would be discussed by the public and what the range of the politically possible would be. Opinion formation became a process that occurred largely within the confines of the party hierarchy and this transformation gave tremendous power to a few leaders. This top-down mode of organization differed dramatically from the Democratic-Republican Societies' vision of independent political clubs dispersed throughout the nation and linked up only through the mechanism of impartial newspapers. While parties institutionalized and made permanent the possibility of political debate and disagreement without resort to physical violence, they also made the messy process of public-opinion formation seem far neater and easier than it actually was.

Finally, the two-party system tended to elide the theoretical difference between electing representatives and participating in a democratic political process. Parties constructed partisan subjects who articulated their political aspirations not in abstract terms, but in terms of their allegiance to a set of leaders. While voters may not have agreed with every element of a party's platform, the party system forced them to choose the best of two options. Parties thus tamed the chaos of contending interests and opinions by channeling them into a bipolar competition with clear winners and losers. Although many voters would remain disgruntled with the policies adopted by the nations' rulers, the results of elections came to be seen as the only authentic and legitimate expressions of the peoples' will. If one had voted, one was represented. While this configuration legitimated calls for expanded suffrage throughout the nineteenth century, it also delegitimated future American democrats' efforts to articulate alternative means of representing the will of the people.

The party system of the early republic was America's unique response to the perils and promises of radical theories of popular sovereignty. The politics of the nineteenth century retained the eighteenth-century language of public opinion, citizenship, and representation, but the more radical implications of those terms largely vanished from public discourse. Revisiting the periodicals of the late eighteenth century—especially newspapers but also magazines as well—points out how radically and rapidly the boundaries of public political discourse expanded and contracted in the age of democratic revolutions. Such an investigation suggests that the emergence of Jeffersonian and Jacksonian democracy in the nineteenth century was not a linear progression into an increasingly democratic future. Indeed, the American definition of a democratic system—one in which parties that were organized in a relatively top-down fashion competed for votes among a slowly expanding electorate—was to a great extent a reaction against the most inclusive and participatory visions articulated by the democrats of the 1790s. This step back from the most radical implications of late Enlightenment, Painite political thought, quite possibly saved the nation from a French-style dissolution. One cannot fully comprehend the version of democracy that survived the 1790s, however, without appreciating the democratic visions that Americans explicitly rejected in that decade.

Notes

1. The Pitt administration, increasingly fearful that domestic radicals were conspiring with the French to foment a revolution in Britain, imprisoned and tried a large number of political organizers and activists in late 1793 and 1794. While many of these people were acquitted, several were deported to Botany Bay, thus becoming martyrs to the British democratic cause. Their crimes usually involved little more than disseminating Paine's writings or organizing a political club comprised of nonelite subjects. American democrats reprinted the transcripts of these British radicals' trials and covered their actions and fates at great length in their newspapers.
2. For recent examples of this argument, see John Brooke, "Ancient Lodges and Self-Created Societies: Voluntary Association and the Public Sphere in the Early Republic," in *Launching the Extended Republic: The Federalist Era*, eds. Ronald Hoffman and Peter J. Albert (Charlottesville: UP of Virginia, 1996), esp. 311–12, and Matthew Schoenbachler, "Republicanism in the Age of Democratic Revolution: The Democratic-Republican Societies of the 1790s," *Journal of the Early Republic* 18 (1998): 237–61.
3. Newspapers were not the only source of foreign news and ideas. Many of the new magazines that appeared in the 1790s also contained digests of the latest reports from Europe. This essay focuses primarily on newspapers

and their editors, however, because they were much more explicit and aggressive in putting this news to political use.

4. For a discussion of the myriad political implications of popular sovereignty, see Jürgen Habermas, *Between Facts and Norms: Contributions to a Discourse Theory of Law and Democracy* (Cambridge: MIT P, 1996), esp. appendix 1, "Popular Sovereignty as Procedure."
5. Qtd. in Richard Hofstadter, *The American Political Tradition* (New York: Knopf, 1948), 6–7.
6. "Address to the People of the United States," *American Museum* 1 (1787).
7. David Williams, *Lessons to a Young Prince* (Boston, 1791), 30.
8. Democritus, *Greenleaf's New York Journal*, March 29, 1796.
9. Thomas Paine, *Rights of Man*, part 2., in *The Essential Writings of Thomas Paine*, ed. Sidney Hook (New York: New American Library, 1969), 243.
10. Qtd. from Gordon S. Wood, *The Radicalism of the American Revolution* (New York: Vintage Books, 1991), 363–64. Joyce Appleby put it well when she described Wood's version of democracy as "a lot of elbowing competitors in a capitalist economy and no participants in a public debate about what is natural, what is just, and what is true." In "The Radical Recreation of the American Republic," *William and Mary Quarterly*, 3d. ser, 51 (1994): 683. Michael Zuckerman's article in the same journal (693–702) and James Oakes, "Review of Gordon Wood, *Radicalism of the American Revolution* (unpublished paper in possession of the author), have also informed the reading of Wood's book given here.
11. This quotation appeared in "An Essay on Man" in the *American Universal Magazine*, July 24, 1797, 101–3. Lee had been a member of the London Corresponding Society until he had to flee England in 1795 under threat of prosecution for sedition.
12. They went by many different names, but here this term denotes them all. The best overview of these societies is still Eugene Link, *Democratic-Republican Societies, 1790–1800* (New York: Columbia UP, 1942). For a thorough list of the major work on the Democratic-Republican Societies, see Schoenbachler, footnote 2. Albrecht Koschnik has convincingly interpreted the Democratic-Republican Societies in the context of the debate over the role of voluntary societies in the new republic in "The Democratic Societies of Philadelphia and the Limits of the American Public Sphere, circa 1793–1795," *William and Mary Quarterly*, 3d ser, 58 (2001): 615–636.
13. *Greenleaf's New York Journal, & Patriotic Register*, March 29, 1796.

14. (Philadelphia) *National Gazette*, December 19, 1791. Thanks are owed to Albrecht Koschnik for bringing this article to the author's attention.

15. The most radical critiques of the insufficiency of representation came out of France. For example, John Oswald, an 'Anglo-Franc,' argued in 1793 against those who claimed that the people "cannot deliberate except by their Representatives. Now, if the nation can deliberate by proxy, they may also assemble by proxy, and decide by proxy, and thus the whole Sovereignty of the People will dwindle down to . . . a voice and nothing more; sound without sense . . . I confess that I have never been able to consider this representative system, without wondering at the easy credulity with which the human mind swallows the most palpable absurdities. Were a man seriously to propose, that the nation should piss by proxy, he would doubtless be regarded as a madman; and yet, to *think by proxy*, is a proposition which we hear not only without astonishment, but even with approbation." John Oswald, "The Government of the People . . ." in *Political Writings of the 1790s*, vol. 4, ed. Gregory Claeys (London: W. Pickering, 1995), 95–103. This particular essay apparently was not reprinted in any American newspaper, but there are many that make similar arguments about the radical possibilities of popular sovereignty and the limitations of representation.

16. Williams 29–30.

17. As many commentators have noted, one of the key goals of *The Federalist Papers* was to contain the more radical implications of the concept of popular sovereignty. The debate over the public described in this paper occurred before the range of possible meanings and applications of this vague concept had constricted.

18. This phrase comes from *Rights of Man*, Hook 242. The distinction between representation and democracy was a frequent topic of discussion in the opposition press of the time, with representation always described as a diluted form of democracy. Over the course of the nineteenth century, the gap between these two concepts became a much less frequent object of analysis.

19. Sean Wilentz and Michael Merrill, eds., *The Key of Liberty* (Cambridge: Harvard UP, 1993), 167.

20. This account of Manning also differs from John L. Brooke's in "Ancient Lodges and Self-Created Societies," 311–12. Whereas Brooke situates Manning in the context of the popular politics of the 1780s, one can argue that his plan also bears the powerful stamp of the utopian and universalistic ideas about communication, rights, reason, and popular sovereignty that marked the radical movements in France, Britain, and Ireland.

21. Although most magazines were aimed at a more-educated and hence well-off audience, some politically minded magazine editors endorsed similar ideas about the democratic possibilities of print. See, for example, the *American Universal Magazine* (Philadelphia, 1797–98), edited by radical British émigré Richard Lee, and *A Republican Magazine or Repository of Political Truths* (Fairhaven, VT, 1798), edited by James Lyon, brother of the illustrious Jeffersonian Democrat Matthew Lyon.

22. Qtd. in Jeffrey L. Pasley, "The Two National *Gazettes:* Newspapers and the Embodiment of American Political Parties," *Early American Literature* 35 (2000): 55.

23. This same December 19, 1792, paper featured a poem that saluted "THE DEMOCRATIC CAUSE" in Europe and America. This early use of the unmodified term *democratic* in this particular context demonstrates the extent to which people like Freneau associated "democracy" with the argument that the role of ordinary citizens in the daily business of politics should be augmented.

24. This is almost nine months before the first American Democratic-Republican Society was formed.

25. *National Gazette* (Philadelphia), July 4, 1792. Emphasis in the original. It is important to note that the Friends of the People was a moderate organization founded by elite British reformers. They did not necessarily see their political societies as a permanent part of the political process; rather, they saw them disappearing once a reform of parliament was achieved. The Americans who read contemporary newspaper descriptions of their project, however, had no way of knowing that, because opposition editors chose to excerpt those parts of their public proclamations that used highly universalistic and utopian language. Unlike the Friends of the People, the political clubs that formed in America never articulated a clear goal that, once achieved, would eliminate the need for constant political action on the part of the people. On the Friends of the People, see Albert Goodwin, *The Friends of Liberty: The English Democratic Movement in the Age of the French Revolution* (Cambridge: Harvard UP, 1979).

26. *National Gazette,* July 21, 1792.

27. This argument about the cosmopolitan self-conception of the American democrats of the early 1790s is developed more fully in Seth Cotlar, "In Paine's Absence: The Trans-Atlantic Dynamics of American Popular Political Thought, 1789–1804" (Ph.D. diss., Northwestern University, 2000), chapter 1.

28. The Democratic-Republican Societies may have been reluctant to identify themselves with earlier, revolutionary examples of collective political

action because groups such as the Sons of Liberty probably conjured up, for some Americans, visions of mob rule and a lack of tolerance for opposing viewpoints. American democrats wanted to identify their project as dedicated to abstract reason rather than embodied, collective force. Because of this, the actions of their Revolutionary predecessors raised some problematic issues for them that they probably preferred to avoid.

29. *General Advertiser* (Philadelphia), August 4, 1794.

30. *Greenleaf's New York Journal,* March 15, 1794.

31. Bache had printed a similar proclamation from the Friends of Parliamentary Reform in Dublin on March 1, 1793.

32. Bache sold copies of the radical French Constitution of 1793 for six cents in his Philadelphia bookshop, and his fellow opposition editors advertised it for sale in their papers. The primary way in which the literature surrounding the Edinburgh Convention got to America was in the transcripts of the leaders' trials. These texts contained more than just trial transcripts; they also included long passages of "evidence," in other words, excerpts from the radical texts that these reformers had circulated. The reports of at least seven separate treason trials were reprinted by American democrats. On July 21, 1794, for example, James Carey wrote his brother Matthew from New York telling him of his intentions to print an unusually large run (one thousand copies) of Maurice Margarot's treason trial because Muir and Palmer's trials had "had rapid sales here," Lea and Feibeger Collection, Historical Society of Pennsylvania.

33. *General Advertiser* (Philadelphia), May 16, 1794.

34. *Greenleaf's New York Journal,* October 18, 1794.

35. Ibid., March 8, 1794, and January 14, 1795.

36. This address appeared in the *Philadelphia Gazette and Universal Daily Advertiser,* December 29, 1794, and *Greenleaf's New York Journal,* December 31, 1794.

37. Qtd. from *Greenleaf's New York Journal,* July 9, 1794. The *Greenleaf's New York Journal* of January 7, 1795, contained an even more explicit parallel: "The British government have sent several members of their constitutional societies to Botany Bay; would the agents of a free people do the same? The butchers of George the IIId have embezzled and torn in quarters, by wild horses, Watt and Downie, for speaking against the abuses of government; would the administrators of America commit such horrid outrages against humanity in this country?"

38. *Greenleaf's New York Journal,* December 27, 1794.

39. Ibid.

40. These essays first appeared in Webster's (New York) *Minerva* and then in revised form in his pamphlet *The Revolution in France, considered in respect to its progress and effects.* New York (1794).

41. See Bache's (Philadelphia) *General Advertiser* of August 4, 1794, for a representative example of this argument.

42. This phrase comes from an essay in defense of the Democratic-Republican Societies in the *General Advertiser* (Philadelphia), May 16, 1794.

43. *Gazette of the United States,* July 21, 1794.

44. Ibid., October 21, 1794. This piece was excerpted from Noah Webster's *New York Minerva.*

45. *Annals of Congress.*, 3 Cong., 2 Sess., 899, 902, 906.

46. Ibid., 906–7.

47. Ibid., 923–28. Ames's argument about the impossibility of public politics closely resembles that which Abbe Barruel would put forward in his 1797 *Memoirs of the History of Jacobinism*—one of the key texts of both the European counterrevolution and America's anti-Jacobin hysteria of the late 1790s. On Barruel's argument about public politics, see Amos Hoffman, "Opinion, Illusion, and the Illusion of Opinion: Barruel's Theory of Conspiracy," *Eighteenth Century Studies* 27 (1993): 27–60, esp. 32.

48. J. S. J. Gardiner, *Remarks on the Jacobiniad. Part First* (Boston, 1795), 17. Gardiner's friend Joseph Dennie wrote a series of similarly critical stories about overly politicized, ordinary citizens for the *Farmer's Weekly Museum* and then collected them into a pamphlet titled *The Lay Preacher* (1796).

49. Hezekiah Packard, *Federal Republicanism, Displayed in Two Discourses, Preached on the Day of the State Fast at Chelmsford, and on the day of the National Fast at Concord, In April, 1799* (Boston, 1799), 28.

50. Nathanael Emmons, *A Discourse, Delivered May 9, 1798. Being the Day of Fasting and Prayer throughout the United States* (Wrentham, MA, 1798), 15, 6.

51. Abbe Barruel, qtd. in Vernon Stauffer, *New England and the Bavarian Illuminati* (New York: Columbia UP, 1918), 216–17.

52. Timothy Dwight, *Duty of Americans* (1798), in *Political Sermons of the American Founding Era*, ed. Ellis Sandoz (Indianapolis: Liberty P, 1991), 1385–6.

53. Packard 28–29.

54. [William Brown], *Look before ye Loup; or, A Healin' sa' for the Crackit Crowns of Country Politicians, by Tam Thrum, an Auld Weaver* (Philadelphia, 1798), 5–9.

55. Such interpretations of the Jacobins' Enlightenment project are still highly influential. The work of Francois Furet in France and Gordon S. Wood in America tend to interpret the radical Enlightenment discourse of the 1790s much as the Anti-Jacobins of the late 1790s did—as an intellectual smoke-screen for self-interested, proto-totalitarian demagogues. Recent work by French historians Isser Woloch and Jean-Pierre Gross provides a more nuanced interpretation of the relationship between Jacobin ideology and practice. For a compelling critique of Furet's interpretation of the Revolution, see Isser Woloch, "On the Latent Illiberalism of the French Revolution," *American Historical Review* 95 (1990): 1452–1470. See also Isser Woloch, *The New Regime: Transformations of the French Civic Order, 1789–1820s* (New York: Norton, 1994), and Jean-Pierre Gross, *Fair Shares for All: Jacobin Egalitarianism in Practice* (Cambridge: Cambridge UP, 1997).

56. The following account rests primarily upon Jeffrey Pasley, *The Tyranny of Printers: Newspaper Politics in the Early American Republic* (Charlottesville: UP of Virginia, 2001). While he has convincingly demonstrated the role that newspaper editors played in bringing partisanship to the center of American politics in the late 1790s and early 1800s, Pasley's focus on explicitly partisan activity aimed toward winning elections has obscured the more utopian political ideas of the early 1790s. While most of the printers of the late 1790s and early 1800s were content to leave the basic institutional structure of the polity intact, their more utopian-minded predecessors had explored more fundamentally transformative visions of the role of the press and political associations in public life. It is perhaps worth noting here that the three printers who most vocally advocated radical publicity—Benjamin Franklin Bache, Thomas Adams, and Thomas Greenleaf—all died before the end of 1798. The passing of this generation of democratic radicals undoubtedly contributed to the demise of their particular vision of the political public sphere.

Sharon M. Harris

The *New-York Magazine*

Cultural Repository

The *New-York Magazine, or Literary Repository* was the longest-running monthly periodical of the late eighteenth century, beginning its publication in January 1790, running without interruption for eight years, and then concluding with the December 1797 issue. Its editors, the well-established publishers Thomas and James Swords, had a clear vision of what role the *New-York Magazine* would play in the recent proliferation of periodicals. Although the Swords brothers' father, Thomas, and elder brother, Richard, had been Tories during the Revolution, the younger sons became ardent patriots. After the Revolution, they established themselves as booksellers and printers in New York City. They became the publishers for the Episcopal church, printing editions of the Bible, the *Book of Common Prayer*, and *Swords' Church Almanac.*[1] As was true for many early periodicals, they modeled their new magazine on a British publication.[2] An article published by the Swords brothers in the first year of publishing the *New-York Magazine* cited the *Gentleman's Magazine* as a model; that reputable London periodical had begun by publishing "histories of the learned men in modern times, and short abridgements of their works . . . [which] required some vehicle to convey them to posterity."[3] The editors of the *New-York Magazine* discovered therein a model for their own magazine's content:

> . . . the monthly magazines have opened a way to every kind of inquiry and information. The intelligence and discussion contained in them,

> are very various and extensive; and they have been the means of diffusing a general habit of reading through the nation, which, in a certain degree, hath enlarged the public understanding. . . . The magazines that unite utility with entertainment, are undoubtedly preferable to those which have only a view to idle and frivolous amusement.[4]

While this model served the magazine well in its own time, it has been the point on which later critics have dismissed the historical standing of the magazine. The *New-York Magazine* has received little critical attention, even in studies of early periodicals.[5] Often sidelined by critics' assertion that it included too many excerpts from published books and other periodicals rather than original materials, this magazine was in fact the only monthly being published in the state of New York, and it entered into some of the most controversial and influential debates of the period.[6] In fact, publishing a wide variety of excerpts was a common practice among eighteenth-century periodicals, as the essays in *Periodical Literature in Eighteenth-Century America* demonstrate. More important, what the editors chose to publish and who its supporters were suggest a great deal about the political and cultural moment in which the *New-York Magazine* appeared and the ways in which its attention to these moments helped it survive for such a long time.

As David Paul Nord has discerned through an examination of the periodical's first year of publication, the subscribers to the magazine were not only the social elite of New York, as would be expected. Half of the subscribers constituted this anticipated readership—professionals and merchants;[7] but the remaining half were shopkeepers, artisans, and nonskilled laborers, including a gardener and a washer.[8] This is especially unusual considering the $2.25 subscription rate for the magazine; while average for the time, it was a prohibitive price for many families,[9] but the *New-York Magazine*, through its readership as well as its editorial practice, attempted to be a truly republican periodical. As Nord demonstrates, the magazine followed the typical themes in its construction of post-Revolutionary republicanism. The editors advocated virtue as public virtue, presented a suspicion of luxury, and articulated the power and democracy of knowledge itself.[10] The latter point is one of the most important perspectives of the periodical and is reiterated in every issue. As one columnist, "The Friend," asserts in the March 1792 issue, it is "necessary in every free state, for the people to keep a strict watch over their rulers, and to examine their conduct with a candid, but a critical eye"; it is through education that "anarchy or licentiousness" in public life will be thwarted.[11] As the subtitle of the magazine suggests, it was to be a *repository* of useful knowledge—literary, historical, and political—for an increasingly educated populace.

Building on Nord's analysis of the first year of the *New-York Magazine* and its commitment to republicanism, this essay examines the eight years of the periodical's publication in view of the sometimes radical positions that the editors presented in its pages, which complicate an understanding of the magazine's alliances as the political atmosphere of the country changed. With subscribers who included President George Washington and Vice-President John Adams, the periodical's commitment to Federalism was evident, especially when, for more than a year, it serialized sections of Adams's *Defense of the Constitution of Government of the United States of America.* Also worth examination are the magazine's political and social commentaries by which it defined itself as part of the new republicanism, including its emphasis on all things French and an early commitment to their revolution; its attention to women's roles in society and, most notably, to women's writings; its opposition to the enslavement of African Americans (countered by its extremely negative commentaries on Native Americans); its support of the rising anti–capital punishment movement; and its commitment, in spite of critical assertions to the opposite, to publishing *original* American literature, especially poetry and drama.

Many Americans in the 1790s were supporters of France's revolutionary efforts toward dethroning the monarchy and establishing a republic; indeed, if the political leaders of the time were cautious supporters of the French Revolution, popular opinion was much more ardent in its support. As Simon Newman has noted, "celebrations of the French Revolution . . . were so enthusiastic as to make condemnation by the government and its supporters all but impossible."[12] In what was surely a marketing as well as political decision, the editors of the *New-York Magazine* supported the desires of the populace for French political independence. In line with their emphasis on history as an important and necessary element in the education of the citizenry, they published numerous historical narratives, but none so much as those that attended to the history and literature of France. The Revolution in France had begun only months before the first issue of the *New-York Magazine* appeared. That first issue included "The History of the Dutchess de C—, Written by herself," an excerpt from *Adelaide and Theodore; or, Letters on Education* (1784) by Madame de Genlis. Equally typical of what would appear in later issues is "The Observer. On the Means of Preserving Public Liberty," an essay that supports a U.S. constitution—"a written basis on which national habits will be formed"[13]—and the education of the citizenry. The author uses France as an example:

> At the present moment, France is an instance of its influence—
> The wealthy subjects of that country are come enlightened, and thus determined to be free. O France! I love thee and thy sons—when my nightly supplication forgets to ask a blessing on thy great exertions,

> and on thy councils, I shall lose my claim of being a christian.— August Empire! Many of thy sons are among the learned; how often have I drank improvement and pleasure from their pens; but I fear, greatly fear, that the vast mass of thy subjects are not sufficiently informed of the nature of freedom, to receive from Heaven and preserve so rich a gift.[14]

This article demonstrates Stanley Elkins and Erin McKitrick's argument that in the early years support for the French Revolution reflected the ways in which that support nourished Americans' own sense of legitimacy in having so recently established itself as a constitutional republic.[15]

Subsequently, French authors' works appeared in several issues each year, including texts by Montesquieu (February 1791); Monsieur De La Villette's *Triumph of Truth* was serialized, beginning in June 1793, as was Sterne's *LaFleur*, beginning in January 1797; additionally, the expatriated English author Helen Maria Williams' writings concerning France appeared in the pages of the *New-York Magazine* (essays in December 1791 and January 1792; in later years her work often appeared in the poetry section). Historical accounts continued with equal frequency, including essays on Jeanne d'Arc's execution (March 1791); a serialized "History of the Rise and Progress of the French Revolution" (May–July 1791); a serial essay on Burke, Paine, and their opposing opinions about the French Revolution (July–December 1791); the "Petition of Madame Guillon" addressed to the National Assembly of France (November 1791); "Account of the Taking of the Bastille" (February 1793); assessments of the decline of Lafayette's reputation in France (July 1793); accounts of arrests in France after the Reign of Terror began (February 1794); and even the "Uses and Abuses of French Music" (April 1794). It was, however, in the *New-York Magazine*'s early support of the radical contingency of the French resistance that the periodical differs from many of its contemporaries, especially since it was also aligned with Federalist politics. Newman asserts that in 1791–92 "celebrations of the French Revolution engulfed the festive calendar of the early American public, overwhelming the annual rites commemorating the anniversaries of Independence Day and [President Washington's] birthday," but that supporters of the Federalist party "refused to participate in rites commemorating the French Revolution."[16] Perhaps this was true of public festivities, but it was not so in the pages of the *New-York Magazine*. Though ardently Federalist in their commitment to the U.S. Constitution, the editors of the periodical were much more in line with the Democratic-Republicans in refusing the Federalists' position of being "extremely wary of the radical impulses of the French Revolution."[17] Perhaps the best way to describe the position of the magazine in this period is in comparison to what Saul Cornell has termed the "middling democrats."[18] If the Swords brothers did not move to a truly anti-Federalist position in their political sympathies, the articles focusing on France reflect the middling democrats' concerns about restricting the powers of the executive and judicial branches of the government and strengthening the legislatures. As Cornell argues, "Federalism was crucial to the middling idea of democracy. . . . The farthest-sighted thinkers among middling democrats also recognized that an energetic public sphere nurtured by an active press could help liberty to flourish in such a federal republic."[19]

The process of change in the *New-York Magazine* began with rather common essays—works supporting France as a means of arguing for the exceptionalism of the United States and in support of "the most perfect Constitution that ever blessed the world";[20] articles such as "View of the Bastille," which also sought to inculcate "a reverence for the principles of a free constitution like our own," was the lead article in the April 1790 issue; and poetry on the anniversary of the French Revolution (September 1791). The *New-York Magazine* was the first illustrated periodical in the state, and the April 1790 issue includes a copperplate engraving of the Bastille.[21] But the periodical soon moved its attention toward more radical positions on the French Revolution, including the serial contrasting Edmund Burke's conservative opposition to the Revolution and Thomas Paine's reply to Burke, defending the actions of those resisting the monarchy and tyranny. The French victory at Valmy was the impetus for large public celebrations of the Revolution in New York. In 1792, for instance, the Tammany Society successfully petitioned the Mayor of New York City to hold a "*Day of Jubilee*" in honor of the successful battle.[22] By January 1793, the editors of the magazine were publishing Joel Barlow's critiques of the French Constitution, in which he argued that it degraded France to make property an element of representation; "the only basis of representation in government," he asserted, "should be *population.*"[23] Although the editors published President George Washington's proclamation in 1793 that the United States would "pursue a conduct of friendly and impartial [*sic*] towards the beligerent powers" in the war that developed between France and Austria, Prussia, Sardinia, Great Britain, and the Netherlands,[24] the *New-York Magazine* did not maintain a stance of neutrality itself. As the split between the moderate Girondists and the radical Jacobins became more evident in America, the magazine published several articles strongly in support of the Jacobins, beginning with an article about the origins of the Jacobin Society in the October 1793 issue.[25]

This alliance most clearly demonstrated the magazine's interest in reflecting popular opinions. Indeed, Federalists largely believed that support of Jacobin doctrines was a sign of allegiance to anti-Federalism. George Washington had condemned the Democratic-Republican Societies as corrupting influences that perpetuated "a leveling democratic impulse" such as had "inspired Anti-Federalists and Jacobins."[26] While the author of "Origin of the Jacobin Society" has concerns about the number of "distinguished members in point of talent and character" who have left the society, he is present on the day that a resolution is made in relation to Lafayette.[27] The general who had been so beloved by Americans during their revolution was now under siege because of his anti-Jacobin remarks, charging the group with having become "a distinct corporation in the middle of the French nation, whose power it usurps, and whose representatives it subdues."[28] On that day, the author of "Origin of the Jacobin Society" reports, the society proposed the "most universally agreeable motion that was made while I was present . . . that a price should be set on the head of M. la Fayette, and that *chaque citoyen pût courir fus;* which is as much as to say, that any body that pleased to murder him should be rewarded for doing so."[29] The *New-York Magazine* was clearly playing to popular public sentiment. In 1793 the populace had made clear its position in a widespread celebration of Bastille Day—so extensive that Columbia College canceled classes on Monday, July 15.[30]

The magazine's willingness to support the French resistance's actions must have come under fire as additional reports of the Reign of Terror reached America. In the editors' preface to the January 1794 issue, they remark that they have been accused of bias in their political writings, but they insist they have maintained a strict impartiality, an assertion that was rather audacious, considering their essays not only on the French Revolution but also concurrent commentaries on slavery, capital punishment, and so on. But a periodical that had published Adams's *Defenses of the Constitution* undoubtedly surprised some readers in their Democratic-Republican response to the French Revolution. In April 1794, however, the first criticism of the Jacobins' extremism appears in the pages of the *New-York Magazine.* The anonymously authored "Remarks" is a response to a pamphlet that had been published in New York on the French Revolution, asserting that "'this severity [the recent violence] is absolutely necessary to accomplish the revolution.'"[31] Not true, asserts the author of "Remarks": "it is necessary to accomplish the views of the Jacobins."[32] While agreeing that the "first revolution" did not go far enough in challenging the old institutions of the monarchy and priesthood, the Jacobins' condemnation of the moderates is too extreme for this author. The moderates *were* republicans, after all, he asserts; "their great crime was, they were *federalists*—they believed so extensive a country as France would be best governed by a constitution similar to that of America."[33]

In the pages of the *New-York Magazine,* any suggestion that a constitution was not the best system of governance had always been seen as a threat to America's standing in the world and to the national self-construction under way. But a few years into its publication, the magazine continued to be less profitable than the editors had hoped; issues, beginning with volume 5 (1794), were considerably shorter than they had been in the first four volumes, and the danger of advocating *too* radical a position left it even more vulnerable financially than it already was. Further, its patrons were largely ardent Federalists on other issues. These factors combined to have a decided effect of the content of the periodical: after April 1794 the interest in reporting on France or including French literature in the *New-York Magazine* diminished to such an extreme that nothing of significance appeared for nearly two years. They even remained silent about the extraordinary response of the citizens of New York City to France's victory in Holland in 1795. As Newman reports, "Over 500 citizens dined in celebration in New York City, after which they marched to the home of the French Consul bearing a liberty cap and a live liberty tree, which they then planted on the pedestal on the Bowling Green that had once supported a statue of George III."[34] Though the New York newspapers covered the event, nothing about it appeared in the *New-York Magazine*. By this point, France's declaration of war against England as well as Holland had made many political leaders reassess their views of France, especially since the United States' economic link to England was essential to its sense of well-being. It was not until 1796 that items about France and French culture began again to appear in the periodical's pages, and they were within the venue of safe subjects and often presented a feminized perspective on the French: excerpts from Sterne's narrative, as noted above, and a now-sympathetic sketch of the "Sufferings of *Madame* Lafayette" (emphasis added), a historical narrative of "Madame Roland's Last Letter to her Daughter" before her execution, and a character sketch of Charlotte Corday, who was executed for the murder of the radical leader Jean-Paul Marat. No other articles about the political situation of France appeared in the pages of the magazine before its demise in December 1797.[35] The shifting sense of America's relation to France and of the economic situation of the periodical resulted in a swift alteration of its political views on the Jacobins, bringing the editorial practice of the periodical securely in line with the moderate Federalist perspectives of the period.

If the editors of the *New-York Magazine* had for several years been supportive of the radicalism of the Jacobin Society, they presented a much more conflicted attitude about another major theme in the periodical: the role of women in society and women's writings. Part of the international philosophical debates about the differences between political orders had turned on the issue of what representations—or lack thereof—women would have under a republican form of government. Although the *New-York Magazine* presented several articles that challenged the status quo of women in the new republic, they also perpetuated many stereotypes and traditional attitudes toward "the fair sex." This was, of course, in keeping with the times. As Linda Kerber has noted, "The new nation . . . witnessed the development of an ambivalent ideology concerning the political role of women. . . . The central architects of the new female ideology were women," including Judith Sargent Murray, Susanna Rowson, Hannah Webster Foster, Mercy Otis Warren, and that important group of anonymous women writers.[36]

That writings by three of the four named architects of this new ideology—Murray, Rowson, and Foster—appeared in the pages of the *New-York Magazine* should not be overlooked.

In the first issue of the periodical, the editors ran articles that clearly aligned the magazine with a conservative view of women in the Republic. "On Women," purportedly by a woman, censured the female sex for their habit of gossip, for reading novels, and other foibles that are depicted in gendered terms, and the anonymous author cautions women, "Carefully avoid every thing that is masculine, as it takes off from our sex."[37] In the same issue an "Essay on Education" from "A Subscriber," who is also purportedly a woman, advocates education for women in somewhat more progressive terms because it is "conducive to piety, . . . morality and happiness."[38] Claiming that women "are exempted from the duties of public life," the author does attest to women's intellectual abilities, which they may "display . . . with pleasure to ourselves and advantage to others."[39] She concludes, "we may now speak and write with propriety without the imputation of pedantry. . . . Many daughters have done wisely, but thine, O America! excel them all."[40]

Advice literature for women abounds in the pages of the magazine, with such essays as "On the Choice of a Husband" (in the first issue) and "An Oration on the Question, 'Which is the more eligible for a Wife, a Widow or an Old Maid?'" in August 1793; the answer to the latter is an old maid, of course, since that choice would allow the most women to experience marriage. Also featured are essays that suggest there are "natural" differences between the sexes, which are rendered through examples typical of the conservative perspective of the period. For instance, a reprinting of "Characteristic Differences of the Male and Female of the Human Species—By Lavater," an uncommonly long essay for the periodical, claims, "how much more pure, tender, delicate, irritable, affectionate, flexible, and patient, is woman than man."[41] Women are "*the counterpart of man*, taken out of man, to be subject to man; to comfort him like angels, and to lighten his cares"; "*Man stands steadfast—woman gently retreats*"; "Man is serious—woman is gay."[42] Equally gendered is "The Taming of a Shrew," in which the male author asserts that there is a need for "'taking a woman down in her wedding shoes,' if you would bring her to reason."[43] He then recounts the experiences of a daughter in an acquaintance's family who was known for her "high temper"; her new husband cures her by insisting he himself has a high temper and creating in her "such a terrible apprehension of his fiery spirit, that she should never dream of giving way to her own."[44] After several examples of how the husband "trained" his wife, she becomes, admirably in the author's opinion, "the most meek and humble woman breathing."[45]

At the same time, however, the magazine began to publish a substantial number of writings by women. Essays that ran counter to the conservative vision of women's roles in society appeared in equal measure with their counterparts. "Marcia," for instance, published an essay in the December 1790 issue on "Female Vanity." Vanity is the foible for which women are most criticized by men, she asserts, but it is men's own emphasis upon a pretty face that forces women to attend excessively to their appearance. If men would value "an understanding, cultured and improved by education and judicious reading; a mind raised above the common weaknesses of their sex; a heart susceptible of the finest impulses of humanity, and manners suited to domestic oeconomy . . . they will soon find that many of those hours usually spent at the toilet, will be devoted to the acquirement of useful knowledge; and thus the mind expanding, new light will enter, and vanity decrease proportionably."[46] Also countering the conservative vision of women's roles in society were the occasional short pieces the magazine ran on female heroism. "Female Heroism Rewarded" (October 1791) recounts Congress's decision in 1779 that Margaret Corbin should receive disability pay for being wounded in the war when she took over her husband's post after his death; and in "Female Heroism" (June 1792) Deborah Gannett's petition to the Massachusetts legislature for a pension is supported, since she served in the war for three years as Robert Shurliff. The essays on heroism, however, always look to the Revolutionary past.

Essays advocating female education were always welcome at the *New-York Magazine*, as was true for most early periodicals. The magazine published such articles as "On Female Education. By a young Lady, a Student in a Seminary in Beekman-street, *New-York*" (September 1794) and Mary Hays's "On the Independence and Dignity of the Female Sex" (April 1796), balancing the more conservative essays that had appeared in the early years of the magazine. Indeed, an essay by "Jenny Sarcasm" on "Rights of Women" attacks men for talking about "their rights, while the *rights* of women lie neglected"[47] and Clara Reeve's "Causes of Female Celibacy, with a Vindication of Old Maids" did appear in the magazine; much more challenging positions on women's new roles in a republic were occasionally published in the pages of the *New-York Magazine*. In the February 1793 issue, the editors offered an excerpt from Mary Wollstonecraft's *Vindication of the Rights of Woman*, one of the most discussed and influential texts in the emerging movement for women's rights.[48] Unlike some other periodicals of the day, the editors allowed Wollstonecraft's arguments to stand on their own. The editors of the *Lady's Magazine; and Repository of Entertaining Knowledge*, for instance, published excerpts from *A Vindication of the Rights of Woman* but interspersed criticism within it to distance themselves from the text's radical demands.[49] In the December 1796 issue, the editors of the *New-York Magazine* also published an excerpt from Wollstonecraft's letters written when she was traveling in Sweden, Norway, and Denmark; they preface the excerpt with the comment, "The following extract from this work affords a beautiful specimen of

[Wollstonecraft's] lively fancy and tender sensibility."[50] Although the piece begins with the typical travel narrative's remarks on the beauty of the region she is visiting, Wollstonecraft quickly turns to her real concern—"the extreme affections of my nature"; she notes that although she tried to stem her affections, she "must love and admire with warmth or I sink into sadness."[51] It is an unusual piece on female sensibilities, as it moves far beyond the norm of the idea of woman's affections—without the usual call for moderation.

If the *New-York Magazine* waffled on its views of women in the new republic, it never wavered from its opposition to slavery. Though the New York Manumission Society was the primary organization of the antislavery movement in the state, initial consequences of the increased antislavery efforts of the period were devastating—in 1788 the legislature had passed its first comprehensive slave code since the 1730 act. The new code sought to emphasize the legal basis of slavery; its one concession to antislavery proponents was to make it illegal to buy a slave if the intent was to export him or her. The fine for doing so was one hundred pounds, and the slave was to be freed.[52] Suddenly, it was the abolition movement itself that came under attack. In the 1792 gubernatorial campaign, John Jay's having served as president of the New York Manumission Society became a point of attack for his opponents, in spite of the fact that the aims of the Society were actually quite conservative and that, while serving as president of the society, Jay had still owned slaves.[53] Through perseverance and a campaign that spread throughout the state, however, sentiment swung back in favor of the antislavery argument. Again the press and periodicals played an important role. This time arguments against slavery not only employed the usual themes of justice and liberty, they particularly emphasized the theme of "public good" that ought to outweigh faulty laws. A writer in the *Argus* proclaimed that "slavery was incompatible with the Declaration of Independence and therefore '*Every Negro in America is this moment of right, a freeman.*'"[54]

As the northern states debated the idea of abolishing slavery, the most influential arguments were for gradual manumission, but the *New-York Magazine* went much further. As early as August 1790, and covering much the same time frame as its accounts of the French Revolution, the editors began running articles on the subject, beginning with "A fancied Scene in the African Slave Trade" by Thomas Clarkson, the well-known British antislavery activist. The use of his name alone would establish the magazine's position on the subject, and in this piece he articulates the history of slavery and the realities of the slave trade, concluding with the injustice of the enslavement of Africans in European countries. A note accompanying the essay asserts, "It is an elegant, sensible, dispassionate, and eloquent performance, and speaks conviction in every line."[55] In the November 1790 issue, following the editorial pattern of presenting historical accounts of the major issues they wished to advocate in the periodical, the editors published "The Original of the Appellation of SLAVE, as applied throughout Europe and America to this day," which argues that it was the Christians of Saxony who originated the term through their treatment of the Slavi and Vandals in 1162.

Margaretta V. Bleecker Faugeres was the first American contributor to the debate in the pages of the *New-York Magazine*.[56] Though it is surprising that a single woman would be the first American contributor on the subject, her background made it a premier issue in her life and in the development of her thoughts on how the concepts of liberty and justice were being formulated in the new nation. Bleecker Faugeres had lived her entire life in or near the two largest slaveholding regions of the state, Albany and New York City, and her family had owned slaves when she was growing up in Tomhanick, just a few miles northeast of Albany. To oppose slavery was in line with her other radical political propensities, as will be noted later. An ardent opponent of *gradual* manumission, Bleecker Faugeres published an untitled essay in the June 1791 issue of the *New-York Magazine* in which she challenged Thomas Jefferson's racist ideologies: "Notwithstanding what the learned Mr. J— has said respecting the want of finer feelings in the blacks, I cannot help thinking that their sensations, mental and external, are as acute as those of the people whose skin may be of a different colour."[57] While Clarkson's "fancied scene" was set in Africa, Bleecker Faugeres was interested in exposing slavery in her home state and in the region where she was raised. The narrative scene is set in what she describes as "the interior parts of the state."[58] Through the story of a slave who dies before he is manumitted, she articulates the dire consequences of seeking only the gradual freeing of slaves.

Other essays, such as "Copy of a letter from an English Slave-driver at Algiers to his Friend in England" (October 1791), suggest that slavery by the English in the West Indies is far worse than anywhere else or assert that whites' demands for luxuries, such as their "fetish" for sugar, perpetuate the system of slavery, as in "A Fable for Sugar Eaters. The Bee and The Negro" (January 1792). The influence of the Enlightenment argument that the races' different skin colors were rooted in climate differences by geographic location is evident in the pages of the *New-York Magazine* as well. In "Account of a Person born a Negro, or a very dark Mulatto, who afterwards became white," Charles W. Peale recounts the changes in skin color of a Maryland slave, James; born of a black mother and white father and with black skin, at age fifteen, Peale asserts, James's skin began to change color until the present, when it is "of a clear, wholesome white, fair and what would be called *a better skin* than any of a number of white people who were present at different times when I saw him."[59] Typical of antislavery arguments by whites in the late eighteenth century is Peale's sense of white superiority, not only in the recognized assertion of "*a better skin*" but also in the unacknowledged "wholesome white"; as with most of the nineteenth-century abolitionists, white antislavery activists of the eighteenth century rarely argued for full equality or were able to move beyond their own sense of privilege and superiority. But the Swords brothers continued to publish essays on the subject of the cruelties and injustice of slavery, including "Hanno, or, A Tale of West-Indian Cruelty" (April 1793), "The Slave—A Fragment," and "Negro Trade—A Fragment" (both published in February 1797) and to advocate educating African Americans as a part of the brothers' desire for the education of the entire citizenry, such as in their notice "Account of the Free African School in the City of New York" (May 1793). Just as would be the case with their position against capital punishment, they believed that opposition to slavery was necessary to create a truly egalitarian republic.

If the *New-York Magazine* was solidly in support of the abolishment of slavery, its position on the relationship between Native Americans and the new republic was anything but laudatory. While they ran some typically romanticized tales, such as "A remarkable Story of an Indian Warrior and a Young British Officer" (January 1790), in the early issues of the periodical, political tensions between the United States and several American Indian nations were soon reflected in the magazine's selections. Articles about the need to "civilize" the Indians began to appear. In May 1790, for instance, the editors reprinted a segment of John Daniel Hammerer's "Account of a Plan for Civilizing the North-American Indian." Hammerer's plan was developed in the prewar years; with the support of the governor of Virginia, Hammerer entered Cherokee Country, intending to enact an experiment to "civilize" the indigenous peoples. Hammerer asserted that the traders in the region thwarted his efforts to assimilate the Cherokee by educating them in "moral virtues and christian doctrine."[60] The unusual aspect of Hammerer's argument is that such indoctrination would fit the Cherokee to "intermarry with our planters, and become profitable members of the *British* commonwealth."[61] Subsequent articles would shift from assimilation to, eventually, the extreme of war. For instance, in a series entitled "The Club," the anonymous author asserted in January 1792 that criticism of the government's policy of the western army against the Indians was "cruel and unjust."[62] He insists that no hostile measures were taken "until amicable endeavours had failed. . . . The truth is, that the greater part of the people of this part of the country, are but illy calculated to judge of the propriety and necessity of this war";[63] distance gives them safety and security, and they cannot comprehend the danger to the western settlers.

Gov. George Clinton attempted to calm the U.S. residents of the region, and the Swords brothers published his comments in their ongoing column "Domestic Occurrences" (January 1792). They introduce the issue by referring to the "action between our army and the savages."[64] However, Clinton notes,

> Complaints having been made to me in the recess, by the Oneida and Cayuga nations, of intrusions made upon the lands reserved by treaty for their use; justice and good faith required that I should exert the powers vested in me by law, for the removal of the intruders, and this has accordingly been effected, to the satisfaction of the Indians, in the manner mentioned in the letters from the sheriff of Herkemer county, which you will find among the papers delivered for your information. It is worthy at the same time, of the consideration of the legislature, whether it would not be more compatible with the mild spirit of our government, to commit this business in future to the ordinary magistrates, which in the present condition of that part of the country, it is conceived may be done with safety.[65]

But on a national level relations were increasingly strained. Later that year the *New-York Magazine* published President Washington's speech of November 2. Addressing the conflict between the United States and Native Americans "north of the Ohio," Washington explains,

> some threatening symptoms have of late been revived among some of those south of it. A part of the Cherokees, known by the name of Chickamagas, inhabiting five villages on the Tenesse [*sic*] river, have long been in the practice of committing depredations on the neighbouring settlements. It was hoped that the treaty of Holston, made with the Cherokee nation, in July, 1791, would have prevented a repetition of such depredations. But the event has not answered this hope. The Chickamagas, sided by some banditti of another tribe in their vicinity, have recently perpetrated wanton and unprovoked hostilities upon the citizens of the United States in that quarter. . . . It is not understood that any breach of treaty, or aggression whatsoever, on the part of the United States, or their citizens, is even alledged as a pretext for the spirit of hostility in this quarter.[66]

He will not act rashly, Washington asserts; but he cautions that the citizens of the region must be ready for the possibility of war, and he requests congress to better fund the enforcement of laws in relation to Native Americans.

Subsequent articles in the *New-York Magazine* maintain a tense tone of concern about the dangers and inferiorities of Native Americans.[67] In "Anecdote of an Algonquin Woman" (October 1795), the author seems to be the rare voice of support for Native Americans in the pages of the *New-York Magazine*. "The vices and defects of the American Indians," he begins, "have been, by several writers, most unaccountably aggravated, and every virtue and good quality denied them."[68] But this assertion is immediately followed by the comment that "the following anecdote of an Algonquin woman we find adduced as a remarkable proof of their innate thirst of blood."[69] The Algonquin woman is taken captive by a group of Iroquois, who strip and bind her; when she has the opportunity to escape, she stops before doing so to kill one of her captors. The author's opinion is that the killing was an unnecessary act of violence. The magazine later published Franklin's "Curious Remarks concerning the Savages of North-America" (December 1796), but its final comment on Native Americans is the "Barbarities of the Northern Indians" (January 1797), which is an excerpt from Hearne's study of the Eskimos. In the early federal period, the editors of the *New-York Magazine* suggest that relations between Native Americans and the United States were deteriorating rapidly rather than the involved parties finding any paths to reconciliation, and they clearly place the blame on the "innate" savagery of the American Indian.

Far more progressive was the magazine's position on capital punishment. As with its essays on antislavery, the editors' opposition to capital punishment remained consistent over the years of the magazine's publication. The ideals of the American Revolution, an emergent liberal theology, and the development of the penitentiary all influenced the change in attitudes about capital punishment in the years from the Revolution to the 1790s.[70] Arguments began to emerge that "social influences, not depravity, caused crime and that reformation, not retribution, should govern punishment."[71] While many ministers who had long sermonized on the threats of capital punishment as deterrents to corruption continued to support capital punishment,[72] public figures such as William Bradford and Benjamin Rush came out in opposition. The *New-York Magazine* was again invested in a radical debate, this time siding with those calling for an end to capital punishment in the United States. In the early issues of the periodical, essays on imprisonment reflect the increased concern for how criminals were to be treated in the new republic. "On Imprisonment," for instance, asserts that "of all the evils to which mankind are subjected in their peregrinations in this world, perhaps those which result from imprisonment are the most deplorable,"[73] and concludes that, while it is probably impossible to eliminate the need for imprisoning criminals, it is within the government's and citizens' power to alleviate the worst aspects of confinement. A subsequent article, however, offers a romanticized vision of prison life. In "Visit to the Bettering-House, or House of Correction" (December 1792) located in Philadelphia and run by Quakers, the author asserts that it "is properly named; because, contrary to the ordinary effect of hospitals, it renders the prisoners better."[74] In fact, the author proclaims, the prisoners are so happy in their confinement that they never attempt to escape. The author shifts his argument as much to an antislavery argument, with its attendant praise of whites, as to an advocacy of the establishment of prisons:

> blacks are here mingled with the whites, and lodged in the same apartments. This, to me, was an edifying sight; it seemed a balm to my soul. I saw a negro woman spinning with activity by the side of her bed. Her eyes seemed to expect from the director a word of consolation—She obtained it, and it seemed to be heaven to her to hear him. I should have been more happy, had it been for me to have spoken this word: I should have added many more. Unhappy negroes! how much reparation do we owe them for the evils we have occasioned them—the evils we still occasion them! and they love us![75]

Although not explicitly arguing against capital punishment, these early essays were important contributions to the idea that imprisonment was a viable alternative to execution for capital crimes.

Within six months, however, the magazine had turned to explicit arguments against capital punishment. The first such essay appeared in April 1793, an excerpt from a piece by William Bradford. Subscribing to the philosophy of Montesquieu and Beccaria,[76] Bradford agrees with the principles that the sole purpose of punishment is to prevent crime, that any punishment that is not absolutely necessary "is a cruel and tyrannical act," and that penalties must be appropriate to the act; these principles "serve to protect the rights of humanity, and to prevent the abuses of government."[77] Like most eighteenth-century opponents of capital punishment, Bradford waffled on the issue of murder, but he argued that execution for murder was applied differently from state to state and especially across the classes of U.S. citizens; therefore, it was doubtful that it actually acted as a deterrent to crime.[78] An essay by "Valentine" in January 1794 made the argument that murder was the worst representation of the depravity of man, but he includes murder in his opposition to capital punishment, arguing, "Would it not be a more rational punishment, instead of inflicting death on a murderer, to condemn him to hard labor in a prison for the remainder of his life, and the product of such labor applied to the use of the widow or children of the person murdered?"; it would be "a continual warning to others."[79] Further, he argues, most religious arguments in favor of capital punishment are misguided: "The advocates for the punishment of death for murder generally cite the scriptures in support of it; I would advise them to examine the precepts of the New Testament, and the fourth chapter of Genesis, where I find the murder of the good, the pious Abel, although perpetrated by his brother out of malice and envy, was nor [*sic*] punished with death, and GOD himself was *Judge.*"[80] In the new sense of republicanism, "the mild spirit of our government," as George Clinton had termed it, could not reconcile itself with the violence of execution. The positions still being debated today had their origins in the 1790s—and the *New-York Magazine* clearly positioned itself in opposition to capital punishment.

For all of its attention to the political and social debates of the period, the *New-York Magazine* had always envisioned itself foremost as a *literary* repository. If the editors waffled over women's public roles in the new republic, they found no impropriety in women's increased activity in the field of literature. Women writers now recognized (or, in the case of Margaretta Bleecker Faugeres, *should* be recognized) as some of the most important of the period also began their careers in the pages of the *New-York Magazine.* Although typically overlooked by critics of Judith Sargent Murray's impressive career, she published a "Description of a Journey to Bethlehem, Pennsylvania" in the August 1790 issue;[81] it was signed with the pen name by which she would become widely known, "Constantia."[82] This letter of a trip Murray took with her husband during his travels to promote Universalism in America is an account of the Moravian community that focuses on women's notable activities in Bethlehem. She details the women's industrious lives and, at great length, the advantages of their female seminary, which offers advanced courses for young women. Although written as an epistolary travel narrative intended for the edification of family members, the letter allows Murray to write a lengthy advocacy of female education, a theme that would dominate her subsequent writings.

In the September 1790 issue, the editors published the first section of the serialization of Ann Eliza Bleecker's *History of Maria Kittle,* a narrative about the real-life capture and return of a woman from New York during King George's War (1744–48).[83] The piece was continued over the next four months and was the first serialized fiction by an American writer to appear in the pages of the *New-York Magazine.* Over the next several years, Bleecker and her daughter, Margaretta V. Bleecker Faugeres, would become two of the most prolific and important contributors to fiction and poetry in the magazine. Bleecker's narrative of German immigrants, *The Story of Henry and Anne,* appeared in the April and May 1791 issues of the periodical, and her poetry became a staple of the early years of the magazine as it sought to develop its commitment to American literature. Toward the end of the periodical's run, when novels were being produced in the United States, the editors published excerpts from Susanna Rowson's *Inquisitor* (April 1796) and *A Tale of Truth* (May 1796), as well as from Hannah Webster Foster's *The Coquette* (September 1797).

It was in the poetry columns of the magazine, however, that the *New-York Magazine* made its most original contributions to American literature. In the first issue of the periodical, "The American Muse" was a two-part section devoted to poetry; one section was presented as "Original Poetry" by American authors and the other, "Selected Poetry," published reprints from well-known English and European poets. It was the "Original Poetry" section that would become the staple of this section of the magazine, and Ann Eliza Bleecker's posthumously published poetry first appeared in the second issue of the magazine (February 1790) and then regularly over the next several years, complementing the publication of her historical narratives, *The History of Maria Kittle* and *The Story of Henry and Anne.* While a few notable American male poets appeared in the poetry pages of the *New-York Magazine*, including Joel Barlow,[84] the section was dominated by female poets. In the early years, a poet using the pen name "Imona" was very popular; and soon thereafter "Marcia" surfaced as a poet whose works were published often in the pages of the magazine.[85] But the premier poet of the *New-York Magazine* was Margaretta V. Bleecker Faugeres, the same person who had published the antislavery essay. This important author of the late eighteenth century has been almost completely overlooked by scholars of early American literature—and regrettably so. Her prose and poetry filled the pages of this periodical, and the Swords brothers supported her work not only in the magazine but by publishing a collection of her work combined with her better-known mother's works. *The Posthumous Works of Ann Eliza Bleecker, in Prose and Verse. To which is added, A Collection of Essays, Prose and Poetical, by Margaretta V. Faugeres* appeared in 1793. A significant portion of its contents had first appeared in the pages of the *New-York Magazine.*

Bleecker Faugeres's political perspectives complemented those of the magazine—she was opposed to slavery and to capital punishment; she was an ardent supporter of the French Revolution and the Jacobins; and she was interested in poetry and drama.[86] When her mother's poetry first appeared in the *New-York Magazine*, it was presented with a note from "Cecilia," the first of many pen names Faugeres used over the years she published in the Swords brothers' magazine. Because she was publishing essays and poetry so often in the periodical, she developed a system of designated pen names: "Antonnetta" for her essays and "Ella" for her poetry. By September 1790, "Ella" had become a main feature of the poetry section, so much so that poems addressed to her began to appear in the poetry section as well. Alfred, the author of the first of the "To Ella" poems published in the magazine, praised her beauty but lamented the unhappiness of humankind. He asks, "Why be a slave at man's controul?" and ends the poem, "So great a paradox is man / He wont be happy when he can."[87] In the next issue, Faugeres replies with "To Alfred," countering her admirer's negative view. While the world may be "a cheat," Ella remarks, "No pow'r exists, by reason sway'd, / Who has not had, In Life's gay run, / His share of happiness display'd."[88] She insists, "Let man not then condemn the fates / For evils he himself creates."[89] She also resists the casual use of the term *slave;* in her poem the slave is "hard labouring at the oar" and intelligently recognizes the cursedness of his master's gluttonous lifestyle.[90]

This pattern of publishing poems by Ella, having other poets address poems to her, followed in the next issue by her response became a significant portion of the "Original Poetry" column. In December 1790, for instance, Bleecker

Faugeres published "To Aribert" by Ella; it is followed by a "To Ella" poem from "Cymon," in which he announces that, since she will not correspond with him, he will publicly ask for her advice. He is sure she can cure him of his wounded heart, having lost the woman he loves; he concludes that he will "yield to sweet Ella my warmest affection."[91] Her response in the January 1791 issue, "To Cymon," asserts that only time will cure his broken heart, but she acerbically adds, "But excuse, if I doubt your sincerity, where / Your 'warmest affection' you tender to me; / For the vows pain extorts are so fragile, I fear / You'll forget the fair promise as soon as you're free."[92] By March 1791, Ella has become the lead poet in the "Original Poetry" column, and poetry by both Bleecker Faugeres and her mother appeared in the June, July, September, October, and November 1791 issues. The editors clearly understood the value of their native-born poets; they began to mention Ella periodically in the "Notes to Correspondents," which came at the front of the magazine. In January 1792, for instance, they observed, "*Ella's Friendship* and *Calista's Apostrophe to Sensibility*, are worthy the pens of these fair daughters of the Nine."[93] Whether because there was concern that she was appearing too often in the magazine or for some personal reason, she used another pen name, "Caroline," in the May 1792 issue when she published the poem "To Ethelinde." A response from Ethelinde appears in July, and Bleecker Faugeres responds again in September. In the same period, she is publishing poetry as "Ella" and essays as "Antonnetta."

Although Margaretta V. Bleecker Faugeres did not die until 1801 and she published a few important works after the appearance of the *Posthumous Works* in 1793, her writings did not appear in the *New-York Magazine* after that year. The split between her and the magazine may well have developed when the editors softened and then abandoned their support of the French revolutionaries. Deeply committed to the cause (she married her French immigrant husband, Dr. Peter Faugeres, on Bastille Day, 1792), she wrote several pieces in commemoration of the Revolution. Though she has disappeared from the literary history of the United Sates, the French have long honored Faugeres for her contributions on the subject. Entries on her appear in nineteenth- and mid-twentieth-century French national biographical encyclopedias. Her alliance with the anti-Federalist governor of New York, George Clinton, suggests her political agendas on U.S. governmental policies may also have been more radical than her editors' positions.[94] By mid-1794, very little original poetry was published in the periodical and none from their usual poets. The magazine turned its attention to theater and published a few dramas; indeed, as has been well documented, it became the most welcoming of the late-eighteenth-century periodicals in terms of theatrical issues,[95] serving as a prelude to the city's future importance in the field of theater. But its contributions to American poetry suddenly waned. Readers, however, did not forget the importance of Bleecker's and Bleecker Faugeres's contributions to the success of the "Original Poetry" column. In November 1794, for example, "Harold" published a poem "To Adeline" that began with an epigraph from one of Bleecker's poems as published in *Posthumous Works.*

If the goal of the *New-York Magazine*'s editors was to advocate republicanism, to disseminate a wide range of "useful knowledge," and to become the premier monthly periodical in the region, they accomplished those goals—and in no arenas so fully as in its political commentaries and its poetry. In doing so, it gives one a broad overview of the political and artistic avenues into which Americans were expanding their influence in the 1790s. The unique nature of periodicals allows one to view this expansion, and its inherent interest in constructing a fluid and extensive meaning of all things "American" and "republican," as it develops month to month, year to year. As the longest-surviving periodical in early America, the *New-York Magazine* is less important for its attention to originality than it is to the processes through which the development of those ideas occurred.

Notes

1. Kenneth Scott and Kristen L. Gibbons, eds., Introduction, in *The New-York Magazine Marriages and Deaths, 1790–1797* (New Orleans, 1975), n.p.
2. The *American Magazine*, the *Lady's Magazine; and Repository of Entertaining Knowledge*, and Philadelphia's *Weekly Magazine of Original Essays* are other examples of periodicals modeled on successful British publications. See Karen K. List, "Magazine Portrayals of Women's Role in the New Republic," *Journalism History* 13 (Summer 1986): 65.
3. "Of the Rise and Progress of Magazines," *New-York Magazine* 1 (May 1790): 256.
4. Ibid., 256–57.
5. Edward Chielens's *American Literary Magazines: The Eighteenth and Nineteenth Centuries* (New York: Greenwood P, 1986) makes no mention of the *New-York Magazine*, while John Tebbel's *The American Magazine: A Compact History* (New York: Hawthorn Books, 1969) gives only a half sentence to the magazine, noting it was published one month longer than Isaiah Thomas's *Massachusetts Magazine.*
6. One of the most dismissive critiques is presented by William Loring Andrews, who asserts, "there is nothing in the literature of the *New-York Magazine* that, if it had been totally destroyed, would have proved a serious loss to posterity or to the world of letters" (*The Old Booksellers of New York, and Other Papers* [New York, 1895], 60). Mott is one of the

exceptions, considering the *New-York Magazine* one of the "four most important magazines of this period," with *the Columbian Magazine: or, Monthly Miscellany*; the *American Museum, or, Universal Magazine*; and the *Massachusetts Magazine; or Monthly Museum* as the first three.

7. Subscribers included George Washington, John Adams, Anthony L. Bleecker, John Jay, and Baron Stueben. Although primarily a New York periodical, it drew subscribers from Halifax, Nova Scotia; Edenton, North Carolina; Danbury, Connecticut; Philadelphia; Antigua; and Virginia.
8. David Paul Nord, "A Republican Literature: Magazine Reading and Readers in Late-Eighteenth-Century New York," *Reading in America: Literature and Social History*, ed. Cathy N. Davidson (Baltimore: Johns Hopkins UP, 1989), 126.
9. Frank Luther Mott, *History of American Magazines, 1741–1850* (New York: D. Appleton, 1930), 34.
10. For a discussion of the typical themes of post-Revolutionary republicanism, see Nord 115–6.
11. "The Friend—No. II," *New-York Magazine* 2 (March 1792): 155.
12. Simon P. Newman, *Parades and the Politics of the Street: Festive Culture in the Early American Republic* (Philadelphia: U of Pennsylvania P, 1997), 7.
13. "The Observer. On the Means of Preserving Public Liberty," *New-York Magazine* 1 (January 1790): 24.
14. Ibid., 25.
15. Stanley M. Elkins and Erin McKitrick, *The Age of Federalism* (New York: Oxford UP, 1993), 309.
16. Newman 121.
17. Ibid., 125. For a discussion of the Democratic-Republican Societies, see Seth Cotlar's essay in this volume.
18. Saul Cornell, *The Other Founders: Anti-Federalism and The Dissenting Tradition in America, 1788–1828* (Chapel Hill: U of North Carolina P, 1999), 82–83.
19. Cornell 119.
20. M. Mercier, "Anecdote," *New-York Magazine* 1 (April 1790): 204.
21. See Andrews's *The Old Booksellers of New York* for details about the periodical's illustrations.
22. Newman 136–7.
23. Joel Barlow, "Barlow's Letter to the National Convention in France, on the Defects of the Constitution of 1791, and the Extent of the Amendments which ought to be Applied," *New-York Magazine* 4 (January 1793): 23.

24. George Washington, "President's Proclamation," *New-York Magazine* 4 (April 1793): 194.

25. This entire issue is rife with articles on France, including "Account of the Trial of M. Cazotte" (601–2) and "Account of the Massacre of the Prisoners of Versailles" (614–5).

26. Cornell 196–97.

27. "Origin of the Jacobin Society," *New-York Magazine* 4 (October 1793): 600.

28. Ibid., 600.

29. Ibid., 600–601.

30. Newman 140.

31. Qtd. in "Remarks," *New-York Magazine* 5 (April 1794): 235.

32. Ibid., 235.

33. Ibid., 236.

34. Newman 148.

35. *New-York Magazine*'s silence and demise comes in the midst of loud public discourse on the subject. The *Albany Sentinel*, for instance, began publishing on July 4, 1797, and was an outspoken opponent of the Jacobins. In a January 1, 1799, editorial, the *Centinel* notes, "A Jacobin paper of late date contains some pathetic wailings about the *liberty of the press.*" The piece concludes, "Out of it, then, ye pack-horses of sedition and insurrection—away with you to *France*, and try the Gallic air of *liberty and equality*" (3). Alternatively, the *Gazette Francaise et Americaine*, published in New York City, thrived from July 1795 to December 1797. Printed in French and English columns, the *Gazette* reported on daily events in France and counted its readers as those "already acquainted" with the radical perspective on the Revolution (July 15, 1795, 2).

36. Linda Kerber, *Women of the Republic: Intellect and Ideology in Revolutionary America* (New York: Norton, 1986), 11.

37. "On Women," *New-York Magazine* 1 (January 1790): 17.

38. "Essay on Education," *New-York Magazine* 1 (January 1790): 40.

39. Ibid., 41.

40. Ibid.

41. "Characteristic Differences of the Male and Female of the Human Species—By Lavater," *New-York Magazine* 1 (June 1790): 336.

42. Ibid., 336–37.

43. "The Taming of a Shrew," *New-York Magazine* 2 (March 1792): 131.

44. Ibid., 131.

45. Ibid., 132.

46. "Female Vanity," *New-York Magazine* 1 (December 1790): 695.

47. Jenny Sarcasm, "Rights of Women," *New-York Magazine* 5 (April 1794): 713.

48. Women's private writings are especially telling about the influence Wollstonecraft's text had. See, for instance, Sharon M. Harris, ed., *American Women Writers to 1800* (New York: Oxford UP, 1995), and Kerber. In Mary Hays's essay in the *New-York Magazine*, "On the Independence and Dignity of the Female Sex" (April 1796), one sees how Wollstonecraft's language has been incorporated with cultural currency: "Objections are also made against the vindication of our rights," Hays observes, "under the pretense, that by enlarging and ennobling our minds, we shall be undomesticated and unfitted, (I suppose is meant) for mere household drudges" (203). Hays posits the educated, intellectual woman against such an image.

49. List 66.

50. Mary Wollstonecraft, "From *Letters*," *New York-Magazine* 7 (December 1796): 648.

51. Ibid., 648.

52. Arthur Zilversmit, *The First Emancipation: The Abolition of Slavery in the North* (Chicago: U of Chicago P, 1967), 151–52.

53. Ibid., 165–66.

54. Qtd. in Zilversmit 178.

55. Thomas Clarkson, "A fancied Scene in the African Slave Trade," *New-York Magazine* 1 (August 1790): 464.

56. Margaretta V. Bleecker did not marry until 1792. However, to avoid confusion with her mother, Ann Eliza Bleecker, I use her married name throughout this essay.

57. [Margaretta V. Bleecker Faugeres], untitled, *New-York Magazine* 2 (June 1791): 338. In the version of this essay published in the 1793 edition of *Posthumous Works*, Faugeres explicitly names "Mr. Jefferson" and titles her essay "Fine Feelings Exemplified in the Conduct of a Negro Slave." See Margaretta V. Faugeres, *The Posthumous Works of Ann Eliza Bleecker, in Prose and Verse. To which is added, A Collection of Essays, Prose and Poetical, by Margaretta V. Faugeres* (New York: T. and J. Swords, 1793), 268–70.

58. [Margaretta V. Bleecker Faugeres], untitled, *New-York Magazine* 2 (June 1791): 339.

59. Charles W. Peale, "Account of a Person born a Negro, or a very dark Mulatto, who afterwards became white," *New-York Magazine* 2 (November 1791): 635.

60. John Daniel Hammerer, "Account of a Plan for Civilizing the North-American Indians," *New-York Magazine* 1 (May 1790): 272.

61. Ibid., 272.

62. "The Club. No. XII," *New-York Magazine* 3 (January 1792): 6.

63. Ibid., 6–7.

64. "Domestic Occurrences," *New-York Magazine* 2–3 (January 1792): 60.

65. Qtd. in "Domestic Occurences," 62.

66. George Washington, "President's Speech," *New-York Magazine* 3 (November 1792): 699.

67. Jeremy Belknap published an article on the skin color of Native Americans, following the same argument as the earlier essay on African Americans. Citing the Count de Buffon, an advocate of the geographical argument for skin color, Belknap asks, "That the blackness [of Africans and the East-Indians] mentioned is the effect of climate is generally admitted by philosophical writers . . . [so] why are not the original natives of America, within the same latitudes equally black?" (197). He offers no conclusions but articulates one of the disturbing questions for Enlightenment advocates of the climate/geography argument for the distinction between the races. See Jeremy Belknap, "A Differentiation on the Colour of the native Americans, and the recent Population of this Continent," *New-York Magazine* 4 (April 1793): 197–9.

68. "Anecdote of an Algonquin Woman [From Leadsum's *History of the American Revolution*]," *New-York Magazine* 6 (October 1795): 619.

69. Ibid.

70. On the anti–capital punishment movement in late-eighteenth-century America, see David Brion Davis, "The Movement to Abolish Capital Punishment in America, 1787–1861," *American Historical Review* 63 (October 1957): 23–46; Louis P. Masur, *Rites of Execution: Capital Punishment and the Transformation of American Culture, 1776–1865* (New York: Oxford UP, 1989); and Wayne C. Minnick, "The New England Execution Sermons, 1639–1800," *Speech Monographs* (1968): 79–89.

71. Masur 5.

72. Between 1777 and 1798, nineteen execution sermons were published, of which eight focused large proportions of their text on arguments in favor of capital punishment; none of the texts opposed the practice (Minnick 88).

73. "On Imprisonment," *New-York Magazine* 5 (September 1794): 569.

74. "Visit to the Bettering-House, or House of Correction," *New-York Magazine* 3 (December 1792): 714.

75. Ibid., 716–17.

76. Montesquieu's *The Spirit of Laws* (1748) and Cesare Beccaria's *Essays on Crimes and Punishments* (London, 1764; first published in America in 1773 in New York), as well as Lockean thought in general, were the most influential texts for Americans of the 1790s who opposed capital punishment.

77. William Bradford, "Extract from Bradford's Enquiry how far the Punishment of Death is necessary in Pennsylvania," *New-York Magazine* 4 (April 1793): 226.

78. Ibid., 230–31.

79. Valentine, "When the Penalty exceeds the Offence, it is not the Criminal, but Human Nature that suffers," *New-York Magazine* 5 (January 1794): 36.

80. Ibid.

81. Murray published occasional poetry and essays as early as 1784, but scholars have missed the publication of this long letter in the pages of the *New-York Magazine.* See Sharon M. Harris, ed., *Selected Writings of Judith Sargent Murray* (New York: Oxford UP, 1996), and Sheila Skemp, *Judith Sargent Murray: A Brief Biography with Documents* (New York: Bedford, 1998).

82. In the editors' "To Correspondents" notes in October 1792, they remark that Murray's "The Gleaner No. II, is come to hand, but unavoidably postponed till our next" (n.p.). The second of the Gleaner series' articles actually began Murray's serialized novel, *The Story of Margaretta.* It did not appear in the November issue, however, and no other writings that can be identified as Murray's appear in the *New-York Magazine.* Murray remained a columnist for the rival *Massachusetts Magazine* until its demise.

83. Although this narrative is typically identified as fiction, this author has uncovered the actual events in the life of the Kittle (or Kitlyne) family. This subject is more fully substantiated in Sharon M. Harris, *Executing Race* (Columbus: Ohio State UP, 2005).

84. Barlow first appears in the poetry section in June 1792 with "The Conspiracy of Kings"; he does not appear again until January 1796, when "The Hasty Pudding" is published.

85. Imona's poetry was very sentimental and often melancholy, such as "On Miss—, paying the Tribute of a Tear to a Scene of Distress" (October 1790). Marcia's poetry was much more serious in its subject matter than Imona's. "On the present Situation in France, and the Influence which the Independency of America had in producing the Revolution" is typical of her work (January 1791).

86. Some of Faugeres's radical works appeared in the *New-York Magazine*, including her arguments for immediate manumission of slaves (discussed above); but other works were published elsewhere, in periodicals or books. Most notable are her anti–capital punishment poem, "The Ghost of John Young" (1797); her poems honoring the French Revolution, which appear in *Posthumous Works;* and her historical drama, *Belisarius* (1793), also published by the Swords brothers.

87. "Alfred," "To Ella," *New-York Magazine* 1 (September 1790): 546.

88. [Margaretta V. Bleecker Faugeres], "To Alfred," *New-York Magazine* 1 (November 1790): 603. This was not a vapid remark by Faugeres. Although a member of the elite Dutch families of New York, she had not had an easy life. Her childhood was overwhelmed by the war, including a desperate flight from the family home when Burgoyne's troops marched toward Albany, during which her only sibling, a younger sister, died; her father was taken captive (and subsequently released) by the British when she was ten years old; and her mother died when she was only twelve.

89. Ibid., 604.

90. Ibid. This poem is immediately followed by another of Faugeres's poems, "Written on a blank Leaf of Col. Humphrey's Poems—by a Lady." No name or pen name accompanies the poem, but it is included in Faugeres's section of *Posthumous Works.*

91. "Cymon," "To Ella," *New-York Magazine* 1 (December 1790): 724.

92. [Margaretta V. Bleecker Faugeres], "To Cymon," *New-York Magazine* 2 (January 1791): 92.

93. Editors, "Notes to Correspondents," *New-York Magazine* 2–3 (January 1792): n.p.

94. As late as 1798, Bleecker Faugeres continued her support of Clinton. For a Fourth of July oration by Clinton, she wrote "Ode," which was set to music and performed for the occasion. Yet the ways in which people's political alliances are often not conformable to a single party or movement (just as

was true of the editorial position of the *New-York Magazine*) is clearly evidenced in "Ode." Though supporting Clinton, she enters into the cult of Washington discourse that had emerged by the end of the century. The poem thus praises "the favorite son of Fame: /. . . WASHINGTON, the brave and wise" ("Ode," in George Clinton, *An Oration, Delivered on the Fourth of July, 1798* [New York: M. L. and W. A. Davis, 1798], 16).

95. Mott asserts that the magazine's column "The Theatrical Register" (November 1795–April 1796) as a "series of reviews of the New York stage was probably written by William Dunlap [and] is the most important body of dramatic criticism in an eighteenth century magazine" (55–56). See also Bowman's essay, which analyzes "The Theatrical Register."

APPENDIX

American Periodical Series, 1741–1800

Below is a list of the ninety magazines—weeklies, bi-weeklies, monthlies, quarterlies, semi-annuals, etc.—that are included in the American Periodicals Series (33 reels of microfilm), plus select daily, semi-weekly, and weekly newspapers. Those referenced in individual essays in this collection are identified by an asterisk. Both magazine and newspapers were known to change names, content, and even circulation periods, often in an attempt to create a more commercially successful product. Some newspapers even lapsed into "occasional" publication.

In compiling this list, we have (except as noted in individual essays) attempted to use titles as they first appeared historically or, later, were most consistently identified with a particular newspaper or magazine. For additional newspaper titles and background, see Clarence S. Brigham's *History and Bibliography of American Newspapers, 1690–1820* (Worcester, MA: American Antiquarian Society, 1947).

The American Apollo (Boston, 1792–94)
The American Magazine and Historical Chronicle (Boston, 1743–46)
The American Magazine (New York, 1787–88)
The American Magazine and Monthly Chronicle for the British Colonies (Philadelphia, 1757–58)
The American Magazine, or General Repository (Philadelphia, 1769)
The American Magazine, or a Monthly View of the Political State of the British Colonies (Philadelphia, 1741)
The American Monitor: or the Republican Magazine (Boston, 1785)
The American Monthly Review (Philadelphia, 1795)
The American Moral & Sentimental Magazine (New York, 1797–98)
The American Museum, or, Universal Magazine (Philadelphia, 1787–92)
The American Musical Magazine (New Haven, 1786–87)
The American Universal Magazine (Philadelphia, 1797–98)
**The American Weekly Mercury* (Philadelphia, 1719–49)

The Arminian Magazine: Consisting of Extracts and Original Treatises on General Redemption (Philadelphia, 1789–90)

**Aurora* (Philadelphia, 1794–1820)

**The Boston Evening Post* (Boston, 1735–75)

**The Boston Gazette* (Boston, 1719–98)

The Boston Magazine (Boston, 1783–86)

**Boston News–Letter* (Boston, 1704–1776)

The Boston Weekly–Magazine (Boston, 1743)

**The Boston Weekly Post–Boy* (Boston, 1734–75)

The Censor (Boston, 1771–72)

**Die Chestnuthiller Wochenschrift* (Philadelphia, 1790–94)

The Children's Magazine (Hartford, 1789)

The Christian History (Boston, 1743–45)

Christian's Monitor (Portland, Maine, 1799)

The Christian's, Scholar's, and Farmer's Magazine (Elizabethtown, New Jersey, 1789–91)

The Columbian Magazine: or, Monthly Miscellany (Philadelphia, 1786–90)

The Columbian Museum, or, Universal Asylum (Philadelphia, 1793)

Courier de Boston, Affiches, Annonces, et Avis (Boston, 1789)

The Dessert to the True American (Philadelphia, 1798–99)

**Der Deutsche Porcupein, under Lancäster Anzeigs–Nachrichter* (Lancaster, Pennsylvania 1798–99)

The Experienced Christian's Magazine (New York, 1796–97)

The Free Universal Magazine (New York, 1793–94)

**Gazette of the United States* (Philadelphia, 1790–1804)

Ein Geistliches Magazien (Germantown, Pennsylvania 1764–72)

**General Advertisor* (Philadelphia, 1790–94)

The General Magazine, and Historical Chronicle, for all the British Plantations in America (Philadelphia, 1741)

The General Magazine, and Impartial Review, of Knowledge and Entertainment (Baltimore, 1798)

The Gentleman and Lady's Town and Country Magazine; or, Repository of Instruction and Entertainment (Boston, 1784–85)

The Gentlemen and Ladies Town and Country Magazine: Consisting of Literature, History, Politics, Arts, Manners, and Amusements, with Various Other Matter (Boston, 1789–90)

**Greenleaf's New York Journal* (New York, 1794–1800)

**Der Hoch–Deutsch Pennsylvanische Geschicht–Schreiber* (Germantown, 1739–77)

The Humming Bird, or Herald of Taste (Newfield, Connecticut, 1798)

**Independent Chronicle* (Boston, 1776–1820)

The Independent Reflector (New York, 1752–53)

The Instructor (New York, 1755)

John Englishman, in Defence of the English Constitution (New York, 1755)

The Key (Frederick Town, Maryland, 1798)

The Lady's Magazine; and Repository of Entertaining Knowledge (Philadelphia, 1792–93)

The Lady & Gentleman's Pocket Magazine of Literary and Polite Amusement (New York, 1796)

The Literary Miscellany (Philadelphia, 1795)

The Literary Museum, or Monthly Magazine (West–Chester, Pennsylvania, 1797)

The Massachusetts Magazine: or, Monthly Museum of Knowledge and Rational Entertainment (Boston, 1789–96)

The Medical Repository (New York, 1797–1800)

The Methodist Magazine (Philadelphia, 1797–98)

The Monthly Magazine, and American Review (New York, 1799–1800)

The Monthly Military Repository (New York, 1796–97)

The Monthly Miscellany or Vermont Magazine (Bennington, Vermont 1794)

The Musical Magazine (Cheshire, Connecticut, 1792–1801)

**National Gazette* (Philadelphia, 1791–93)

National Magazine; or, a Political, Historical, Biographical, and Literary Repository (Richmond, Virginia 1799–1800)

**Neue Unpartheyische Lancäster Zeitung, und Anzeigs–Nachrichten* (Lancaster, Pennsylvania, 1787–97)

The New American Magazine (Woodbridge, New Jersey, 1758–60)

**The New–England Courant* (Boston, 1721–27)

The New–England Magazine of Knowledge and Pleasure (Boston, 1758–59)

The New Hampshire Magazine or the Monthly Repository of Useful Information (Concord, New Hampshire 1793)

New Hampshire and Vermont Magazine and General Repository (Haverhill, New Hampshire, 1797)

The New–Haven Gazette, and the Connecticut Magazine (New Haven, 1786–89)
The New Jersey Magazine and Monthly Advertiser (New Brunswick, 1786–87)
The New Star (Hartford, 1796)
The New Star. A Republican, Miscellaneous, Literary Paper (Concord, New Hampshire, 1797)
**The New–York Gazette* (New York, 1725–44)
**The New–York Gazette, or Weekly Post–Boy* (New York, 1747–73)
The New–York Magazine, or Literary Repository (New York, 1790–97)
**The New–York Mercury* (New York,1779–83)
**The New–York Journal* (New York,1784–93)
**Minerva* (New York, 1796–97)
**The New–York Weekly Journal* (New York, 1735–40)
The New–York Weekly Magazine; or, Miscellaneous Repository (New York, 1795–97)
The Nightingale (Boston, 1796)
The North–Carolina Magazine; or, Universal Intelligencer (Newbern, North Carolina 1764–65)
The Occasional Reverberator (New York, 1753)
**The Pennsylvania Gazette* (Philadelphia, 1728–1815)
The Pennsylvania Magazine: or, American Monthly Museum (Philadelphia, 1775–76)
The Penny Post (n.p., 1769)
**The Philadelphia Gazette and Universal Daily Advertiser* (Philadelphia, 1794–1802)
The Philadelphia Magazine and Review; or, Monthly Repository of Information and Amusement (Philadelphia, 1799)
The Philadelphia Minerva (Philadelphia, 1795–98)
The Philadelphia Monthly Magazine (Philadelphia, 1798)
**Die Philadelphische Zeitung* (Philadelphia, 1755–57)
Das Philadelphisches Magazin, oder Unterhaltender Gesellschafter für die Deutschen in America (Philadelphia, 1798)
Porcupine's Political Censor (Philadelphia, 1796–97)
The Religious Monitor, or Theological Scales (Danbury, Connecticut 1798)
The Remembrancer, for Lord's Day Evenings (Exeter, Massachusetts 1797)
A Republican Magazine; or, Repository of Political Truths (Fairhaven, Vermont 1798)

The Royal American Magazine, or Universal Repository of Instruction and Amusement (Boston, 1774–75)

The Royal Spiritual Magazine; or, the Christian's Grand Treasure (Philadelphia, 1771)

The Rural Casket (Poughkeepsie, New York 1798)

The Rural Magazine (Newark, 1798–99)

The Rural Magazine; or, Vermont Repository (Rutland, Vermont 1795–96)

Sentimental & Literary Magazine (New York, 1797)

South–Carolina Weekly Museum, and Complete Magazine of Entertainment and Intelligence (Charleston, 1797–98)

The Tablet (Boston, 1795)

The Theological Magazine, or Synopsis of Modern Religious Sentiment (New York, 1795–99)

Thespian Oracle, or Monthly Mirror (Philadelphia, 1798)

The Time Piece; and Literary Companion (New York, 1797–98)

The United States Christian Magazine (New York, 1796)

The United States Magazine, a Repository of History, Politics and Literature (Philadelphia, 1779)

United States Magazine, or, General Repository of Useful Instruction and Rational Amusement (Newark, 1794)

The Universal Asylum, and Columbian Magazine (Philadelphia, 1790–92)

The Vigil (Charleston, 1798)

The Weekly Magazine of Original Essays, Fugitive Pieces, and Interesting Intelligence (Philadelphia, 1798–99)

The Weekly Museum (Baltimore, 1797)

**Der Wöchentliche Philadelphische Staatsbote* (Philadelphia,1762–79)

The Worcester Magazine (Worcester, 1786–88)

CONTRIBUTORS

SETH COTLAR is assistant professor of history at Willamette University. He is finishing a book manuscript on American popular thought in the age of democratic revolutions that will be published by the University of Virginia Press. He has published essays on transatlantic radicalism and conservatism in *The Revolution of 1800: Democracy, Race, and the New Republic* (U of Virginia P, 2002) and *Beyond the Founders: New Approaches to the Political History of the Early American Republic* (U of Virginia P, 2004).

PHILIP GOULD is professor of English at Brown University and a past president of the Society of Early Americanists. His most recent work is *Barbaric Traffic: Commerce and Antislavery in the Eighteenth-Century Atlantic World* (Harvard UP, 2003).

TIMOTHY D. HALL is professor of early American history at Central Michigan University. He is the author of *Contested Boundaries: Itinerancy and the Reshaping of the Colonial American Religious World* (Duke UP, 1994) and coauthor, with T. H. Breen, of *Colonial America in the Atlantic World: A Narrative of Creative Interaction* (Longmans, 2003). He continues to explore the interaction among theological ideas, religious experience, commercial growth, and cultural change in seventeenth- and eighteenth-century America.

SHARON M. HARRIS is the Lorraine Sherley Professor in Literature at TCU. She was editor of *Legacy: A Journal of American Women Writers* from 1997 to 2004, founding president of the Society for the Study of American Women Writers, and a founding officer of the Society of Early Americanists. She has edited numerous anthologies, including *American Women Writers to 1800* (Oxford UP, 1996), and editions, including *Early Women's Historical Narratives* (Penguin, 2003). Her most recent critical study, *Executing Race* (Ohio State UP, 2005), examines race, class, and the law in eighteenth-century American women's narratives.

MARK L. KAMRATH is associate professor of English at the University of Central Florida, where he teaches early American literature. He has published several essays on Charles Brockden Brown and his era, and is coeditor of *Revising Charles Brockden Brown: Culture, Politics, and Sexuality in the Early Republic* (U of Tennessee P, 2004). He is on the editorial board of the Charles Brockden Brown Electronic Archive and Scholarly Edition, and he is currently completing a study of Brown's historicism, forthcoming from Kent State University Press.

LISA M. LOGAN is associate professor of English and director of women's studies at the University of Central Florida, where she teaches American and women's literature and feminist theory. She has published several essays on early American women writers, including Mary Rowlandson and Harriet Prescott Spofford. Her current project is a feminist study of early American women's cross-dressing and authorship.

CARLA MULFORD teaches early American literature and culture and Native American studies at Pennsylvania State University, University Park. The originator and founding president of the Society of Early Americanists, Mulford's work in canon reformation is evidenced in a series of articles in the field and in her anthology *Early American Writings* (Oxford UP, 2002), and the collection of essays *Teaching the Literatures of Early America* (MLA Pubs., 1999). Her primary era of inquiry for the past few years has been the eighteenth century. She is currently writing a book on Benjamin Franklin and early modern liberalism.

BEVERLY J. REED is assistant professor of English at Stephen F. Austin State University, where she teaches early American literature and is the director of composition. She has published on Louisa May Alcott and *Frank Leslie's Illustrated Magazine.*

CHAD REID is a Ph.D. candidate at the University of Connecticut. He received his M.A. in history from New Mexico State University (2000). Reid's current interests include the reading and rioting of laborers in eighteenth-century New England and New France.

FRANK SHUFFELTON teaches American literature at the University of Rochester. He has written widely on early American literary topics, with a particular interest in strategies of authorship, and has edited volumes on the American enlightenment, ethnicity in early America, and texts by Thomas Jefferson and John and Abigail Adams.

JOHN SMOLENSKI is assistant professor of history at the University of California, Davis. He has published articles in *Prospects: An Annual of American Cultural Studies, American Quarterly,* and other edited collections on early American history. This article is drawn from his current book project, titled "Friends and Strangers: The Evolution of a Creole Civic Culture in Colonial Pennsylvania."

ROBERT D. STURR is an associate professor of English at Kent State University, Stark Campus. He has published "The Presence of Walt Whitman in Ha Jin's *Waiting*" in the *Walt Whitman Quarterly Review,* as well as an article on Ha Jin in the *Dictionary of Literary Biography.* His research focuses on representations of the American Revolution in both literature and political rhetoric and currently involves a study of the mythologies surrounding the life of John Paul Jones.

W. M. Verhoeven is professor of American culture and cultural theory at the University of Groningen, The Netherlands. He held the Charles H. Watts Chair in the History of the Book and Historical Bibliography at Brown University, 2002–3. He is editor of *Revolutionary Histories: Transatlantic Cultural Nationalism, 1775–1815* (Palgrave, 2002) and coeditor with Amanda Gilroy of *Epistolary Histories: Letters, Fiction, Culture* (U of Virginia P, 1999). He is currently general editor of a series of ten anti-Jacobin novels for Pickering and Chatto, as well as a series of the novels and selected works of Thomas Holcroft. He is also writing a monograph on British radicals and American land speculators, *Westward the Course of Empire.*

INDEX

Periodical Literature was designed and typeset on a Macintosh computer system using QuarkXPress software. The body text is set in 10.5/12.5 Filosofia and display type is set in Old Claude. This book was designed and typeset by Barbara Karwhite and manufactured by Thomson-Shore, Inc.